SEA BATTLES ON DRY LAND

METROPOLITAN BOOKS

HENRY HOLT AND COMPANY

NEW YORK

HAROLD BRODKEY

SEA BATTLES ON DRY LAND

ESSAYS

Metropolitan Books
Henry Holt and Company, Inc.
Publishers since 1866
115 West 18th Street
New York, New York 10011

Metropolitan Books is a registered trademark of
Henry Holt and Company, Inc.

Library of Congress Cataloging-in-Publication Data
Brodkey, Harold.
Sea battles on dry land: essays / Harold Brodkey.—1st ed.
p.   cm.
Collection of previously published essays.
ISBN 0-8050-6052-9 (alk. paper)
I. Title.
PS3552.R6224S4   1999   98-46248
814'.54—dc21   CIP

Henry Holt books are available for special promotions and premiums.
For details contact: Director, Special Markets.

First Edition 1999

Designed by Kate Nichols

Printed in the United States of America
All first editions are printed on acid-free paper. ∞

1   3   5   7   9   10   8   6   4   2

CONTENTS

SEA BATTLES ON DRY LAND

CELEBRITY

AND

POLITICS

TRANSLATING BRANDO

The Marlon Brando who appeared on a special ninety-minute edition of *Larry King Live* last week is the Brando we have come to expect: overweight, vulgar, and boring, and then abruptly passionate and intelligent, with his youthful face gleaming in all the fat. King was deferential, but he wasn't spared Brando's antics. Brando mocked his host for sweating under the lights, and at one point even tweaked King's nose. He kept propping his puffy bare feet on an ottoman in full view of the camera. And at the end of the program, ever the Godfather, he kissed King on the lips—a Mafia gesture indicating that a suitor has behaved well and is accepted into the gang.

Was Brando disgusting? Mostly, yes. But the screen clips of his finest moments that were dropped in before and after commercial breaks during the program said more about him than he did himself. When Brando first emerged as a star, in the late forties, it was amazing how instantly many theatergoers and critics and people in the theater recognized the way he had of existing in the present moment. Except in the case of the occasional comedian (Buster Keaton, say, physically, though not, of course, in speech), this hadn't been seen before.

Brando's mumbling was said to be "real," as if the impetus to speak were occurring then and there and had not been written in a script. His brutish explosions of anger, his displays of vanity onstage were seen by pretentious and unpretentious reviewers alike as having an immediacy new to the theater. And although many critics complained, the public acclamation and the box-office draw were noticeable at once.

More openly than movie acting or book reading, theater presents a series of moments in some kind of sequence. The moments are real enough as performance, but their degree of reality in giving us the scenes of a story—the degree and kind of stylization of the story—forms most of what is called acting. The pursuit of reality, the self-conscious attempt at realism, was more than a century old when Brando first appeared; from Balzac to Einstein you can draw a fairly clear line. Brando, Norman Mailer (whom Pauline Kael links to Brando in a well-known review of *Last Tango in Paris*), Leonard Bernstein (whose musicals were *real*), Richard Avedon, and countless others—John Berryman, for instance, and Robert Rauschenberg and Jasper Johns, and Paul Taylor—all emerged at roughly the same time, and all of them, with various lacks or deficiencies and various skills and abilities, worked within a frame of extreme realism. You could say they worked counter to modernism. Of these artists, Brando was the most directly perceived by the public—the most fully *welcomed* and perhaps the most influential.

Brando has written a 486-page autobiography entitled *Brando: Songs My Mother Taught Me*, with the help of a writer, Robert Lindsey. On *Larry King*, Brando stated that he had been paid an advance of five million dollars for the book, which he kept calling "an exercise in freedom." Almost simultaneously, a third-person tell-all biography entitled simply *Brando*, which is more than a thousand pages long and was written by Peter Manso, has come out. Unfortunately, Manso's book is unreadable except in short bursts. Manso, in my opinion, has no sensible view of Brando. But he has a great deal of largely unexamined information, much of which is grim and unsettling.

Brando's own book is readable, and for someone my age who has been affected by his work it is often gripping—although it is obviously self-serving and in every respect that I have any knowledge of seems factually misleading. But let's call it a lie, for it is clearly a performance, which Manso's book is not. Brando is an actor and has lied for a living all his life—lied and presented a simulacrum of truth. It is widely held that he was "truthful" in his work. He seems to dislike acting now—because of the human elements, the immediacy, the slipperiness of effect. People say of Brando that he seems to have experienced a living death—that his life was a horror. His book says that this is not so.

Still, the more Brando lied, the more he conveyed a sensation of truth. Stanislavsky, the Russian theoretician of acting, who was Chekhov's director, uses the idea of translation to suggest the process by which you transform something in yourself into stage effect and aesthetic truth. (To act using yourself is very different from trying to talk about yourself to an analyst, but it is not so different from writing about yourself.) Brando was taught by Stella Adler, who studied briefly with Stanislavsky, and by Elia Kazan, who was influenced by Stanislavsky.

It is difficult to talk about Brando's stage performances, because they varied from night to night, and nobody saw every one of them. Looking back, one can easily guess that he was interruptible—that his performances were infinitely fragile. They were like translations in progress. My memory is that in the late forties, when I was in college, and the gossip about Brando had started, some of the comment was about how tricky or erratic he was in his full glory. And opera singers and musicians— with singular exceptions, such as Glenn Gould—were entering a period when they were like workhorses. Richard Tucker and Zinka Milanov and Birgit Nilsson gave and were said to give "rousing" performances, whatever their mood.

Brando was a scene-stealer and was strong-willed and ruthless beyond belief, but he was never a horse. Either the performance flickered with inspiration or he was merely sexy. Every once in a while, Brando would do a final or overall translation of a role—always flawed but classic. And, like Philip Roth, he asserted that he was *playing a role*. But to me it seemed that Brando was only playing himself, in an autobiographical epic about an American soul. And, either because of his Celtic background—he is largely Irish, he says—or for some other, intangible reason, he seemed from the start to be doomed to go to hell, unrescuable. Brando worked from himself, as all actors do, but he did it differently. He took something homeless and naked from Tennessee Williams's plays (Brando, who is seventy, hasn't yet done a Eugene O'Neill play) and from the very air and reality around him, and though it can be said that he is telling the truth when he claims that his acting is not autobiographical, in some deep, resonant way it is, because of the degree of improvisation in it and the disrespect for all that has been done in acting before him.

The way his book is put together suggests that he is somewhat talented as a writer but a bit wild. And the movement in language toward a coherent argument—the melody line of meaning—is beyond him. Perhaps in acting you have to be raw but veiled at the same time, but he can't manage this for long on paper.

In his book, which jogs one's memory of him much more than the Manso book does, the first and last thing one feels—feels with surprise—is that he seems to have almost always existed as the lone figure in the universe, despite his having a family, his not being an orphan. He *says* he was an orphan in some sense, and I believe him. He was the pure and barbaric new solipsist, who existed—even in a performance, even in the part of a story that is beyond words—above and to one side and behind and below the words. He was pictures and text, a temporal animal, so clever that he seems demonic while remaining at least semi-irresistible—and not passively so. He was not an adorable self sitting still. He was as active and energetic as Puck.

I see myself in Brando's book, and that is natural, since he was the first male star to emerge in my adult life (when I was eighteen). Brando taught me something about maleness; it is the man's world that Brando's good work treats and embodies. His father, Brando says, liked hookers. He was a hard drinker (though not as serious a drinker as Brando's mother, who was an alcoholic), and seems likely to have been abusive. In one of the semiautobiographical improvisations in *Last Tango*, Brando tells a stock anecdote of a son humiliated by his father. The tale involves cow manure being on Brando's shoes at a party because his father made him milk a cow when he, Brando, was already dressed to go out. We can guess at the son's rabid and contemptuous ambition to escape from humiliation into the topmost stratospherics of triumph—to become the greatest of all time, as it were. But Brando can act certain things that he cannot write about clearly. At one point, he says, "The power and influence of a movie star is curious: I didn't ask for it or take it; people *gave* it to me"—as if such fame were possible without some desire on his part. The mixture of truth and not-truth, the shock to a reader who accepts the gesture of a statement that cannot be true, recurs over and over in the book. Though Brando did not finish high school, he has always claimed to have read widely and with some care. But his performances are not brainy—are not primarily even verbal. He says he is intuitive or "mostly" intuitive. So why is he playing at being a brainy person?

Did Brando ever play an intellectual? Was he ever in a movie that had an intellectual in it? Could he have done George in Albee's *Who's Afraid of Virginia Woolf?* Could he do Prospero now? He did an extremely famous semi-intellectual movie, *Last Tango in Paris,* and he did a self-consciously political intellectual movie, *Burn!* And he was far from out of place or clumsy in either one. What was frightening (for me) was a vampire quality he had in those roles, as if he were feeding his performances with bits of flesh and mind ripped from the directors of them. This borrowing or stealing parts of developed selves, often with malice or cruelty, is also boyish-childish, semiadorable—which is what an orphan learns to be in order to gain shelter. And if I say that what Brando ripped off was mostly faults and rottennesses; if I say that his characterizations (or translations) are mostly junk assemblages, I am placing him among the fifties talents, among the artists. Brando lays this out without actually saying it: Brando is a kind of junk figure—worthless, he says. (He cheats on that by being politically active, by doing good. But good in this world is usually tainted.)

Part of Brando's persona as an actor is that he is a swindler and a rapist and a bully (of a certain kind), a murderer, a madman. He says these are characters. That is, these are not traits of one central figure. The liar who tells the truth *in a way,* while being a real man, was the standard role for actors in this country in the thirties, before Brando. Brando wasn't the first of the new generation of actors. Montgomery Clift was. (He offered sensitivity and a profile in someone middle-class; he was a kind of American Leslie Howard.) But the morality of Clift's characters was never in doubt. Nor were their manners. Brando's questionable morality and the questionable morality of his art, its graffiti quality, its shitting-on-you wildness: all this was new. And so were Brando's eyes: clever, androgynous, hauntingly threatening eyes, somehow also soft and weak, satyr / American-storm-trooper eyes (though they are less famous than his profile). He seems to have worn glasses at one point. His hair was darkened for *A Streetcar Named Desire.* For most of his career, he had the same makeup man do his hair and his skin. As early as the movie version of *Streetcar* (1951), he was notorious for having too fat a can. (Clift, when he wanted to dispraise a performance of Brando's, said he had noticed Brando's fat ass—meaning that the actor Brando wasn't being magical.)

For me, Brando is a self-invented, one-character actor who does the separate selves in himself as characters. He was in many ways a kind of unknown soldier—not dead but dead-souled, as a result of the Second World War. Tennessee Williams, according to a letter printed in Brando's book, saw this quality in Brando from the start. Williams wrote Audrey Wood, his agent:

> I can't tell you what a relief it is that we have found such a God-sent Stanley in Brando. . . . It humanizes the character of Stanley in that it becomes the brutality or callousness of youth rather than a vicious older man. . . . A new value came out of Brando's reading which was by far the best reading I have ever heard. He seemed to have already created a dimensional character, of the sort that the war has produced among young veterans.

Brando says that on the famous visit he made to Williams to read for the part he did not sleep with Williams. People in New York thought he had. Williams continued to see Brando in terms of incarnation and reincarnation—the soldier Orpheus, for instance—and most of his plays after *Streetcar* seem to me to have parts written for Brando, but Brando never acted in another Williams play. (He did do the film *The Fugitive Kind*, Williams's adaptation of his play *Orpheus Descending*.)

The American-spiritual, or national, quality in Brando—his representing someone we were indebted to, his new take on the working-class father of the country—was a very important cultural invention. This serviceman quality lasted as long as Brando could project sexuality, and then he became a post-Bogart hard guy who never had a chance and yet was hugely triumphant—Superman *père* and the Godfather and Kurtz in his kingdom.

For people who saw Brando in anything he did when he was young, the overwhelming first effect he created was one of sexual presence. The fifties were supposedly not a highly sexual time. Yet Brando and Mitchum and Russell and Bardot flourished then—odd precursors of the sexual revolution of the sixties. Was it the war that brought these people to a boil and then brought them forward? Brando had worked with Katharine Cornell and Tallulah Bankhead by the time he appeared in *Streetcar*. He is not very talkative in his memoir, but both of those women were bisexual and they were romantic presences of a considerable sort—Cornell regally and Bankhead temperamentally—and he says he reacted positively to neither of them. I say he absorbed their quality, masculinized it slightly, dirtied it, and went a bit out of control with it. Elizabeth Taylor, in *Reflections in a Golden Eye* (1967), attempted a portrayal of sexuality, but she is a pretentious junior harridan in comparison with Brando, who is playing a frustrated and murderous repressed-homosexual major—God, the story lines back then!

I am not discussing Brando's androgyny. I take androgyny for granted in everyone. But Brando took over the vanity and posing and sheer willfulness of a good-looking woman and developed a deconstructed version—an antiversion of a diva's romantic sexuality. He gave it a male twist, using the rigorously male energy of his director Elia Kazan. Kazan, a much better director of men than of women, was a bitter, potent, philandering man—and this found marvelous expression in Brando, who could actually embody those qualities physically, in glances and posture and walk. Brando became—in a sense, in part—a surrogate Kazan. And there you have the sexual icon that dominated the stage and screen and the imagination for twenty years. In *On the Waterfront*, Brando added a weird—and weirdly beautiful—other element: a quality of being a hero-victim, a sacrifice.

It was because of Kazan that most of the ingredients of Brando's force as an actor were without class bias, class identity. It is not clear if Kazan knew how much of him Brando was putting onstage. From the beginning, Brando's theatrical persona was meant to be responsive to everything and everyone, was promiscuous.

Promiscuity has dimensions of self-loss and of addiction and of *Arabian Nights* storytelling; it whispers of a story constantly renewed. The image of promiscuity as noble and fated (as dirty but real) still has power in the militantly homosexual community and among some practitioners of S and M and some literary critics. Brando presented this image openly and head-on. To say metaphorically that Brando's mischief fathered later rebellions—Elvis and the Stones, gay liberation, and "Black is beautiful"—is to indicate some of the abiding power of that youthful work of his, or, if nothing else, how accidents of the spirit of the age favored Brando. (I prefer the idea that Brando was a great inventor.)

By the time he made the movie version of *Streetcar*, Brando, as I said before, was fat in the rear. In an interview with Truman Capote, published in this magazine in 1957, he said about his sudden success that one morning he "woke up . . . sitting on a pile of candy." A punitive sexual quality hovers over Brando's image as he ages, in *One-Eyed Jacks* and, especially, in the sequence in *Last Tango* which involves anal sex.

Despite the plot of *Last Tango*, which for most viewers, I would guess, has no interest whatsoever, the movie is something like *Der Rosenkavalier* for the sexiest male star of his day. Pauline Kael, in her review, seems to have announced a truth obliquely: that Brando coming apart with age and decay, like Brando obese and dying, would still be a star attraction, would be one of the wonders of the time. Surely this is in part the point of the movie—that Brando can play a man his own age as if he had had a lifetime to prepare for it.

Kael once drew a distinction between tall actors, like Jimmy Stewart and Gary Cooper, and the noticeably short ones, like Brando and Cagney. She argues that the tall actors hide in goodness in order to shrink themselves, but the small ones are nasty. Perhaps for short men sexuality is more likely to be represented by competitive promiscuity. Short men are more overtly violent because they feel cheated. Kael doesn't say that tall actors make an effort to reduce the menace, while short ones crank it up, but that, I think, is one way to understand Brando: he was less menacing because of his size and was allowed or encouraged to be more menacing, to be the heroic-demonic short guy, an heir of Cagney.

Postwar promiscuity rested on the escape from the horrors of war and the nervousness in the shadow of extinction from the bomb. It rested also on the medical advances made during the war, the control of VD and of pregnancy. There are technical aspects to male promiscuity, a mastery of difficulties, a degree of access to information, and a free schedule and a great deal of attitude. This is all pre-AIDS.

Promiscuity also protects you from individuals. In a certain sense, if it is to preserve itself, it cannot work sexually.

Brando is not said to be or to have been sexually fake. People who claim to have known him don't derogate him sexually. In the fifties, certain women had sexual rank because they'd had Marlon, and they told you—they offered themselves tantalizingly in that manner. The quotes in Manso's book about Brando's sexual performance are mostly concerned with his sensitivity and with his actual physical touch. In the movie *Street-*

car, there is an astounding close-up of Brando as Stanley, when he is strug-gling to take Vivien Leigh in an act of rape, and his face is that of a satyr. It is a brilliant piece of work—but perhaps inept for a moment of rape. His look suggests malice and danger but not violence and control, not physical control. It seemed to me he was saying in facial gesture *I know you* or *I have you*. In his later movies, he does not claim this sexual authority.

Brando and Manso both suggest that Brando likes control, likes the feeling of webbing or enshrouding another mind. He seems to have escaped from a childhood in which he was out of control and too pretty and without education—escaped into a sense of empowerment that is, after all, contingent, and ultimately unsatisfying to him.

Brando *was* pretty. Then his nose was broken in a bout of boxing with a stagehand during the run of *Streetcar*, and that made him beautiful. Slightly different versions of the anecdote are printed in Brando's book and in Manso's. Irene Selznick, who produced *Streetcar*, told me that Brando had been hard to light—he had been too pretty for the part of Stanley.

She also said that he was undisciplinable onstage after the first weeks of the show, and that that had frightened her. Brando's way of being fully involved onstage had a Zen quality, mixed with an obvious narcissism and touches of lunacy and cruelty. Everything he ever did had an element of mockery. Selznick said that Brando hated Jessica Tandy, but so did the audience, at times. Selznick said the play was magical. She became concerned about possible litigation, because Williams's contract did not permit anyone to make changes in the script. She dragged him to the the-ater to see what Brando was doing in the part. Williams wasn't bothered at all. "Leave him alone," he said, according to Selznick. "The audiences like him. The money is good. The play will be printed and saved—if it can be."

Selznick denied having discovered Brando. She gave the credit to Kazan and Williams. The text of *Streetcar* before Kazan and Brando altered its meaning represented a kind of social reality and aspiration that she understood. She disliked Brando, the androgynous and sensitive lower-class or classless brute—the actor without tradition, without old-fashioned glamour or chivalrous responses. He was so talented and so strange and so inward that he seemed to be a mythological creation. After establish-ing Brando, Kazan worked with other male dreamboats, including Tim

Everett, James Dean, and Warren Beatty. But, in the odd way that things
turn out, they were considered to be offshoots of Brando, not of Kazan's
direction.

Whether Brando did or didn't have an initial innocence (it seems he
didn't), he was a blatant exhibitionist, and not a democrat but a star—not
only a peasant but a great figure. And once he had become a looming icon
on the screen he received an unnatural amount of attention. Anyone interested in the contemporary world will probably buy or borrow the two
Brando books and a number of videos and will take a look at the phenomenon. Brando is not like any other star. Clint Eastwood and Greta
Garbo are similar to each other as movie presences—Eastwood is as postcoital as Garbo in manner, and as cranky and as melancholy—and Monroe
resembles Mae West, combined with W. C. Fields and Shirley Temple.
But no one is like Brando. For example, Eastwood is committed to action,
while Brando is condemned to it.

Brando in his early movies is an unforgettable face atop a semi-
inflated, loosely disciplined body. I don't know how important he has
been. Jack Nicholson conveys a post-Brando sheer nuttiness about the
demonism of sexuality and self-importance, often ironically, and so does
Sharon Stone, in another style. And, once I start thinking about it, I see
Robert Lowell as Brandoized, and I see John Irving and Nureyev and
Montserrat Caballé and Maria Callas as Brandoized, too.

No one greatly helped his or her own career by appearing in a movie
with Brando. In *The Missouri Breaks*, an Arthur Penn movie of the seventies, Brando in a dress, a transvestite, was the most sadistic and most
feared killer in the West. It is a very strange take on the American Western. And it does not explain itself. Penn uses Nicholson to represent comparative goodness, and the movie does not recover from that mistake: it
should be about shades and variants of evil. But instead it is unsentimental where Brando is concerned, and sentimental at the core.

Part of what Brando is as a male diva is indiscreet and extreme. Sex
with its unphotographable internal hydraulics and its equally unphotographable heats and progressions of response is beyond a Hollywood
story and is perhaps beyond the camera except as pornographic detail,
mere information. But Brando can act this. He began as Cherubino, an
adolescent sex fiend. He progressed to Figaro, working-class sensibility
and successful sexuality. He moved on to Almaviva, the corrupt count or
duke or godfather.

In American movies, sex, like society and community, is over-glamorized up or down as good or evil, and is briefly glimpsed through a haze of stylish misinformation and ignorant mannerism. This is very strange and may be what gives American movies their quality of fantasy. And this is what Brando works counter to. He seems obsessed or crazed, he is so unyieldingly anti-bullshit. Brando did not at first buy into the myth of his own sexual stardom. Stars tend to be boastful and expectant toward the possibilities of sex for themselves, and sexual actuality often makes them sullen, disappointed, angry, and sexually conspiratorial and hugely self-destructive in sexual matters.

In someone as actively sexual as Brando, it is perhaps to be expected to find a sense of truth and so great a degree of self-centered solipsism. The willed nature of overt sexuality in a promiscuous and public figure—in Magnani or Errol Flynn or Mailer—the impostor element, the elements of swagger and of hallucination, and the oppression of performance leads to hatred, to rage, to an angry or sullen self-exposure, very un-English, very unlyrical. The exquisitely overstressed anguish (and anguished cruelty) of self-discovery, starting in childhood or used to mark the end of childhood, was Brando's gift to American and then world culture, and it dominates the way articles in the media are written.

Our acceptance of the senseless, operator, dreamlike Oz of the movies doesn't mean we are cheated by them. But, even with all the power of movie illusionism to help him, Brando never seems to *love*—not in *Sayonara* or *Reflections* or *On the Waterfront*. That absence of love in him was part of the teasing sharpness of projection he had—part of the icon. It is doubtful whether Brando was capable of portraying love, or even obsession, on-screen—brutal or not, with a man or a woman. Though he hints at but denies solitude, Brando is magnificently obscene as someone alone, a sort of embodied will taken from his own daydreams and played on-screen and then abducted by the world.

The Manso book details various aspects of this. Brando mentions it in his book but doesn't give accounts or examples. Between the two books, we are left with a sense of a man who earned between fifty and a hundred million dollars, much of which was stolen or lost. A man who slept with a couple of thousand women, perhaps several thousand, and with a hidden number of men. A man considered the best actor of his time. In his case the Dorothy-in-Oz thing of being a movie star is a concomitant of an unclassical and pragmatic narcissism, an emotional isolation. In his book he seems to be saying that his triumph occurred among artificial creatures—that other people were fabulously unreal and meant little to him. In his life he seems to have found more reality among people of another culture, people less successful, or among the other sex—among women as sensitive, mad-for-him bimbos. He seems to have seen other people as unenlightened.

The maybe innocent inability or unwillingness to project any real feeling or desire toward anyone else becomes in Brando's work a kind of sadism mixed with masochism. He explores this in *One-Eyed Jacks*—a bad movie with a great many insights in it. The worldwide romance with Brando was clearly an S and M business—as it was with Bardot. For me, the resonance of his popularity is always there, in any consideration of his art or of his purposes. After Brando's success came, it was not clear whether his isolation was a sophisticated sense of the world, a form of heroism, a screen fantasy of male independence (the inevitable result of talent, stardom, and intelligence), or a cry for help.

Brando may have been emotionally recalcitrant, but he was not recalcitrant material as an actor. He was a supreme technician, and was superb as a director's surrogate—just as he was superb as our surrogate. It was also clear that he was morally-amorally one of the mass, a mass-man. This contradiction was never resolved in his movies or by those who wrote about him. Bertolucci saw it, but I doubt whether he actually directed Brando. Bertolucci is not a mass-man, and he made the mistake of casting Brando in *Last Tango* as an expatriate in Paris who is down on his luck.

In that movie, Brando presents sexual failure as the failure of life to have meaning, as the sexual failure of *capitalism*. He ate the subject up and spat it out—a socialist, vanity-struck Dorothy in the sexual Oz of the postwar world. But his defiance and pride are not those of an expatriate failure. The betrayals by women and the bestiality of women are presented belligerently in Brando's performance. Brando parades guilt, dissatisfaction, and a sort of infantile sadism—a tantrum of resistance to his own masochism, perhaps—and he does grand-but-grungy soliloquies, but what I see is an extraordinarily powerful personality being punitive and suicidal because it is *time*, because the biological clock is running out for him. The movie consists of scenes as self-conscious as the musical num-

bers in *An American in Paris*. But what survives in memory as the dominating image is the aging and enraged Brando.

I think Brando failed to be a defeated expatriate—failed even to be
defeated by age—in *Last Tango*, just as he is undefeated in his so-called
autobiography. He emerges as undefeated even in Manso's assault on him.
Brando's book is full of present-tense moments and of long-term sweep-
ing remarks. He is trying to hide himself in a performance separated from
theatrical time and sequence, and he succeeds. Brando says in his book
that he likes to talk, but he gives no examples. Manso doesn't, either. He
relies on Capote's interview with Brando. Most of the meanings Manso
suggests for Brando's actions and most of the interpretations he offers of
Brando's character are hinted at in the Capote interview (which he quotes
substantially): the self-involvement, the self-created royalty, the tinge of
ignorance. But the interview itself seems dated.

The traits ascribed to Brando can be ascribed to Garbo, too—and to
Alice Faye, for that matter. Even Myrna Loy was accused of them. It is
possible to argue that the older Brando's performances consisted largely of
a world-weariness, a cold irony or disillusion that was perceptibly asexual
or anti-sexual—a contemptuousness toward sex that you found in some of
those women stars.

With Brando it is also possible that meaning is derived from a faded
Catholicism and is genuinely hellish. Evil rules the planet. But Brando is
ambiguously dark, since a suspect optimism and utopianism appear in
him and in his work. Like most other fifties figures, Brando spent enormous amounts of time in analysis, but Brando Faustianly chose to be the
father of a largely unverbal dogma. Brando in a movie, as onstage, inserts
bits of business, cadenzas that express, nonverbally or in clumsy speeches,
his own theories and views of life. Brando as a god? Control of the screen
by men makes them figures of sexual fantasy. One might argue that
Brando exists most successfully in the realm of the lively hallucinations
that accompany sex, the tales one tells oneself to make fucking work or
while masturbating.

Power in an aging man is a valid image—as valid as the loss of power.
Brando with jowls and tough, slightly crazed eyes became an image of
money and power and pained and eroding self-satisfaction.

. . .

I never knew Brando. But one time, in New York, my agent and Irene Selznick arranged adjoining house seats for Brando and me at *The Entertainer*. Laurence Olivier was terrific in a tiresome piece of work about the collapse of the British Empire. ("*Who cares?*" I muttered.) As a seedy music-hall entertainer, Olivier put on a superbly interesting performance. Brando, beautifully dressed, was hunched down in his seat and gave an impression of startling tininess—not that he was so tiny, but he had a colossal power of projection, which worked even at close range. His hands were small. He had a Baryshnikov-like authority, but a very different sort of masculinity—less noble and more impish.

He did not laugh or breathe or applaud in any way that drew attention. He watched and studied, and occasionally he and I looked at each other. My wife then, Joanna Brown, did not like Brando's work, and she paid little or no attention to him. In his book Brando says that Olivier did not "play down" in terms of accent. He meant that Olivier did not directly act out social class. But no one had before Brando. And that wasn't the issue with Olivier; the issue was the fourth wall, was self-consciousness at being a performer. Wonderful as Olivier was, his performance was a glorified *reading*, not an embodiment. But, I repeat, it was wonderful.

"It's not hammy," I said to Brando, with a kind of amazement, at intermission. People had gathered in sufficient numbers in both aisles so that it looked too difficult to make a try for the lobby and a cigarette.

"No. It's really good work," Brando said, in the most educated and class-ridden and modest way you can imagine.

"He really hates it," I muttered to my wife, on the other side of me, and she said, "I do, too."

The crowds inched forward. Certain brash or enamored souls led the way. Suddenly they were all around us. But it was a polite crowd, a theater crowd. Brando gave autographs and responded to compliments and was not mocking.

He said to me, "I'm sorry about this."

When the bell sounded to signal the end of intermission, Brando said to the gathered crowd, "We don't want to hold up the play." The crowd then mostly scattered. A few people went on staring and sighing at him. He sighed, too, and hunched down. The lights went off, and Brando scrunched in his seat and became tininess itself again.

At the end, he said, "I wouldn't do it this way." Which was kind of obvious. Olivier not only played directly to the audience but used British theatrical culture as a context and kept the characterization at a sliding distance, entering it more fully sometimes than at other times. At no moment did he stop being Olivier doing a music-hall turn. I have never been more *entertained* in the theater, and I said that to Brando. I said I was knocked out. "But it's a stupid play," I said.

He said, "Yeah"—meaning, as far as I could tell, that the play had no truth in his and my sense. (I say "my" because I was influenced by him.) The play was meant to have tidy language that rose to symbolic truth and poetry. But this was overmatched by Olivier's crass poetry of stardom. He gave a great performance, of a nakedly seductive sort. "I will tell him he's wonderful, and I will mean it," Brando said, sighing very heavily, as the autograph seekers and admirers gathered again.

Olivier, around the end of his playing actively sexual men onscreen, costarred in *The Prince and the Showgirl* (1958) with Marilyn Monroe, the woman who was the measure of fifties male sexuality. The combination was a curious one. What Olivier knew about sexual attraction and what Monroe knew about it did not match up. Monroe knew nothing— or, rather, cared nothing—about consequences. She seemed to be far wilder than Brando. She was Miss Unafraid, Miss Un-Freud, a free woman. Both she and Olivier used a subtext of humiliation in their acting. (Olivier's Heathcliff, his Maxim de Winter, his Henry V, his Richard III, and his Archie Rice have that British poetry of humiliation and subordination.) Monroe used the good cheer in the face of degradation which she projected in the comedies she did. She never showed that she hated humiliation.

Brando usually did show that he hated it. He complained of the humiliation in being an actor. His rage, unlike Olivier's and Monroe's, was not beneath the skin; it was clearly visible on the surface. The ambiguous Olivier, with his vast technical resources and intelligence, made filigrees out of male humiliation. Monroe was monstrous with wet-lipped satisfaction and as-if-low IQ and with delight—with her own sort of playing for keeps. Just as Brando did with his costars and directors, she humiliated Olivier, wiped him off the screen. (What an odd Dorothy *she* would have made.) Most of the pleasure of the movie is in her dominance over Olivier's intelligent talent, over greatness, over perceptible culture. Brando was a similar construct onscreen. It may spring from innate humiliation, this relentlessness. (The reason for it in Brando is not clear from either book. In the Manso he is judged to be a demon. In his autobiography he presents himself as someone perennially young who was not empowered by youth. That can't be true, can it?)

To use Monroe to see Brando is not eccentric. Monroe in *Some Like It Hot* played a mostly bright-tempered gold digger, a woman who was imprisoned in her sexual persona and freed from sexual pressure at the same time, who was self-hugged and flauntingly open—who needed no one and accepted everyone. This description could easily be applied to Brando. Monroe was jollier on the surface than he, but there was the same devouring thing in both of them. I imagine that people they went to bed with didn't have to be sexual; Brando and Monroe would be sexual for them. A man *became* sexual, plugging into Monroe's unjudgmental, priestess-of-sexual-gluttony welcome. It hardly mattered what any man's sexual lacks or merits were. What mattered was her magic. So, too, with Brando.

For me, Brando is a point at which definitions begin. He is one of the basic tautologies of our age. If you ask people to talk about him as a performer, the most common response you are likely to get is *Brando is Brando*. He seems nowadays to be more admired as an artist by men than by women. But he has been a force for equality, for miscegenation of all sorts.

When Brando lost his sexual vanity and his power of sexual suggestion, everything changed for him, but he has kept on going in a kind of loony autobiographical momentum. As an old man Brando seems a bit automatic: not manipulative so much as still automatically vivid, still automatically irresistible. (Genuinely so; I do not mean this ironically.) I suppose he is trying too hard, with death being so near. Everyone around him—parents and wives and lovers—has robbed him of money and pride, or tried to. His autobiography is intelligent, and, as I said, the more he lies the more a sense of truth emerges. The lifelong performance on his part of very strange notions of rage and self-pity and pity for others, of absolution for the male at the soldier level and absolution for himself, continues in his book and will continue, it is clear, until he dies.

1994

WHY IS
THIS WOMAN FUNNY?

No one of my friends could understand why I wanted to write about Carol Burnett—not that my friends are so much alike or that they make up a New York group—but Carol Burnett seemed an unlikely enthusiasm for me. Partly, of course, that was because of the sort of man I am or seem to be, but partly it was that even in television terms, Carol Burnett is not what my friends would expect me to watch. My friends liked *Laugh-In* when it was new, have maybe one violent program they addictedly watch, or they gaze at old movies. (I think movies on television lose an essential part of their glamour: the figures on the screen have to be big, and I have to look up—I think that is in order to reproduce childhood spying, spying on the grown-ups, seeing what the grown-ups, the freed-of-restrictions, the starring souls do.)

Burnett's audience presumably consists of people in or from small towns, people more poor than rich, less educated rather than more, women more than men, children more than grown-ups—the peripheral, the half-mad, the violent; also, the self-loving, the complacent, the odd, incomprehensible people of Middle America, those who are not in the mainstream of money and power. Only by stretching several points do I fit in with the rest of her audience—if this *is* her audience, and not simply a New York-ish view of who watches Burnett—but actually it is a fine audience for a comic, in some ways . . . and a dreadful one in others.

The thing about Burnett is that at moments—and not very often—she engages in a kind of total and ruthless, infuriated at-the-way-some-people-are, peripheral-person's explosive burlesque, hostile, honest, cold-eyed, like someone saying, "A lie is a lie, and you're lying." It is done as comedy from the odd vantage point of a folk performer, as was the work of Chaplin and Fields. When Burnett works in that vein, it seems to me she is gross, demonic, American, and possessed of comic genius.

But Chaplin's comedy, its use of cannibalism (in *The Gold Rush*), bullying, alienation, poverty, and the threat of death, was coated with a gentle, self-loving sweetness that becomes more palatable to me as I get older. Fields's lazy silliness marred everything he did, as well as being, like his essentially passive bitterness—he can barely bestir himself in many senses to act—close to the center of what made him marvelous. At times, he was merciless, not just toward villains but toward women, children, and himself (he was often kinder to the villains than to the women he dealt with): he was often semi-loathsome. Burnett is never self-loving, never lazy, and not particularly passive. She will go farther than Fields—with a woman's extremism—and be entirely loathsome—but funny.

For me what is *funny* is something that undoes my sobriety entirely, upsets me, upsets my balance so that I laugh and keep on laughing to the point of pain, and am unable to stop laughing. I realize I got that definition of *funny* from the movies, from experiencing that kind of laughter at the movies. As a child, I first laughed at the Marx Brothers (and knew, without knowing the word, they represented anarchy: they represented people who did not study, who were not middle-class). Then there was early Bob Hope; in his first movies, so my perhaps defective memory informs me, he was usually frightened, easily gulled by cleverer, more *grown-up* people—but he kept on wisecracking. I must have been ten years old or so at that point. Then Danny Kaye came along at a time when I was gawky, and he took gawkiness to a point in his early movies where I fell out of my chair in the theater and lay on the floor laughing. Then there was no one. I thought it was me—and perhaps it was. I was probably more in the mood for Garbo. Then when the glare of romance died down, I started hunting again for that ancient laughter. But Danny Kaye had taken up pathos by then, Sid Caesar had too, and Bob Hope had become, in his comic persona, a prosperous corporation executive, who joked and was a swindler and was apparently semi-impotent with women. There was Lucille Ball: she was the best; she set up enormous contraptions of circumstance, that then trapped her, and I laughed, but the show she did was based on a fantasy of innocence: Lucy lied, stole, envied, did various kinds of harm, but she was always innocent. Innocence, like pathos, is a form of self-pity, is a claim that *these things shouldn't be done to me*, and that claim dries up my ability to laugh, even when watching people as skillful as Nichols and May. This is because the sympathy it inspires depresses me, and also because it is unlike the sympathy with struggle and demolition that underlies the hilarity of my childhood and that I still occasionally pursue.

I cannot remember a single episode of the interminable *Lucy* series although I must have seen a hundred or more, but I do remember a skit Burnett did five years ago, although I may not remember it correctly— and I may not be able to make it funny.

Burnett came out of a bedroom dressed in a rumpled bathrobe; it was clearly early in the morning, and she was either a housewife or a maid: it was something of a toss-up; she had a look of servant's malice, of taking shortcuts, of no middle-class illusions; on the other hand she had a kind of knotty pride like someone who'd escaped becoming the prey of her husband. She was an unclean winner, and fairly detestable, but it was okay (I thought it was funny) maybe because she radiated a cheater's determination to survive. She seemed to be a woman of primarily underhanded persistence. It seemed odd and unsettling and funny to me that in this context, a television show, Burnett would pantomime a housewife in that way.

Burnett picked up a basket of dirty laundry, carried it across a frighteningly white, barren kitchen, put the basket down and opened the lid of a washing machine. At that time there was a commercial in which a very muscular, hairless male arm came out of a washing machine brandishing a box of detergent. The suggestion was more or less that a woman could harness the strength of a powerfully built male, could get such a man inside her washing machine to labor for her there. Burnett crammed dirty clothes in the machine, they were tossed out again, and Burnett put them in again, they were tossed out; she peered into the machine, and the strong, hairless, male arm came out, formed a fist, and slugged her in the jaw. She fell to the floor, then crouched there on her hands and knees looking—sickened but enraged—at the hairless arm waving out of the opening of the machine; she *plotted*; she got up and, with a combination of deception, of creeping and swiftness, got the dirty laundry close to the machine (behind her back I think), whipped it into the machine, slammed and locked the lid, and maybe showed a little satisfaction with her dirty pool. Then she turned on the machine; it shuddered; and it began to grow—as in the other commercial. It rose up and up, hit the ceiling, plaster came down. Burnett snarled, I think. Then she shrugged, maybe, and trudged to the sink, opened the window above it, and hundreds of doves flew in, some settled on her hair, on her shoulders; the kitchen was filled with birds; she beat at them; her face became horrified as if at the quantity of guano being deposited not only in her kitchen but all over the world; and she cowered, as anyone would have. She brushed off the last dove, straightened up, looking weakened but not defeated, and she went to the icebox, leaned in, and a huge crown was thrust on her head. She backed out struggling and holding and eating a cracker with margarine on it. Struggling to get the crown off, she had a face of great bitterness. She did get it off; she slung it violently away; and she went back to the washing machine which among clumps of plaster sat there, having returned from its former size. She cautiously tiptoed to it, opened it and, ducking her head, grabbed her clothes out of it and slammed the lid shut again. She went out in the backyard to hang the clothes up, and you heard hoofbeats, galloping, and saw moving past the kitchen window the white Ajax knight, I think. There came a terrible scream. A pause, and then Burnett staggered back into the kitchen, holding a lance that runs through her. And she died.

In a parody of a spy movie that Rita Hayworth did called *Gilda*, Burnett dances in a strapless black dress with a slit up the side and in long white gloves to signal information with her hips to the Allies. As she dances, something comes over her, and she wig-waggles information with a demonic exhibitionism. When she is shot, she does not die quietly: she spreads her arms, her fingers, and she shrieks, making it quite clear it hurts.

As a nagging slattern whose husband vaguely threatens to hit her, she effortlessly, while chewing on a snack, tears the telephone book in half. Lady Bird, Lynda, and the other one were, in sketches, given the voices of maniacs, sweet but barely in control. Mrs. Nixon with a frozen and imbecilic and supremely tortured smile was a woman of limited intelligence who had become catatonic sometime ago. Burnett seemed to manage to embody the unpleasantness of the world, politicians' wives, soap-opera pretensions, all of that. Some of her work was quieter and still funny:

there have been a number of husband-wife skits of that sort. But her horrors were very special. To some extent they were like George Price cartoons, and to some extent they were like the women in W. C. Fields but done by a woman, placed at stage center, and exaggerated into a ballooning heartlessness. Some people I spoke to said of those skits that they were too shocked watching them to laugh; they were merely aghast. And it seemed obvious to me, she could not go on doing those skits, or ever do many of them on television unless the American audience was a good deal unlike what it is widely held to be.

It seemed especially likely that she would not go on doing this sort of thing when her program was switched from 10 P.M. Monday nights to 8 Wednesday nights: an earlier audience meant, in television tactics, more sweetness, more amorphousness. The whole thing in fact mystified me: why was she doing this on television anyway? It seemed to me odd that a woman known for her niceness should be doing this at all. I couldn't believe the American audience would stand for seeing women caricatured and examined in this way, or had the American public grown up at some point while my back was turned? It seemed to me that American comedy fell into two categories: it was either self-pitying, or it was essentially moral, like Burnett's. But most of what she did was not like the stuff I wrote about above: did that mean of her, let's say, fifty writers, one wrote that stuff? Did her husband occasionally talk her into doing these things? I didn't think there would be any direct answers given: if it was, in the opinion of the people working on the show, an advantage to advertise this facet of Burnett's work, it would have been done by now. Clearly (I said to myself) for television purposes, her image as a nice person is more important to the program's survival. Anyway, it seemed to me very odd no one had looked into this.

The PR man who met my plane in Los Angeles remarked that his accountant said his Cadillac was as cheap for him to drive as a Volkswagen would be. He spoke to me of Miss Burnett's niceness; he did not mention her comedy. Her particular PR man, who is assigned to her show, seemed to have difficulty hearing my questions. He too spoke of her niceness, not her comedy; I asked him about the comedy, and he said, "She still makes me laugh." We went to the studios to have lunch with Miss Burnett's husband, Joe Hamilton. We were early and waited in a small office. Miss

Burnett came in and we were introduced. I am not quite sure why I was scowling. Perhaps her extreme friendliness nettled me: I do not like to be nudged.

She said, "Hi. We're going to get together later in the week, Rick says we're going to have *lunch* together. I'm really looking forward to it, tell me what you'd like to eat and we'll have it." (Rick was the PR man.)

We looked into each other's eyes with what seemed to me the overwhelming truth of our nonacquaintance. I said I did not care what we ate.

She said, in what was perhaps a determinedly friendly way, "There has to be something you'd like—now tell me: we'll have it. . . ."

I raised both eyebrows and tried to think of what would be easy to cut, that one could eat without paying much attention to it, and that would not splatter. "Hamburgers?" I said.

"Oh good," she said. She was wearing sneakers. She said, "I'm glad—we'll have those." She repeated that she was looking forward to talking to me, and she bounded out.

When she was gone, the PR man said pointedly to me, "What did I tell you: Carol's a real sweetheart. What's different about her is that she really likes people."

I said, "You have no idea how unreal all this is to me," and I sat down to make notes on the above exchange.

Her husband, Joe Hamilton, who is the executive producer of the show, is good-looking in the style of the five best-looking boys in high school—if you went to high school in the early 1940s. He had an air of decency, no pretensions, no signs of nervousness; he did seem unreachable, inward, well-guarded. He did not look like an educated man. He seemed to be well-ordered and someone I would want to like me—I thought it was unprofessional to want him to like me, so I was stiff and—ah—relentless in manner.

At first, in answer to my questions, he said such things as "We try to do good comedy." What do you mean by good comedy, Mr. Hamilton? "You can always get what I call a cheap laugh," he said, "by having Carol pretend to be caught naked in the bathtub: that isn't the sort of thing we do."

I asked him if he ever theorized about comedy, and he said no, Carol did it some, more than he, not a hell of a lot, though.

I said I thought some of her comedy was savage. "Savage?" he said. "I don't think that describes what we do."

I asked him if he would mind describing his wife's comedy. He said, "I wouldn't say Carol was a comedian. She's an actress who does comedy." I asked him to define the comedy she did as an actress. Hamilton said, "Well, she can't just be funny: she has to be a comic character, it's what the character does that's funny: it has to be realistic. . . ."

I asked him if "realistic" did not, considering the way the world was, mean being sharp or unpleasant. He looked at me. "That will come out of the character."

I asked if he would say all her comedy was kind. He said, "We upset some people, we upset somebody all the time. We try to use taste. . . . You know, I've never had an interview like this before."

I asked him if I could ask him what he thought of other comics—I figured asking him that was giving a sort of comedy Rorschach. He said, "Go ahead." I said, "Chaplin." He said, "I don't really know his work or remember it very well." Fields: "He was mean, he was *very* mean." (And he made a slight face of distaste.) The Marx Brothers: "Groucho was the best—he made it all work." Bob Hope: "A good joke teller?" Zero Mostel: "Very, very good—but a little too much." Mort Sahl: "Mort Sahl when he started out was the funniest man in the world." Streisand: "Funny and unique, but she's too slow working on something to be funny on television." Johnny Carson: "I don't think he is a comedian."

It seemed to me he liked verbal comedy with some acidity, some anarchy to it, but that he liked his satire well-grounded, that is, not in madness, but in sanity; you can interpret the Rorschach differently if you want to. Certainly, he was no fool.

Then he asked me if I really thought some of his wife's comedy was cutting. I said I did and that she did this only a small percentage of the time. Then I asked him if he'd ever thought how little self-pity there was in her comedy compared to the work of any other living comic. If, in a slapstick sketch, she fell or was hit, she was not put upon or merely hurt, or sweetly hurt, but she became angry or murderous, or merely ignored the pain. He said, "That's interesting. I think that's true—at times. I think I've noticed that but I never really said to myself that was what she does. I'm not sure she does it all the time. I *partly* see what you mean." He said, "This is a very strange interview. . . . What else do you want to know?" And he laughed.

The next day I went to see the man who is listed as being "supervisor" of the comedy writers; he is also listed as producer of the show.

Arnie Rosen is from Brooklyn. He has dark hair cut short, a dark beard, closely trimmed, and the sad, sharp eyes of a man who has at some time in his life been tormented but has subsequently been soothed.

We talked for a while and then I asked about the savagery that there occasionally was in Burnett's comedy, where did it come from? Rosen said, "No: that's wrong. Not savagery. It's sweeter than savagery." Then what terms would he use? He said, "Well, maybe Carol would be uncomfortable to think along these lines but we know pretty well, don't we, that the basis of all humor is cruelty." He went on, "Good comedy writing means you fit the skit to the performer—to Carol—and to whomever she's doing the skit with. So I have to qualify what I said. The basis is cruelty but you don't have to go all out—" What did he mean by cruelty, I asked. "You know, pie in the face, falling on a banana, or a one-word thing: realism. But we do all kinds of humor—not just that." But you said the basis of all comedy was cruelty. "Well, more or less." Is the crueler comedy funnier than the other? "I tend to prefer some of the more biting sketches. . . . I like the nag, George and Zelda, those are indictments. And the Carol and Sis sketches which are really about the marriage between Carol and Harvey—we do some skits where what is dealt with is anger and hostility in the wife. . . ." I said that it seemed he and I looked at the comedy in the same way and he said, "If you say sharp, we're in agreement, but you said savage." I said, "Maybe I'm wrong."

To the, ah, comedy Rorschach, he gave the following answers: Chaplin—"A genius. The father of us all. Great. Very great." Mae West and W. C. Fields—"I like them. They built good, solid comic characters; Fields was excellent as the likeable villain." Marx Brothers—"Yes and no: if you talk about the great moments, the peak moments, for those moments yes, a strong yes, I like them, I admired them, but on the whole, no." Bob Hope—"Radio, yes. But since then with limited interest." Red Skelton—"No." Lucille Ball—"A fine comedienne—as Lucy."

He said, "I don't want to knock *Laugh-In*. What they do is good; but it's just criticism. They don't act anything out; they just give lines. We try to reach for the real thing—or maybe that's too strong: we reach for a reflection of life—a percentage of what we do is that. . . . I'll tell you what I think it is: I think a lot of Carol's comedy is survival-oriented. You take a woman like that, a girl, with the childhood she had, and people, no one ever thought she was a beauty, there's going to be that survival drive or there's going to be nothing. . . . You take a woman, a person, who never shows temper, who knows what outlet there is in the work: who can say? Think what you want to think. I don't say she does this. Maybe she doesn't do it consciously but you can think it's there if that's the way you like to think. But here is a woman who is very intelligent, *very* intelligent, and she is *addicted* to comedy. . . ."

I asked him if a lot of what she did was really his comedy. He said, "Sure, some of it's me but that's because I've worked with Carol for years. . . . I used to do the Phil Silvers show, *Sergeant Bilko*. . . . To some extent Carol thinks like me now. . . . We try to keep the characters she does sympathetic—"

"The nag?"

"Well, but everybody's seen her or knows her or has an aunt like her, and don't forget that's not Burnett, it's a character Carol is playing. . . . Carol hates to play forceful, mean dames: she has to be talked into it. . . . You have to remember, this girl is an actress, she can do anything, she's the most talented performer in America today: she sings, she dances—"

"Not all that well."

"But well enough for someone who's as funny as she is. She's pretty good."

I asked him if he had to keep the audience in mind: "We have taboos: we're never obviously cruel, never obviously biased; when she's in a skit, we try to make it palatable." I asked him about the giant salami Burnett had carried in a nag sketch and he said, "I think that was Carol's idea. . . . She enhances things." I asked him if she read Freud and he said, "It's hard to tell what she knows and doesn't know. . . . You say we're savage: I don't think that's the word. But when we find a target, maybe there's a little of the feeling of seek and destroy. . . ." I asked him to give me examples: "The Johnson and Nixon sketches we did were mean parodies. . . . And the Doris Day one: Doris Day's son wrote a letter of complaint about that one. . . . You wouldn't believe Carol could do Doris Day. She was the distillation of phony virginity. She sang the most syrupy *Que Sera, Sera*. Her cheerfulness was—there are no words for it. . . . We want to do a Kissinger takeoff with him more concerned with his image as a ladies' man than with affairs of state. He's being interviewed by the Burnett character, and his secretary comes in and says, 'Jill St. John is on the hot line. . . .' Maybe you won't find that sarcastic but our viewers will. . . .'

We're working on a sketch, a Carol and Sis, where Harvey wakes up in the middle of the night—in a sweat. He dreamed he died, and Carol's period of mourning was eight minutes; she has an affair with the pilot next door and the lawyer who was Korman's best buddy. . . . We don't hit every time but I wish people would just come out and say this was a good, sharp, incisive, intelligently written show."

I went to see a run-through of the show for that week. Burnett seemed underkeyed and very much more skillful and sharp in her timing than on television. Some of the physical comedy was very funny, the pratfalls. The same routines on television two weeks later seemed flat, slow, and unferocious.

As she worked, and during the pauses, in the run-through, she was pleasant to everyone, apparently unself-conscious, and she did not seem to arrogate to herself any prerogatives. It seemed to me, however, that her pleasantness was considerably shallower toward some people than to others; it was graded. The PR man was sitting next to me, and I murmured to him, "I would like to begin the piece, 'I dislike Carol Burnett as a person.' "

He said, urgently, "That would hurt her very much."

I was willing to bet the world was largely defined for her by her mind. Survivors trust their minds more than their emotions—you can love unwisely and still love well, but you can't think unwisely and still think well, or so they are inclined to believe. I knew she said to interviewers that both her parents had been alcoholics, that she'd grown up with her grandmother, that they'd lived in one room in a boardinghouse in Los Angeles. In New York, when no one would hire her, she'd put on a revue with other young people who'd had trouble getting started in show business; as a result she got nightclub work, sang a song called "I Made a Fool of Myself over John Foster Dulles." She sang with such rapacity that she won some recognition at once; she did nightclubs for a while; the man who wrote the song for her works for her now. She did daytime television, and then she was asked to go on for an ailing Martha Raye on a nighttime show, a show Joe Hamilton produced. Miss Burnett learned Miss Raye's lines and all her comic business in a few hours and said to the PR man (he told me), "You'd be surprised how fast you can learn when you're hungry." She was a success to the extent that she became a regular on the show she had replaced Martha Raye on. She did an off-Broadway musical called *Once upon a Mattress* and engaged in publicity stunts and got the show to Broadway. Then Comden and Green wrote a musical for her, *Fade Out, Fade In,* another reprise about a girl who becomes A Movie Star. She was a hit, as I recall, but the musical was not; still it ran; but about that time she had married Joe Hamilton, who had eight children from a first marriage; and she hurt her neck or her leg, or both; I don't remember: she left the show amid rumors of temperament and God knows what all. Broadway brouhaha. She said in interviews then that she'd hurt her neck, she was in pain. There was ill feeling among the sponsors of the musical who somehow blamed her marriage for her abandoning the show. Without her in it, the show folded. Then she rusticated for a while. She did some television specials which were successful, and about five years ago she began doing her hour-long variety show. Her marriage is reputed to be an exceptionally happy one. . . .

I went to her dressing room. She is not photogenic, and she has a great deal of physical magnetism, which is to say she is attractive. There was about her at first an odd mixture of charisma and extremely careful modesty.

She said, "I'm in awe of you."

"Don't be," I said, crisply. "I'm a bumbler." (I assumed she was being tactical in her flattery.) I said, "Your PR man said if I wrote a piece that began, 'I don't like Carol Burnett as a person,' you'd be hurt—is that true?"

"Yes."

I asked her why, how could that be? I could be any sort of New York neurotic, or half insane, or someone who loathed her lifestyle, or have some mysterious purpose that made me not open to her personal worth. She said, "Yes. But you'd met me, you spoke to me: it's not that you read a book I wrote; when somebody is a performer, it's themselves they're offering, and I don't care what anybody says, it hurts when that's rejected." I asked her if she wasn't used to being rejected by some critics and some people; after all, she was a star and—

She cut in, "I'm not a star. There are only about five stars in the world." Who, I asked. She thought and said, "Well, there are more than five—I don't think I want too much to go into that." She has a pleasant laugh; she laughed. "Do I have to go into it?" I asked her what she meant by star. She said, "Longevity: if I'm still around in twenty years, you can call me a star." I asked her if she minded talking about comedy. She said, "I know you have very interesting theories about it, and I want to talk about it, I'd be very interested, but to tell you the truth, I've never thought about it much."

I asked her if she had any general, overarching ideas about what was funny, any formulas about comedy. She said, "Well, I think the same things make people cry but different things make people laugh. For example, in a sad thing, if someone dies, everyone is sad, but not everyone finds a pie in the face funny." What things have you found make people laugh? "So many things. . . . I don't know how to put it. A voice—usually a voice, and—I don't know what to say. I think what it is, is we all laugh about people we know. . . ."

A little later she said, "I know when something is funny because I think, *that's true.* . . . I shouldn't sound so sure of myself. I *think* I know when something is funny because I—no. I know when *I* think something is funny because I think that."

I asked her what sort of comedy she liked to do, and I think she was, amiably enough, putting me on when she answered, "I never thought about these things before. I'd say mostly satire, comments on human nature, things like that, people's foibles."

I wondered if she often used words like *foibles.* I asked her if satire was not often a bit harsh or unkind. She said, "I don't think it's unkind—its just comedy."

We talked a bit, and then, wanting to get at what aroused the satirist in her, I said, "Well, let me ask you about the queen of England: how would you react to meeting her?"

"I guess I'd be thrilled."

"Would you curtsy? Let me explain. Jackie Onassis, when she was Jackie Kennedy, refused to curtsy, she said it was not for her as an American to do that, and so she shook hands with the queen."

"No, I wouldn't do that. I'd do the other. I'd do it *all.* When in Rome, I guess. I think I'd hire a teacher and really learn to do the curtsy *right.* It would be fun to learn, and I'm good at learning things: I'd learn to curtsy very well. I like doing things that are educational, I like to get into things where I don't know my way around, where I have to learn, where I'm not sure of myself. I don't know enough. I need an education. I like to be among people and pick things up from life. I—"

"But how would you feel about the affectation?"

"Well, I did the queen of England once."

"You did!"

"Canada wasn't too thrilled."

"What bothered them?" I thought she'd have to mention the element of caricature.

She said, "My skirt. I had a miniskirt with the British flag on it, and well, you know, comedy has to be a little exaggerated, it has to be a little left of center or no one laughs— Oh! That's what you're getting at. No, no. All it was, was I looked just like her and I—well, they were upset."

"Was the sketch hard on her affectations?"

"Oh *no*. . . . I don't think so. . . . But things were exaggerated—to make it comedy." She smiled and clasped her hands in front of her.

"Have you by any chance met the queen of England?"

"Me? How would I ever get the *chance*?"

"Your show is shown in England."

"You think *she* watches? I'm not exactly what you'd call a *household* name in England. . . ."

"What do you mean by left of center, or by *exaggerated*?"

"I don't know if this is what you want but what I like is when it's real, the more real it is, but in a dumb situation—you have to have the dumb situation, and then what I like is the *logic*. . . . I go with the logic of that character in that dumb situation."

"But the *left-of-center*, and the *exaggeration*?"

"That's in the logic."

"And when you mug, that isn't exaggeration?"

"I mug if the skit isn't comfortable for me. Then I might do anything."

I asked her what she meant. She said she couldn't do some skits. I told her Arnie Rosen had said she could do anything. "Did he say that? That was nice of him. I can't, though. I can't play nervous, frightened people. I hate to play—hate is such a strong word: I don't like—no. I *find it difficult* to play, oh, you know, nervous Nellies. Now Don Knotts can do it. But I can't."

"Arnie said you prefer to play shy women, that you have to be talked into playing forceful, mean women—is that true?"

"I don't know. I don't think so. Not as far as I know."

Her manner had changed but I hadn't noticed when or why. . . . I said I'd seen a tape of a sketch in which she played a shy, nervous secretary.

"That was the hardest sketch I ever did! I couldn't get into her, I couldn't get *near*. I didn't know what to do so I just played Tom and Jerry."

"What?"

"The cartoons—the Tom and Jerry cartoons: first you do this, then you do that, she does things. . . . Some of the things she did were funny—lifting the bottle to hit him and there's no top on it, and it runs all over her head, that was funny I thought, but I didn't understand that girl. . . . To tell you the truth, I don't *start* with, I don't work from the *inside* out: I do everything backwards: I work totally from the outside in—they have to tell me what she looks like, what's she going to wear, then I figure out how she walks, and if I'm lucky, then I can get inside her and do some good things. I used to feel defensive about working this way but I hear a lot of the good English actors—people like Olivier—work that way, and you can't say *he's* not a good actor. So I'm not defensive about it now."

"What would you like to do as a performer?"

She said, "I'd like to do hour-and-a-half shows. And movies, of course. I'd like to do movies very much. So I could get into doing three-dimensional comedy—what I'm doing now, I'm lucky if it's two-dimensional: it's slash, splut, the thing's there, or it's not, and that's *it*."

I asked her why she didn't do hour-long sketches on her show then, and she said they didn't write them for her. I asked why she didn't insist on having them written for her. She said, sort of smiling, "I do what they tell me to do. . . . And we do longer sketches sometimes: we call them 'epics'; they run about twenty-five minutes. . . . I like doing them very much."

I told her if I seemed rude, she had only to murmur I ought to desist, and I would, of course, but meanwhile, wasn't it *her* show, why did she do what "they" told her to do? (I ought also to say that by this point, I showed no disbelief in anything she said; the atmosphere was one of our being friends.) She said she didn't think it was right to tell people what to do, "And the people who work here know what to do—that's why we hired them. Why did we hire them if we're not going to listen to them? You hire people you can work with and who know what they're doing, and then you're silly not to listen to them. . . . They know more about comedy writing than I do, they know what's possible, what's not. I'm lucky: I work with good people whom I trust. . . ." I said but after all in the end it was her show, her name, she was the star; she said vehemently she was not a star. I said, "Well, what are you then, how would you describe it?" She said, "I'm successful in show business at the moment but tomorrow I may be gone. . . . So far television has produced only one real star—Lucille Ball."

Then I asked her about money (a star=money). She said, "I'm not a good talker about money. . . . I think all of us in this field are overpaid, way overpaid. Of course. . . . Those of us in this field who make it, who had nothing as kids, go one of two ways when we get it: they watch every cent, maybe they spend it but they *watch* it go, they know where every cent is, they think about it. Or they can't think about it at all, it doesn't make sense to them; as soon as it's there, when there's enough there has to be enough—you have to know it's going to be there for a while—you like go to sleep, you don't think about it, you don't *like* to think about it. These people can't handle it, they don't understand it. My business manager talks to me about money and I try, but I really don't understand a word of it. I know it's all in my head but what can I do? Let him put it somewhere and do things with it but don't tell me about it. I won't understand anyway. When he talks to me, my head goes blank. My eyes are open but I'm asleep; I don't hear a word. Once I put my head down like this and snored—he was not amused."

Along about this point, she asked me if I would like to stick around for the rest of the afternoon; she'd be in and out of the dressing room, we could talk off and on and have dinner later. After that, there was a change in her; she'd jump up and move around, and she didn't always look at me when she spoke to me. We had had lunch by then—turkey sandwiches. I asked her if she minded personal questions. She said, "Well, let's try. Try and see."

I asked her if she minded talking about religion. She said, "No. I was raised as a Christian Scientist, my grandmother was a Christian Scientist—and you know what? There was this idea in Science about never giving up—maybe I got it from there—never having a negative attitude. You know, I've told people and it's true I never thought I wouldn't make it, it just never occurred to me I might not—that thing I have about not playing nervous, defeated people, I wonder if it came from that? Do you

think it did? . . . I'm not a Scientist now. I believe in God—but a whole
religion? That's too much. I can't go all that—I don't think I'm religious
anymore. I—that's all."

"I'm getting really kind of prying but are you bringing your children
up as Catholics?"

"Yes. But more for historical than religious reasons. . . . You know,
you told Joe the characters I played never got defeated, never acted
defeated even when they were. I think that was my grandmother. I never
once questioned where I was going when I was starting out. I never questioned it that I would get there. You know what else helps you think
positively? Psycho-cybernetics." I asked her if she believed in psycho-
cybernetics. She did not stiffen but she said with small silences around her
remark, "I like it, yes." She was, I suddenly saw, not someone who liked to
be teased at all, not someone who could bear an inferior position; or I
thought I saw it. She is in earnest; she can be playful, I would imagine;
but if you tease her or don't take her seriously, that's it. She is very intense,
I think, about living her life, about enjoying her life. I asked her if she had
ever been analyzed. She took on a student's air and looked at me as if I
were a Wise Man from the East. She said, "No." Then she averted her eyes
and said, "I—" Then she said, "No." And looked at me.

I asked her if she'd read any Freud. She said, "Very little." I gazed at
her. She said, "I should read more of him." She sounded very, oh, tenta-
tively intellectual. I still looked. She said, "I don't know much about
Freud. I'm really ashamed I don't read more—" She offered me the last. I
said she didn't have much time for reading. She said, "Oh I have time. I
only work thirty hours a week. I don't read enough good books. I mean to
do something about it. But I never get to it—I'm lazy."

"Would you describe yourself as uneducated? Or stupid?" (She was
still closed in from my disinterest in psycho-cybernetics, but now suddenly, she opened up again.) She said, "No. I'm very smart. . . . But I'm
not well-read. . . ." Pause. "I think I'm very, very smart." I said, "I do too.
How much Freud *have* you read?"

"Some—but not enough that I'd come out and say I knew what he was
all about: I read a little and then I stopped."

"Why did you stop?"

"I think he's dumb! Well, not dumb, but the things he says about the
ladies are dumb. He's very mean to the ladies, and who needs that."

"Would you say the queen of England was affected?"

"She has a different life. I wouldn't judge her. I'll stick by what I said earlier—I'd be honored to meet her. I'd learn how to curtsy, I'd practice— I think it's a hoot to meet different people." I looked at her but her eyes were fixed on the wall. She said, "I like to go into places I wouldn't get to go into if I didn't have this show, I like doing special things that I get to do now, I like to see things I wouldn't ever have gotten near if it wasn't for all this: I don't want to miss any of that. And I learn from those things. I like to see people as I told you, I can learn from people, from what they do, from the things they do, and the things that happen from that. What I like, I really like it, it's what my education is, I like life to educate me."

"Do you use what you learn for satire?"

She sat up straight and said, "No!" She looked at me firmly: "I wouldn't do *that*. . . ." She looked away. "Maybe some. Not much. Maybe a little. I don't know . . . yes. I guess I do. But not coldly. I don't do it coldly. Never coldly."

Of the people I know, those who watch her with any regularity have all spent part of their youth in small towns; I was born in a town with forty-five hundred people in it, and grew up in a suburb of forty thousand people. Something in Burnett's comedy, in her herself, had always struck me as small-town, some note of flat common sense, of flatness, some note of determined democracy, some element of belief in politeness, and so on; but she'd grown up, so far as I knew, in Los Angeles.

I asked her—she was in and out for the blocking—if she minded a little biographical poking around. She said, "No, no. Go ahead. I like the way you come at me." I glanced at her; she glanced back. I said, "Where was your grandmother from?"

"California. We lived in California."

"Was she from California originally? Where were her, ah, roots?"

"I—I'm not sure. Arkansas. I think Arkansas."

Then I asked her what she was ethnically. She said, "I'm not sure. I'm a lot Irish, and I'm part Indian. . . . I didn't know my father when I was old enough to ask him who he was so I'm not sure what he was. . . . My grand-mother said my mother's side of the family, on that side we were Irish and English and there was Cherokee blood. . . . I think my father was German and French and English—and I think Irish too. I'm not clear about it."

"You said in an interview that I read that your mother was witty. In what way? I mean what was her wit like? What sort of things did she say?"

"Barbed. She was very barbed. She just peeled away phoniness. . . . She had a violent temper about those things. She had a violent temper."

"Do you ever get mad?"

"Not if I can help it . . . I do sometimes, I guess, and I get very distant, very sweet-bitchy; everyone starts climbing the walls; I get disgusting. I hate it when I'm like that—I get unattractive. . . . The thing about me is I always have to be in control—of myself: that's as a comic too; when I'm working, I have to know what I'm doing. . . . I can't work if things are out of control. . . ."

(So her comedy is self-conscious but she uses some set of terms for herself very unlike the terms I used trying to describe what she did.)

"Both your parents were alcoholics?"

"Yes."

"Do you have any memories of the 1930s? Like I remember vacant lots and—"

"Sure. We were in Texas then, I was still with my parents. There was yellow dust in the streets. I can remember almost everything. Here's something I never forgot: I was four or five, and there was a boy, he was eight, about eight, maybe seven; and he took me for a ride on his bicycle. I thought it was his bicycle, but what I didn't know was the bicycle was stolen—he took it from in front of the movie theater—" I think she said her father ran the movie theater "—and when I got home, my father was mad, really mad—because I guess he thought I knew it was stolen but I really didn't. He beat me—on the bottom. I always remembered that. He'd never raised his hand to me before, and I loved him. I loved him very much. . . ."

"Did your mother ever hit you?"

"My mother? Sure. She cuffed me around all day long. She'd give me one for this and one for that, and she'd give it to me like, 'Here's one for what you're gonna do next. . . .' "

"Didn't you mind?"

"No. She was a mother. . . . And it didn't last long." Then I understood her to say, "When she got bad, she sent me to live with my grandmother."

"You mean when she knew she was getting worse, getting out of control, she didn't want you exposed to that violence, she separated herself from you?"

"No. It wasn't like that. We all lived across the hall, in the same building, my grandmother and us. My father'd gone away then. My grandmother lived across the hall. I just went across the hall at first."

"But was there a particular reason when you moved in with your grandmother?"

"I don't think it was clear—it was a thing that happened gradually, no one knew it was happening exactly. It was just that my mother wasn't there much. My grandmother was very strict. My mother was there less and less."

"In that interview I read, you were quoted as saying you missed her."

"Well, I could do things for her now. I could afford to have her treated, to get good treatment, the really good kind, the stuff is there—what else is it good for? Money. I just could do things for her now, that's all I meant. I'd like to. I'm stronger, I understand more than I did—maybe I could—I just wish she was around now when I—when everything's—everything's, well, it's hardly bad now, everything's all right, it's pretty good, and I could help her maybe. . . . I don't say I *could*, I'm not conceited about that, I don't say I could do anything, that would be conceited, but we could try things. I think it would just be great if she was around—you understand what I mean, don't you?"

She was called back to the stage for more blocking. While she was gone, I thought about asking questions that would establish some connection or association in her mind between violence and love, being cuffed around and being loved, and then another set of associations of order and the positive approach and so on to survival, but I thought, the hell with it.

What it was for me was that I disliked being a reporter in any way that set me at cross purposes to Carol Burnett's enjoyment of her life.

I was exhausted and seduced, and I liked her a lot. I had sense enough to realize a great many people felt this way about her, and to withhold committing myself entirely, but I did like her, too much to pursue the other thing, or, for that matter, to talk about anything she didn't show signs of wanting to talk about.

She bounded back in after a while, saying, "You're making my mind work, Harold. I'm really interested now in this thing about comedy." (Of course, she knew, by then, I'd been subjugated.) "If you stick around for dinner, by then I'll know what I think—maybe. But I talked to Harvey while we were waiting around for that dumb dance number to get going—isn't that a dumb dance number? I really don't like it. The only thing that would save it is if at the end I'm standing there taking a bow and I get a pie in the face. . . . And Harvey said comedy always is about hostility, optimism, and never being defeated. He did Chaplin's walk to show me, and it really was a very optimistic walk. Harvey said comedy was mostly being undefeated: when you're defeated, it's tragedy. . . ."

I said no, a lot of modern comedy was defeated: Nichols and May, Lenny Bruce, even Bob Hope. Hope's comic personage was a corporation man, a thief of petty cash, and his character was entirely determined; a lot of the comedy was that he had no free will, if you put a blonde in front of him, or money, he had to take it, he had to fall. I asked her if she didn't like the dance number, or if she wanted a pie in the face, why didn't she have them change the dance number? She'd been listening to my blurred and heavy-handed exposition about pessimism in comedy, and she went on looking at me: "Change it? How?"

"Just tell them to fix it."

"They don't listen to me, they don't pay any attention to me about things like that." She dropped onto the couch. "And they're right. I'm wrong a lot: I just think it would be funny to have that dance—you didn't watch on the monitor? Well, it's just us being adorable and saying, Here We Are Again, and being just so charming and so sure we're lovable, and that everyone is glad to see us, and I'd like to stand there at the end being welcomed and—you know—and I'd get a pie in the face—"

"Well, tell them that." (I had assumed the role of adviser: it is a kind of stupidity that I am particularly given to.)

She said, "I did. They didn't seem too thrilled."

"Well, why not insist."

"How?"

"Throw a tantrum, stamp your foot."

"No. There's no excuse—none at all—for temperament." She made a face. I said it wasn't temperament, it was quality control. She said, "I think temperament is sick. Look, Harold, I don't know everything, nobody does, nobody has the right to say, 'I know,' or, 'Do this.' Everybody has to go to the toilet—do you know what I mean?"

"Sure, but don't you ever protest?"

"Oh sure. I'm *not* helpless. I'm not a shrinking violet. Me? No. I don't just *stand* there. . . ."

"No? What do you do?" (By this time, my manner toward her had become, at least by my standards, sycophantic.)

"Well . . . I hate the charwoman bit so—"

"God, I can't stand it either."

The kindness with which she looked at me! Oh well. She smiled and said, "See: we agree about some things." She patted my knee, leaned back, and said, "I told them I didn't like doing it. What it is with me is that I hated it quasi-philosophically." I looked at her; she did not grin or anything. She said, "There's no reason for me dressing up as a charwoman. Of course, it's very popular, but I don't think I play it well; it feels dead to me; I feel embarrassed doing it. I don't know why people don't notice when I'm dead sometimes. You did, though. . . . They only set her up as a real character about four times in four years; they gave her four pantomimes to do that I liked. I mean she didn't just come out and sing, she was part of a skit—do you call it a skit if it's a pantomime? One that I loved doing, she fantasized herself a burlesque queen—I could get into that. I think when I like things, I do them better. There's something for me to do dressed in those old clothes, to be *her*, if she's going to imagine herself a burlesque queen, but I can't just use her to ask for sympathy. . . . What I think is, if I don't like what they give me to do, or if I can't get a grip on it, I'm sort of a quitter. I don't know how to play it and I tend just to walk away from it. I play it but I'm dead in it. I can't help it. That's the way I am, and it's not a good way to be. So I just do those skits the way they're written but I don't think I do them right, I don't bring anything to them, I think they end up just lying there, being very dead. I don't think I'm the only person in the world who's like this. I can see in everyone here they're like that. When they're turned on by something, things develop. One time when that happened, it was so funny because we could feel it happening, it was so obvious. We were doing a ham-actor sketch, and I was a ninety-four-year-old star or something on her seventeenth, twenty-fifth farewell tour, and I'd fifteen or forty face-lifts, and we discovered she couldn't move her face, she was too afraid it would fall, she didn't want to say her lines out loud; every line started to feel funny: I didn't know what saying that line would do to my face and I was so suspicious, so—well, it was funny. And the audience liked it too."

"Would you say that skit was somewhat sarcastic about, ah—"

"I don't know. I *liked* doing it. I don't always know what's in a skit. I like doing the stronger comedy, but some skits, you know, that I didn't think were funny? Well, when we got to the final taping, in front of the audience, they were. They worked."

"Will you really wait for the final taping to see if a skit is any good, to see if it will work? Isn't that a considerable chance to take?"

"Oh, we take chances around here every week. You know, I wish I could just let loose and do everything they gave me full out but I can't. Sometimes I wish I didn't have to be in control of myself. Sometimes I wish I were another sort of person, but for me control is everything. But I like taking the chances we take: it helps keep the show alive. It keeps us from going stale. You'd be surprised how little I've thought about any of this. . . . I'm really interested in what I'm gonna say. . . . I'll tell you the truth that you probably won't believe, but I've only just started going to production meetings. I've just begun to express my views."

"Are you pulling my leg?"

"No. I only started going last year. Also, it was I didn't want to be pushy. What happened was I woke up one day and thought, I don't know how the show is put together, I don't have the first idea, and I asked Joe if I could *observe* some of the production meetings, and he and Arnie said, 'You're welcome to come anytime you want to.' So I went and now I'm saying more and more—I'm saying what I like to do as a performer, and sometimes it works out in material I feel better with. What I'd like to do is more movie parodies. What I mean is, that I've been lucky these last four years that they've found things for me to do without my going into it, but I guess what it is, if you don't throw up because I sound like Goody Two Shoes, is that I'm growing up. I've been slow. I can be very slow. I'm not all that confident. I didn't *want* to go into it before—to tell you the truth: I liked having it done for me. I was grateful. Whenever I did have an idea—which wasn't any too often, my friend—they usually liked it, they'd let me do it. Three years ago I had an idea for an epic. There were two songwriters, a boy and a girl—" She has nearly total recall. "The guy was Mel Tormé, and I was the girl. They were both songwriters but their songs were terrible. They were like half songs. They do their songs for Don Rickles but he kicks them out of his office because the songs are so bad. Then they realize if they put their songs together, they're not so bad, they're pretty good. So they become a success. It was basically a parody of Dan Dailey–Betty Grable movies. Then the other woman comes on and takes Mel away. He can only write half songs that are terrible again, and some hoods come in to hear the score he's working on for a show they're going to back, but it's terrible, and they push him around. So he goes on the skids. The girl meanwhile takes off her glasses and becomes a singer and a star. She gets to be very famous. Then she's leaving Ziggy Flofeld's theater with some people, and it's snowing and she's all dressed in furs, and this guy comes up in rags and begs for a handout. It's Mel. She says no and he falls flat in the snow, he faints, but we walk away, the snow is falling, then I stop and say, *'That man looked familiar.'* The camera comes right in to my face, which is busy having memories and feelings as I think it might be that guy. So I turn back and kneel down and lift his head up and look into it very closely; I get closer and closer to it—because I don't have my glasses on—and then I say, 'No, it's not him,' very matter-of-factly, and I drop his head back in the snow, I just let it go, and I get up and when I walk away I step on his ukelele, the ukelele he sings his songs with to beg with, and I break it. . . . I gave the skit to the writers, and they liked it, they fixed it up, but mostly they used it as I'd written it. . . . I guess I did that maybe three times in four years. Maybe I can do more. . . . What it's been, Harold, is I've been lazy. I haven't been using my mind. Now I'm starting to go to production meetings and it's toning my mind up."

I asked her what she thought of Chaplin: "It's like what Harvey said: optimistic, undefeated." Fields: "I feel terrible about this . . . but he makes me uncomfortable. I saw half of one of his movies once but I left. I have not sat through one whole movie of his so far. I suppose that's terrible." The Marx Brothers: "I haven't seen their movies since I was a child. They scared me. Clowns do that to me too, scare me. Clowns are physically mean." Bob Hope: she merely nodded. Jackie Gleason: "I don't know." Jack Benny: "I like him. It's so beautiful what he does, the way he sets up things that aren't funny at first, but when they keep coming back, he makes them funny, and they get funnier: it's beautifully worked out comedy. And he reacts so beautifully, to what the other characters do. I like that. I admire him." Nichols and May: "Well, there's no one like Elaine May. She may be the best. I think her characters are the best acted that have ever been done, so real you just can't bear it, and then that twist, that going left of center or whatever you should call it, that makes it funny." Mike Nichols: "I only met him once. He wrote one of the things Julie and I did, and he was there. He was caustic. He scared me."

The interview got more scattered. She came and went. I asked her, "You said you wanted to do movies?"

"Yes, but the producers, the movie people, they think because you're in television, you're some kind of bastard. . . . You can't work with somebody who looks down on you. You asked me about temperament a little while ago: I'll tell you what's wrong with it—you don't get good work from people with it, so it wastes money."

"Would you say you were addicted to comedy?"

"I like to do it—I like it a lot."

"Marijuana?"

"I never took any, I never needed it, I never tried—I'm not one for drugs."

"Would you say you've gotten pretty much everything you've gone after so far?"

She winced. "Some of it. Maybe a lot of it. Yes. I'm not sure. If I say yes, it makes me sound like a pushy person, and I don't think I am. But I'm very determined. I don't know what to say."

"Would you say you were more a realist or a fantasist?"

"I'm a realist but I fantasize. I fantasize a lot. I get inside my head, I get so into my own thoughts that sometimes I pass Joe in the hall and he says hello and I don't even know it's him, I walk right past him, and then I wake up, and I'll turn around." She went out and came back. She said, "It's interesting to me about comedy. I've been thinking and it seems to me what it is with me is the first seasons I was groping, I was finding myself: now I know pretty much what I'm about." And that was? "I like good, strong comedy." And that was? "It has to have a fresh premise and be written consistently so I can latch onto the character and it has to be longer."

"That's all?"

"That's how I think."

A little later, I asked her, "Freud remarked when he was fairly far along that most people were filth."

"Did he say that? They're not that bad."

"Would you say people were more good than bad?"

"Do I have to answer that? Well, there are more good people than bad people, and it's a shame the bad ones get to a station in life where they can influence people."

"Then your comedy is about a minority of flawed people?"

"I didn't say people were entirely good. You asked the question in a statistical way, and I gave you a statistical answer."

"Do you think people are fairly awful at least at times?"

"It depends. Will you stay for dinner? I'm still thinking about comedy."

She went out and came back. I asked her if she was willing to be unhappy if that seemed likely to help her do work she thought was good. She said, "You mean a director who made me cry to get a performance out of me? That's not the way to handle me. He wouldn't get anything: I'd get stubborn and resist him, I'd get closed in. I wouldn't be able to react in any other way."

I said no, I meant would she be willing to be miserable for five years in return for doing work she really admired. She said, "Not if it hurt someone else: there's always someone else, Harold. Always."

"But if there was no one."

"Oh, then I'd do it in a minute."

I asked her why she wasn't stubborn about doing skits she didn't like, but she would be stubborn about being made psychologically uncomfortable. She said, "That's the way I am—I don't really understand myself you know."

At times she spoke in the sentence structure and inflections that I use.

Joe Hamilton came in and said they had decided to cut the dance number. Burnett asked him, "You don't want to use it and end it with me getting a pie in my face?"

"No. What's the use: it's bad material—it's a piece of shit."

I said, "Should I write that down?"

He said, "Why not? We talk dirty sometimes."

I asked him if it wouldn't be better after a long day if I didn't go with them to dinner, then everybody wouldn't have to watch what he was doing. Joe Hamilton said, "We don't mind being watched. We eat beautifully."

Eight people went to dinner, six in the Rolls, and Miss Burnett and I went in the Mercedes 280 SL. I didn't take notes in the car but my memory says she said something like this: "You know, Harold, I've been thinking, and what it is, I think you overrate me. My comedy—you go into it too deeply. I wish all that was there but I don't think it is. I don't insist on this or that in it, it's just comedy, there's no medicine box—no, there's no soapbox to my humor—I like purely physical humor too, you know, and—"

"But even in slapstick there are always implications, there's a frame. Your comedy for instance is always about what you think of as good sense—"

"No, no: you put that there. Or Arnie puts it there. A lot of what I do is just silly, is just physical, I like it like that: what I do, Harold, is I go after laughs. I've thought about it, and I would like to be the way you think I am, but I'm not there yet. I'm flattered you think I'm good and that you see those things in what I do but I don't see it."

"In some of the things you do. Do you remember a sketch you did last year with Rita Hayworth? You were a tourist from the Middle West and you were monstrous, you—"

"I wasn't. She wasn't. I see people like that all the time. They come at me—believe me, they're real. I—"

"I didn't say she wasn't real. I just think that at some point you must have said you were going to show a really trampling, egocentric, monster of a woman, and you were going to show what she was like. The voice you gave her was accurate; it was frightening; it wasn't a funny skit but it was damn cruel and—"

"No, no. I didn't mean to do that. If that's what happened, then the skit didn't work. The skit didn't work anyway. I remember."

"But you had a purpose in doing that skit. . . . And in doing the Johnson and Nixon parodies. . . ."

"No, no, I didn't. I sound funny saying I didn't, but I didn't. I just did them. I don't think what you see is there. There may be a lot of things I don't like but I don't think that ever gets into the comedy."

"You don't think it's possible that the temper you never show has an outlet in the comedy you sometimes do?"

"I don't think so. I don't know about things like that. When the comedy's good, it feels good and that's an outlet. Maybe what you say does happen, but I think that leaves out the purely physical things I do. Remember: I like physical comedy."

"But gestures are language. And they're usually violent in comedy and they say things about good sense and fairness and—"

"If that's there, I'm glad. But *I* didn't put it there. It just happened, Harold. Honestly."

As Joe Hamilton had said, he and Carol Burnett ate well, or rather ate nicely. Burnett made a reference to "Fred and Marge" and explained they were imaginary viewers in Nebraska or Alaska who knew everything about television and the machinery—splicing, superimposed camera shots, dubbing, all of that. She described Fred watching a show and saying, "That's a beauty: Marge, did you see that tape splice?" Marge says, "That third camera is a slowpoke on the zoom lens, isn't it, Fred?" I asked her if she intended doing a Fred and Marge skit. She said, "No. Uh. Fred and Marge wouldn't get it. . . ."

On the way back to the studio, she said, "I'd like to be the sort of tough comedian you have in mind. Maybe it's there sometimes. I think I'm honest about things. I think I know what I'm doing—you're just not right—yet. I'm going to try more things this year. But I'm realistic about what we can get, on a weekly show. We'll see. It was nice of you to think so seriously about what I do. I appreciate it. I just don't think you have things quite right just yet. . . ."

At her dressing room, she said, "Don't go. Ask some more questions. I'm not tired."

"I am. I'm worn-out. I'm going home."

She hesitated, came toward me, lifted her arms, and put them around my neck. I put my arms around her, hugged her, patted her. Anything she would have cared to ask me, I would have done, but she didn't ask anything. I said, "Well, good luck. The best of luck." She nodded. On my way out, I bumped into Joe Hamilton, and we shook hands. He said, "It was the strangest damn interview I ever had. You did more talking than I did."

"Yeah I know. But don't tell anyone," I said.

·   ·   ·

The next morning, I telephoned Arnie Rosen. He said, "How do you feel?"

"Exhausted, seduced, admiring."

"What did she say?"

"A lot of this and that but no direct statement about satire, or any of that."

"No? Too bad. But she's a very guarded woman."

"She struck me as being ferociously intelligent."

"Well, that's it. She is. And when you're that much smarter than anyone who's ever been near you, you have a lot of caution."

"Well, thanks a lot."

"Next time you're out, call."

"I will."

It seems to me it makes sense that someone like Carol Burnett might not want to play the role of public (and part-time) moralist or Occasional Genius or any public role except the one she thinks most productive and most protective for her. If she wants to be taken merely as a performer, that's fine with me. At dinner, I asked her if she remembered doing a skit about television commercials and she said, "Oh, did you like that? Joe and I wrote it. . . ." A woman might not want to go all out with a talent and material basically violent, concerned with and focused on betrayals of various kinds. Why should she? I watch her program and think as I sit through the harmless stuff, the dull stuff, the okay, empty stuff that she's happy, and I wait for the other order of stuff. Those moments when she gets around to demolition. They're something.

They really are.

1972

THE LAST WORD
ON WINCHELL

I suppose what I mind most in this country at this moment is its implacable gullibility, its pseudo-hard-hitting, impassioned credulity. Take the instance of Walter Winchell, a newsman who had great journalistic power and success over several decades. Men who became movie stars—Cagney and Bogart—modeled their styles and their approaches to roles and their voices on his persona. Movies (*Okay America*) were written about him. He was extraordinarily public—as visible and audible as President Roosevelt. Pretty much at the height of his fame, he began to crack up, bit by bit. And, bit by bit, he sneaked off the stage into near oblivion as a rich, somewhat nutty old-guy Jewish businessman with no special role in history—you know the type, unclear about who they are and what they did, and inclined to simplify?

He wrote an autobiography, which was published posthumously, but left no coherent account of his tremendous popularity and its effect on the country. Neal Gabler, in his book *Winchell: Gossip, Power and the Culture of Celebrity,* tells us, "By one estimate, fifty million Americans—out of an adult population of roughly seventy-five million—either listened to his weekly radio broadcast or read his daily column, which, at its height in the late thirties and forties, was syndicated in more than two thousand newspapers; it was, according to one observer, the 'largest continuous audience ever possessed by a man who was neither politician nor divine.' "

Another estimate of Winchell's audience, in the 1943 edition of *Current Biography*, puts the number of readers and listeners at twenty-seven million, and another source has the number of papers syndicating his column at around eight hundred. Winchell and his contemporaries knew that he was popular, but no one could ever quite prove or measure his political or cultural power except in terms of circulation figures. Susan Sontag made the formulation to me that, in America, once you were famous you were famous until you died, but your status went up and down all the time. Winchell's status was never high. One can say that, well, Jews and women rarely had status in those days, but some did: Supreme Court Justice Benjamin Cardozo and Pearl Buck, for example. And such figures as Sinclair Lewis and Lou Gehrig and Ronald Colman had status in spite of being popular.

During the years before the Second World War, the chief thing about Winchell was that he was not respectable at a time when respectability was a cultural and moral essential. He had charm (of a kind) and a rare sense of excitement and drama. He was a truth teller of a folkish sort, a sniffer-outer, a tipster, with his nose in the wind. His column often consisted of items gleaned from late-night cruising, chasing after New York City cops when they were called to crime scenes (he had a shortwave radio in his car, and a special arrangement with the police). Or he sat and drank at the Stork Club, picking up bits of gossip. His snarling and cynical and opinionated manner, his flaunted readiness for a fight, we see nowadays in Bob Dole, Newt Gingrich, and Rush Limbaugh, in the practice of an American politics of the impolitic: a form of realism.

Winchell didn't invent the modern gossip column, as Gabler and others assert. Gossip in the press predates him by at least half a century. What he did was revivify a dying form. He made it commercially viable on a grand scale. As for a "culture of celebrity," there is no culture without some sort of celebrity. Modern celebrity may have been invented in Paris during the French Revolution, with the sudden importance of the other-than-the-aristocratic. The public statement of thinly substantiated private information precedes the invention of the printing press. It goes back at least as far as Aristophanes. The cult of personal fame was perhaps given its modern form by Sarah Bernhardt.

Winchell grew up in Manhattan and left school after the sixth grade. He does not seem to have been educated or protected by his family or to have belonged to a family tradition. He began writing in 1919, in order to break the boredom of a national tour in second-string vaudeville houses. He was a singer and a dancer—a hoofer. He wrote a one-page news sheet offering information for other performers about whatever town he was in. At some point, he added "gossip," stuff about people, and found a market in trade papers. He spent two years freelancing and two more years as a full-time reporter for something called *Vaudeville News*. He already had a following in 1924, when he moved to a regular New York paper—well, not so regular. The *New York Evening Graphic* was published by a rich health-food and exercise nut named Bernarr Macfadden. Winchell's column was a mixture of elements, and he was more popular than the paper itself. In 1929 he moved to the *New York Daily Mirror*—a Hearst paper, not a respectable paper—and again he was more popular than it was. His bosses there could not tell him what to do. They could interfere with his copy, but he had the clout to fight them. He had a very cheap operation. He always said that he didn't pay for tips from informants. He stayed at the *Mirror* for more than thirty years, which is inexplicable except as an act of independence—a street person's independence.

Winchell became the most famous columnist in America and in the world, and no one owned him. Hemingway wrote, "Winchell is the greatest newspaperman that ever lived." But his writing isn't easy to come by nowadays. Gabler tells us in the "Note on Sources" at the end of his book, "I bought Winchell's own bound volumes of his *Mirror* columns, the complete scripts of his radio programs. . . . I have donated all of this to the Billy Rose Theatre Collection at the New York Public Library for the Performing Arts at Lincoln Center, where it is currently being catalogued (hence the inexactness of many of the citations)." Winchell's status is, apparently, still low.

Winchell was a Gatsby type, but he was compulsively talkative and he had no social aspirations—on the contrary, he was sought after by social figures. He had no Daisy Buchanan. He liked showgirls—classless, spirited, and, again, without social aspirations. The party was in nightclubs—was wherever he was, so to speak. His view of society, which society down to its lower levels found so persuasive and so detestable, was genital. He believed in the moral hairsplitting and fineness of the upper caste as pictured in Henry James to about the same extent that we believe Bill Clinton to be a virgin.

The tone of social skepticism in Winchell was a large part of what made his columns and broadcasts work. Here's a sample from the early thirties, which was quoted by St. Clair McKelway, in this magazine, in a 1940 "Profile." The two items appeared four days apart:

> Mrs. J. Loose who has more money than her Loose-Wiles plants have biscuits and Vice-President Curtis are blazing.

> The line on Monday about Vice-President Curtis and Mrs. Loose of the biscuit company "blazing" . . . Well, the Trib yesterday refuted it by saying that Mr. Curtis denied he was engaged or going to marry . . . Who said anything about engaged or marriage? Can't a vice-president get That Way about a girl without marrying her?

This disrespect became part of the thirties—part of the style of the decade. From early on Roosevelt was allied with Winchell and his audience. Roosevelt came into office with the help of radio and national touring, and the help of big-city machines and bosses and Southerners. The United States after the Second World War—the nation that was said to have Americanized the world—was a Roosevelt (and Winchell) creation, and was not the old or traditional America at all.

When I was young, you had two major social classes (as now again, since Reagan): the people who mattered and the trash population. If you like, you can name a third class, of those uneasily in the middle, but actually behind their facades of respectability they fit into one of the two other categories. You had a country two to three times larger in population than England or France or Germany, but much less well organized or centralized. People had root cellars and iceboxes, and no down coats, and Washington was a small Southern town. Almost every populated center had a large belt of farms near it, and there was an urban-rural multiculturalism underlying our politics. Ethnic divisions were extreme and often violent. We had little, compared to today, in the way of *national* structures—just the railroads, the radio networks, a few newspaper chains, such as Hearst's, and the "national" magazines. There were also national political parties, but the most fervent politics remained local—the province of local sheriffs and judges and newspapers. People were not as nomadic, and they stuck with their jobs, and the local storekeepers and police knew you. (This led to a terrific amount of sexual freedom if you were "respectable.") Sears, Roebuck and Montgomery Ward and the five-and-dime may have been all you had in terms of national merchandising. Most of the roads had been laid out for horse and buggy, and some took right-angle turns to follow property lines. Where I grew up, in the Midwest, some country roads were made of brick. (I've always thought that the yellow brick road in *The Wizard of Oz* was a wet brick road between corn-fields, reflecting sunshine.)

The rich, the people who mattered, were (with some exceptions) arriv-istes, newcomers to power since the Civil War. They were terrifically genteel—at times. Gentility was a constant issue. Various groups at the top of the heap covered for one another. Much of the fiction of the time—not James but Edith Wharton and Theodore Dreiser—spoke of this hypocrisy.

Newspapers *were* power and blackmail: they printed scandal, often unsubstantiated. The careful newspapers were always few in number. America was not gentlemanly except as a quality of longing. I was adopted by a family that was well known in a small Illinois town called Alton. The adoption was not, I think, legal. My adoptive mother was a Daisy Buchanan type—although Jewish—and once, when she had me with her and couldn't find a parking spot, she left her car in the middle of the street, blocking a trolley line, and told the traffic cop to take care of it, and he did. When we moved to Saint Louis, in 1934, we had no connec-tions, and even as a young child I could feel the difference. Joe Brodkey, my adoptive father, used to go back to Alton once a week just to sniff the memories of the time when we had been *influential* and had had *position*.

Winchell allied himself with actors (who had been considered outcasts and somewhat disreputable) and then with journalists and gangsters. He had nothing to do with respectable America, and the national audience, such as it was, had no interest in respectable America, either. It went to the movies, followed big-league baseball, listened to *Amos and Andy* on the radio. Let's call it a kind of social self-consciousness, an individual and mass identification with Chaplin's tramp—which was an identification of oneself as a nobody, as someone not in the loop. (In truth, though, every-one was in some sort of loop in those days, through ward politics or an ethnic organization or church or the PTA. Or one had access to the upper-level loop through marriage or town gossip.) As a disreputable figure who said what he liked, Winchell was part of an American tradition: the poor and actors had always been subject to gossip, and so had Democratic Party politicians, as far back as Andrew Jackson and his much-insulted wife, Rachel.

The thing about going back in history is that it is difficult to keep your sense of scale. If everything in the past is like a toy, then the scale is wrong. In actuality, people were people then, and the future was unknown. The twenties' high-literary sense of life as a party for cynical depressives—which you find in Hemingway and Fitzgerald and in Edna St. Vincent Millay and, in a nightclubbing and emotional sense, in Winchell—meant a flight from small-town existence, from that violence and peace, from encountering your peers in church or at meetings of the Elks. It meant rejecting your parents. The party was sophisticated, a rendezvous at the edge of Hell—outside the law, outside of Prohibition. Winchell kept this sense of a party through much of his working life. (Hemingway and Fitzgerald did, too, writing about it in ways that tried to reflect eternity in willful and giddy transience, and you can use your sense of Hemingway and Fitzgerald to picture Winchell, use their exhaustion and Hemingway's reputed insanity to imagine his.)

My guess is that the source of Winchell's famous style—his swiftness and nastiness and outspokenness—was the Bible, with its air of truth. Winchell's idea of a story was Jezebel in five lines. He used no schooled rhetoric at all. His riffs depended on rhythm, brevity, and mocking parody, in ways reminiscent of song lyrics and vaudeville. Not simply because his work was entertainment but because in a country with so many ethnic divisions and a maddening variety of manners of speech, show-biz vernacular was the only common language.

Winchell *was* show biz, was a placeless American, someone who could not be kept down on the farm after he'd seen Paree. And his homemade journalistic jazz vernacular was not a language that could claim correctness or purity any more than twenties clothes could. Such language was used to separate the "lowdown" on someone from the "truth" about someone. "Truth" was fancy and hypocritical. The "lowdown" was the opposite. It was not a language for Congress. It was not imposed. It was noncoercive, and it was defiant or defensive, impudent, sassy, and vulgarly subject to self-will, which is to say style.

Winchell's razzmatazz, which depends for its effect on rapid changes of attention—he could cover fifty topics in a single brief column—has a modern-day counterpart in rap, since rap is, among other things, opinion filtered through show business and personal style. When his influence was at its strongest (from, say, 1932 to 1942), his style was tough baby talk à la Bogart and was more formulaic than it had been in the twenties: "It was the first party I had gone to since I got my long pants and some sense, but it was all veddy lifted-pinky and ho-ho rather than ho-hum." Pure high-flying gutter. And no one is left out. Winchell (I think) never wrote from a posture of superiority. Both his lack of power and his enormous influence come from the fact that he was shouting "Listen!" and then pointing to FDR or someone else whose speech had authority. He was more doorway than podium, more carnival barker than the show itself.

In Gabler we find this: "It was Dorothy Parker who once quipped, 'Poor Walter. He's afraid he'll wake up one day and discover he's not Walter Winchell.'" Of course, Parker's quip depends for its point on Winchell's immense popularity. I seem to remember that Parker, very drunk, sometimes said, "My tragedy is that I am not Dorothy Parker, and I never was." (She once said to me, "Stop looking at me. I'm old and dull. I'm not funny anymore. You want me to be funny. Leave me alone.") Winchell's constructed persona was based on his being truant, on his autonomy, and it granted us, the citizen audience, our autonomy. It was all a massive dose of liberation. Winchell didn't deal in dead men's and women's greatness and in memories of greatness. He was absolutely topical. Now. Our lives. Winchell's two great interests—the structures that underlay the popularity of his work—were sexual reality and conspiracies. His métier was the folksy deconstruction of officaldom and of lies about class differences. He had a fine sense of headlines. He didn't tell the "truth" except in a sportive or arch manner, and even then he didn't do it because he was truthful by nature. He dealt in other people's lies. J. Edgar Hoover is said to have assigned agents to listen to Winchell, because he had so much information.

Gabler presents one especially vivid detail about Winchell talking on the radio: Winchell liked to broadcast with his pants undone. Exhibitionism? A kinky reaction to the splendors of radio fame? According to Winchell, it added to his already terrible nervousness, his stage fright, and helped increase the urgency and drama of his voice on his broadcasts. His vocal pitch was an octave higher than usual when he was on the air. Winchell's verbal style—its childishness—was like the childishness of Hemingway's and Gertrude Stein's styles, and like Fitzgerald's juvenile tone, and like the scowls of gangsters. It was a late-night style, and his "friendships" were late-night, too—were with Mark Hellinger and Texas Guinan and Damon Runyon and Sherman Billingsley. Texas Guinan may have been the inventor of having a party sense of life without illusion. She was the one who used to greet people in her speakeasy with "Hello, sucker."

Gabler says that Winchell dealt in implication and fey language rather than stock journalese in order to avoid lawsuits, since it was difficult to pin down an implication. Winchell often said that he had been trying to hide his illiteracy. But if you consider his sense of conspiracy and of sexual shenanigans, and also his distrust of high style (as British) and his use of a low, invented style, and consider his popularity, you can see that he had great literary impact. Writers who were growing up when Winchell flourished—Thomas Pynchon and Norman Mailer and Don DeLillo—show his influence. You can also see the shadow of his shadow in Peter Matthiessen's novels and Richard Ford's and Robert Stone's and Cynthia Ozick's, but in those writers the derivation is diluted by faith and by a stylistic denial of contemporary speech and by a noticeable literariness, a claim of not having arisen from the vernacular.

What Winchell signified by leaving home and being himself and deracinated and outside a tradition—by being accepted and hated and reconstituted as a person of unique influence—was the effectual savagery of freedom. Not many of the *good* writers of Winchell's time were concerned with such freedom; they advocated religious and political dogmas and self-sacrifice. Winchell's individualism was urban, just as Ezra Pound's was Western and rural: Pound's country-boy dialect and his knowingness, his hot scoops on high culture, come from the same roots in a provincial society as Winchell's patter. Where Pound chose T. S. Eliot and Mussolini, Winchell chose Roosevelt.

Winchell's phenomenal daily and weekly popularity probably reflected the fact that his was the most fully developed *populist* intelligence in the country—which means that he was extremely valuable to Roosevelt. You could almost say that Roosevelt stole bits of method and tone from him. Winchell himself is a clue to public reality, to national life before it was clearly realized that we had such a life—and perhaps, outside of media response, we didn't and still don't have much in the way of national life.

. . .

Winchell's opposition to Hitler was no small thing. Gabler writes, "Acting out of his sense of revenge and his fear of anti-Semitism, Walter took on Hitler in 1933." He wrote regularly about the activities of pro-Nazi groups and funneled information to the FBI. Hoover was so grateful that he assigned agents to protect Winchell, beginning with a speaking tour in 1934. Hoover explained to one of his men that Winchell "has been very active in the anti-Nazi movement and feels there may be some efforts to cause him harm or embarrassment." The Mob also gave Winchell protection for a number of years. Of the successful popular figures in the Western countries, Winchell was the most consistently and blatantly and disrespectfully anti-Hitler. Hitler's influence was enormous. People are moved by success. People in the Midwest said *"Heil!"* half as a joke. Kids goose-stepped. The *idea*, whatever its quality as idea, was in popular motion, stirring the world. The extent to which Fascism and Nazism constituted a style—greatcoats, guns, and cars; hats and postures and faces and parades—and their overt S and M and violence held a deep, blind fascination. The aura of invincible ruthlessness and the threat of apocalypse were satisfyingly mocked—at the time—by Winchell's calling Hitler a fairy, for example. Such remarks were accusations of inauthenticity in Hitler's heroic persona. Where I lived, there was a sense that the rich—some of the very richest families—felt that Nazism rose from the people, from the *mob*. The rich took Nazism to be "the trash people" disciplining themselves. If these Nazi groups were vile, it was thought that their vileness was limited, and that a limited but well-ordered vileness suited the world, which was evil.

In a sense, between 1932 and 1936 the party of the twenties turned into a lawless political brawl. Winchell's column was then being published in the *Washington Herald* by Cissy Patterson, a photogenic rich woman with nerve, who bought the paper in 1939 and merged it with the *Washington Times*. She was very neurotic, a right-winger, an isolationist, and, apparently, pro-Nazi. Gabler tells us that in 1941, at a party for the British ambassador, Patterson confronted Winchell and demanded, "Why the hell don't you quit looking under the bed for Nazis?" Winchell retorted, "Mrs. Patterson, why don't you get another boy?"

Gabler also says that Patterson described Winchell in print as suffering from "a chronic state of wild excitement, venom, and perpetual motion of the jaw" and as a "popgun patriot," a "grimy clown," and "one of those whispery, furtive characters who used to pop up from nowhere to ask if we'd care to buy some spicy French postcards." Gabler goes on, "One headline called him a 'Cockroach.' But these were less worrisome to him than Cissy's main line of attack. She began editing anti-isolationist and anti-Nazi items from his column, frequently killing the column entirely."

One of Patterson's other writers, Georgiana X. Preston, called Winchell a "twisted, inferiority-ridden soul, perpetually sick with hidden shame over his past and origins," and a "marred vessel that many of us had an unconscious hand in fashioning." Subheads were "How Winchell Is Like Hitler" and "He Has a Foxlike Face."

You can see how real the anti-Semitism was. Perhaps you can guess how exciting it was, in a provincial society, to have such violent and dangerous politics to be part of.

Gabler describes FDR seducing Winchell in the course of a ten- or fifteen-minute meeting a week after his 1933 inauguration, by playing on Winchell's longings for stature: "However brief the meeting, it had its intended effect on the outcast from Harlem. . . . 'Winchell developed a blind adoration for FDR,' Walter's friend Ernest Cuneo later wrote." But I doubt that Winchell, bad man and exploiter of gossip and whatever else he was, was simply floored by a prep-school accent. Winchell and Roosevelt both had considerable judgment. It is very likely that an alliance was set afoot between them. Shortly after the meeting, Winchell began to do columns about the dispossessed and the starving, and the idea of Eleanor Roosevelt's daily column, which began appearing in 1936, may have been derived from the success of Winchell's column. She championed some of the same causes but in a very different—more elegant—verbal style. Gabler says that Winchell was resented for his role, that the "grievance against Winchell was the control he exercised over his social and intellectual superiors and what that control portended for the élites." This was actually truer for the Roosevelts, in their fairly well-documented war with their own caste. Winchell never claimed to be more than a columnist, a *newsboy*. Gabler defines Winchell's career in the nineteen-thirties in terms of religion:

[Winchell] called himself an "intuitive" Jew, but his Judaism ran deep. . . . He suffered a vulnerability about being Jewish, a sense that "underneath, they're all anti-Semitic." To him, it was always the latent motive of his enemies: They had to destroy the powerful Jew.

But Winchell was identified as a Jew chiefly in terms of being anti-Nazi; in this sense, Roosevelt himself was often accused of being a "Jew." Furthermore, it is not possible to be purely Jewish; one's mind wanders, one slips into being merely a person. Winchell was a *popular* Jew, and the Hitler question was not simply a Jewish matter. From where we stand now, we tend to see Nazism in terms of the Holocaust, but, of course, the Holocaust hadn't occurred yet. Hitler and Nazism were incompletely known, partly because they hadn't fully acted. The potential actions contained in them, the changed world they might bring about—all of that lay latent, as yet unclear. Hitler was the charismatic leader of an increasingly powerful state, and through the mid-thirties his opponents were still discreet and basically reasonable in their objections to him. Hitler's ideas and actions were feared and held in awe; his wildest remarks and political maneuverings were treated with what seems to us now a shocking amount of respect and restraint. His governmental programs and his willingness to wage war were the most pressing issues. Winchell grasped early on the extent to which Hitler was a menace, not just to Jews but to *everyone*, to life as we knew it. His attacks on Nazism did not diminish his enormous popularity—his popularity grew—and this indicated a "market" for anti-Nazism, indicated changing public feeling. No other person played such a role; no one propagandized against Hitler with such lowdown ferocity. Just this one cheap journalist.

Historically, this trembling-nerved, loud, and heroic Winchell is invisible. But he was visible everywhere in this country at the time. He was, paradoxically, one of the people who mattered. He was the buzzmeister, the chief nerve of the American republic. Ernest Cuneo, the troubleshooter among the insidemost insiders at the White House, said he believed that Winchell "was carrying the fate of the Nation with him every time he went to the post," and added, "He was the only man who could simultaneously elevate FDR back into the White House and meet Goebbels . . . down in the gutter and stomp him and his lies into the mud."

Everyone knew Winchell was a hero.

. . .

Roosevelt and Winchell: two loners, widely hated and popular. Was it Roosevelt's inborn taste or an unavoidable tactic or the result of his relationship with Winchell in a country where the print media was dominated by Hearst, Luce, and the McCormicks—all of them suspicious of him as commander in chief and opposed to his tactics and his overall strategy—that led Roosevelt to wage war by gradually convincing the populace that war was what it wanted?

People have said over and over that the Hitler war was the last just war; that is, they have credited the evil of Hitler with the comparatively moderate amount of disillusion with the war afterward. And it left us the political legacy that "greatness" is determined by the evil, the demonic quality, of the enemy. All that seems perverse. Roosevelt, in his conscienceless way as a leader, waged war with the consciousness (and wit) of an intelligent man. To some extent, Winchell's columns before 1943 can be used to indicate what Roosevelt was thinking—his process of selecting a program, a policy. The great stumbling block to any direct policy was American weakness. Folly and boasting aside, there were many people who believed that we could not beat the Germans. In the sentimental jargon of the prewar era, we were just people, not a people. Was it a pacifist society? It was, largely. Before Pearl Harbor, a culture had been evolving of extraordinary respect for individual lives, and this was broken—never really to return (so far)—by the war.

Skepticism and selfishness and survival were part of American culture in ways that militarism and discipline and self-sacrifice were not. Utopian virtue, moral pleas—even among the cynically disreputable— were powerful elements. Roosevelt threw all those conflicting attitudes out, bathwater and baby. We did have a class of armaments manufacturers and of military families, largely Southern, but we had such flagrantly lousy military equipment—by the spring of 1940, our few tanks were armed mostly with machine guns while many German tanks carried heavy-duty cannons—and such a lousy and out-of-date peacetime army that Roosevelt reorganized everything. He was, in a sense, what he was so often accused of being—a playboy. And he was insanely overworked, insanely set on winning.

Roosevelt *seemed* to let the army define itself and the ways it wanted to fight. This meant that there was almost unparalleled media coverage of the front lines—a tremendous flow of information. In response to this, and because much of Congress was isolationist before Pearl Harbor, Roosevelt established an unusual degree of secrecy—and, for the first time, found himself the center of favorable and pleading media attention. Winchell played a smaller and smaller part in the overall picture. He became simply a home-front propagandist and a supplier of domestic infotainment—which is very odd, if you think about it. Well, there are two oddities: Winchell's staying away from battlefront reporting, and Roosevelt's undercutting Winchell's position and, in a broad sense, taking it for himself. Media reports about the war, the merits and/or the vanity and stupidity of the commanders, the quality of war matériel—this particular approach became the dominant thing, because it was what interested us most. What undermined Winchell's preeminence was that he did not do that stuff.

But why? Why allow yourself to be cut off from your own mass audience? From your own quality as a newspaperman? Or as a construct? A few years before, Gabler reports, in 1938, Winchell had announced that Roosevelt would run for a third term, and his language suggests that he and Roosevelt were in relatively close touch at the time. ("The President feels the nation needs him in the White House for another four-year term.") By late 1942, war news was more important than Winchell's news, although it was understood in Roosevelt's camp that in 1943 Winchell would begin preparing the public for Roosevelt's run for a fourth term. That was useful work but not important; it was scut work.

As I remember it, Winchell's slide from preeminence was perceptible as early as the landings in Northwest Africa, in November of 1942. He was, if you will forgive me, a purveyor of yesterday's Roosevelt. Gabler reports that Roosevelt and Hoover wanted Winchell to keep on fighting the isolationist elements in Congress and in the media. But Winchell knew that he could not compete with battlefront reporting. People talked. They said that Winchell was slipping or wasn't good anymore. Edward R. Murrow and Ernie Pyle and the photographers for *Life* were good.

In Hollywood's wartime movies, you can see this shift in our narrative unconscious. You can see the switch in story lines from lone-wolf figures like Bogart in *Casablanca* or *Passage to Marseilles* to platoons in military or air force stories, and you can see John Wayne and Errol Flynn (supposedly a Nazi sympathizer) do selfless dialogue that would have made Texas

Guinan sick. In the movies, Van Johnson was the archetypal serviceman. Or Gene Kelly, with his face redesigned from movie to movie until
he got it right. Hollywood wartime musicals still reflected Winchell's
1920s world—show business and Broadway and cynicism. But that was
escapist stuff.

Perhaps Roosevelt's shenanigans—his political and military genius—
broke Winchell's heart. Or, to put it another way, reality broke him. The
automatism that set in—the robotization of his responses—was so extensive that it is possible to say he was a dead man from then on. Popular, yes.
But weird. And not important. He was out of it, and he never was in it
again. The heroism, the big-timeness vanished from the legend. And the
having a good time and the gossip remained. The short guy who went
with tall showgirls remained.

Actually, Roosevelt's undeviating will to success was not so different
from Winchell's. (Or Eisenhower's.) He waged a deft war, waged it expensively, but did not bankrupt the country in terms of either blood or
money. And he didn't change his style much—this wasn't something that
was stage-managed. It wasn't *image*. It was the extraordinary, bloody success he met with.

Of the major Allied wartime leaders, Roosevelt was the only one who
died before the war ended. It is surprising how few leaders die in wartime.
Tension and blood seem to keep them going. I am just guessing, but I
think Winchell's collapse or withdrawal into pettiness and Eisenhower's
stony manner after the war are related. They both had to do with the killer
instinct and its exercise, with the fear of success and then the reality of
success in war. The knowledge of the god-awful way people act (their
greed, their vicarious or direct violence), and of the youth and helplessness
of those who died, leads to shame—shame and what is now called denial,
a sort of macho, still functioning, white-male autism. Everyone sort of
went mad.

It's just a theory. But you can't imagine how strange it seemed, at the
time, that Roosevelt died before the end of the war. Of course, he knew
about the camps. And, yes, he was ill, and he was a cripple. But he was
Franklin Roosevelt, and he had conquered the world and had more sheer
power than any other creature in history. Was it unbearable? Was he
ashamed? Just as a human thing—do you know what I mean?

Each of the spectacularly lit and photographed wartime leaders-as-
symbols—Chiang Kai-shek and Franco and Stalin and Churchill and

Hitler and FDR—had a huge, androgynous vanity. Is there an answer to what has happened to us in these male pinups of the achievement of great power? Imagine being the cause of literally innumerable deaths—say, fifty million, all told, in that war, or even more, if you begin the calculation earlier in the 1930s. Something of each man was visible in those posed photographs: in one case, something of the mutt aristocrat; in another, the immovable father; and then there was the alternately stern or laughing deviant, the Oriental general, the self-invented and crippled American.

For me, by the time of Yalta Roosevelt was half mad in his photographs. In the Yalta group photograph, his expression has a self-mocking quality and a touch of horror. He is wearing a cape and has a cigarette in his left hand. Churchill sits on one side of him, Stalin on the other. They look like pets on chains. Roosevelt's role in world history, in the defeat of Hitler, had a blood-chilling quality, and an absolutely top-flight cleverness. He looks like the cat who swallowed the canary. He looks as if he were in an advanced state of shock and disbelief: the atomic bomb he'd ordered into existence was simmering on the stove.

This didn't keep him alive. This didn't keep him going. But let's say that Roosevelt's brilliance broke Winchell. What the story amounts to, really, is that Winchell fell out of love with fame and with history in a peculiarly American manner. The rest of his life consists of his hanging on, without much in the way of fire or desperation visible, and of a long, slow retrenchment until he wound up, in Gabler's words, a "ranting King Lear," haunting the Stork Club—a man who, in his own mind, had backed off from Roosevelt and politics and war, and remembered with the most intensity an episode involving gangsters—the slaying of a single man, Vincent "Mad Dog" Coll, or some such thing.

After 1943, when the stench of glory arose, a datedness hung over the politics of the thirties. And America was so unbelievably rich that all history was mocked. All the money in the world wound up here. But it was truly odd how when the war changed—when it turned into our crushing everyone—Roosevelt sort of evaporated. He went off and died almost a thousand miles from Washington. He had been with an old girlfriend; his wife and children were nowhere near him. It was not the usual stuff of legend.

It was funny how when Roosevelt was gone you realized that no one else in public life was interesting. Winchell certainly wasn't. Perhaps, in the end, Winchell was a grieving-widow type, like Mamie Eisenhower, who lost her small-town husband to the war and then to his "greatness," and who by some accounts became an alcoholic. I have almost no postwar memories of Winchell except as someone cracked, as a fool.

I did read his column from time to time, but it had no life. And not much influence. Sometimes he had good inside information, but not often. He seemed to admire Eisenhower, who was said to have a gift for being placatory matched by an obscene toughness. Perhaps Winchell grew to be like Eisenhower in that way. In a sense, neither Roosevelt nor Winchell made it through the war, the crippled Prospero and his rat-a-tat-tat Caliban.

Then it was the fifties. We Americans, ex-rubes, ex-bumpkins, ex-hicks, walked very carefully in our ad-hoc new America, the one powerful, rich country in the world, a quasi-socialist utopian state with good public education, good hospitals, nearly full employment for white males, a country with quotas for Jews in most occupations and with lower-level jobs for blacks. There was a sense of community, which had come to us from Roosevelt and the war.

Of course, utopia is a crock of shit. But it was hard to deny its douceur, which was not that of the upper classes but that of pushy, not especially educated men. Truman and Eisenhower were both regular guys, wonderfully uninspired—again, walking dead men. Except in terms of pop culture, this happy state of prosperity was a cultural defeat of the deepest imaginable kind, since nothing from the past could carry over into it—not Spartan simplicity or high ethics or upstate-downstate politics.

We tried to go back in time. Women were sent back into the kitchen—and into waist cinchers. The country made suburban noises. But the Roosevelt legacy was so complex and generated so much power and aroused so much ego that moral cowardice and personal safety and corruption and self-doubt and unlimited greed became national characteristics and national virtues. No one knew how to act. It felt as if this were a country consisting entirely of recent converts, and everyone went on tiptoe. McCarthyism came—first it was an attack on the upper-caste white Protestants that Roosevelt distrusted, and then on show-business figures, and then it became a move toward a popular coup. Winchell allied himself with McCarthy and publicly attacked Truman and Stevenson, calling them "un-American."

It was not an era of clear thought. Eisenhower tacitly backed McCarthy and then withdrew from him and then destroyed him. The veterans' right to have a McCarthy—to protect the Roosevelt legacy long enough for them to get rich from it, too—seemed very clear, but that didn't make any of it bearable. It seemed to be a function of a semiutopian mass society that it be unlivable.

In that society, Winchell was a memory figure. The Luce magazines had imitated Winchell's tactics and improved on them—a process that culminated later in the creation of *People*. You could even say that the *Times* gradually became, in its lengthy way, a version daily and on Sundays of a Winchell column. Improving on Winchell and sneering at him, attacking him in a twenty-four-part profile in the *Post* was like smoking your father's brand of cigars. But it wasn't much said that Winchell was imitated—it was journalism. It was God speaking through inspired editors.

What happened to the notion of celebrity was paradoxical: there was a demystification, based on the mystique of success, but a success that anyone could have. This new social reality did not concern the most interesting lives but lives that anyone could live (depending on how well you were groomed and how good your publicist was). In our rich democracy, anyone—Nixon, Kennedy, Carter—could be another Roosevelt, and anyone could be a Winchell and was. You didn't need the authentic one.

Winchell didn't like to appear on television. The visual has an obstinate obscurity, a riddle quality, an ambiguity that went against his grain. Winchell's legacy was everywhere, but was unnamed. Gabler writes of him, "All that would remain was this image of an angry, mean, foolish old man railing at the fates that had betrayed him."

Winchell had a Job aspect and a Noah aspect and a bit of Lot's wife in him, too. He railed at fate, he fought it, and he won for a while—and, of course, he lost in the end. And it broke him.

It is practically everyone's story.

1995

THE WOODY ALLEN MESS

1.

Woody Allen. Well, let's start with notions of madness and sanity—of normalcy. Or let's just mention them and say we'll keep them in mind; and then let's mention the irresistibility of a movie star as an object of affection and of sympathy, an irresistibility before and after the fact, in the person, in the person become a symbol, in the glamor attached to the now famous but partly hidden person inside the glamor, moods and all.

Let's attach that to money, spendable, disposable income with almost all elements of display and amusement being deductible as business. And legal untouchability—sympathy will protect a star although perhaps not completely. A movie star is welcome nearly anywhere in the world, among the richest and most fastidious and most public and powerful people, at least for a while, no matter how he or she acts, since the image is familiar and the fleshly encounter, even if it includes decomposition and scandal—acted out, palpable image-deconstruction—is of interest for the anecdote and the experience.

And most people in any class of society are sophisticated enough to deal with immediately scandalous behavior.

Then we must add in the force of so many people who are willing to be sycophantic or who are looking for scandal and for opportunities of black-mail and subservience for the sake of the advantage. A star is a constant target for gangsters, for bullies, for climbers, for more or less ordinary people looking for a chance or for a thrill. This leads to defensive and imploded systems, compensatory arrogance, self-protective dominance, and extreme self-concern. Those, too, become part of everyday reality for the star.

The self-discipline and immense strain of performing, the skin hardened to criticism, the long habits of big-time and independent and lonely decision and superiority of power, superiority of life (plus the drugs and natural stimulants necessary to work long, tense hours on a usually murderously coercive and exploitive schedule) present us with a problem requiring close attention, which is that certain sorts of behavior are within the range of *the normal* for a movie star and not for us, especially if the star, man or woman, has the status and degree of public meaning of being "legendary," of existing as a common or universal term as a human object, a Garbo, a Hayworth, a Chaplin, a Woody Allen.

Imagine the rights, the privileges of an ancient duke but nowadays in our present-day near anarchy in a movie actor from Brooklyn.

An actor's power is not royal, is not set by law. It rises from a partly bribed electorate, and it is PR'd and merchandised and interfered with throughout its existence, but it is still very real.

A common enough phrase is, after all, *Hollywood royalty.*

An actor's power exists within the movie business, which consists of a great many absolute fiefdoms. And the movie business has no history. It is self-invented, improvised.

Male violence, male will, male sexuality, capricious personal (but not political) corruption, and clever plotting and suicidal risk taking: among the "great" movie stars have been a number who exemplified that sort of personality as stars and whose publicity suggested they were somewhat that way offscreen. Probably the most famous and strongest image of that was Humphrey Bogart's. Allen in the movie *Play it Again, Sam* (which was a play first), offers us Bogart as his tutelary deity and as the actual secret self of a small, funny-looking, nervous man.

Allen has been almost spectacularly forthright in portraying elements of himself and of his life but always in a sentimental fashion.

. . .

Reading about Mia Farrow and Woody Allen gives me the willies, but that is because I am an adopted child. Well, an adopted child grown old; I am sixty-one at the moment.

For twenty years now, I have been writing in the voice and persona of a character named Wiley Silenowicz, who was adopted at the age of two, greatly damaged, ill, silent, beaten, semiautistic, starved. He was adopted into a family where there was a blood child already in place. The resemblances to the actual situation in Mia Farrow's household are obvious. In the stories and in *The Runaway Soul*, the novel told by this narrator, physical and romantic abuse, erotic and moral trespass, are the recurringly central, major actions.

Being adopted is a more romantic situation than being a blood child. The tie is personal. The love isn't based on genetic duty. Instead, choice and exoticism, foreignness, are there from the start. Everything is contractual. Emotions are acted out in good performances. Or in weak ones. This produces a different order of intimate relationships. Every single act has a moral and contract-carried-out quality. Or not.

The emotional reality is nearly indescribable. In one story, "S.L.," Wiley relates what happened in the hour when his future father decided to proceed with a legal adoption.

Wiley says he is telling a marriage story. He says he has two characters and that the child is an active part of the scene although not in a way a grown-up would be.

But a child knows about protection and seduction, about emotion directed at him and about responses to that emotion. He has a sense of amusement and comfort, a damaged but active sense, a childhood sense of those things. He has an already partly dismissed memory of such severe horror that to remember would be to crack up.

The father, S.L., in his monologues in front of the child condemns himself in a number of ways talking about himself as a man, a bit of crook here and there, not really a crook, just an American businessman, a good-looking man, a lecher, moody, wounded in the First War, a man of cynical temper.

He talks some about his unsociable melancholy and his bitterness and how ugly the world is, and how men are mistreated.

Of course, he is talking about the costs to him of protecting a child, one perhaps permanently damaged.

The only way he can bring himself to accept this role, this privilege and burden, is through love—he loves the child's innocence. This innocence is unlike the dirtiness and self-willed assertiveness of the rest of the inhabitants of his world.

His love is based on an unreal notion of children and of personality and of what is possible. It amounts to a form of castration imposed on the child. The child has to satisfy the adult male's notions of a contract in which the child's innocence and responsiveness are necessities.

The compromises of a grown-up life—its lecheries and its sadnesses—are not, on the face of it, things a child can understand. But, in order to be sheltered, the child, without knowing what he is doing, learns early on to be seductive and commanding, to use pain and tears and charm and responsiveness to comfort adults and to offer meaning and purpose to their lives. The child knows, senses its power, a slight power but a meaningful one.

I think we lose touch with childhood realities because the mind is trained later in language and in how to think in ways that make much of what goes on in childhood invisible.

The man decides he likes the child. The child accepts the whole shebang.

I'm going to quote the end of the story here to show what I think is the central emotion in Allen and Soon-Yi and in Farrow and her other children.

He is running toward the gate of the park: I see the torn rooms of the out-of-doors. Dad says, "NO," [to the squirming child he almost drops] *and refolds me in his arms, defining me as Error and A Fool and someone he wants bodily near him, someone whose bodily welfare concerns him; it's interesting and I start to laugh. The moment is unideal, semi-ideal, this one particular moment. The child's laughter passes: I am silent, very silent. The feeling as S.L. moves rapidly in the still thin-bodied but now fattening gray-black air (I mean rain) is of contented fright, a distanced kind of staring at the world. In the world at this moment, in what is contained in it, the future hovers like the mist-hung air. But the kid knows only a general and civilized imperfection and hope. The shrewd-hearted, prying-eyed kid in his shrewd-hearted torpor is being carried home.*

Transposing that paragraph and those elements gives me a potent sense, potent to me, of what the emotional reality might be for both Soon-Yi and Woody Allen, the sense of finding a home.

2.

If one takes *Manhattan* and *Annie Hall* as variations of *Lolita* and of *Of Human Bondage*, then one can assume Allen sees his masculinity as that of a luckless predator-victim, not an uncommon attitude or state of mind in males. We can also assume he is modified patriarchal—a movie director and a Jew—with almost Hemingwayesque-Bogartian notions of women as rescuers, as causes of heroism, as toys, killers, objects of reward.

Then if you decided that Allen, a very clever man and a movie star, is prettifying those things in himself (as Hemingway did) and making them photogenic, comic, sympathetic, if you think he is fundamentally lying in his work even in its obvious semihonesties, then you might think you can feel from your own experiences and with your own powers of sympathetic projection the polarities of Allen's sexual reality in relation to women. Then you might feel his sexual presence to be obstinate, darkly but comically supremely insistent, exhibitionist, unashamed—since as a victim and a nervous man he is primarily innocent—and self-absorbed, self-willed, and very, very knowing, successful at getting his own way and avoiding victimization and yet victimized from birth, terrified. And always being taught a lesson in either misery or in happiness dependent on a woman.

One can deduce, perhaps wrongly, the center of his desires as outdoing others in the Humphrey Bogart realist-cynical self-destructive frame, dominating and castrating—and greatly admired—a man who does not want to be cynical. Consider for a moment Bogart's male costars and second leads—he wipes the floor with them. And usually they are weak as performers. And often the roles themselves are of drunks or old guys or fools-for-women who get shot by women.

Consider his screen persona and personal reality as an outcast from society, as a leader of the rat pack, a group which included Sinatra, Farrow's first husband and a world-famous lecher, and Peter Lawford, who married a Kennedy and who apparently pimped Marilyn Monroe to John and Bobby. Consider Bogart's late-in-life marriage to the young Lauren

Bacall. Bacall was a girl then, but a girl of power, a powerful waif—a femme-fatale-waif on the loose, in an updated Dietrich mode.

Allen seems to like women of power who are also loony with nerves and waiflike. Farrow was the most famous waif-femme-fatale—a reversal of the same Bacall effect—of her time; she is too old and experienced now. Allen, in a semi-Bogart manner, seems to see himself as loving foolishly skinny-skimpy, bonily boyish or simply bony-faced, lonely, intelligent, orphanlike girls, or waifs, ones of frail glamour, of exoticism, an exoticism of helplessness.

It is not so different from Chaplin's tastes, from the blind girls in Chaplin's movies, the waifs, from the pathos and gleaming beauty, the note of immanent mockery by society of the attachment, the sweet harmlessness of the tie as Chaplin—a bit self-righteously presents it—and from Chaplin's tastes in actual life.

Allen is, in his screen persona, sexually terrified while manifesting a rather ugly sexual obstinacy—but in an American democratic context. He doesn't pursue princesses or heiresses. And he doesn't make movies about Europe or use Europe as a setting. And he makes no pretense to culture, only to reading and to show-business culture.

In America, partly because of Chaplin, because of frontier heroics and upper-class heroics in the fictions of the nineteenth century, such male clumsiness is intrinsically moral. Such a man, such a clumsy man, such a nervous fool is not a seducer.

It is more a case that the demons are against him than that demons are in him.

But such a clumsy fool can't become a movie star. Allen's style, one of high intelligence, in its antipublicity, in its tonality is that he is not a movie star. But he is. His style so far has not been that of someone who has sold or lost his soul, but rather that of someone who so suffers that we are impressed by his celebrity and admire (and love) him in an ugly way. We would not pay attention to him if he was not famous—and famously ugly.

He assures us he is ambitionless, idle. He assures us that he is grotesque. He practices, in general, a vengeful mockery *sweetened*, a *sentimental* demagoguery usually in *likable* proportions. He presents himself as a *likable shrewdness* reacting to the world.

This persona is presented as being incapable of evil or as being evil only because the world and its inhabitants are hunting him down. Which is revealed two ways, the first being comic: the *schlemiel*—with *schlemiel*hood explained as being this purity, this absence of evil. The second way is aesthetic, as Chekhovian, an artist, a man of understanding and depth, a genuinely profound soul, subtle, sad with knowledge of human flaws, human viciousness, but subtly kind. I don't think this second sort of presentation of his guiltlessness has ever been accepted in America. In America the second part has been something you indulge in Allen's work in a heartfelt way as a fan, as in accepting Elvis Presley's ultimate goodness, sweetness, kindness, innocence.

Presley and Chaplin were, of course, more popular than Woody Allen; but I want to use them to draw a graph of a kind. The technical reality of being lovable on-screen and large-scale means keeping in active existence something childlike and hugely or totally outgoing, seeking approval, i.e., innocent, victimizable—and ultimately victimized.

Famous as they are, they are us. The daydream lies not in their quality but in our meeting them.

In the foregrounds of their lives is the *technical* reality of being lovable in such a large-scale way for so large an audience and at the edge of legend and always of enormous scandal. Were they—like Salinger, say, among writers—exploiters of the young or were they drawn to their own images, to equals of a kind, or helpless superiors whom they could rescue?

How deeply movie popularity becomes rooted as conviction of one's own virtue varies but it seems to occur inevitably. The belief in their own, even Christlike, innocence is profound. Chaplin used doctrinaire politics and a personal fastidiousness—and his marriage to his last child-bride lasted until his death. But he never doubted his own high morality, it seems. Presley used his folkishness and his outgoingness on stage; his lack of middle-classness, of inhibitions, attitude, snobbery, or pretense. Allen has used his political and comedic decency, the "warmth" and kindness in his work.

Chaplin and Allen project the innocence of small, ugly, sensitive men, deeply combative, violently comic, inordinately ambitious. They insist on their humanity, their connection to us, their being moral light-bringers. Technically, in their comedy, they use alternations of humiliation and success.

3.

For an adopted child, as Wiley Silenowicz learns, the infidelity, if I might use that word, in leaving home or in tiring of adoptive parents and wanting to leave them as loving outsiders, is more final more quickly and more shockingly—more emptily—than in a blood tie. The adoptive tie can hardly be other than a variant of a love affair or of a marriage. Which is all the more reason for careful erotic coldness since an adopted child—in Wiley's view—longs for the regularity of a real home.

An adopted child doesn't carry the shadow of his adoptive parents inside himself. If he is kicked out, he falls into freedom or loneliness in a special way. The pressures to behave, to respond "romantically," to be an ideal companion, to do what's asked of one are correspondingly greater. The adopted child is bought by safety and money and by parental emotions very differently—he is is more conscious at all times of what is going on psychologically.

Then, in overt symmetry, as in all instances of love, rage and rebellion match in intensity the degree of consciousness and of conscious belonging. The whole thing is nerve-racking and scary—and close to psychic singularity—because the stakes are so odd. The tie really can be broken.

Now Woody Allen—a sad, successful man growing older, the irresistible glamour of his rights to happiness of some sort—and the disparity between the reality of his success and power and the humble schlemielhood of the character he portrays which exists in life, too, so that he is awesome and accessible—and the exotic waif, the rescued adopted child, now possibly a rescuer, see in each other the chance of a home at last.

But that disparity in Allen, as in Chaplin's portrayal of tramps in his movies, seems dishonest and menacing, even mean-spirited, too greatly self-licensing, self-righteous, and ruthless. Too emotionally knowing. And the adopted child's brought up to be a real illusion, to return conscious love and loyalty.

But how do we know we aren't jealous of them? It was my experience as a child that a lot of people around us were jealous of us.

The creation of a home and then maintaining a home is not a given or a set or a stable thing. It is culturally determined and economically determined and emotionally determined, and all sorts of circumstances affect it. Soon-Yi cannot know what she is getting into although she may know what she most needs. In a sense, she preserves Allen's presence in her family just when he was about to drift away. Of course, it turns out many of the others in the household are excluded, but not necessarily. They would be included if they accepted the situation.

And Allen, an enormously successful, immensely well-read, tremendously self-conscious man, untethered from ordinariness and under fantastic pressure all the time in the writing and making of movies and in performing and in life among his fans—his fans and his dependents—gets what he wants. That's the whole point of being able and talented. The very real unreality of everything for him is compounded by his power to alter superficial reality, not always superficially either. But so is the power of an adopted child to be what is desirable in a person in relation to love, the absence of greed, and the like.

Nude photographs—the Polaroid camera makes this easy—of lovers in compromising postures are how rich or famous or wickedly calculating people protect themselves by having evidence of the willingness of the other party to engage in "mature" sex. Allen may have thought it necessary to protect himself in that way. It goes with being a movie star vulnerable to scandalous publicity and with an adult life of temptation and of watching others and himself succumb to temptation, caprice, will, temper, what-have-you.

One forgets what life-and-death matters these are in individual lives. But part of the patriarchal setup is to take responsibility for lives interfered with, is to forestall tragedy while causing dislocation by the imposition of will. Considering what a compromise life is, the patriarchal compromise isn't always so bad. But often it is.

I suppose we can't help watching and judging and talking out loud and in print about this event. I think abuse and molestation are widespread, are common. Childhood and boyhood and girlhood, adolescence and late adolescence are intimate matters in a family, and children are provocative—and temperamental. A lot of grown-ups are mad, loony, semi-loony at least some of the time. Perhaps all of us are.

Children sometimes throw themselves at houseguests or show off erotically to an excruciating extent. The grown-ups don't behave. Sexual trespass and intragenderal revenge and power broking are common.

. . .

In the real world, the moods of a movie star who is also a writer-director and an accomplished comic, the mind and attitudes of such a star are not ordinary and not always wrong, even when scandalous. Sometimes such a man or woman is right. And we're wrong. Sometimes two stars fighting with each other are both right. Such cultural and moral diversity is to be expected, all romanticism aside.

The let-him-who-casts-the-first-stone-be-without-sin argument of Christ prevents too-quick a judgment especially if you believe in the unconscious mind. And no nation now has a large percentage of *respectable* families.

This does not mean that moral disapproval and ethical distaste are impossible. It means they ought to be expressed without self-righteousness.

The star's sense of gender in a child, his views on the relations of women with men, his sense of what is owed him, his sense of what life really is, his sense of his own success are big-time matters: they are already part of the culture. Thomas Mann, I am told, writes in his diary that he mounted his son Golo while the boy slept. The boy had already declared himself homosexual.

Family reality includes such matters. The irresistibility of famous parents when they choose to exert themselves and reward you, their child, with a day on the set or a meeting with someone you admire or with jokes and warm attention and physical closeness, or the similar decision or caprice or compulsion to be demonic is part of the picture, if I might be permitted to put it like that.

From the adopted child's point of view, sibling rivalry between children who are not genetically related is abusive. And romantic. Rage and competition, the wish to be the one most loved, the favorite, isn't balanced by the usual fear of alienating one's siblings or mother (assuming that the father is the one being pursued because he is the most powerful).

At best, an adopted kid is always only half in a family, always half out of it. This is because everything existent defines itself by where it ceases to exist. A blood child *is* the family whether she or he likes it or not. The adopted child can leave and, indeed, in most instances, such a breakup—a return to the real family, a return to the primary culture, a marriage that won't suit the family's view of things, that lies outside the family's capacity to accept cultural diversity or to accommodate to it—is always vaguely in the air as a fear.

This too leads to romantic abuse depending on what the members of the family want from you and on your response to things.

4.

Allen's movies are very forgiving. He is a great forgiver although he doesn't quite forgive the scandal in being dense and good-looking and rich. He never shows women who know their way around, who are not waifs, except as destructive powers, neurotic harridans.

He is less sentimental than Chaplin, more like Bogart but in a comic mode. He is a bourgeois American Jew, not music-hall lower-class British. And he is hardly a Yankee. In life he has made the women he was connected with, each one, a star of considerable magnitude. The *waif* thing has been illusion, symbol, acceptable pornography until now.

He tries to embody the power of sensibility. It is a dreamlike power that matches the power of women. It deals with the audience in the theater. It acts out the sensibility of the audience. His audience has identified itself with him too directly and now is carried into guilt.

The dreamer's power has been as often treated in American fiction and poetry as it has in European and Asian work.

While liking a lot of what he did, I have always been partly put off by Allen's work, tending to find the comic construct of the dreamer's power to be false. How innocent is any celebrity who presents himself or herself as a dreamer?

The moment-by-moment reality of making a movie is not a dream, and it is not dreamlike. The requirement of picturing motion, motions of faces and bodies and of stories that will, in becoming popular, become cultural presences, and the mighty and petty tinkering that comes into play, the planning, and the matter of making use in sheer immediacy of momentary advantage are the opposite of dreaming.

This illustrates the movies' paradoxical dilemma, which is that they are self-provingly and expensively real right there in front of you on the screen—there they are making dreams and willed projects real while being dreamlike.

Dreamlike means self-willed and centered on the self. This introduces a note of the absolute. Fame, the size of the screen, the amounts of money are real and are, in a bottom-line way, pretty much ultimate nowadays. No other degree of fame is quite so famous or so personal. Little else except large real-estate ventures and wars and major weaponry cost as much. No other representation of the human figure in motion is so large.

The movies have a hidden bitterness at the failure of the world to be absolute and to be discoverable by the peering lens in an absolute and final way. And every movie displays its connection to the paradox of cinema's unholy joy that the world is not absolute, is subject to story, to talent, to wit and to force and to comedy. Furthermore, because so many people depend on the efforts and profit from the success both financially and mentally—as the audience—or think they benefit, it is difficult if not impossible for semibenevolent, or benevolent-seeming, money and power and popularity not to see itself as virtuous. As noble. And exemplary.

Violent degradation in the movies is a curable, solvable hell. Most conditions in the movies are. Even documentaries that are a bit less utopian tend, propagandistically, to present evils as solvable by direct, bold, heroic, dangerous action.

How much this sentimentality is commercial and how much is essentially ego, which is to say self-love, and how much is it the self-righteousness mentioned above and how much is true are hard to say. It is open to argument.

One definition of evil in practical life is the dark possibility of final humiliation. But humiliation can be taken to be the admission of error. As social intelligence. You can't be educated without being humiliated. Allen's version of a happy ending is to have violence humiliated by humiliated innocence, as in the present circumstances.

5.

Allen as a moviemaker or a writer has not shown any interest in the slow death of the soul, in what becomes of the soul in the course of becoming part of the mechanism of success or of half-success. He does not deal in the growth of corruption as the loss of the self. He deals, I think, in what are despicable universalisms, each of which gets its comeuppance after proposing itself as the real authority. Among the excitements of modern success he sees that, with the help of psychoanalysis and money, one can live the personal absolutism of advertised or movieish dreams-come-true. The love and attachment—and sexual response—of an adopted child is just this sort of dream-come-true. This is opposed to the rebellious night-mare-horror of reality pictured as neurosis—suburban or unsuburban. The middle-class authority of *modern success* has attracted and tormented and misled many.

Allen presents his character as one of aggressive fatalism. I think this is a variation on the Bogart-Chaplin sense of the male but changed into something peculiarly Allen's own, a figure that has a working absolutism of belief, of hope, of Freudian fate.

He often suggests that his voice can't afford this madness. The self-congratulatory nature of his feeling of safety inside the events of his movies and his sense of humiliation alternate in a sort of seesawing abso-lutist incoherence: comic and a confession of nightmare at the same time. This never takes on the character of grief and greatness as in the work of Kafka. Allen suffers and wins out.

Allen offers as his final merit his powers of representing grace—happiness, blessing—in this world.

6.

To speak about the scandal directly is to say what others have recently said. Mia Farrow has a long history of scandal: her tie and then marriage to Sinatra when she was the age her adopted daughter is now, her taking Previn away from his wife, whose public rage and despair were highly publicized in their time.

Her alliance with Allen, her displacing the other women in his life, and her highly publicized eccentric lifestyle have also had an element of scandal. She is a movie star herself although not a popular one, and she is the daughter of a minor movie star. That she has been shaped by this, that her sense of family and of behavior has been shaped by this, seems not only likely but as unarguable as such matters can be.

Allen's public behavior during the scandal seems intelligent, forth-right, unfaked. But certainly he can fake such behavior or summon it up in himself. He does not blame himself, and he is not, at the present moment, guilty or defensive in manner. But Allen's actions with the girl—taken as romance—are unacceptable ethically, let alone morally.

. . .

The relation of an adopted child to a parent or stepparent is often, in the absence of the blood tie, romantic in nature. Parental love, protection, sharing a private language, all tend to have a romantic reality. This is a source of pleasure and it is a danger.

Touching a child warmly, a hug—a tone of voice, a good-night kiss—if the grown-up is not cold and austere, has a personal quality that springs from context and from the nature of the person and of the child. Men can rarely escape a faint or strong aura of being sensually abusive, whether with dogs and horses, friends, or children. It is a reflection of their size, voices, their active natures. The point at which such an ever-present physical reality—an inescapable one—passes over into being ill-advised and then into crime, those two points are relatively simple to define.

In the first case, it has to do with the mind and thoughts of the man, the use made of his affectionate response to the child, the use in a given moment. If we assume this is always anomalous if it is affectionate—and not more than slightly cold or bullying or morally self-serving—then you have, usually or often, a self-righteous father and a family atmosphere of considerable privacy or private in nature, somewhat permissive, somewhat disciplined, ingrown. If the self-righteousness is too great, if the father's self-love—and permissiveness toward himself (and not necessarily toward the child, although often the child is bribed)—we can argue unconscious molestation.

But the criminal element occurs when certain physical criteria are met, when certain physical acts are consciously performed.

Bathing or wiping or toweling a young child is an intrusive and intrusively erotic act and cannot escape being that. I have written about this. But while it is inevitably and always done individually—that is, in the manner and with the emotions and overt and covert purposes of the person doing it—while it always induces not a *normal* response but an individual response within a frame of allowable behaviors called *normal*—it always has aspects of the other, of the inevitable general case, of the *this is not acceptable behavior.*

Comedy, a comic attitude—a joking tone—"Are you naked, Little Pudding? Does this tickle? Don't move around so?"—may be taken to defuse the thing but it does not defuse it actually. So it is subject to accusation.

Let me put it another way, a mother or a father, taking personal care of a child, is guilty, on the face of it, of abuse.

If both parents have a history, as they do in this instance, of love affairs between older men and younger women, the danger, not of neurotic intrusion, but of cultural intrusion, is all the greater. *Normal* equals *permissible*. They are not normal people. Permissible has rewardingly and tormentingly been different for them.

7.

We entered the story as observers in medias res. What we think of it and what use we make of it in regard to our own behavior is separate from how we react to Soon-Yi, Farrow, and Allen. They have to be assumed to know, in part, what they are doing. Our curiosity has to do with defining what is acceptable in the modern community, which is not much like the communities of even fifty years ago. Allen's and Soon-Yi's invention of a home should be allowed to work itself out.

We, mere watchers, may be assumed to be jealous busybodies but we are also thinking of ourselves, and we can find the actions not only odious but as commenting on and defining much else in the man and in his work and in the actress and in her work.

I'm ending this piece ambiguously. This whole situation might prove to be at least half acceptable in the end.

Right now, though, although it doesn't concern me and isn't my business, I hate it.

1992

THE KAELIFICATION
OF MOVIE REVIEWING

Life, you may have noticed, everyone's life, is a matter of reviews. Everyone reviews your jokes, your cooking, your house, your haircuts. Movies, of course, get reviewed formally. And a movie review is not a simple matter. Not a modern review. You want to know a little about why they're written the way they are?

Lionel Abel, the *Partisan Review* man, the critic, is in his eighties. He drew my attention to the Woody Allen movie, *Husbands and Wives*, saying, "Harold, putting all the crap aside, it's a good movie. It's as interesting as a novel. Actually, it's more interesting than the novels I've read this year. It's smart. And it's about something. It's about de-ethicized sex, you can say it's about the comedy and the calamities of de-ethicized sex. In the absence of God, of course. I have to say it's aesthetically unsatisfying. I walked out at the end with an empty feeling because the movie fails as art. I need an aesthetic form in a movie. But this is an interesting movie."

What he said didn't sound like something that a reviewer influenced by Pauline Kael such as Terrence Rafferty would write. Mr. Rafferty in fact disliked the movie. And what Lionel was saying wasn't anything Andrew Sarris would say.

For the young among you, I should explain that the *Partisan Review* brought high culture into American discourse. Mary McCarthy and Elizabeth Hardwick were first unleashed in those pages.

. . .

Social historians see this as a development stemming from the influx of educated anti-Fascist Europeans in the 1930s who came to this country when the term highbrow hadn't yet been coined; there had been no need for it. Under this influence Sigrid Undset was replaced in time by Flannery O'Connor, and J. P. Marquand and Pearl Buck by Nabokov and Hannah Arendt. The careers of Leonard Bernstein and Norman Mailer, Jackson Pollock and Arshile Gorky, John Barth and Robert Coover became possible.

Call it a rebellion from the top down, or a status coup or the end of American parochialism, but the Anglo-Saxon cultural ascendancy was displaced. They really didn't know enough. American universities quite suddenly became good. The literary canon was rethought. And everyone wanted in. To some extent the sixties spread this culture in a popular, or common, form. Everything that the rich and the educated allowed themselves, such as adultery and an interest in trash movies, became commonplace. Even conservatism. You didn't need breeding or money. Or even intelligence, as we know.

Everyone in the country rebelled one way or the other and claimed intellectual success and standing, often in the robes of borrowed high culture. The central cultural fact, however, is that no self-sustaining and continuing form of discourse on any level arose; and the substance of high culture is discourse.

Pauline Kael emerged some decades back with a conscious program of separating in her criticism talk about movies from high culture. Hers was not an attack on high culture or an appropriation of it. High culture claims to know and propagate eternal verities, but it is chiefly a bunch of people—in this country, on the East Coast—who have dubious title to it, anyway. It is reputed to have—it is supposed to have—heartless standards of merit. It asks over and over, *Is it good?* But it is unable to define what is good: *complex, intelligent, with "profound" moral concerns.* Good try.

Ms. Kael's credo was that movies were merely a popular form and vulgar; and that nothing was at stake in them except pleasure, money, style, fame, and sexual daydreams. Movies, she said, were unliterary and meaningless and socially irresponsible, thank God. They were meaningful in terms of the immediacy of their effect as thrilling popular entertainment, not only in themselves, but in the whole daydream machinery of publicity and infinite fame. To be available to their real audience, movies had to stop pretending to be social comment and ideated or ideological. That was glop.

Ms. Kael single-handedly established the sub-elitist transitory moment as the measure, that it was always to be taken as trashy—as human—with no interest in uplift, thank God, but only in the melodramatically intense procedure of giving people what people really want. She is a very short woman and very intelligent but thoroughly unreasonable. She is masturbatorially intelligent—and successful. She has no sense of society or of family and the French cinema of the 1960s, when Mr. Allen was young, is not set inside a framework of fate.

But she may be the very best writer who ever lived at descriptions of dramatic actions, of what-is-there, of what actors are doing. Her class bias and her sense of preferred subject matter—it should be grungy, raunchy, universal in that sense—are a workable recodification of the democratic common denominator.

The trouble is that the justified success of her arguments and opinions meant that moviemakers in their cowardly way lost interest in showing society as anything except something to be overturned, as in a Marx Brothers movie, because that was thrilling and strong flavored, and any other approach was weaker in the new view of things.

Ideas disappeared. And movies aren't great vehicles for ideas: Ms. Kael was right. And with ideas went issues. The limited subject matter and inarticulate intelligence and nearly lunatic and often infantile opinionatedness of contemporary movies is the result.

Toward the end of her writing regularly, she became a rebel against her own program to some extent.

I repeated to the Los Angeles literary critic Michael Silverblatt what Lionel Abel had said and asked if Woody Allen had done something new in his movie. I have to talk about movies before I go to them or I am likely to have a very eccentric response to them. I want to think what everyone else is thinking. Michael Silverblatt is forty years old and lives in Los Angeles, where he has a radio program dealing with books and where he works in the movies as well. He is a former student of Mr. Abel's; Norman

Mailer has described him as the best critic and best reader in the country at the moment.

And he is something of a disciple of Pauline Kael's. Mr. Silverblatt also studied with John Barth and Dwight Macdonald. The heady mixture of mentors is apparent when he talks, as are echoes of Los Angeles and New York. On the surface Mr. Silverblatt has retro style, but he is current, and I listen to his opinions.

He said, "Lionel is right, but, uh, uh, you're wrong. This isn't something new in movies. By the way your novel is on the coffee table in the living room. Uh, uh, but it's funny. Months pass in the movie, and your book is still on the coffee table." He said that what Mr. Allen did was uncommon in American movies but was not new. "The French did it a lot," he said. I'm mimicking his voice: "And the French have given up making serious movies, at least for the moment, so it's good to have this. But it's not as new as you think."

I went to the movie to see my novel make its film debut. In society, it is possible to speak the truth, if you should want to, only if you are not in need of favors. But it is socially permitted to speak it on the occasion of a scandal.

How do you write about a movie that is doing something quite new? Ms. Kael and Mr. Sarris and Mr. Abel and the others are no help. Inheritors' English and inheritors' ideas can't handle a new thing.

And it isn't possible to invent a new critical approach all at once. Mr. Allen has made a movie entirely opposed to Ms. Kael and almost mocking toward Mr. Abel and his ideas; and this movie shows no interest in Mr. Silverblatt's generation and its notions of the inarticulate.

The primary structure of the movie is that of a talky, would-be literate Hollywood romantic comedy of the *Adam's Rib* and *All About Eve* and *My Man Godfrey* sort. But the surface is Freudian except that it is relativist—a further shock, a Nouveau Roman sense of objects and a fair use of French cinema of the 1960s, when Mr. Allen was young, is not set inside a framework of fate or of sociological or ecological shtick or flat-out hopelessness or flat-out hope. The movie isn't about the corruption of society or of the characters.

Mr. Allen's people this time around are set in motion relative to one another and to the era and to their own qualities in a movie clearly in a post-Kaelian mode. The movie and the story are in their hands. The infamous camera movements make nausea real. And comic. The speeches are communicative. Language failure is not the issue here.

Mia Farrow as Audrey Hepburn is scarifying, although, as a psychological matter, she should be given grounds for her confidence—something like motherhood and money—so that her quiet bullying can be seen as modest all in all, even as reasonable although unlivable. Sidney Pollack as a gonadal Spencer Tracy is not maddened enough. Judy Davis is. She imitates Bette Davis, Bette Davis married to Spencer Tracy and set free for a while to have a life apart from Tracy. Mr. Allen as a brainy, funny-looking Tony Curtis, a sweet New York guy, needs more poison in his character but he is fairly convincing as a good man.

The characters in their web of relationships and their words are, as characters-in-a-narrative, fully enough realized that one wonders about what is not shown or said about their lives.

Each scene is about knowing and discovering. And about exploring. Nothing is granted to mystery or to unknowing except why these people are unhappy: This is Chekhovian and generous.

The unconscious is not explored. Life is. The characters are rational. They have problems. This is profoundly funny and unsettling. Chaos is not a possibility for them—this is very New York.

In place of showing the world of seasons, Mr. Allen offers his awareness that this is a movie. That the movie-as-a-movie is a stand-in for the world is—*profoundly*—shocking.

The death of a marriage is the death of the strategies of speech, of an era of one's life. The move toward silence is affecting.

Mr. Allen as a relativist is still too much of an absolutist to see life as holding different paths. He avoids showing minds opening. He doesn't deal in terror as instruction.

A *good* movie is not good. Or bad. It is a ground of thought, a source of named feeling, of wandering sensations, of thought about what life is and what it might be.

This movie is not Chekhov. But it's good. And it's new.

1992

HOLLYWOOD CLOSE-UP

Stars, right? And, as always in America, money as the background. The Academy Awards show gives us stars. It does it by gender—presenting men one way, women another. Women? The most complex, strongly illuminating, slightly off-duty images of what at the moment is felt to be attractive in women may be the prime demonstration of the show: warmth, charm, liveliness, bone structure, talent, what have you. That these women represent some sort of peak of their gender is indicated by the fact that just sighting one of them on the street or getting out of a limousine gives point to a day and becomes a long-term anecdote for many of us.

The Academy Awards treat these peak men and women mostly in a suburban country-club way, showing what is acceptable (desirable) and attractive in women, in men, often darkly or perversely. The show is codified, like the American country club itself, so that a lot of it can be fully understood only by insiders—while it is seen symbolically or as romance by outsiders.

The awards, in their six-decades-long history, have steadily had a WASP bias. In the 1930s, the secret count was how many Catholics won an award. Except for Paul Muni, the Jews were a minor part of it all; John Garfield, Edward G. Robinson, Sylvia Sidney, Paulette Goddard—none of them won an Oscar during that time. In a society without much in the way of accurate social reporting and with no tradition of a social sense of itself, one of the few glimpses of its actual social reality—who was loved, who was envied, who got invited, what people looked and dressed like more or less at the top—incomplete as that glimpse was, was offered in this movieland ritual. In this idea of the top, in this besieged and yet still, for a moment, triumphant country club, with its mass market and democratic base, and its WASP bias, we see male notions of protected daughters and wives. And daughters and wives gone *a bit wild*. And we see, from year to year—usually in off years—one or two examples of the unprotected outsider-woman, the bandit-woman, in feathers or leather or in feathers *and* leather. If you're old enough, you may remember the mother-versus-whore, nice-girl-versus-slut games of Oscar shows in the past.

The trouble this year with the awards, whose theme was supposedly "Oscar Celebrates Women and the Movies," was that the oblique signals and hidden references were too simplified and the overall treatment was too numb, or too dumb. There was no frisson, no scandal, as a conscious, sly thread through the show. Perhaps unconsciously, most of the complications in the way women are regarded (and in the ways women regard themselves) got lost in a general haze of condescendingly respectful bimboization of some of the stars and an acknowledgment, dim but perceptible, that some (odd-looking) women exist not without but a bit beyond sex, beyond expensive T & A and beyond even ladylike tits and ass.

The key moment actually occurred near the start of the show, when Watusi-legged, six-foot, very white Geena Davis—with her enormous, Betty Boop head—came out wearing a long dress with an apostrophe-shaped cutout between her breasts showing that they were supported by naught but their own youthful hubris. And she read off the teleprompter a tribute to what women supposedly learn at the movies about being women: by golly and by gum and by God, they learn how to be women *in movie theaters*. Not through birth or nurture or social pressure but at the goddam movies. It was a sort of *Time*-essay version of Hallmark-greeting-card prose about woman-in-general being instructed at the cineplex. It was not a speech written by a woman. The moment was not subject to rational enjoyment or even rational interpretation. Written by a man, it was a blast of conceit and a country-club recitation of what a locally attractive woman, a sex object circa 1953, would be if one didn't think too much about it. And it was acted out, illustrated: the lighting was such that a slightly paradisal glow was cast on the inverse parentheses of the inner curves of Davis's breasts while she recited "to shoot from the hip, to tease and uplift, to be villainous, wily"—at one point Davis gave an involuntary, embarrassed grin at the mass of words, like tadpole eggs, that she could do nothing with, and the big-boned Betty Boop head swung a bit toward the horizontal, as if to enter an animated cartoon, an entirely willed, unreal, malely sexual world.

And this is Geena Davis, the woman who played in *A League of Their Own* and *Thelma & Louise*. She specializes, it's true, in the less damaged and more dependent woman—she is almost a strike-breaking scab in this feminist era. But in her acting is something amazingly full-blooded, temperamental, depth-filled, liquescent, sometimes scorchingly far out, which combines with a hint of abandonment to mindlessness, to an endless near-death or suffocation as a woman. So, this is Geena Davis, a tremendous young talent of considerable fascination and ambiguity, and she is given a cretinously sentimental speech about how a woman learns to be a woman in a movie theater, while a haloing light illuminates her cleavage. She is reduced to the synecdoche of tits, and to being a good sport, this movie star in a clearly gilded cage mouthing nonsense. We don't analyze as we watch, but on some level we know at this point that the awards are tendentious, not subversive or honest or complex, just argumentative; and that they're not going to help us in our lives this year. We don't turn off the set, but we turn off our minds: we start reading between the pixels; we watch in a more distant way and think the awards stupid and feel a restless itch for something we can't name. We know we're being cheated, even if the show is free.

That's what was on TV sets around the world. But that isn't quite what I saw. I didn't see the awards show most of you saw until a week later. At the time, I was in the Dorothy Chandler Pavilion, with its ninety-five-foot-high proscenium, watching, along with twenty-six hundred other people, a show only bits of which were telecast. And what I saw was good, surreal, as strange as hell, full of shadows and low points and high spots and never dull. (Earlier, I had seen some of the rehearsals, in their usual messy warmth, while sitting in the first or second row among the placards set up in the seats around me with photographs and names of the big shots who would sit in those seats.) Actually, I saw a show that the producer, Gil Cates, and the director, Jeff Margolis, never saw. Of course, they'd seen the run-through and the dress rehearsal. But they were in "the truck" during most of the performance, picking images from the fourteen interior cameras and the seven exterior cameras they were maneuvering, and putting together the television show that such a large chunk of the world saw.

Whatever the offscreen finagling among the Hollywood samurai to control parts of the show and to make use of it for publicity and to dispense favors or exact vengeance, whatever the big-toothed, well-barbered, notoriously barbaric sharks did or didn't do, the show as it occurred in the theater was warmhearted, unhysterical, not particularly egoistic—except, maybe, for Barbra Streisand, and she had reason, as we shall see. The crew and the orchestra and the choreographer don't have a lot of rehearsal time, and they don't bullshit about the quality or lack of quality of the songs, say, or about the merit of what they can accomplish, of what can be staged, under the circumstances. But the level of admiration for stardom and what goes into it, the outright near-love for the professional skills and magnetism on parade, the interplay between celebrity and the weird amusements of the audience on this occasion, and the implications about human limitations and superhuman show-business souls, are stunning. And effectual. They wrap you in show business in the friendly way of those old M-G-M musicals with Rooney and Garland.

Even the admiration for the stars as they make their way into the theater past the fans and the reporters is more moving than horrible, more paradigm of something than parody of stardom. The feelings are heartfelt, tactful, and particularized, star by star, reporter by reporter. Gregory Peck, wearing too much makeup and looking as if he were about to be laid out rather than about to perform, had a gloriously friendly look and genuinely feasted on the attention. Some of the older women—Sophia Loren, for one—had a special Cinderella burden, a time limit to how long they could feel safe about how great they looked, so that their warmth was a bit crimped at the edges compared with Peck's. Or Bob Hope's. Hope spent a certain amount of time singing to himself.

Streisand came into the awards brouhaha already on the gender warpath, because of the Academy's having slighted her last year as director of *The Prince of Tides*. And when she showed up at the rehearsals she made special use of their warmth and folksiness. She demanded a trailer—one with viewing equipment. Then she came onstage not in old clothes or daytime clothes but dressed for the awards. She tried two dresses, one low-cut and one not so low-cut, and the one not so low-cut was a Donna

Karan, someone told me. She had her bit onstage in each dress taped. She asked the rehearsal audience if it thought a gold necklace or a diamond necklace would look better with her dress. "If I wear diamonds, they have to change the lighting of the whole set," she said. She taped her statements about women directors and about directors without gender a couple of times onstage, working with the show's producers; offstage, she revised and rethought what she was going to do. Working from tapes that showed on television monitors what she looked and sounded like, she wrote and rewrote what she was going to say. She adjusted her makeup and her voice—and her necklace—to fit what she was going to do during the show.

Elizabeth Taylor is neither stupid nor foolish, and never—or rarely—foolish about the effect she makes on or off camera. She is a movie star, and she is of a different generation from Streisand. Taylor isn't fascinated by technology or at war with the media—she isn't at war with the world or with people's attitudes toward women in the same way that Streisand is. Their rage and energy spring from the same root, but Taylor isn't interested in television—few movie people are—and she isn't a recording artist who has learned about audio technology, fighting all the way. For her, the TV screen is too small compared with a full-size movie screen; it can't convey space or movement, or glamour, to the same extent—at least, not yet.

In the theater during the ceremonies, one saw the small, lone figure of Elizabeth Taylor come out on a very wide stage, into a lot of brightly and imaginatively lit space, in front of a lot of faces in an audience that one was part of: there were a lot of us and one small *her*—a famous her, in a kind of flesh-colored peignoir. One seemed to see her drawing on her strength of will under the weight of the world's attention, felt mostly as antagonism, or as sexual intrusion—a wish to see her fail, to watch as she loses her looks or this immediate battle, to see age gouge her and a change of styles make her look cheap despite the jewels. In the theater, in the full scale of things, her small being confronted that wish as a figure accustomed to fame, a figure more or less fearless. In the theater, Elizabeth Taylor was electrifying—personal and alive, isolated, relentless, and concerned with her own vanity, her own destiny, and with charity on the most practical, least-elevated level.

But in the television close-up, one saw a face entirely out of scale, locked into a kind of golden telephone booth of space; one saw a willful woman, hard at work, losing her nerve off and on in her speech, or else simply drawing on a store of unsuitable facial expressions. One saw someone not alone, someone who for most of her life has not been alone, who has commanded enormous media attention since she was twelve, someone spoiled and so egocentrically self-concerned that the speech was nearly impossible to follow. She seemed almost like a bully in her presumption within the limited television space of the close-up. Her face is so much a medium for the transmission of effect, so famous, and with age and design now so much that of a jeweled, enameled, doll-like creature, not flesh and blood, as when she was young, but still alive and still with aspects of freshness, still so unharridanlike, that a close-up without story or a role for her to play is perilous with other stories—our wishes, our memories, our jealousies, and her always obvious humanity. I mean, it has been obvious since *National Velvet*, forty-nine years ago. She *was* playing a role in the awards, of course—that of a sixty-one-year-old woman loaded with jewels given to her by chubby, sloppy, high-powered men who found her passionate and amusing and world-class desirable, who adored the feisty and lusty and earthy girl-star and luminous animal, a dirty and indomitable spirit.

In the theater, Streisand's speech was a dud—overrehearsed, self-conscious, small in scale. But Streisand, having studied and thought about the matter, and being aware of the ratio, roughly one-to-fifty, of television's power of representing size or space or emotional depth or elevation, didn't worry about the audience in the Chandler Pavilion or about theatrical reality or theatrical effect. She is deep into television representation: she had a significantly appropriate expression when she spoke in close-up; she had a serious and strong set of facial expressions and, clearly, the right voice. And the right movements of the voice. She had studied the tapes and used the rehearsal time well. The speech she wrote, the words she used suited that medium—and the close-up. On television, she was effective, dignified, persuasive, a knockout.

Pauline Kael has argued any number of times that movies have to be seen on large screens; they have to be big; and they're better if they're seen in full movie houses, if there is an actively responsive audience. It does seem that television can't convey the charge a movie carries. To push that a step further would be to say that television can't show what a movie star is—not in full, or even half, radiance and fascination.

In movies, nothing kills narrative quicker than an ill-judged close-up.

Close-ups are a slower range of time; they represent minor climaxes of perception on our part and minor or major climaxes of revelation on the part of the actor. Often the story makes you long to see the calculation or emotion of the actor, so that the close-up is like studying a face in life or is like a kiss or is subtly orgasmic.

Television consists blithely of a mind-obliterating surfeit of meaningless close-ups, to animate the small screen. Most television theoreticians feel that we are constantly judging the honesty, the sincerity, of the face, and of the person behind the face, boring or entertaining us on the little screen. But a meaningless close-up of a star or a near star is a kind of hell of exposure, in which what we as audience see is vanity and social class and pride. Mercedes Ruehl looked as if she were wearing furniture fabric and as if she weren't wearing makeup, which was interesting and unmovielike, bohemianly the wrong social class, not part of the country-club thing at all. No one has ever sported as complicated a haircut as the seemingly emotionally eviscerated, no-eyed, dim-lipped Richard Gere; at a rehearsal, his hair was so layered and fell in so many waves that it suggested the Sydney Opera House. On television, combed out, it was still elaborate enough to distract some of us so that we never entirely heard his fantasia on China and Tibet. Susan Sarandon in gold lamé looked villainous. Jane Fonda in some formfitting swollen raincoat with half a million buttons suggested an unpleasant dominatrix.

A star in public, like the rest of us, is acting out something—sanity, let's say, or dignity, or sexiness. Most stars are so hypnotic that it almost becomes possible to forget that stars are likely to be the most restlessly competitive and uncontrollably destructive people you will ever meet. Consider their mischief, their self-righteousness, their psychic insensitivity to anything beyond their range. They can be and often are insupportable. And remember that stardom is more than ability or will, although will is a large part of it. A lot of what we react to and what draws us is courage, is reckless nerviness. Some of it is a predatory focus on being alive in the risk-laden, irreversible moment: Anjelica Huston coming offstage at one of the rehearsals and saying, "Oh, let's talk—I want to use this adrenaline high."

Two episodes, epigramlike, dealt in tangential ways with this matter of Hollywood stardom: the real thing, as stardom goes, is the Hollywood brand, with few exceptions. Emma Thompson gave one of the best acceptance speeches of the last two decades: clever, a bit dismissive, saying that she was honored to see in front of her the faces that had "entertained and influenced me and thrilled me," and half offering to give back the money that she had been paid for her performance in *Howards End*. The famous faces didn't really respond to either remark. While intelligence is the rule in Hollywood, it tends to be a Hollywood intelligence, which is to say untranslatable, suspicious, uneasy, and parochial—pure Hollywood, country-clublike in its distrust of trained intelligence of an outside kind. Thompson did not offer her face in close-up. She twisted and turned and somehow masked her eyes. She seemed almost facially deformed: a set of dowdy tics, a performance potential, and not so much a woman at all. The American Academy gave Thompson's superb performance an Oscar, but the audience didn't seem to warm to her or to her unstarlike manner.

The other episode was provided by Federico Fellini. First, Sophia Loren appeared, the most ardently admired of the non-Nordic, non-country-club stars of the last few decades. She was wearing a version of the peignoir-type thing that Taylor was wearing. Then she introduced Marcello Mastroianni, in a supporting role to her own diva grandeur. Then there was the dreary montage. I suppose that's part of the hidden politics—not having a knockout Fellini montage that would have brought the audience to its feet roaring. And then Fellini appeared. What a sly-eyed, wrinkled, commanding face. What a scene-stealer. Or, if you like, alpha plus personality. With his first response to Loren, cutting into her speech, telling her drolly and commandingly that she could kiss him, and then moving his head, he obliterated her. Even with the eyes and the gown and the diva manner, he doused her in darkness. He erased Mastroianni. For a while now, we've known that among the greatest starring personalities are directors, whose abilities are visible to us only through their films, through the performances of others. But Fellini did it in the theater, at a distance, and he did it epigrammatically—in a very small space—and did it so that it worked on television as well. He imposed his improvisatory timing and his wit and intelligence in a dominant yet modest, kingly yet Felliniesque way. His eyes did not stay put but kept moving in nonstarlike swiveling scans, almost comic, locating the cameras, judging the temperature of the audience. And, in a language not his own, Fellini stole the Oscar show. He seemed to prove that the artist-mind is, in a way, king, and that the director has final power, because he, or she, is finally not so self-consciously caught in a set persona as a star is.

I mean, his is not a famous face. Surgical intervention and a degree of youth were not the question. Even in terms of expression, he was not an actor, quite: his eyes never did behave for long. He was like a ghost or a road map or an abstract painting of stardom. And he was brief. His whole bit was seamless charm and grace, culminating with his thanking his wife, Giulietta Masina, whom he told to stop crying in a slightly climactic voice. And the cameras swung then to the star's face: she *was* crying. His performance flowed into credibility, into anecdotal greatness, with the real thing, her tears. He entered human credibility through her sweetly magnetic sentiment. Her crumpled joy. None of which was he capable of projecting. He needs a star.

With Gil Cates and Jeff Margolis in the command truck, masterminding the television cameras and choosing and directing the flow of effects and images, Billy Crystal essentially ran the actual performance. His writers were working all during the show, coming up with lines. Crystal is free to do pretty much as he likes, to up the tempo or to slow it, to be silly or dignified, to be outrageous or to play it safe, but he has to react at once. If on television he seemed subdued this year, that was perhaps because he thought the show was going well and he didn't want to take too many chances. And perhaps he has become, for the moment, too much the insider and the big star, like Eastwood or Nicholson—a world male figure. It was in the brash, restless, maybe a bit shy role of the unlikely outsider—the short, not too famous outsider with a pie-pan face a little like the "Have a nice day" face, the outsider breaking in with our connivance and approval—that he did so well as a bridge between us and the glamour and oddity of the Oscars and stars in his first three years. In rehearsal this year, he was a lot livelier physically and he had some of that edge; he seemed then to be without self-love, to be a performance addict. But maybe in performance the size of the audience and the show-biz history got to him. He's more famous now than Bob Hope, after all.

It is nearly impossible to explain the self-consciousness about the size of the audience, the alertness to realities of popularity and success—and the obliviousness of other things—that go into the concentration that carries Crystal along in his performance. He is a borderline great performer, but he is given to holding back and to undoing his showier effects in a kind of pious modesty, a sort of self-anchoring in being a person, and not a star, in the end. He is determined not to be self-destructive. One of his writers remarked to me that Crystal and Kevin Costner are the two least self-destructive stars in Hollywood. Maybe we're gladiatorial, and we want our stars to risk emotional evisceration, insanity, exhaustion, public folly. Crystal constantly lessens the distance between him and us by falling back on schlock and merchandising himself as a sad ego full of longing for more prizes and glamour. It seemed to me in the theater that the more Crystal presented himself as a famished Hollywood ego, the more the audience in the Pavilion liked it. I liked it, too. Of course, Crystal was doing two shows simultaneously—one in the Pavilion and one for the TV cameras that kept sniffing at him from the sides and back. For better or worse, his judgment came from the response in the auditorium and the general feeling backstage during the show that the show was going very well.

The nature of what's at stake for us, even for me, in being part of this huge modern audience, and living in a time when this audience determines a good deal of cultural history, came to an obscure climax at Irving Lazar's party at Spago, a clumsily built stone-and-wood restaurant on a steep slope, with low ceilings and a view of LA. Lazar's party begins as a dinner alternative to the awards performance. You watch the awards on small televisions scattered among the rooms. Some of the bosses are usually there, and a stray studio head with some actual power for the moment—and stars, new and old, and people from the East Coast. The Oscar winners come along after the show and after they've spent a few minutes with the press at the Governors' Ball—not the governor of California, but the Board of Governors of the Academy of Motion Picture Arts and Sciences.

As always happens when I'm in a room full of powerful men, I needed a cigarette. Smoking reminds me of my youth, when it was OK to be a blank-faced bystander, an apprentice. The table I was at was a corner one, with Larry McMurtry, who wrote *Lonesome Dove*, seen by twenty-five million people as a miniseries on TV. It was a good table; no one walked behind you. A guy looking party-bruised ducked into the corner of this corner and pulled out a pack of Marlboros. I excused myself from McMurtry and asked this guy for a cigarette. I lit up, and said, "I needed that. It makes me nervous being the least famous person in the room."

The guy said, "Yeah. I know."

At that moment, Lazar and Barbara Lazaroff, who is Wolfgang Puck's wife, and Elizabeth Taylor and a squat man carrying an Oscar arrived at the table. Larry Fortensky, Taylor's husband and the guy I'd unknowingly bummed a cigarette from, looks a little like a blond Richard Burton. He is clearly likable, with a clouded or overshadowed, nicely self-conscious quality of tenderness and a somewhat nervous manner. Taylor seated herself and started fiddling with her rings; she has very small hands, almost like squirrel paws. She dwindles to discretion in her hands and feet. She has unfortunate coloring for jewelry. None of the stones one can think of—sapphires, rubies, diamonds—really go with her eyes and hair and skin. She had on a remarkable, ice-cube-size emerald ring, but the green, except for being spectacularly impressive, didn't go with her eyes or her makeup. Her very black hair was heavily sprayed, and it looked sticky. It stuck out in a lot of directions and detracted from her very large yellow-and-white-diamond daisy necklace, which looked as if it needed cleaning. Her directness and impatience, the absence of hypocrisy, combined with her glamour, have a certain effect. The obviousness of her temper and her will and her undefeated air and a notable absence of any spiritual quality or yearning—the absence of anything transcendent at all—with her realist's quality of measuring and tasting what is there, her vigor, and her outrageous nerve become a form of sex appeal and beauty.

She seems to be someone who feels no embarrassment at all. Perhaps she gave up being embarrassed a long time ago. Someone at a nearby table remarked audibly, "Queen Liz." Taylor told the squat man where on the table to put the Oscar; she adjusted another ring on her small hands, bent backward very slightly and looked up at Lazar, who, standing, wasn't that much taller than she was seated; she flashed a smile of considerable power but of no personal significance except that it was large and radiant; she straightened up again, was serious, was warm. "I like my Oscars," she said to someone. She seemed entirely unrattled, unnervous, but when Lazar turned away she dipped her head briefly toward Fortensky's chest, and he touched her cheek with his lips and slipped her a bite of pizza.

Fortensky was tender toward her, with a slightly suffering quality of inheld strength. McMurtry leaned forward and told her how much he admired her speech at the Oscars.

I joined in, and said, "Yeah, it was a really good speech. It really turned the audience on."

Taylor looked at me, and it was unsettling, the directness, the swiftness of her decision to talk, her lack of fear. But so was the oddity of her beauty, of her good looks, and of the makeup. Her eye nearest me didn't seem to be pure violet but to be dark blue and partly purple and flecked with brown. She is a hell of a good-looking woman, and is piercingly and burningly alive, but the effect she has on someone my age is complex, because of the passing of time. Her image is complicated with the representation of time back to the late 1940s.

She said of her speech, "Well, I'm used to being a fool. I can do it if there's a reason."

"I don't think you were a fool," I said. I wasn't being tactful—or guileful.

The aggression in Taylor seems to have nothing to do with ordinary ambitiousness but, rather, with her readiness to feel and with her sense of herself as overendowed, and wicked. In her speech she'd said that she knew that good, gentle Audrey (Hepburn) was in Heaven with her children but that her own job was to keep fighting down here, to be rowdy and aggressive—everything Hepburn was not—working for AIDS patients and for a cure. Her small, pretty voice is strongly projected in a narrow range; nothing in its familiar tones is without humor or color, but nothing in her voice suggests wit or any kind of mystic allure or music of longing. And nothing about her says, *I am a nice person.*

"Couldn't you tell that the audience was responding?" I asked her. "Where I was, people stood up. A real jolt of electricity went through the crowd around me."

"I didn't notice anything," she said. "I just did it. I wrote it myself." I understood her tone—and her eyes—to be saying that, if she wrote it, it was worthless, a throwaway. "I just did it."

Now I began to half-grin: "Oh, but surely by now you must know that you know a little bit about audiences."

She never took her eyes from mine; she set her breathing so that we were subtly in step with just a slight syncopation. "I don't know anything," she said. "I know my own limitations. Maybe."

"You don't know how to affect people?"

"As an actress, you mean?" Almost piteously but not whining: "It's been so long since I acted I don't know what I know."

She gives an impression of enormous personal force and will and of almost endlessly direct response—the here-and-now thing—and of a deep capacity for a kind of barking amusement. She's hardly middle class, and yet she is an archetype of a middle-class woman. I said she reminded me in her mere existence of my past. I meant my unreligious past, and how nearly everyone I knew had lived in the 1950s—the here-and-now thing and a distrust of what couldn't be physically known. Sunlight coming through the windows and making the college rooms warm, and oneself lying there and contemplating love versus chastity. We were all a lot like her. No one I knew gave a shit about heaven or hell. We wanted to live. We wanted to be young for a while—we had just barely escaped the war.

She, Elizabeth Taylor, embodies a lot of that reality that you will never tell your kids or grandchildren about. She is us, in that sense.

It can be argued that she reflected the times she lived in. But maybe she influenced them, too. Certainly her life, unsnobbish, hardly ethnocentric, filled with divorces and illness and material triumphs, with its political movements leftward and rightward, curiously mirrors the American decades from 1950 until now. She is us in more than one sense.

Leaving Spago, I followed Angie Dickinson down past the reporters grouped along the stairs. Kathy Bates was coming in, looking a bit whipped, walking slowly, with a large red AIDS doojigger on the lapel of her evening jacket.

"Kathy!" Angie Dickinson said. "Kathy! Kathy, it's Angie. . . ."

It is like high school in a way, maybe as much as like a country club, this stuff with the stars.

Outside, Los Angeles looked, as it often does, as if it were a piece of costume jewelry. It is strange how it has in this century almost unfailingly inspired apocalyptic images in writers and directors. It does strike me as being a city of avid and perpetual apocalypse and moneymaking and of overt sexuality and as being a place of great potency still largely beyond definition or clear description. And as being this more and more lastingly: the real home or center of what is worldwide middle-class right now.

1993

VARIATIONS ON SEX

Ah, beware the hard-eyed, merciless fan. You might say that the will to be beautiful, to be considered beautiful, to be sexually efficacious as an image and irresistible (to a large audience) and to be exploited for it—and then to escape from this exploitation—makes up the history of those people who become Hollywood symbols of the first rank. But if the escape is complete—into success, say, or into experienced professionalism and age—then the whole apparatus of Hollywood illusionism about life and beauty and the movies and us and the stars breaks down. Control and self-preservation, even ease, seem stupid as they age. Actors, men and women both, are said to be ageless, and seen so for much of their careers—uncertainly thirty, tautly forty, liftedly fifty, and so on— if by ageless we mean of no known human age.

But a lot of the older actors start to look alike; they probably have the same surgeon. Errol Flynn, who in a way seemed safe from ridicule because he was so relaxed about himself and his stardom, became something of an international joke as he aged: he seemed not virile but, rather, unimaginative, or insectoid, with pathetic eyes and a foolish laugh. The gauntly beautiful Gary Cooper became fatuous, a manly and sadly tireless boy whose lechery was still clean, jowls and tough, slightly loony eyes and all—and he was too old to be clean that way. Cary Grant was an always sexually available form of male evasion: he never played a role in which what you saw sexually was what you got sexually, you or his co-star. But that image of a man who was attractive yet hidden became too stiffly formulaic as he aged, though he lasted a long time as a viable icon. What he seemed to be hiding then were not depths of sexual response but symptoms of joint pain and creeping exhaustion. The youthfully Bronxy Tony Curtis was sexually glib, and then, as he aged, the glibness came to seem more a response to his own celebrity than to the story in front of him. Cagney's ironic male acquiescence and violent slyness faded in interest, as you might expect in a smallish, potbellied, oldish man. No big star is a snob on-screen, but the audience *is* snobbish, and capricious, which is to say it is capable of punishing the loss of attraction, the loss of a sexual future in the star. Even the skillful Spencer Tracy, who had never been overtly sexual onscreen, lost it.

Of the old stars, Olivier came closest to cleverly denying the inroads of age, I think because he had for so long used humiliation—as Heathcliff, Lord Nelson, Richard III, Othello—as his particular gothic-romantic territory. The British poetry of humiliation, not as rage or failure but as triumph of the human spirit, carried him for a long time. And then, at the end of his playing a fully sexual man on-screen (the joke is a curious one), he co-starred with Marilyn Monroe in *The Prince and the Showgirl*. There was Monroe—as perpetually precoital as Garbo was perpetually postcoital—with her highly professional but self-goaded, joyously half-mad exhibitionism and her overstuffed body, making no admission that life could occur between the promise of sexual bouts. She was flauntedly open, and yet as unreachable by courtship as Brando.

Olivier not only failed to command Monroe's interest but failed to respond to the hugeness of the sexual image she projected worldwide. He should have known that Monroe never made an interesting movie that concerned a relationship, never really played a scene that involved a relationship. What Olivier knew about sexual attraction and humiliation and what Monroe knew about them didn't match; she offered a seeming ignorance of her humiliations, a brainless triumph. What you saw were rival prides, rival prerogatives, rival royalties. And in the rivalry Monroe—who never judged a man on-screen—won out with the audience, and Olivier seemed old and pretentious.

Attempts to co-opt age and humiliation: take Bogart and Hepburn in *The African Queen*. She has written that her friendship with John Huston, the director, was intimate. If she had brought real sexuality to the movie, it would have been much more interesting, more human, and funnier and deeper than it was, rather than having to carry in scene after scene the tremulous sexlessness, the would-be comic chastity of her character—that utterly false chastity that Hepburn, who did better than most Hollywood stars at the age thing, perversely used to suggest age. She was a mess, a harridan head-on, an essentially obstinate virgin spinster. Hepburn's nasal escape from, and superiority to, sex did not embody a change in experience or a lessening of heat but an I-never-had-any-sort-of-experience outcry. It was this quality that made and kept her a star, a radiantly irritating pain in the neck. But could a virgin spinster enslave Bogart? The Bogartian hero—alcoholic masochism, cynicism, and all—was not a sucker. He was superior to his own sexual subjugation (except, of course, as wartime patriotism, in *Casablanca*). I mean, Bogart as slave, sure, but to fleshier women with large lips, Bergman and Bacall. He projected a physical self-assuredness, physically, phallically. He didn't care about many things, he was intelligent and shrewd, and he had talent. He could be old-fashioned about a woman; he was a withholder, a successful one, truly male in that ancient, ever popular sense.

It is curious watching Harrison Ford grow older on-screen. His movies have been more successful, on the whole, than those of any other star, but they have had to be adventure movies, and he has had to be boyish, an action star of a new kind. He cares about everyone; clothes and haircut matter to him. He has a sort of rumpled face—rumpled like Jeanne Moreau's. In seven of Hollywood's twenty-one top-grossing movies, he is a messiah figure, successful in the story but—unlike, say, Eastwood—softly, reasonably so: not a killer.

He has wholesomely adolescent attachments to women—to Princess Leia, Melanie Griffith, to various sirens. He seems classless and, in a way, shapeless: without angst, without even the sensitivity of Tom Hanks. He *is* ironic toward duty, but he always does it. He is effectual but not dictatorial—or tortured. His messianism is along the lines of *A Connecticut Yankee in King Arthur's Court*—someone out of place, out of time, and with special information, not from braininess but just from being an American.

His roles require him to lie a lot and to be the wrong age for the part he's playing. He is a certain kind of honest and impossibly robust impostor, but he is in no way dysfunctional. He wins. He does sex scenes, but the overall effect, somehow, is that it stays in his pants. He doesn't display himself enticingly—that isn't within his range. He has no shadow of sexual ambiguity in any usual sense—yet his roles allow for an emotional acceptance of a kind of quietly healthy, almost Boy Scoutish homosexuality, such that *The Fugitive* can be seen as a homosexual allegory. He is gender-liquescent, unsplendid, deft. So far, no one has become a star playing with him, but Sean Connery wasn't harmed, nor was Tommy Lee Jones, and, because Ford doesn't do much publicity or because he is not publicizable, the media seize on those other guys, while he remains somehow secret, nonexistent. He is purer than Mary Pickford, than Charles Laughton.

Ford was predicted, from a wounded distance, by Fellini, in his movies—but also by the excesses of Pasolini, by Bertolucci and Fassbinder, Godard and Truffaut, and Tony Richardson—as the man beyond limits, the true heir and modification of American heroism, successor to Gary Cooper, the man uncompromised by sexual problems, disappointments, hang-ups.

There is another pathway to this iconography of sex-is-no-big-deal—not European—but leading from John Wayne, when he was getting up there in years, and Montgomery Clift, in *Red River*. The supposedly phallically minuscule Clift, who seems to have suffered over his phallic insufficiency—the p.i. factor—like nobody's business, co-starred only once with the reputedly less than virile Wayne, who never seemed to suffer over it at all but, rather, put out a foliage of half-civilized male beauty and friendly conceit and boastful masculinity that flourished for decades.

Red River, which was directed by Howard Hawks, is a fable, an unreal projection of a pretty son and a potent father reacting to their struggle with each other. In the grip of mad, Hawks-driven magic, the two men (one a great actor, one a great star) parade themselves brilliantly along a fault line of humiliation—the father humiliated by the sensitivity of his son, the son humiliated by the potency of his father—to a state of purity, where sex is no longer the issue. Harrison Ford inherited this purity, and it is not a naive construction, or an unconscious or accidental one. It isn't the untouchability of the star. His screen manner disclaims sexual secrets. But he is also beyond concern about sex. Publicity can't yet touch this quality, and perhaps age can't wither it. We will see.

. . .

It is interesting to look back at Julia Roberts at the beginning of her life as a star. *Pretty Woman*—charming and popular, the most popular expression so far of fucking your way *up*, aloft, in the world—lies, in order to be charming, about the whole procedure. The corporate-raider figure is not someone who has been too busy for sexual love and has been sexually cheated or denied—he is not a sexual fool with a mad sense of power and a narcissistic delight in himself and a fear that he is a freak. He looks far more experienced sexually than the Julia character, the prostitute, far more experienced and further out sexually. Roberts is not given the power that Monroe took in *The Prince and the Showgirl*.

The reversal makes the movie operettalike. A whoring-tycoon Prince Charming is one of the least possible human characters I can think of—like a truly, deeply musical SS man—but the fantasy tickles. The tycoon rescues her, not she him. He does not need her sexually, he sets her free: the naive and honest child of the streets is set free—to shop.

I *liked* the movie. I like this kind of movie, this sort of lie. I like denial flicks—no sex, no sorrow, no death. Or the ones where the men are too manly to be stirred by sex—*Citizen Kane*—and Katharine Hepburn movies and some Audrey Hepburn movies, in which the women are too proud and intelligent to be prey. I like down-with-sex movies, like Fellini's *La Dolce Vita*, with Mastroianni as a desolate bystander. An American image of the desolation of men, while suggesting a rather sorry moral loneliness, is different—is a baseball team on the field, nine men set widely apart, waiting, galvanized briefly by a ball in play, and then waiting again in the sunlight, widely separate and with their own territories and their own thoughts. Or there is the desolation of Bruce Willis, Tom Cruise, Dustin Hoffman, but this is the desolation of fast-talking trespassers, of small, clever men.

Why grow up when you can be as-if-young and rich and famous and powerful and all the rest of it for a long time? Look, perhaps no one and no art form grows up. But you haven't a lot of choices: you get older or you die. Movies have choices. Movies are anticlassroom, antiworkplace. They are time off, time out, masturbatory-hallucinatory, subversive; they are acts of genuine deconstruction, having to do with desire of some sort. Why the hell should they be realistic about sexual cause and effect? Or about humiliation? Or about how men and women change decade by decade? Movies' sexual madness is a great relief from genital logic. (We assume that in the world, too, the stars really *are* sexy and have the best sex and have a regal extent of sexual choice. We "know," suspect, can imagine, that on the plane of daily reality the actors and directors and producers are fucking around all they want. We are startled when it is only about Heidi Fleiss.) Movies play with time, dispense with common sense, they exert but also exorcise the will, they change power, and even biology, around— this is a source, a cause of their popularity, and their popularity alone may be the sign of their great, great greatness. The feel-good element in American movies is the beauty of the indulgence of the will without one's being sent to hell: there isn't an equal counterreaction, except a slap from reality, now and then outside the movie theater.

But movies demand of stars a certain suppleness and availability. You can reorganize the sexual elements, but you have to be young. Responsiveness can't be faked. One sees stars outgrow it and become resistant rather than responsive, obstinate rather than available. This can't be hidden. And when too much intelligence and pain and self-control begin to show—in the face and in the body, in the eyes and in the voice—a kind of dismissal from the kingdom of illusion begins. You have to be a risk-taking and eager fool to be a star in a medium that insists on such availability; you have to be shrewd as hell. A pastime slower but crueler than watching gladiatorial combat is watching the stars deal with or fail to deal with age, and struggle to preserve the slippery images that entertain us so.

1994

AMERICAN MOVIES
AND SEX AND NAZIS AND
MORAL QUESTIONS

In silent movies, comedies or melodramas, actions without speech are concerned in each scene with whose will is dominant. By 1939—the year of *Gone with the Wind* and *The Wizard of Oz*—the game of wills had become more sophisticated. We have the moviemakers' will, the audience's, and the star's or stars' will inside and outside the story. The story is rarely about a conflict of wills but deals in innocence and appetites and in victimization and triumph.

What made American talkies popular is the sheer handsomeness and optimism of their presentation of successful wills. Since 1939, the will is pictured solipsistically: the will of a single dreamer with subsidiary characters.

In actual American life solipsism is balanced by the extreme politicization of everything. Everything rests on deals, which means mutual recognition of a kind but it is not tribal or cultural recognition. It is often presented as a simultaneity of solipsisms, but that approach omits the difference in political skills among individuals.

American imagery and American art are largely solipsistic, Nietzschean, in westerns, in comedies, in such writers as Hemingway and such painters as Jackson Pollock. Stories and public images of the great icons are concentrated chiefly in supremely central near-messianic figures—in movies from John Wayne through Brando to Schwarzenegger. Movies often have a directly Oz form as in *Star Wars*, but so does political iconography. Reagan, Bush, and Clinton are almost entirely seen in the United States through a scrim of Oz imagery. Since 1939, the image of the solitary will has been treated by American movies as the master image of existence for decades now.

Yet, anyone who has ever kissed someone is aware that part of a caress is the experience of the magic shock of another's will. In the presence of two wills, the indeterminacy then of what is going to happen in the interplay, gives a resultant tenderness or warmth its value. The movies' marvelous bullshit—mother versus whore or mother *is* a whore—is a defensive posture toward the fully inhabited world of diverse wills and variegated types. Is this a specifically American thing, a form of American federalism?

Increasingly, this posturing is a problem everywhere. Multiplicity actually exists and monolithic structures are actually myths and unstable ones at that. It is common in popular art and in pornography that coitus is seen through a veiling of solitary will but *that* signifies virginity, a prior and juvenile state before consummation. High art has a formal dependence on two voices at a minimum, the composer's and the performer's, even when the composer is the performer playing for himself. But the formal elements, as in the concerto or the duet or the *pas de deux* or the dialogue are antichurchly, antiabsolutist, are double. Some artists try to get behind this to a single-willed notion, but then you get Wagner and on occasion Beethoven writing very very good movie music.

In American movies, sex and historical events and violence and criminality are Oz. The relation of response and registry to the Dionysian is not part of the American sense of the Dionysian. And not always part of the German sense of it either. The hint, as I see it, is the image of rape being perpetrated by a fool. This is so in both cultures. The American sense is *we will all get together and get drunk and do mad things.* The German sense is *we will get drunk and retreat into the absolutes of the blood.* Neither is rooted in any but a few ancient myths. The modern forms are inane as one can see in, for example, O. J. Simpson's vanity and sexual showiness and isolation.

In America everything is subject to arrangement, conspiracy, corruption, votes, usurpation, and politics, including sexuality up to a point. It would be foolish to say that the American system doesn't work. If you're an American male, you can stick to Heidi Fleiss and ambitious women and bimbos and/or certain sorts of homosexual sex that are over-the-line but which are elliptically solipsistic. You can escape the relatedness of sexuality along any number of Dorothy-in-Oz routes. You can remain solipsistic whether you are a man or a woman.

Women can have a response which is, as it were, automated and leaves the central self of the woman in peace. Or the woman can have a slut self and another self. But Dorothy-in-Oz tends to be unitary or to split into selves only arbitrarily, not realistically. In actuality, most people find sex elusive and mostly dull—they never get beyond solipsism or find a woman or a man with whom they can. Styles in Hollywood temptresses over the decades have indicated that sexual attraction can hint at the end of solipsism, can hint at being understood: Dietrich, Bacall, Garbo, Hepburn, Irene Dunne were all of that type. Monroe, too, but on a more specialized basis. The most impressive of the tempters, male and female, do not seem to have been capable of enjoyment offscreen. They do not seem to have gotten past the power-game-solipsistic structure. The solipsism is a problem and may be felt to be like the tower the princess (or prince) is imprisoned in. The solipsism may be tempting and seem like elusiveness. It may produce an ache in the audience of sympathetic longing. It is a sexy world.

In the actual world, the pivots of sexual story, of emotion and of affectionate attachment recognized and honored, can be quite minor, a goopy smile or a cagy one of the male, his arm suddenly without tension *afterward*. The woman, a Bardot, say, utters soft or harsh French and sort of snorts in this afterward. Or likes to clean house or walk around and pull at her hair and occasionally smile at the man. Each of the pair may drift in a fake solitude in which the other is just a second or two away. Actual sexuality is two-personed, real. Everything in an encounter is inflected by the politics of there being two wills. Two beliefs. One is goaded and tempted by moments in which such politics are in abeyance. And anyone can daydream of an ultimate triumph, of being one-willed, dominant, in control during sex. It is seductive to offer this to someone unless they are daydreaming at that moment of submission. Or of equality.

In American movies, the solipsism, the Dorothy-in-Oz sense of things makes the love story one of courtship dishonesty and then of myth about differences in social class. American movies do not traffic in two-willed, two-personed dramas of emotion.

Consider Marilyn Monroe, a man's woman who never once in her life belonged to a man. In a harsh sense, this sort of thing is an area of fascist dreaming, but it is not European Fascism. A close-up, like a glamour photo, is an image of desolate isolation which elicits infatuation. So did the photographs of Hitler and Churchill during the war, but they both chose to be a racial, rather than a sexual, type.

American movies suggest a rather sorry moral loneliness. For a while now, photographic models and rock (and pop) singers and sports figures and stand-up comics have supplied the dominant images of active sexuality and truer ones. The *truest* public sexual imagery is solipsism-at-the-end-of-its-tether and coming to an end or ending in front of you. To see Jagger on stage when he was young, before he was geriatric, was to see the ways that sexual possibility for Jagger existed. He related to his band and to the audience as possible sexual partners in a directly possible way. He was out there—far out—way out in some special realm of sexual privilege and sexual iconography which obliterated all notions of sexual gentility, a sweaty, crotch-forward, obvious figure, post-Brando, post-Nazi, yet drawing on those images and to some extent on those realities as well. Nazism, like the Napoleonic, influences styles and feelings still. When it does not meltingly fail and fade into a sense of others, it has a tragic feel. When it does fail, we recognize a basic myth that goes back to Hercules and Omphalos and perhaps further. Jagger's sexuality is not a dream, not merely an icon. Neither is that of American comedians, men or women. Their sexuality is tied to actual experience, the (often howled) isolated feeling, the clumsiness of the real.

The Beatles were dreamlike, American movie-like, but as a group, although the group element was lyingly presented. Movies try to be serious and nostalgically meaningless and potently sexual (aphrodisiac) and to boast of the intelligence of the stars and directors and writers, a kind of expense-ridden omniscience. Meanwhile, in the historical moment, our movies define sexual freedom as freedom from interplay and oppressive otherness and negotiation, freedom from reality. A star, an important director, is sexually sought after, sexually indulged. These movies present attitudes as realities and not always foolishly: an attitude, a morale, a spirit, a credo, is real and dangerous in a man or woman.

This Americanized Nazism-without-any-but-a-local-führer, a star or a star director, is, as a philosophical matter, exciting and dangerous and important crap. A pose. A bluff. But so was Nazism. What kind of bluff is this? A bluff that you don't have to grow up, don't have to use your head. Hitler derived far more of his program from American roots and movie imagery than is usually admitted. But he forced each hero into a cadre, then a squadron, then a great mass of heroes.

Now I am going to propose something which will perhaps sound like a perverse joke. But actually I mean it when I say that the 1939 M-G-M movie, *The Wizard of Oz,* is the archetypal modern American movie that shows us the real structure and source of popularity of American movies.

That movie is a charming account of an entirely solipsistic adventure arising from a blow to the head of the heroine. In its chief sections it is dreamed. It has only one "real" character, the dreamer. This adventure is set between opening and closing sections that present real life as poor in money but utopian.

The girl Dorothy has magic powers and a great destiny in Oz. She is accompanied on her adventure by three figures, each of whom represents a form of romantic movie hero but portrayed from the level of fandom and yearning: the scarecrow is a variant of Astaire and Cagney but is not a star. The Tin Woodsman is a variant of such men of steel as Gable and Cooper. The Cowardly Lion of such swashbucklers as Tyrone Power and Errol Flynn. The animal and the toy and the effigy yearn to be figures like the above.

The movie has a solipsistic structure of storytelling but with no great consistency—it could be interrupted at any time. The wizard is real. The movie is set in an imaginary landscape like one in a Disney cartoon with an opening and closing section of romanticized landscape meant to be taken as real but which is not real. In the movie there is a transformation of others into symbols of themselves as the narrator-hero-heroine sees and feels them. Fellini and Bergman have done variations of this using reality or fantasy in a European mode to alter the American device they are so influenced by. Fassbinder as well. And Syberberg of course.

A Dorothy-in-Oz presentation of reality has notable limits in terms of an adequate representation of a complex reality, but it is useful in presenting an emotion and in simplifying a narration and it can be readily identified with as representing our own egocentric subjectivities, and it has many of the structures and effects of our dreams. At the moment, it is the supreme storytelling mechanism in books and movies, more dominant in America than in Europe but more and more popular here.

My colleagues John Updike and Nicholson Baker use only Dorothy-in-Oz structures. In *Schindler's List*, for another instance, history is seen through the eyes and actions of a male Dorothy who finds himself in Oz. Oz in this case is Nazi-occupied Poland, is Nazi reality. The Jews are like the Munchkins in the movie, dwarf-willed and helpless, and they can be saved only by a male Dorothy. This may be historically accurate but it feels dreamlike. The Nazis are as crazed as the Witch in Garland's Oz. Certainly Fiennes is.

One appreciates the distancing and the promise of a happy ending. I ought to say here that a modern-day audience watching a well-made, effectual movie is also in Oz, the Oz of moviegoing and not only the Oz of the country, the context in the film. This moviegoing Oz has to do with making and seeing movies and being instructed by them. The overlap is with the actor in his life and career and not with the character—this is so in America. The solipsism of the story also helps distance the powerful effect of the large figures and scenes on the screen while keeping the effect immediate enough to impart a thrill or frisson, a sense of life in the watcher. The problem in regard to historical accuracy and intelligence is that history consists of the operations of disparate wills and does not have a star director, although we may pray that it does. Madness is a form of innocence, for example, because its solipsism is supposedly beyond the control of the sufferer. Moral behavior, moral actions such as Schindler's, consist of operations within a sphere of equivalent wills, unsolipsistically. All wills are equivalent by means of murder. A superior equivalence survives the crime and is the right of the leader.

The Jews in *Schindler's List* are not shown as having independent wills. They have emotions, neuroses, pathos, but no independence. Schindler had a dictatorship but a small one and destined to save people. The idea of the wills of the Jews, like the idea of their sanity, does not matter in the context of the movie. In fact, in *Schindler's List*, Nazism, persecution, and death are treated as intrusion, as disaster and violation, as oppression ending a utopian state of existence in which there were no pressing moral questions. Spielberg always works at the edge of a presexual world defined as normal or admirable. Updike and Baker have a middle-class American Protestant version of such innocence for men who then regard women as questionable quantities. War crimes and moral peril and moral acts do not figure as points of drama for them. This establishes a baseline of goodness, of pragmatic *innocence*, which supplies pleasure and consolation but which cannot be accurate in the real world. The baseline of innocence that is proposed is not an experience but a lie about experience, which is an idea suitable for fable but not for moral parable and not for a study of history. This idea of an original state of peace or grace has great appeal but such a state never existed even in infancy although it may be defined that way by others around the child.

The convergence of realities in a real situation is treated by having a mutedly messianic, male Dorothy figure observing quite spectacular scenes of violation, dreamlike in their power—Schindler ought to go a little mad. And he is imprisoned in complicity, one would think. But that is not what happens. He is a sane fascist, merely that. And the trespasses against the wills of individual Jews are not shown. I mean the breaking of their wills. In the Nazi reality back then was a certain sexual excitement overall, even a feverishness of such an excitement. It was a bit as if the Nazi promise was of the expression of male will (often said to be German will) in every way.

And this quality accompanied the war and the persecution and the massacres except for one element, which was that of discipline: the will was not indulged but was obeying orders and was constrained in a number of ways by what was, after all, an absolutist hierarchy governing in line with its ability to kill if you disobeyed. The only free-willed things one could do were rebel, die, or conspire.

This is to say, Hitler lied. The massacres were dreadful work. The hunt for excitement, for satisfaction, was infinitely dreary. Some of the balked Nazi-generated sexual excitement and its talk of blood and breeding merchandised sexual superiority and sexual freedom on demand, a paradox and not likely but possible as violation, i.e., only as crime. Combined with this was the excitement and terror of the onslaught of war, which brings various complicities in its wake as well as forms of self-doubt and various fears. The crude sexualization of everything inside an envelope of force and propaganda and horror and then unregarded heroism and the odd, peripheral status of those who committed the atrocities aroused, as in all armies and guards and onlookers, feelings of resistance and resentment, feelings of self-assertion. The political realities of the time had an overtly sexual nature. That emerged most clearly at the end, in the collapse and after the fighting stopped, but it was always there. But it is not in the movie, the tempted fools murdering and being unfed by murder, but then it was too late except in Catholic absolution, which does not always work.

In *Schindler's List*, we know that the male Dorothy will not betray us, that he-she will make the right choices. The star is sexually attractive, not an unappealing and overweight womanizer. We know that most of the large cast have roles that could be written with any degree of madness or sweetness, to convey any sense of character or feeling that was wanted cinematically, since only Schindler/Liam Neeson is indispensable to the story. We recognize the mad dog outbursts and the fear. What we don't see is the true nature of the violations and we do not see the nature of the moral act with its sublimely human ordinariness.

Some intellectuals in America and some in Europe have argued that morality rests on absolute principles, but I do not see how that can be so, although it is true that some crimes announce themselves as such by the boredom and horror you feel as you commit them. It is possible to say that no one should be treated as the Jews were, but in actuality those who mistreated them merited similar treatment, but who could inflict it without becoming like the murderers? Most cultures have traditions of law and argument—which is to say a nonabsolutist sense of crime. Moral issues begin with the plurality of *lives*, with there being more than one life and a very odd, shifting moral reality, therefore. The underlying questions in moral issues always spring from the variety of wills and of fates. A Dorothy figure offers a fixed decency of some kind, which is from quite a different moral dimension, one of assertion and not of observation, but since it asks no questions, it maximizes self-importance and is dreamlike.

At a certain moment Schindler was lost to indecency. He fell in love with a series of actions. It was the registry, in full, starring complexity, of others' lives as real. It had little to do with his innocence as such or his wish to protect the innocence of others. It had to do with acting morally. A movie like this one, which is a reconstruction for those who were not there, changes the nature of the rescue and of the rescuer: the reality was not movielike.

The daydream element in erotica as in battle madness has to do with the training or breaking of others' wills or of one's own. Schindler begins to collect broken wills. Is this erotic for him? The movie is very good about the reality of hearing the screams in the air at the time. Is he in rivalry with the claims of omnipotence of other Germans? Does he have a small quasi-Nazi state, entirely controlled by his will, but directed toward survival? Were his actions a conscious echoing and correction of Nazism?

The pornography inherent in the Dorothy-in-Oz or the Tarzan movies lay in their showing the exertion of a dominant will onesidedly. Others abdicate their wills or lose their right to them because the hero's or heroine's is superior. *Schindler's List* presents a world of hierarchies of phallic will and of indulgence in such will. But the movie director's will is the one in final control. The movie is focused on the *decent* use of such indulgence in the will in relation to madness and innocence. This is very potent, very Hollywood, very untrue.

A movie camera proves something in every scene it photographs. It proves that people were present on camera or not, for instance. But the emotion suggested may not involve other lives except as extras in the scene. As bits of meaning of that sort. And not as real lives, which are not easily knowable, not easily dismissible, not easily comprehended under the rubric of some doctrine or other. This is the real issue between American and European movies. How many figures in *Schindler's List* are figures in a dream no matter how many details about them are presented that give a tingle of life?

Fellini's movies comment on American movies and particularly on this quality of solipsism in American movies. He treats it as the sexual heroism of American movies. His movies start from self-knowledge and physiological shame (one's pale body and its attributes), and then he addresses the supposed sexual superiority of American movies from a drastically hurt, wounded distance in *La Dolce Vita* and *8½*, which are movies that use the Dorothy-in-Oz structure but complicated by sophistication, such as both comic and serious oracles. In *La Dolce Vita*, Mastroianni is a male Dorothy, a bystander but not messianic. He is no one's rescuer but he is a forerunner of Schindler. (That is, the influence flows back, flows back and forth, in an expensive dialogue between cultures.)

But the point of *La Dolce Vita* is that the other characters, the other lives, are not imaginary and uncoercive figments of the mind, nor are they supporting players in the American sense. Or in the actual sense. They are stars, too, often more famous ones than Mastroianni. It is part of the effect of wonder that these characters in their reality are fantastic and artificial in dress and makeup and behavior, often very Ozlike but real. They seem infected with fantasy and history and inflected with reality.

In European movies (except Syberberg's) the national culture fills the screen-canvas behind the stars with lives from edge to edge. The faces of a crowd in Rosellini's *Open City* or in Fellini's *La Dolce Vita* look on from inside other stories at the story we're being told, that the chief character or characters are undergoing.

For comparison: In the scenes in *Gone with the Wind* that concern the burning of Atlanta, the extras are not permitted to suggest lives. They are deaths and numbers, an audience, fragments of meaning, parts of a scene, parts of an effect. So, too, in recent movies filled with explosions. The faces, the degree of reality of the extras obeys the logic of solipsism in an American movie. We expect it in an American movie, that the star's is the only life. It is a form of people's aristocracy, that all the meaning and expenditure of a movie be summed up in a single person as countries used to be in the body of a monarch, so that Shakespeare refers to *France* or *England* and means the king, and Antony addresses Cleopatra as *Egypt*: "I am dying, Egypt, dying—"

In life, no one behaves so neatly as extras do in movies. In life, the rebellious individualism of wills, even in people who are subdued, is everywhere apparent. Part of the Nazi phenomenon was its extraordinary corruption, an absolute corruption, a corruption of everything, a banality of corruption, that interfered with and yet exercised individual will. For a monolithic system, Nazism was extraordinarily confused. The middle level of evildoers felt an exasperation with this chaos. No movie director would permit it. And the movie does hint at this. The nature, the idea (and reality) of patriotism, might try to bring clarity and purpose and thereby ease the confusion. Schindler has performed an act of common-sense orderliness, using helpless, easy-to-discipline Jews to produce goods in wartime. In the jostling of judgments and wills among bystanders, the *going along* and partial withdrawal, in the mix of all the stages, all the individual reactions to the crime of going along with it or withdrawing from it, moral actions emerge. But they cannot emerge for purposes of study and knowledge through the further demonization of an already demonic confusion.

I am saying that while a great deal of truth and of drama were in the movie, the moral issue was not there. I have no right to judge this except as an onlooker. One's teeth are often put on edge when one observes social reality, and sometimes this discomfort becomes final. When this discomfort arises in relation to an aesthetic construct, one writes an essay such as this one. Some such understanding was in Schindler, teeth on edge and essayistic, some such sense of argument, which would have been useful in the movie if Spielberg had used the sexual implications more, the physical disgust with Nazism that I believe mounted year by year and to a high level by 1943. This would have deepened the implications within the movie.

But such an approach, if realistic, would have complicated the storytelling. And to do it unrealistically would have extended the lawlessness in American movie storytelling. Such lawlessness here in this movie is Hollywood at its noblest and most tactful. As in most American movies, the supporting characters have no wills of their own except in the possibilities of conspiracy and suicide. The great crime, so handsomely presented, and the dizzying and dreamlike horror of it have no relation to the other, smaller, undreamlike crimes that form the elements of ordinary life, form the elements of the whole as we know it. The elements of disobedience are concentrated in one figure. A single will controls the sequence of images. Spielberg-Schindler. The continuum of the human is absent. Schindler's *soul*, if I might be permitted to say this, is absent. We see it in the tracks it left as interpreted in America as a male reality. A supposedly inexplicable heroism, I would guess, came as a relief to him. He could breathe.

In the current Hollywood equation, the implicit question is why grow up when you can be as-if-young and rich and supple and famous and powerful for the rest of your life? Well, one grows up in order not to be deceived by such wishes since they are not going to come true. One can see the coarsening, the aging in the stars' and directors' faces, and the denial in the roles of what they know and what they feel.

One grows up in order to escape from daydreams, in order to become, even if briefly, oneself, which means, of course, oneself in relation to others. It is possible, however, that no one and no art form really grows up, that the idea is a myth, a metaphor, the idea of growing up. Maybe people just become madly effectual in different, property-grabbing ways as they age. By property we mean traits as well as money and power. But men and women in the movies, as they age, become movie constructions with lives dimly visible inside the surgery and the costumes. And since movies are anti-classroom, anti-workplace, this seems an unnecessary grimness. But it is the triumph of the will that is shown.

Movies are time off, time out, masturbatory, subversive; they are acts of deconstruction, having to do with desire of some sort. They play with time, dispense with common sense; they exert and exorcise the will; they change power and even biology, into daydream. And this is a source, a cause, for their popularity, and their popularity may be the sign of their great, great greatness. Or it may indicate their massive stupidity.

The feel-good element in American movies is the beauty of the indulgence of the will without one's being sent to hell. There isn't an equal and counter reaction except a slap from the light and air and reality outside the movie theater. American movies *are* culturally dangerous. They give poor instruction. They are historically and psychologically and morally feeble. Extremely feeble.

In European movies the feel-good element is likely to be lyricism and isolation and peace or solitude and an escape to America, to the American West, to just such an indulgence of the will as we've been describing, an escape to the Great Plains, the Great Permission to be alone. For all their faults, American movies may represent fairly the American dream. This stupidity with all its implicit brilliance has been voted into office. Every American movie comfortingly shows the primacy of the dreamer's will. This is philo-phallocentric, pseudo-phallocentric. But, hell, it's popular.

Movies glorify the moviemaker beyond the limits understood before movies were invented, beyond the resources of the Sun King or the talents of John Milton. Hitler comes later, of course. And movies glorify the moviegoer. More of us dwell in the aura and oracular echo and thumping of movie advertising than read books or listen to sermons or read philosophy. Movies fill the empty vessels of longing in us. They do it for a profit. We are X-rated flesh and blood and nearly entirely commercial propositions in relation to our movies.

At my age, after the history that has passed, I wouldn't presume to judge this circumstance. We, the audience, assume the innocence of movies so long as they are not fundamentally intelligent. We accept shrewdness but not intelligence. The degree of unreality in movies and the freshness of their lack of intelligence and of the substitution of shrewdness for mind leads to our cinema having the necessary motto *It's only a movie.*

At moments one loves all of this. A moviegoer's sensibility is far from home and she or he loves and hates the world through images derived from the frantic cultural dominion of movies, that absurd Oz. American movies enthrone the journey and the mental landscape of sexual dreams. Altogether they form a perverse and senseless form like opera. And sexual display, even if indirect, is the music.

One must look at *Schindler's List* through this scrim or veil.

1993

NOTES ON
AMERICAN FASCISM

In America, fascism has never held much sway. We had an example of American fascism in Louisiana under Huey Long and in parts of the North under Lincoln during the Civil War.

American fascism and American leftism are largely undefined in any broadscale way. If we define fascism newly, not entirely in terms of Mussolini's anti-Communist and patriotic movement, but generically, now, as a rule by a strong man outside the structure of usual law of a given nation or state and in the name of national or religious greatness—that is to say, without any other new doctrine except the doctrine of rule and of competitive efficacy and conquest—we have a definition loosely describing what has been attempted here and what now seems possible and even hovering as a near probability.

In the past, the Fascist project drew a following by proposing antagonism to Bolshevism, programmatic anti-Semitism or some other form of xenophobia, and patriotic demands for territorial expansion to accommodate the greatness of the folk. These elements exist in the United States, in a yet more modern setting and in a particular form of contemporary anarchy, along with a loathing for the real or imagined threats in the moral and political doctrines of liberalism to structures of an imagined society. The specter of the dissolution of the folk holds a particular terror especially when the folk never existed or were defined but where the idea of the folk, of the people, had a political meaning.

These are in operation in contemporary forms in various fringe and splinter movements and in various social sectors as usual but also in the major political parties, chiefly and most frighteningly in the Republican Party, in very nearly the same forms through which the rightist and conservative parties in continental Europe became near fascist and, in some cases, rulingly fascist.

Political ideas, in a mirror form, moved from party to party, and much of what is in the Republicans is covertly already embedded in the Democratic Party. Concealed in the Democratic program is a demand for order, for more government, more centralized government. And nothing in the Democratic agenda rejects world rule; and the American political system is ill suited to such a position in the world.

The Republicans are running against foreign dictators and on the platform of American greatness under God—this is to say against Bolshevism in a new guise, and against Hollywood and New York, which is to say, against Jews—and with the only, so-far, half-spoken statement that the world is ours—this refers to international expansion.

Liberalism is held to be destructive and foreign rather than part of the American tradition, which, of course, it is. It is the primary American tradition.

And the cries of the dissolution of the folk are everywhere, not always mistakenly.

Military service, a devotion to militarism, is asked of the major party candidates.

None of this is new. But a number of factors that kept America more or less democratic have vanished. Small-town America has vanished. And the safety in this being such a large country and difficult or impossible to govern closely is gone because now the population is more concentrated and the technological means for close control exist.

It is an anomaly that Fascism, having decisively lost the Second World War and having committed enormities for which the populace paid heavily and having made its followers suffer greatly, has not been thoroughly discredited in the way that Communism has.

Some of this has to do with the glamour of the idea of the reality of absolute power in the persons of the adventurers, Stalin and Hitler, Mussolini and Franco, and the Japanese militarists. This glamour has to do with personal will and masculine notions of meaning.

And the overthrow of the Fascist governments, except in Spain, came about through military defeat and not through operations of the popular will. Fascism was defeated, not discredited, and has its draw still for adventurers, for doctrinaire thinkers, and for large parts of the populace, 30 to 40 percent, in any given Western and industrialized Eastern country.

The acceptance of the fascist idea is a troubling matter. Hannah Arendt argued, in her book *The Origins of Totalitarianism*, that a Fascist state both was and was not a state. Its internal functioning was not that of a state but of some sort of corporate entity in which power and control were never clear but yet were absolute along certain axes of hierarchy. You knew whom you must not affront. The Nazis had three systems of law and had the power and will to operate outside the law as well. This idea has not been discredited by the defeat partly because the idea of corporate efficiency still exists.

The war intervened to prevent the internal economic and disciplinary bankruptcy that would otherwise have occurred. The defeat forestalled and took the place of popular disillusion. But, finally, perhaps, we do best to admit that fascism as idea and as reality is built into modern circumstances and is an inescapable factor as doctrine.

The reasons for this are complex. Fascism offers a sense of personal triumph, citizen by citizen, and a sense of intelligent mastery of the world, first of all by proposing power and dominance as the measure of intelligence, in a simplistic bottom-line fashion, and then by offering power to such vast sectors of the populace as the police and others in the civil bureaucracy, party members, and soldiers. You empower vast, vast sectors of the populace; you empower them officially.

Secondly, by preventing analysis and argument, fascism offers complete legitimation of idea in opposition to experience to such an extent that experience itself seems to be controlled or mastered. Once the principles of utility are largely ignored—except in the case of a utility for the creation of immediate power—much obscurity is removed and the standards for intelligence are changed. That is, cleverness consists in bulling forward and in bullying, in bribery, and in staunch belief, even, paradoxically, belief in cynicism, and not in any other experience or in any complex sense of reality. A sense of achievement and a considerable number of achievements are obtained without measured judgment of any kind. (But one can look back and see a few achievements of Fascism that have lasted—mostly, I think, the transportation networks.)

Defining social reality as power in *this sense* confers standing and rank, including the rank of being intelligent. And good. The role of ego, of individual masculine satisfaction, in political matters is paramount and inspires armies; and the masculine ego is fed by this system in these ways; and a certain number of feminine egos are placated as well.

Once these ego structures are in place, the state is unshakable for a considerable period of time. The desire exists to try this in a non-Hitlerian, non-Stalinist mode. In individuals of ambition, this may now be the dominant mode.

In a successful fascist structure, change and argument do actually stop. And alertness is focused on issues pointed out by government propaganda. Everything is settled, seems to be settled. This fixity, outward and social and inward and private, suggests livability and pleasure, livability and satisfaction, society having been extensively redrawn. Yet since no new doctrine other than that of government has been introduced, society now seems lastingly traditional except to the few observers who agree that politics is omnipresent in all societies, and that political arrangements are dominant and represent often new doctrines, which had been part of the Fascist argument. Fascists do not and cannot ever admit the thorough-going radicalism throughout all the range of ideas and doctrines of their program of government and of national greatness.

Inside a fascist movement the effect of success is of less change except in the direction of order and pleasure, although the radical change has actually destroyed the traditional structures of society and attacks and destroys each bit of remnant culture one by one as time goes on. One might propose that any would-be absolute primacy of government auto-matically, inevitably, means the death of society in every real sense.

Instead of a functioning society, what exists, and exists seductively, is a cannibalistic and partly insane hierarchy of overlapping powers and a single clearly all-powerful hierarchy at the top feeding off the dying and dead social structure it said it would preserve. Competing hierarchies struggle for the loot and the limited and discontinuous profits of the controlled economic functioning. And all of this is judged, legislated, and controlled by the one absolute hierarchy at the top that admits to no legal limits on what it does. Everyone has some small or large number of some-ones he controls. Fascism includes the absolute subordination of women and the control of children. However, this is insufficient so that classes of further subordinates are found—outsiders, foreigners, near slaves.

These necessities of (male) ego are clear in all absolutist structures, not only in the West.

The rewards are a clear political and personal identity from which, or out of which, come a consequent and immediately perceptible power and the perquisities of power even on such a low level as that of a prison guard.

But we are concerned nowadays less with that reality than with the foreshadow and aftertaste of that historical reality, the perhaps black-and-white image of this known from films and books and from one's own imagination.

The retreat from direct experience, the petrifaction of experience—and of social reality—the seeming livability of such social stasis compared to flux, change, and active argument, the fairly exact allocation of power and the substitution of the use and operation of such power for any other social usefulness in considering individual rank and merit, and the lust for clear political identity as establishing one's degree of actual power in the project of establishing some sort of monolithic and efficient state, are apparently of such value to so many people that they will engage in crimes and even die in the attempt to establish such a structure as the govern-ing one.

Absolutism is dreamlike and has little patience with reality. The absolute (or final) decisions it makes seem to be dreamlike or loonily surreal and to have the quality of clarity of a dream.

And absolutism is built into our present use of language. Dream struc-tures made real, or that are attempted in reality, and which omit ordinary politics, are unworkable except as horror.

But some absolutism, some horror, is endemic in our notions of good, in all severe practices of religion, in all second-level uses of logic or of attempted logic.

Dreamlikeness and simplicity are sought after in some of the arts, par-ticularly on the popular level. We must live in the unemendable rela-tivism of reality whatever we believe, but we don't have to admit it.

Fascism has in it a large amount of inherent relativism: ranks and propaganda, for instance, deal in comparisons and comparatives but with a strong and passionate movement toward superlatives, toward an absolute and apocalyptically final resolution.

The role of social class as defined by Marx actually posits the role well-defined social class plays in defining guilt and absolution outside the structures of legality and of the church. Each social class, and each fragment of a social class, represent specific permitted illegalities—poaching, prostitution, embezzlements of certain kinds but not of certain other kinds, different sorts of lying and violence, self-assertion, and the like.

When social classes begin to dissolve and to be reformed in periods of social change, what is first apparent is that in such periods, as people and enterprises fail, the sense of failure is worsened by the implicit guilt and by the absence of social-class absolution that had existed before the period of change to explain and to make bearable ordinary life and its crimes. In the Italian Renaissance, in city-state after city-state, extreme social instability (except in Venice) kept reflecting this during the changes in rulers, changes in sources and realities of true power, changes in technology, and in social arrangements and in the quality of leadership.

The social-class explanation of one's self is a longing for absolution, self-justification, righteousness. This longing invariably leads to an outburst of idealism of an absolutist kind. That is to say, what is invariably present behind the regard for social class is an appetite for fascism of some kind or other.

After all, common sense would tell us that moral issues are complex and tangled. The jury system argues tacitly that all issues are arguable. And they are. And that time changes things. And it does. That adjudication and rights and duties are complex matters.

Not only common sense but almost all culture, literature, history, philosophy, even religion, if studied and pondered, tell us that. The disappearance of common sense and the ebbing of culture and the advance of the dreamed-of and dreamlike are clear signs of social danger.

To speak of the dissolution of social classes in America is to encounter a curiosity of American culture, which is that America does not have and did not have social classes in either the European or the Asian sense. The United States is largely a classless political culture, or classless once you enter the political culture. We have had subcultures rather than classes. The American definition of the market as a mass market indicates this. The specialty markets in America have tended in the past to be supplied from European and Asian sources and to some extent still are. No attempt was made to establish china factories or rug or silk manufacture.

The mass market represented a form of economic citizenship, of enfranchisement of the population in the sense that the people were the primary market. This is very unlike European circumstances and European economic history and is still contrary to much of European experience in all the countries of Western Europe. The Germans with their cars, the Italians with gloves and clothes, the French with perfumes and wines and fabrics, the English with sweaters and formerly with cars, enjoyed considerable affluence dealing with upper-middle-class and aristocratic markets. Indeed, those were the prime markets and in relation to exports and foreign earnings are in many cases still the prime market.

Economic enfranchisement is not a small thing. And then it was further enlarged culturally by the course of advertising, which slowly learned to do mass-market merchandising. American mass culture like the American mass market included everyone. This sense of everyone was, and still is, defective, but no other country has had a form of active citizenship so large or so inclusive except perhaps France since the time of the Revolution.

This citizenship with its various local and national exclusions and its often defective sense of women has and has had very curious social-class realities underlying it. By its very nature it indicates a liquescent sense of social class and an availability of social-class symbols with their corresponding subtext of different sorts of absolutions.

Few people realize to what a degree the United States was not established by a homogeneous folk. Now one says European whites, but the Europeans cannot themselves see in Europe an active category of that.

America has no tribal base. It did not evolve with historical cohesiveness. It was established by revolution and constitution. And it consisted of elements diverse in culture and, especially as a result of the Louisiana Purchase later and the Mexican conquests, diverse in language. Sublanguages—French, Dutch, German, and others—were common in colonial days.

These groups were not melded or educated in any mutuality. Instead, a constitution was devised to set up a political frame that would be dominant. This was a derivation and further development of English experience, although the English do not have a constitution per se. This English idea, and this development of it, is now the most widespread principle of active government in the world.

The American experiment was to say not blood, not tribal identity, not religion or economics, not culture, but a *political system* was to be the dominating principle and the fundamental form of a national existence.

This establishment of secular politics as the guiding principle had no organic inner principle and no secrets to it. It had to do only with principles of secular government and nothing to do with folkish or tribal or religious culture in any sense but that of secular politics. It was established by will on the basis of theory and practical experience in a geographical reality that had had little or no written history.

The system could not absorb any individuals or groups, such as the American Indians, that maintained a different sense of politics. Xenophobia was limited to those who had some sort of group organization that prevented their entering the political system.

The system had cultural roots in Western Europe, in Christianity, in earlier European (particularly German), and in Greek and Middle Eastern experiments in republican egalitarianism, and, of course, in post-Roman, pseudo-Roman, and Roman government.

It was a new construct in a number of ways but let us notice particularly the legal omission of social classes as categories or as social realities. John Adams used a phrase, "the rich, the well-born, and the able," which hints at a classlike order of things but does not name it, and which the English came in time to accept as their own notions of the governing elements of the population.

This construct set secular politics as the basket that contained and judged all the rest. It played the role of the monarch and of tribal history. It was not only dominant; it was in a relativist mode absolute. Politics permitted religion and economic activity and could under no circumstances at all be controlled by either or by anything other than its own evolved laws and by the necessity of protecting itself as the ark of the covenant or as the monarch or as the senate-and-people-of-Rome.

Under Jefferson and still more under Jackson this was worked out in political reality into a monarchical-cultural principle in which the pursuit of politics was the pursuit of happiness—of justice and equity here on earth—and in which everyone, with the exception of blacks and women and children, had the right to engage directly in politics.

This established a multiplicity of centers of power including the separate states with their disparate cultures. What held it all together was a proportionally large middle class. Most of the rich in the North had fled or been driven out. Few of the Southern planters were actually rich except by comparison. It is often said in textbooks that the first rich American was John Jacob Astor in New York. He got rich in the fur trade and expanded his fortune in real estate.

But what is to be noticed is the classlessness of the social reality, a large middle class with many segments and different levels of income, but joined in adherence to the political system and to the economic circumstances that arose from that system. This middle class had no economic or geographical unity. It was relatively coherent in its sense of nation, however.

This new social class—agricultural, mercantile, professional, academic, early industrial—became the American polity. It fought and won the Civil War. It supplied the national identity to such an extent that the rich were forcibly restrained by law by the beginning of the twentieth century for the second time, the first having been sixty years before at the hands of Andrew Jackson.

Ugly and anomalous, blundering and ruthless as the history of the United States has been, that social class and its life and its political reasoning and pursuits became the envy of the world and was what one admired or fled from.

What is happening today worldwide is a reorganization of ancient or new or newish social classes into two social classes: the economically and technologically sophisticated and the failed and unrooted and not sophisticated.

In the United States this is a social revolution of unprecedented dimensions since the sophisticated class includes Asians and assimilated Irish among others, as well as a number of blacks who have not actually been absorbed into the American political system and who do not necessarily want to be.

And the old American middle class is gone, is broken into these two parts. The surviving mass of the American middle class is not cemented by sharing in the political system or by being part of the mass market—which is also breaking up—or by any sense of mutual interests with other parts of itself, but it does share the use of certain institutions—the stock market primarily and the American tax system and, in part, an interlocking web of universities.

This is not sufficient for political and social ballast. American democracy in its local universalism of citizenship and its egalitarianism—always psychologically and politically real beyond the capacity of even the most insightful Europeans to understand—cannot survive a two-tier social structure of such pragmatic force and so visible.

The political reality is that American centrists and moderates no longer control elections or exist as an overwhelmingly dominant force in the society; and no central group combining and overlapping the two new classes has made itself known as the chief power and chief ballast of the political system.

Any opening of possibility is torture to a closed mind but imagine, if you can, the closing of possibility when it was the possibilities inherent in the American system, and only the existence of such possibilities, that made American consumerism, instability and near anarchy, and the wide range of kinds of subcultures not just bearable but lovable to those of us who loved it.

In the United States, we have had no established social classes but only a very great many social groups, not one of which admits to any inferiority. Most lives include a movement among social levels and an exploration of social levels. But this is ending. Over the past three centuries of our national existence, we Americans have had evidence of a very thin crust of actual American social class at the top and bottom of the social scale.

Both those classes are dissolving and are being reformed, the top with newcomers and new fortunes—the great wolves that Gibbon describes in Byzantium in his *Decline and Fall of the Roman Empire*—and the bottom with new elements of the disenfranchised, now often white and not immigrants.

Social change is much easier in the United States than in Europe or Asia. With us, populations shift, cities rise and fall quickly. Columbus, Ohio, was a small city of perhaps a quarter-million population thirty years ago, and now it has about three million. It is a largely white city created by a migration of whites from Cleveland, Indianapolis, Dayton, and Cincinnati. Cleveland has vanished into a complicated urban area as complicated as Los Angeles. Los Angeles and Miami are recent cities.

America has little or no culture of a curatorial nature and no institutions that are reliably conservative. The American Catholic Church is not a force of social cohesion or any sort of brake on change. In American circumstances, it is entirely a radical institution, although its radicalism is not easily to be understood as either left-wing or right.

Its radicalism seems to be vaguely populist, warlike, and largely lower-class. The absence in America of a rural nobility or of large and permanent landholders who control the countryside means that when small farms were no longer supported by governmental regulation and subsidy and began to disappear, the rural population disappeared as such and became roving figures of social unrest. Small towns ceased to function. State politics in state after state lost their character as rural versus urban. And one whole aspect of American society, the free and independent farmer and the small-town merchant and entrepreneur, no longer mattered or, even, could be located in any numbers. Large American farm enterprises have landing strips and computers and deal with large cities. Shopping malls and highways mean that small towns are no longer centers for shopping and supplies. The American social infrastructure, in place since the early nineteenth century, has ceased to exist in the last thirty years.

Probably more land has returned to forest in the United States in absolute terms than it has anywhere in the world since the fall of the Roman Empire.

But, also, we do not have the ballast of a settled rural population. Perhaps 75 percent of our population now lives in suburban circumstances, with more than one large or good-sized city nearby. Suburban circumstances are inherently unstable. These are not old houses, not properties. The population is nomadic. School systems are correspondingly unstable, but not in every suburb. The two-tier system of classes has spread to the suburbs.

The suburbs are more comfortable and safer and offer access to the practice of sports but do not and cannot do much to preserve culture or the interplay of groups and classes that heretofore made up American education in politics, in American political realities.

The reality of American industrial unions is distinctly dangerous as well. Not one blue-collar union is free of gangster domination. A good deal of the support given Reagan by the working class was tacitly to encourage breaking the power of the unions, which used violence in a semi-fascist form to control union members and to guard its investments outside the unions of siphoned or embezzled union funds. Sizable patches of parts of America are blighted still by gangster control. These can be charted by noting where educated whites will not live and where industries will not locate. In Indiana, for instance, respectable whites have fled to the northern tier of counties or areas near Bloomington or to Columbus, Ohio. State police and others commute long distances.

It is not clear how much of long-distance hauling is still gangster-dominated. Successful farmers often band together, hire their own guards, and have their own trucks. The areas where that is the case can be charted by noting where median income is higher than in surrounding rural areas.

Where the nation-state is not an institution, governmental services including that of education can be freely tampered with. American patriotism, the American sense of America, has never been monolithic and has never existed as a direct cultural matter. Politics does not need to define itself and can't be taught in schools. No one knows what America is or what is American. The usual thing is to sense something as un-American, such as collectivism, and to stumble into being sentimental and foolish when naming something as American.

American semi-education and cultural illiteracy is balanced oddly by a media literacy unmatched anywhere in the world. I think it is unwise to speak of American naïveté in regard to the sales methods now in use in American politics. The real problem is in the linguistic-intellectual difficulty of naming the actual issues and actual grounds of decision.

The collapse in the American social infrastructure is mirrored quite precisely in the falling quality of education—what you educate children to do depends on your being able to picture the society you are educating them to enter, serve, and govern—but even more dramatically in the media, in the collapse—to use the word again—of newspapers and their influence and in the great change in radio and television news.

The newspapers could no longer serve local constituencies when the cities fell apart. No newspaper in America that I know of has managed to serve the black constituency yet or, on a lesser scale, the new classes of corporate and civic bureaucracy. To some extent this is a failure of language.

The language frame of most newspapers in the United States is derived from 1920s journalism. Nothing has been rethought. In newspapers, suburbs are still considered near-utopian places. And every year the papers find that their notions of scandal have to be rethought.

But to some extent what we have had in the United States is a failure of nerve on the part of the newspapers. They modernize their coverage largely by changing what they cover, by the topics they cover. They make little visible attempt to reflect the society or to study its changes. The great exceptions are the *New York Times*, of course, and the *Washington Post* and the *Los Angeles Times* and the *Chicago Tribune*.

But Boston hasn't a respectable or reliable paper. The Philadelphia and Detroit and Cleveland papers aren't having great periods, and those are cities wracked by Mafia power, unions, the flight from the inner city, extreme disjuncture among elements of the population at all income levels—by cultural diversity, if you like, by the failure of the melting pot to work, at least in large numbers.

Television has stepped into the breach (after helping to cause the breach by attracting so much advertising money, which it couldn't have done if the papers had had higher standing in their communities) by offering news of all sorts, talk shows that deal with social issues, and documentaries of myriad kinds; by reporting events directly; and by doing all of it in such a way that social identification with the newscaster or the format is often not necessary.

But it is interesting that most of the newscasters and documentary people are folksy and not educated in manner and do relate directly to their viewers, who are taken to be, in all cases, suburban, some quality of suburban, which, statistically, would be the case.

Television has no tradition. And its distinctive qualities of being ultimately local and entirely unvillainous tie it, if not to virtue, at least to a certain caution in regard to lunatic ventures on the left or right. But it has no editorial language, only attitude and faces being tricky or kind in some specific way in each instance. And it is dependent on enthusiasm in the event and in the personages publicized. This means that issues cannot be directly expressed. The Anita Hill–Clarence Thomas hearings had an invisible effect, invisible until the 1992 elections.

What this means is a well-informed electorate but it is well informed only in a way, although in greater depth, and it includes children, the old, and functional illiterates. The common language of public events is genuinely public. But, again, there is no ballast. Reactions can go in any direction and to almost any length. So far television has not shown itself capable of influencing anything editorially. It registers only where the power is now. And it can show the velocity of certain political movements.

It doesn't seem to be, in any way, a force for stability and real judgment.

For the first time in my experience as an adult, the issues in the present presidential campaign spring, so far, almost entirely on personal experience. Such matters as unemployment, violence, gender issues, abortion, more or less government intervention, have devolved into what each voter knows from personal acquaintance.

This is a hopeful sign in many ways, but we should recognize that because the country is so large, American experience is never monolithic. And at times like now, when it is nearly monolithic, the situation is extreme. It is very difficult to discuss the Republicans and their agenda except in extreme terms. They do not have an overt program beyond the slogans of American greatness and American supremacy. The covert program, which seems to involve an attack on unions, on very large corporations, on the American social structure, is so radical as to invite amazement. Nothing was done domestically in the last twelve years in regard to police, transportation, or any civic infrastructure. The army was maintained and a course of almost systematic looting was set in operation with the overt statement that you had to learn to take care of yourself.

This is easily recognized as a pre-riot condition. As I intimated earlier, the closeness of this to situations in Byzantium written about by Gibbon is startling. Very little in America is functioning nationally at a high level. House sales are off, and the recent argument is that houses will not appreciate in value in the future. They are now so expensive that it is very difficult for people in the lower tier to buy a house, or very much of a house, even if they have inherited money.

And it will be very hard for them to trade up. This amounts to an extreme devaluation of the savings and gross assets and net worth of the larger part of the economically unsophisticated part of the country.

The stock market is doing well, however, but the market is tricky at the moment and shows signs of becoming genuinely international, which means unpoliceable. The government does not support American manufacturing or American exports except in very sophisticated ways closed to outsiders.

The two classes are tied to America, are invested in America, in two very separate ways.

The stock-market class lives in protected enclaves. This is something that started in the United States a hundred years ago. They have their own social discipline and their own access to education, to private education. They use the highways in a limited way. They have two houses. They fly. They travel. Their primary source of information is not television. Their primary commitment to America is to their particular portion of it and the lives it supports or confers.

The unrooted class is tied to America because their skills and emotions are not readily transferable. Their language, their habits, everything they do is American and is tied to America. Their chief avenue of education is the military. They may try to stay in the same districts in which they grew up but often those districts are bankrupt, or having been bankrupt, are now gentrified with a new social structure that tends to exclude them.

The question of disenfranchisement (like so much else) rests on matters of comparison. The judgment of what is available and how to avail oneself of that availability, if it exists, now rests for the disenfranchised class on television and movies and on the lifestyles of popular entertainers who have risen from this class.

The members of this class have no base and no leverage except the vote. Statistically, they are in the majority now, whereas until now, the middle class, in its various ranges, was the dominant political force. The national wish of the disenfranchised class, white and black, would avail itself of the egoism of a single all-purpose leader who seems likely to be successful if that leader did not socially shame them, but was like them.

Since they are unrooted, and since any sense of rootedness now, under modern circumstances, would be factitious, they show an absolute hunger for absolutes. Absolutes suggest land, rootedness, and meaning. Fascism, more and more, is offered as a supervention of the national interest or as the properest form of it. Put another way, every sect and social splinter in certain sections of this society are set on coups to seize power; and the large, passive American middle class is in disorder, is split into two classes.

What is the process by which a situation in which everyone is voting according to personal experience leads to a strong political movement in which the flight from experience is absolute? Well, just that. The absence of overriding political ideas becomes a demand for such ideas because the uncertainty of being without ideas is insupportable.

Absolutism leads to death, to deaths. Death as meaning, death as glory, death as nihilism, but death: one can be in command of death, one can inflict it, or daydream of inflicting it; life itself, any community, is beyond imagination or control at the moment. American writers, the post-Hitler generation of American writers, for twenty years now, have unconsciously or consciously been trumpeting some form of dictatorship, absolutism, and death as a sign of their seriousness (and not of their infantility as it more readily seems): Stone, Bloom, Sontag, Barthelme, Theroux, Mathiessen. Realism has come to have the meaning of a sense of evil violence and of deaths and of nothing else.

It was in the 1930s in America that the political process began in reflection of the European movements—perhaps one should say the seductiveness of the European movements. On the high governing level, as was widely known and discussed at the time, it began with J. Edgar Hoover and with Franklin Roosevelt. Roosevelt took charismatic one-leader lawless leadership quite far, but like Lincoln, in this if not in every way, Roosevelt had a sense of America and of the media and of the population that he manipulated but did not terrorize and control.

Much of what he did as president, much of what he accomplished, however, is probably best understood as a translation into those American terms of popularity of what the European dictators were accomplishing.

The worst and most damaging legacy of his policies was the labor unions, which were not defined in terms of responsibility or of public examination. From the beginning, leftist or rightist, they had quasi-fascist structures.

The next step in this direction came from the Kennedys. One might say the "tradition," brief enough, but from 1830 on, was thoroughly broken by those able men who simply had an inadequate grounding in the "tradition."

That is, they were not necessarily rebels or innovators by nature but did understand their media support to be for outsiders, for the as-if newly enfranchised . . . That is, they could not be part of "tradition."

The anti-middle-class movements of the 1960s successfully introduced popular violent tactics for the first time since the Constitution was adopted. The opening of American political culture once again after 150 years (since Burr) to adventurers and to twentieth-century lawlessness-based-on-idea received enormous encouragement from the worldwide media success of Henry Kissinger, who operated—one might say, of course—more thoroughly outside the political tradition than even Nixon, who operated far enough outside it to have to resign.

But more and more enterprises and projects adopted quasi-Fascist structures. Public figures of the other sort, beginning back in the 1950s, with Adlai Stevenson, were considered weak. Something similar was happening in the American world of ideas. More and more dogmatic adventurers were appearing with arguments weaker and weaker in terms of actual merit but with more and more realism as charismatic, quasi-Fascist merchandising and propaganda. The misbehavior of the government and of large corporations marched apace.

It is hard to know whether the cold war or the ill success of the adventurers—none of them had major triumphs in any real geopolitical or military sense, and none of the literary adventurers did either—or the mass of America, the huge middle-class center, or a democratic momentum, chiefly held the country together. Perhaps all those elements entered in.

But what was clear was the erosion of the political culture or a more and more successful redefinition of it. Presidential nominations and the elections themselves increasingly had the atmosphere and reality of near coups, of plotting and seizure. No major figures emerged in this period but only successively diminutive presidential aspirants. One could guess at the decline of America, and one could track the democratic process of leveling great concentrations of power in the programs of the parties as an attempt to increase the power of the not very powerful politicians.

One could theorize self-comfortingly that democracy protected itself by refusing to let strong figures into public office at a time when the society was in greater and greater disrepair as the monolithic center, the great American middle class, began to fragment culturally, and as the American mass market began to break down as well.

But one could also see it as failure and as slow decline. In one sense, it didn't greatly matter as long as the cold war lasted and kept Japan and Europe dependent on American weaponry, particularly nuclear weaponry. Kissinger had forged the shoddy, second-rate, but lasting, political structure, which, along with the oil rise (the formation of the Arab cartel), quite clearly forestalled but predicted the exact shape of the American decline.

Reagan was, of course, the droll genius or demon who carried out the dismantling of those structures of American society, many dating back, however, only to Roosevelt and the 1930s, that created what stability we had. And the attack was on corporations, as well, because they had long since come to terms with internationalism and a modified statism and because, in some cases, they represented more intelligent and more extensive and realer power than the new office holders.

The usual Republican looting took place but on a wider level than ever before in history. And there was no great public outcry. The dismantling had wide popular support. Economic suffering was limited because of the earlier momentum. But the attack on the unions involved not only turning a cold eye to the infrastructure of American manufacturing and transportation—since nothing could be done to restore those infrastructures without making use of union labor—but the tradition of inviting foreign investment, to control the power of American companies and to help break the unions.

The desire to rule and the form that ruling took were the modified quasi-Fascist forms of the postwar years but taken much further and with much more ruthlessness and with much clearer evidence of the disorder and weakness of the media, and of the complicity of a majority of the electorate in such a program.

George Bush, like Reagan after the first two years of his presidency, and to some extent even then, has operated largely without Congress and without much reference to American domestic reality as it existed when he took office or as it now exists.

Instead, his and Reagan's periods of office seem to represent that sort of attack on the nation itself that is the hallmark of fascism coming to power.

The terms of American disenfranchisement and of American rights and the power that one has to enfranchise oneself through education or violence or sexual connection have changed and are much more unstable than before, but that is, in part, because the enfranchisement is taken for granted by most groups and is denied only secretly. Or socially.

The rejection of blacks so far is very real but it hasn't been obdurate. The relation of blacks to the dominant culture, white, now partly Asian, has been uncertain, more usually one of rejection. Put it another way, the grounds for federalism and the means are not clear since the majority of the outcasts, if we call them that, no longer want to adopt white middle-class culture. They want the consumer goods, the money, the medical care, the choices, and the police protection, but they do not want to accept the dominant culture.

This is very largely true for the first time since the Second World War; and the chief reason for it is that it is no longer the dominant culture. It no longer represents the core of the mass market, and it is not the chief repository of the powers in the political system.

Not only that, while the dominant political half is the less literate half, the educated half is less and less interested in that old culture except as a repository of privileges, ideals, and success.

Community: self-rule but under a noble or a business hierarchy as in a free city (the European model); nothing like the American communities ever existed. The attack on that community by liberals had to do with a number of things: the liberalization of the treatment of the working classes and the poor and the ease of rule, the fact that the governing bureaucrats did not come from such communities and did not understand the importance of preserving them.

The majority of such communities now in existence are rightist, sectarian, militaristic, armed, and economically beleaguered. We don't have the statistics—we haven't yet established this category.

And former union members, for instance, are accustomed to violence and oppression, tyranny and rule by violence and corruption, and are looking for a strong man.

Social class by pretension is still real and is still of importance. But it has a flaw: it is not interested in honesty and perhaps cannot recognize it. Corruption is necessary in Europe for intercourse across class lines, for communication between rulers and ruled across class and culture lines. But in the United States, it is the common language of most dealings not set by professional ethics and not carried on within a small group of like-minded people. There are two major reasons for this; one is quite surprising. Politics here rests on the wills of so many people that corruption has to be widespread. You can't pay off one person and be done with it. The American system is economically sound up to a point, but it leaves, always, a residue of longing for a more centralized system. Secondly, honesty is not part of the code of any social group I know of, but rather it is limitations on dishonesty and on certain kinds of dishonesty that are part of the code, and those limitations are inexact and have more to do with style and manner, with unspoken rules. The country largely functions in this shadow area of uncertainty of claim, uncertainty of rank, uncertainty of actual unspoken practice.

No one has yet charted, even in a novel, the actualities of the structures of power in this country. One good reason for that is that they are constantly shifting, are always up for grabs. Historically, one can point to the era after the Civil War until the First World War when power shifts occurred every year, and new power centers emerged with startling frequency and rapidity and in great numbers.

It was said the country was ruled by money, but it would be more accurate to say it was ruled by rapacity, by an opening of the rules to rapacity, to an open situation of national looting and the establishment of fortunes and business enterprises and a national infrastructure of production and transportation.

The looting has recurred ever since under every national Republican administration, except perhaps Eisenhower's. The Democrats contrarily have sought to preserve some sort of national community made up of lesser communities and to restrain the looting while taking a wide rake-off over the multitude of laws and regulations such a course involves.

The Republicans under Reagan and Bush, and to some extent under Nixon, did not support any industry or aspect of national existence. The simplicity of their programs and the dependence of those programs on having a figure to merchandize them to the country, or, to be less tendentious, a figure whom the country would accept, have begun to have a pre-fascist look, but that is peculiarly American: America is its own enemy and semi-anarchy is created as American, but actually it is created as part of the dismantling of the usual national community to establish an equivalent of the situation at the top—a situation to permit a lower version of the looting at the top—among the lesser economic groups.

Every city has its police, and most states have theirs. Each county does.

Each state has a militia. The American military is quite large and is not actually part of American society across the board but only of certain sectors of the society. More and more of American life is compartmentalized and not localized. Without roots such compartments are hard to examine and are often without a sense of responsibility for land or people.

Again, the resemblance to Byzantium is striking. Byzantium was ruled by a series of strong men who seized power. The royal heirs nearly always did not inherit. The consortiums of power put together by the strong men were reasonably representative; and the plots had to be carried through with some skill. Succession by usurpation was recognized after a while, and after a while, the usurpers often came from families that had supplied usurpers before.

Every large business, every rich real-estate enclave, every large mall, has its guards.

Can the political system here survive the dilution of the power and the meanings of states and cities and the disappearance of a comparatively stable rural population? How much violence and order are necessary to rule so unhomogenous a society and to deal with the realities of the country and of the world? What is the meaning of so large a military and espionage establishment? The hidden history of America is not so hidden, and we know it to be imperial.

The only functioning national institution, functioning with a high level of organization, is the military. At this point, even liberals might accept a limited-term dictatorship. There are not enough power centers that are roughly equal or trying for equality or superiority to guarantee a democratic continuance. The power centers now in existence are remarkably dependent on national legislation. State-based power centers are, on the whole, remarkably crooked.

Ethnic diversity, the new federalism, have not resulted in a new sense of community or in a workable sense of America. Some of this is the failure of New York intellectuals and of the movies, of clerics and of other leaders. They have not made a sufficient attempt even to begin to try to understand the community. They use old forms, they use idealism and absolutism to draft a position, they fail to observe what is here.

In moments of redefinition, as in the 1930s and 1840s and after the Civil War, this country does become remarkably unstable with all sorts of splinter groups of great passion and strangeness.

In the past, the size of the country, the emptiness of social reality, made the country a nonconductive mass. That is no longer true. The population is concentrated, and the technological means of control, of unity, are in place.

The American world empire represents a new federalism, but the old federalism is cracking up at home in this fascist strangeness of attack on diversity. What will emerge will be a new form, a bit Communist, perhaps in a Spartan, puritan mode, but it will be popular, even if with a rightist surface.

1992

BOX POPULI

In last Thursday's presidential debate, the second and probably the decisive encounter, Hollywood's cynical political comedies of the thirties made their long-delayed entry into the real political world. The oddity, or grotesquerie, went well beyond the debates-that-aren't-debates problem, to the media, and, more specifically, to the men in the media. The hunger for bloodshed, the wish for the candidates to mix it up, the conventions of putative evenhandedness, perhaps even an abiding wish to protect Bush in certain ways from his younger, more virile challenger, seemed to guarantee inadequate and nearly mindless comment, adding up to a point-blank refusal to accept Clinton's clear superiority in the debate. It's hard to know whether the media men refuse to deal with the issues and facts Clinton so relentlessly discusses because they don't know much about these matters, or because such discussion has been out of fashion during the reign of the conservatives and they've wanted to stay in step, or because of some misplaced sophistication about campaigns, campaign lies, and the realities of governing.

The lack of dignity of the *Donahue* format was simply denied by John Chancellor and others, who were impressed but inarticulate about what they saw. Chancellor said, idiotically, "The big story tonight is certainly Bush's unaggressiveness." One newspaperman even judged Perot sadly: "He wasn't funny tonight."

No one I heard on the night of the debate except David Gergen and Robin MacNeil on PBS, and no one I came across in the local papers the next morning except Maureen Dowd in the *Times* and Lars-Erik Nelson in the *News*, remarked on the triumph the occasion was for Clinton. The morning TV shows seemed to have caught up and caught on, but the admissions were, on the whole, either grudging or hesitant.

If there is no name-calling, if some sensible talk is heard, that is enough for the occasion to be called dignified. But in truth the spectacle was shabby and grating—and human. Ross Perot behaved like a fool, reciting the schedule of his TV half-hour slots. He is bankrupt intellectually, and he loses his aura of common sense when his desire to sell himself gets too strong for him. Clinton was loose and used his personality, which is that of, guess what, a populist prophet in the line of Truman and William Jennings Bryan, but educated and New Age. Bush is an aging Shakespearean figure, caught by his own history, betrayed and abandoned by nearly everyone; he is possibly ill, most likely worried about scandals breaking and to come. He seemed concerned chiefly not with gaining one more victory—some of the commentators said disapprovingly that Bush had "no fire in his belly"—but with establishing his place in history, his own human merits as they will be seen by history, and the triumphs of his Administration as he sees them: he wants them understood and memorialized. Carole Simpson, the moderator, was nervous and intrusive and assertive—but without result, since she couldn't get any of the candidates to talk directly about race. Clinton used voice tonality and body English, a different kind of *Read my lips* thing, to imply indirectly that he was concerned about racism and would attempt to do something about it, although not as liberal scolding but as a matter of American community.

Of course, it isn't easy, it may not be possible, with men of power caught up in a competition for office, to get them to answer directly. We saw a dance of politic responses, during which Clinton emerged as stronger, more confident, and more interesting than his fading rival; and Bush, for the only time in the last twelve years that I know of, actually spoke as himself—although from behind the Bushman mask. He is an aristocrat of an American sort and is simply baffled in the face of ordinary American middle-class life. He hopes to win on abstract points of competence, on being the exotically superior figure you can—or must, in the end—trust.

To win overseas, as he claims to have done—giving no credit to history, or even to Reagan—the country had to undergo sacrifices. Bush couldn't speak of that; the childlike nature of America prevented him. He is a deeply secretive, devious man, trained in business and in the CIA. The condescension in the man, the sense of his own greatness, the sense of his own background, dominated every gesture and every speech. He addressed the audience as if they were children. He apologized for using the word "portable." Such a big word! And, "When we went out to South Central in Los Angeles—some of you may remember the riots there." He tried to keep his eyes visible, but they closed down to slits almost at once. He was also small-minded and untrusting—a combat pilot in very truth—whose tactic over and over was to focus on some small, safe, winning thing. When he was asked to talk about health care, he focused on malpractice suits. His strength of will was visible, and so were the limits of that strength. The tactics and strategies that brought him to the White House have burdened him with a history he himself distrusts.

As Clinton may have foreseen but certainly understood while it was happening, all this greatness alienated a directly human, involved audience, who were concerned for themselves and their lives and didn't give a damn for Bush's place in history. Democracy at work means that Coriolanus is despised. The camera shots of Barbara Bush were terrifying: she looked ugly and savage—beaten in one sense, even grieving, but indomitable, indomitably malevolent, in another sense. She seemed to be a Greek figure of baffled rage. But she, too, seemed human. One senses that she considers her husband to have overseen one of the greatest military-nonmilitary triumphs in history—the collapse of the Soviet Union—and that what she sees now in the terrifying American populace is silence and jealousy, human and low, without regard or gratitude for her or her family. The price of high office, the ambitions and betrayals of assistants and underlings, the isolation—these things have told on them both.

It is the prophetic element in Clinton that has seemed so slippery and sometimes sleazy and then so impressive. He worked the audience, and although after a while this was a little unctuous and phony, he seemed almost inspired in conveying his message of committed ordinariness and of hands-on government favoring the statistical mainstream, the standard middling mass. It was clear and not entirely implicit that he is offering us a type of corporate state on the Scandinavian order, but not so idealistic or so culturally framed. Rather, ours would be directly tied to our electoral realities, to the conditions and fevers of the statistical mass, the center classes and elements of the upper-level working classes, omitting the rich and the poor, although not without sops thrown to each, and omitting the nutty fringes that Bush has embraced.

Clinton also seemed to be implying that he would concentrate on the new elements in the mix—women and educated blacks—with the purpose of changing the educational levels of the country, reinvigorating the schools, restoring rural and small-town infrastructures, and offering inner cities enterprise parks and self-government. He is some kind of populist prophet, by God.

Bush's heroic-pitiable last line about choosing him for crisis management is why Europeans have thought all along that he would start a Bush brush war in an attempt to steal the election. But it was the old, crinkly, nobly rich, insufferably petty, sly fighter pilot talking about the one thing he does well. That was all.

But the media's initial reaction was to ignore what we in the viewing audience saw—what we recognized in the faces and events, what we heard said by the public and by the candidates, and the way they said it. And in the media's first, dreary, self-protective interpretations, Clinton's clear-cut victory and the audience's less clear-cut triumph were unacknowledged, invisible.

1992

A FRIGHTENING CHASM
BETWEEN THE RULERS

The debates are over. But the grotesque drama of the candidates, Old Bush and Young Clinton, lingers in the mind along with the televised reality of the voters as audience. The citizen-audience in its dual role as polled television watchers and as on-camera questioners in the second presidential debate was a new version of the people, as in government by the and for the and of the. . . . An unclassical mob, to use another ancient term, they were clearly outsiders—ill-informed, ill-educated but media literate. And—pardon the rhetoric—these Americans had hardly anything visibly in common with one another and almost nothing in common with the power seekers and power wielders running for president.

In their television role as players once every four years, the people mumbled stiffly. They weren't great show business discoveries, any of them. They were expressive, though. And what they expressed—and not unconsciously, either—was the very great, towering, frightening gap between the rulers and the ruled in this country.

I'm old, or at least not young, and what I thought was most unsettlingly dramatized was a return in part to the situation in the 1930s and 1940s, when the citizenry was often referred to as the little people by the propaganda of the Fascists, the Communists, and the democracies.

Sickening then, it is disturbing now, the condescension, the sheer distance in education and power and vocabulary between the sons of bitches on top—including the media, which includes me—and the cannon fodder, the instruments of national greatness, the sweet canaille.

The condescensions of the manipulators and the commentators, with their professionally common touch, the staging of the debates that weren't debates, the candidates' notions of themselves as saviors—including the militant Mr. Perot—contain so much contempt that what this public performance brought out in the open—I think—was something that might be called a pre-fascist state of things.

Some of it is in the overt mudslinging. Some of it is implied when any attempt is made to say anything. Some of it is in the improvised and even revolutionary forms of the campaigns, again including Mr. Perot's.

It appears that the media—specifically, the men in the media—are the chief enemy of sense and reason in any and all political matters. The most often named enemy now is not the system or even governmental corruptions and stupidity but it is us in the media: we're the enemy.

The media have too much regard for sports metaphors to lose respect for any clever SOB who has a license to practice public manipulation and who has any history at all of success at it. And by extension, then, they have too little respect for the national realities that concern those without gross political power in their own names, who are invariably taken to be part of someone else's power, cogs in the machine, and outsiders in the game.

For the men in the media, only gross power is power. Power determines real citizenship and actual franchise. But this is out-of-date and has been since the Second World War. And perhaps before.

Those of us who don't write journalism or who are just beginning to write it find ourselves to be in rebellion in this matter.

In the debates, Mr. Bush and Dan Quayle enacted "real" alphahood for the little people. Topdog, born-rich, birth Republicans, officer material in a populist society, Mr. Bush and Mr. Quayle came out like mad-dog fighter pilots. They seem to be offering militant leadership and themselves as administrators of the militant national will and as caretakers of national greatness and national values, offering leadership as a ruthless feistiness of the very rich.

But murderous wimps are still wimps. And four years of lies are still four years of lies. And the Democrats struggled early in the debates to address us wounded beta-level beasts with a disturbingly wooden simulacrum of humanity that was almost, not quite, worse. I say worse because it was so damned unconvincing.

Mr. Perot's presence, his acerbic looniness and bottom-line obstinacy, illustrated the degree to which Mr. Bush and Mr. Clinton were stumbling along in the ugly improvisations of an American presidential campaign speaking almost entirely in coded dishonesties.

The debates weren't debates, but exercises in comparison shopping, popular oratory and high school election contests, with notions of character, pugnacity, and popularity being the points of comparison. This was what the voters and Carole Simpson, the moderator of the second debate, rebelled against. A functionally appropriate media should have set up some sort of sensible order a lot earlier.

But it is itself committed to old mechanisms. The politics of this shopping-mall era suit this strange nation—and it is a strange nation. A realistic sense of this would, at first until it became popularly accepted, seem eccentric and even crazed.

Mr. Bush, a conservative, reinvents America and constitutional law at will, as he does definitions of truth and notions of expediency. Mr. Clinton, the eternal student-running-for-class president, political greatness and American destiny whistling in his head, invents one governmental possibility after another depending on polls and theories and on the phrases that come to his mind. He seems ignorant of the country's consistent rejection of presidential populism in the last one hundred years. The collapse of the sixties included the collapse of Lyndon Johnson's often brilliant attempts at a Great Society.

With no cultural restraints in operation, the players in our politics try everything and risk nothing and look like fools. In the early debates it was all now we'll find out what floats, what sinks, what stinks. What a horror. Pragmatism without history—without cultural restraint—and the great vivacity of individual ambitions led to the wrestling and snarling and promising and sniffing-their-way-to-high-office of the candidates, sniffing at the monstrously many-headed citizenry that in turn was sniffing at them.

Let's face it, we're a hell of an electorate: the dispossessed and the possessive, the haters and the blandnessmongers, the armed camp suburbs and the utopian suburbs. And S&L looters and would-be S&L looters and the denizens of the shadow economy. Never underestimate the cranky rebelliousness of American ambitions. None of the average Americans shown on television or quoted in the New York papers that I saw were among the ferocious Americans—maybe a majority of Americans—at least partly stained by illicit actions.

The candidates are going for their votes, too. The media have a complex or neurosis about responding to new circumstances. Mr. Clinton is too untested, too young, too new a type in national politics for them to risk liking him. It is possible that the media are consciously helping Mr. Clinton win by bringing Mr. Bush down—sadistically making the wimp go through hoops, flaying and mocking the Coriolanus figure. But they are unwilling to risk praising Mr. Clinton, and that is worrisome.

Perhaps they want to have a clear path for attacking him later, to restrain him in his youth if he wins. They want to give him no mandate for social change. But they sure as hell want him to be tough.

The backlash to Johnson's progressivism, the reactionary social regressiveness of the last twelve years of American government still exists in the media, unchecked, uncorrected for.

In power terms, by covertly helping Mr. Clinton, the media seem to want to keep him tender and hanging on its words. The aficionados and cold-eyed observers of male power—and maturity—and of the political arena, at the summit of the American state, are not working for political and cultural change but only to get that fool Bush out of office and to get a stronger man in.

As a result, the last twelve disastrous years—and the Great Event, the collapse of the Soviet Union and the Communist and advanced Socialist left, with its full range of meanings—have gone too thinly unreported and largely unanalyzed. The media are prepared, man by man, to twist and turn and go right or regressive rather than face contemporary reality and new ideas and new approaches to that reality.

Harry Truman won without media support or approval, and he governed without it, as did Abraham Lincoln, for that matter, in the greatest of all such national examples. But I believe the situation is very different now.

The media are the voice of the population, but actually have been acting as the voice of one given part of the population only, the middling middle class up to the top, and then only in the largest and richest cities, and even then favoring the two seacoasts—not the Gulf Coast.

Well, let's give the men in the media credit for the last twelve years. Or blame. Let's let George Bush escape indictment as a tool of hidden and overt historical forces and of the psychological politics of the actual shenanigans of Americans wielding power. He is just George Bush.

Whom to vote for? Traditional left- and right-wing governments as we've seen lately have what amounts to the same drive toward the disenfranchisement of the large mass of the population. The only interesting possibility is to lessen the distance between the governed and the governors, and that can be done by lowering the governors or elevating the governed. The first path to try is educating up, along with a program for controlling cash-transfer individualism. That indicates Mr. Clinton.

Unhappy? Welcome to an American election.

1992

WIT

AND

WHIMSY

SHY MWM WRITER, 61,
SEEKS CULTURAL ELITE

Let me introduce myself. I am a sixty-one-year-old white male who lives largely on a macrobiotic diet which I cheat on. I am a shy man who was something of a recluse for twenty years, shipwrecked on Manhattan in an advanced state of unsuitability for what passes for educated or intelligent or economic life nowadays—post-Eisenhower intellectual-literary life and love and what-have-you.

I'm told now that I had those twenty years a tremendous, pulsating, earthshaking underground reputation—as a writer, as a man, as a lover, a dinner companion, a bastard—but no one told me that then. (Mike Nichols had a routine in which he named songs for a musical version of *The Song of Bernadette*: One song was "Why Do You Tell Your Beads When You Don't Tell Me?")

When the publicity started, I was fifty-five or fifty-six years old, and the violence in the publicity startled me, especially the accusation that I was famous. Until then I'd had to produce my driver's license if I wanted to pay by check in a bookstore. Some of it was a joke. The issues, I think, were drawn from the lives and politics of other people and of factions that had little or nothing to do with me or had something to do with me but not much.

(I mean some powerful literary journalist might want to affix a repu- tation for power to me because I told him powerlessness is the strongest daily sensation I have. And he couldn't write fiction, or thought he couldn't, but he had power coming out of his ears. So, he did ascribe power to me as ironic mockery. Or perhaps I had the power to hurt his feelings. Who knows?)

My reputation, when it surfaced, was partly like Moby Dick coming up for air and vengeance. And a little bit like King Kong waddling in a papier-mâché jungle and fated to die on the Chrysler Building—in love not with Fay Wray but with Anna Karenina and the American public.

It was something quite rare and strange, a journalistic birth of a reputation begotten by Dismay on Incredulity.

It's still pretty strange. People I had never met wrote pieces implying close acquaintance—and historical accuracy, as if my history were well known, well documented, and, of course, it's not.

But the history like the literary discussion concerned only my *reputation*. To mix genders a bit, it was as if I was the last coed.

I have never said any of the things attributed to me in print. I did one live radio show once—with Diane Rehm in Washington—which I did not know was live until I was halfway through it, and the phone rang and I realized it was a call-in show. Anyway, I was later told that at one point, the sound engineer in the booth exclaimed, "Hey, the son of a bitch is telling the truth. . . ."

In self-defense I read little of the publicity: It is like a roomful of aunts or of fraternity brothers all commenting on my haircut. But I was advised to read one piece, and in that piece, my reputation was mentioned in every paragraph. It clearly stirred the essayist—the reputation. The work was never mentioned in any frame except that of an Orthodox American-Jewish right-wing opinion of it, a rather odd frame of judgment for a work in English; but the essayist-reviewer did not consider himself a practitioner of multiculturalism. He felt himself to be central, even biblical (and absolute) in reference to what people had written or spoken hurriedly, casually, about me or my work. The Smart Jew Sweepstakes, maybe. It's true, I think, that Americans are culturally very advanced in matters of publicity and public reputation. People at my old gym (I'm now too old for a gym) used to discuss the publicity with verve and at length until I gave up going to the gym. A lot of people want to discuss your publicity with you. Reputation may be the major American art form.

.   .   .

Well, I confess I am a snob, as any self-respecting son of a junkman would be. If you think back over the last five decades at the misguided projects that our columnists and thinkers have touted, you might decide that snobbery was called for. And I'm not a fan of middlebrow stuff. A writer in the *New Republic* not too long ago referred to "the art of middlebrow"; but the point of middlebrow is that it is not art. It is safe. It is defensive. And mythological—it starts with the notion that advertising shows a normal world, and a true one, one that actually exists.

So, middlebrow is not usually on target—not usually accurate as reportage or reliable when discussing theory. It sells Utopia (normalcy as the happy ending) and social-class flattery, flattery of the folk, *echt* or mixed, high or low.

The writer in the *New Republic* referred to this unlikely "art" as "proficient" and "creamy. . . ." If you take words seriously, if you take seriously the reality that discourse means something, intends something, refers to issues, then you wince when someone throws words at a subject carelessly. Middlebrow is sturdy and intense and has kind of middling craftsmanship. It demands too little to require *proficiency* of technique. Real proficiency, of course, is hardly ever "creamy" but is jolting or thrilling and articulate. "Creamy" is a special quality, thick and sleepy, bonelessly rich, maybe frothy—high-toned, decadent, that sort of thing—or it is indigestible and poisonous because it has gone bad.

A certain confusion enters here because fake middlebrow can be highbrow—Dreiser some of the time. Fitzgerald, but only when he gets the glamour-death ratio right.

But a few truisms come in handy: Sentimentality is not emotion but is the substitution of self-love for all other possible emotions. Shrillness is not a sign of intellect. Or of judgment. (It usually indicates bad nerves and a weak vocabulary and limited powers of reason.) People who prefer to feel and to have their feelings toyed with by sentiment or by fake highbrow or by cheesy lowbrow rather than by good stuff are traditionally in this country called *boobs* and *mediocrities*. I am a traditionalist in this regard. One can be moved and lured by stupidity but that is a particular taste.

Middlebrow has a terrible propensity to become low-level and dangerous kitsch entirely without truth except for the truth of its own, often shocking, success. Our sympathies may lie with just that quality; but our trust in what it says should be limited.

The question with some of the very junior *middlebrow* writers is not whether they are good writers or not. They are not at the level where that is a question at this time. The question is whether we are interested in moral dwarfs. (Perhaps in my next column I will describe my least favorite contemporary moral dwarf.)

In the piece about middlebrow "art" was the statement: "We now profess to be above art that provokes only saturated feelings." What "we" can the writer honestly mean? He is not talking about the mass audience. And he can't be talking about an intelligent one. No one intelligent would ever make such a remark. *Above* art? And what are *saturated feelings*? It sounds like something requiring a diaper. He's talking about a good sub-cathartic weep, maybe—in other words, about sentimental crap.

We judge written and enacted or performed work of all kinds by its valid portrayal of true feelings and of dishonest feelings and by its showing some responsibility in evoking feelings (or an honest coldness and lack of feeling). We judge political oratory this way. Not all kitsch is bad. Much of Matisse and Picasso plays with kitsch . . . sometimes not well, sometimes illuminatingly. I hope in a future column to discuss the Cornered Rat Postmacho kitsch of some male book reviewers and of some books, and how kitsch-macho now has the force of social law for some among us who ought to know better.

In the matter of feminism, I hope to do a column on how in my country the old women have all vanished. Think of it: We *have no more old* women. . . .

In terms of politics, I hope to popularize the notion of keeping score, to point out how often, for instance, Daniel Patrick Moynihan has been right.

In terms of culture, the *cultural elite* itself, in its greed and ambition, has become Dan Quayle–like toward cultural elitism and has adopted a lowest common denominator intellectual standard. I hope to attack that.

I intend to argue that English as a language is very peculiar and rests not on rules so much as on an ear for language, an ear for accuracies of expression, and a comprehension and some knowledge of the many complex systems of grammar available in English. (John Updike's book *The*

Witches of Eastwick has a foolish grammatical error on the high school level in the opening sentence; the discussion of it would have to be whether he has the right—and the proficiency, creamy or otherwise—to make such a solecism as an addition to the language or if he has, at times, a tin ear.)

A Cultural Elite is judged by the work it praises and the work it preserves and the work that it causes to come into existence. A so-called Elite is dismissible and contemptible if it is not part of a great movement or of a project of reason or part of a great city's continuing greatness.

And Dan Quayle, as part of his vigilant support of family values, recently pushed through an OK for the sale of nuked food, without FDA investigation. Your kids and mine will soon be eating unidentified fetal matter that can turn into a cancerous future. This is hellish. And where is the intellectual outcry?

All right, all right.

A year or so ago, someone tried to explain to me the difference between the West Coast and the East Coast as being the difference between John Wayne and John Simon.

I'm from the Middle West.

1992

THE WEATHER OF
THE SPIRIT

Travelers' advisories offer cautions about weather, and perhaps the weather of the spirit needs advisories, too. I think visitors to the city, to Manhattan, should be given warning that the city poses certain hazards to your mood, your sense of the world. For instance, in midtown at midday most color tends to disappear, and you get a bone-colored clutter: a clutter bustling, bleached, and dirty—dust-smeared glass, streaked aluminum, discolored brick, dirty concrete, potholed asphalt. Of course, if you look closely you can see that the city is not entirely a colorless mess, but the order and the colors don't stand out.

Take midday midtown reds—they are everywhere: in the signs on the sides of buses, in the folksy script announcing Bojangles', in the chunky letters spelling out "Burger King," in the "Express" of "Federal Express" (on white trucks), in the signs taped to the *Times*-dispensing machines that say, in white letters on a red ground, "Find Your World in Ours." But these advertising reds, like the reds of the stoplights and taillights, do not operate strenuously in the large white glare. Part of the reason is the way colors behave in bright light: diffusion and suffusion are limited, and so colors drown in the spectrum's imperialist, or total, white. Part of the reason is the discoloration of the air. Part is the bulk of the buildings: large, very large, continuous areas of streaked monotone, which, together with the blind glare of a just about uncountable number of windows, jolts the eye, probably our cleverest receiver of signals, and maybe the one most easily appalled. Or disappointed. I mean, nature intended the eye to be easily attracted—to be easily amused, so to say—and to discriminate among fragments and variations of texture and surface. It has no natural reason to study anything as stony and as monolithic and as unvarying as so many of our buildings.

Perhaps part of the architectural intention here was to startle and oppress the eye, commemorating immense power by means of brute geometry—in this case, solid rectangles that are simply immense. I would, I think, like to wallpaper many of the larger buildings for the sake of the amusement and health of the eye, and of the spirit of visitors as well as my own.

Then, too, one must be prepared for the daytime effect of so many windows—windows carried to such heights, all of them blind and gray, and without any suggestion of being looked out of. Glass is everywhere—fragile, disconsolate, uncomfortable, too vulnerable to produce the effect of masonry but often used for masonry, and giving the perverse impression at midday of needing to be shaded: a citywide impression of squinting shutteredness (in the midday brilliance and soot) and of a lack of color. Glass does have color, of course; it often looks green or blue. Much of it seems slate gray in daylight. Yet I would say the effect is of no color, of neutrality. Emotionally, the effect of so many blind windows is of blindness. Be prepared.

The city goes on seeming bleached—without color or charm or romance—until late in the afternoon, when a carnal and carnival flavor takes over. The streets change, and so do the hallways and rooms inside the buildings. The enormous blind-windowed monoliths are no longer nearly no-color; they are the color of shadows and of late yellow light. And the sky often turns memorable blues. I have seen twilights that were even bachelor's-button blue. A great blue. It's then that the reds come into their own. They emerge from their daytime careers of sluttish advertising and begin to glow and live as color, flirtatiously, seductively, juicily. We then have an evening spring, with luminescent poppies appearing everywhere. The taillights of cars begin to be, I swear it, heart stirring. And the white of automobile headlights around eight o'clock in the dark is a courageous white. The prettiness is enough to soothe a troubled mind. Anyway, the reds proliferate, they spring up everywhere: neon bar and hotel names, record stores and painted signs, and the traffic lights and, now, irresistibly glowing taillights. The windows gleam with varihued lights. They no longer have the quality of masonry, are no longer blind. Walls look like walls. I find the sense of party then to be convincing. A poetry of parties, maybe. The New York reds—the taillights and stop-lights and neon—proclaim this, and they shine until the sky itself takes on its nightly red tinge, and New York City vanishes into darkness.

1987

A MAN ENRAPTURED
WITH THE SEASONS

This time of year I think of as marking the return of buttonholes. No more the lisp of easy summer fabrics and the swift slide and snap of elastic, no more the lisp of the moister summer breezes. Not many butterflies, but buttonholes and buttons come in small autumnal swarms. If I regard buttonholes harshly, it is because they mean you have to think when you dress—you have to get the buttons and the holes matched and in the right order. This is a matter of technical propriety held in some esteem ever since first grade as a mark of social ability, not to mention social class. It is very schoolish, and to get the holes and buttons mismatched, so that everything is lopsided, is, ah, pathetic, and indicates more absentmindedness and a greater extent of social unfitness than one would like. Buttons are first-day-of-first-grade propriety come again.

If I ever build a pyramid as a memorial to anything, it will have as its approach an allée of statues of crouched and uncrouched glasses-wearing first-grade teachers of the type old-fashionedly known as battle-axes. I'll have no smiling, lipstick-wearing educational-arts youngsters, or light cruisers, among my dreadnoughts. All propriety, ferocity of demeanor, and able relentlessness, the crouching ones, alphabet lovers to a dame, will be fastening buttons to buttonholes before the startled gaze of be-sphinxed (which is to say, hypnotized) children, first-grader size, caught by historical duty, stunned by the end of summer, and over-whelmed by the mathematical and social complexities of the button.

It's not that I think summer is perfect. I think summer is demented. I would argue that August is a misnamed month. I wouldn't say it was august; I'd call it intimate and bad-breathed and unlaced. People who are dressed up in August in an august manner strike me as eccentric. I can't believe I'm sharing those melted thirty-one days with them. But I wouldn't say September is well named, either. It's not the seventh month. September to me is when I go back to school, not in memory but in a kind of classroom-and-school-corridor sense of dutiful language. I lay aside my summer language and refurbish my phrasing with spiffier terms and autumnal and businesslike inflections. I use a sharper rhythm than any that August encouraged or permitted. My purposes, my moods are sharper. It is often said that the air and the light develop an edge in September. Well, so do I. It is as if I had got up from lying on a beach towel and by the time I got back to the house were re-established among my contradictory usual duties (to earn a living, to be human and a citizen, to be a family person). This is reflected in my language. Sprawling and out-flung summer jabber—"What a clear day, nice wind, isn't it? You going out in the sailing dinghy?" A sentence apt for a semi-absurd romance with the weather and a sailboat; but facial expressions and sighs for a tropical and boyish and flirtatious season won't do now. I grow terse and silent; I have things on my mind. Syntax, the sailor, yanks itself into a posture of intellect, sort of. "Fine clear day. Well, up and at 'em." I think the Spirit of Efficiency is summer laziness chilled and goaded into what might be called having a practical heart.

I suppose I'm absurd and aging. I never used to notice the seasons in verbal detail or name the details of living in them, or with them, or along-side them—however it should be said. Sunlight abbreviates itself; it hangs, like the apostrophe in a contracted *won't*, among the architectural details of a porch or on the facades of houses sternly unporched. The buzz and mumble and details of summer, insects and the importance of shade and the nuisance of glare are erased. A child I knew said once that the cold weather bit butterflies. The air has a bite. It bites butterflies. A waspish tang and the seeming jocularity of morning temperature indicate the departure of wasps and the seriousness of fall. Tweed and corduroy nudge me along the cusp of Libra. Autumn's buttery days are crisp.

The people in my family become precisely headlong in their tempos and ambitions just at the time when grass grows more slowly. Plants are fragile and seem to be careful. Leaves seem to be pre-emeritus. I need all things to be grammatical and deft. I long for careful language and scheduled utterance. In many ways, the climate known as temperate is rough. Energy, and maybe wickedness, spill from rested folk.

Let's rename the months:

August—The Sprawler
September—School-and-Cool
October—The Red Ox
November—Unpack Your Scarves
December—The Time of Firewood
And so on.

Now, a climate with seasons has often been derived by writers who feel that civilization is both mannerly and ruthless—essentially Mediterranean. I prefer the spiritual urgency (along with the hypocrisy) of a culture of puritan seasons. I tend to consider a cold edge to warm light a defect in the natural charity of the light; and since autumn in this latitude is rife with defects in this way, I consider those dreadnought early teachers of mine—and my parents—to have been prompted to considerations of charity in the course of rectifying the defects of charity in the natural world. Doesn't the fall prompt feats of attention that tend toward impulsive but serious charity? Human summer, unaugust and intelligent, perseveres in the charity the weather lacks. I have always thought that was why this was called a temperate climate.

1986

THANKSGIVING

Looking back on Thanksgivings in the past and thinking about the recent one is a little like turning your head in a fast-moving car. Whoops! Look at that. Zip, zip. The Pilgrims in their stockade, with their buckle shoes and their moral postures, and the nearly naked Indians, about to be dispossessed (but some will take large recoveries through lawsuits three centuries later), bringing corn and fish and turkey—or whatever it was in 1621—became this year a gathering of a nervous, somewhat bookish tribe, edgy but happy: ten people, four of them related by blood, the rest related by marriage or just related. One of us said it was more of a party than a Thanksgiving. Two couples were flirting, and we played poker after the meal and no one got too competitive. The center was the mother of the baby. It was she who was attached to everyone directly. She looked terrific. Cheerful.

We didn't go outside this year and pass a football around or toss a Frisbee. This was partly because it was cold and mean out and we were in an eleventh-floor loft downtown on Walker Street, and partly because we started talking. We couldn't watch the games on TV, because the baby would flick channels unless someone scared him off, and no one wanted to do that.

A Thanksgiving retrospective includes the years when the men—and sometimes the women—in various settings, various eras of my life, went outside to take target practice after the meal. We did that the year of the Cuban missile crisis, and once during Korea, when we thought the war would spread. There were few years without a crisis—none, really. Small arms seemed a safer, or more bearable, evil than the Great Bang, so we gave thanks with small arms.

The last year we discussed the Pilgrims at Thanksgiving, to the best of my recollection, was 1959. And the year before, or two years before, my wife and I went outside to the car to play some good music—Elvis, I think—and get away from the supermarket-bought food and from the textbook self-righteousness, which was actually a sort of bitterly ironic nostalgia for heroism of a sort different from that which had put the food on the table.

The last year we put marshmallow on the sweet potatoes was 1968. That was the end of my thinking I'd had a palate in childhood. I mean, there was no point in dredging up childhood tastes as an act of rebellion or of piety. Still, every year we think about pieties of diet and pious meals one way or another—variants of kosher. A college professor of mine used to argue that the Puritans had been Judeophiles and that New England Protestantism had a Jewish cast. The trouble is I can't remember which professor. Anyway, at that point in the 1960s we wore beads and smoked pot, and we made conversation and decided that some childhood tastes were lousy.

What year did we substitute goose for turkey? Was that part of a step-up in social class or part of an attempt at more authentic folk cooking? Was that the year I issued the ukase "No fancy turnips. Do them plain or let's dump them. We're commemorating hardship and charity here"?

What year did we attempt Thanksgiving in a restaurant? What year did we stop thinking about having it at someone else's house? Our children were fighting with us one year: "We could go to Paris. We could try Saint Bart's." What was the last year we went to a working farm and chose the bird and got semifresh corn and a pumpkin from the field of an honest-to-God rural person?

The last Chinese-checkers game, the last Thanksgiving before part of the afternoon was spent in front of the television, were when? You can think, if you like, about the flowers you've had, and about the fruits-of-the-earth arrangements you've attempted, and the photographs you've taken of the family at Thanksgiving that refer to or avoid referring to Norman Rockwell. He looked like a Puritan. He was an icon. He was—

is—one of those artists of a certain rank, like Sousa and Eugene Field and Stephen Foster, and maybe Irving Berlin and Margaret Mitchell and Cecil B. De Mille, who are something like signed folk art. They're awfully close to being part of what we are as Americans at Thanksgiving time, as are those half-anonymous car designers who came up with the post-war Ford and the Mustang and the Cadillac with tail fins. I'm grateful for tail fins. And all my cars. I'd prefer a world of bicycles, and intend to work toward one, but I have been grateful for the cars that got me to Thanksgiving.

I like the way people talk when they're playing poker. This year, it was jokes again and talk about the Great Depression II and Kondratieff cycles and whether the baby was in the phase of parodistic formations. We discussed Dylan and Johnny Cash—prototypical Americans. We played some Beatles song. I thought about Walt Whitman and Emily Dickinson—those are my kind of Puritans. They and Louis Armstrong—we played two records of his—represent America to me. So do Scott Fitzgerald and the movies of Buster Keaton and what we have of Balanchine. Also Bernstein and Billie and Bogart. Elvis, Roosevelt, and Lincoln.

A few Thanksgivings back, some of the kids in my apartment building played in the street with the kids from the welfare hotel at the corner. Indians and Pilgrims, in a sense. The hotel has since been upgraded, gentrified, turned into condominiums. And the urban work of getting the turkey and getting it home and getting it cooked, in the uneasy truce between feminists and male chefs and with kids underfoot and who knows what—it's a small epic, but it's a small *American* epic. And everyone being good-looking and healthy and alive one more year. And the new television set. The fretfulness of the world economy. Another year of Reagan. Arms control. The death of American farming as we've known it. May as well accept it all at the moment as not being worse. May as well accept those stories of how the caretakers have to remove all the BB shot and slingshot missiles fired into the Macy's balloons.

1987

A GOOD BLIZZARD

The night before the first of two recent snowstorms, I looked out of an acquaintance's office window at the winter twilight around the grandly lit RCA Building and I saw what looked like the intrusion of black into the deep-blue cup of the sky, suggesting some kind of beautiful invasion by cold, black space. Then, when I went outside, the dark in the streets had a genuinely wintry blackness, and it did seem that the darkness of uninhabitable space was settling down on us in ticklingly cold, harshly rigid folds. It was clearly presnowstorm. The next morning, I woke to miles of busy air outside the windows of my fourteenth-floor apartment—an endless cataract in slow motion of gray, wind-driven shredded fluff. Sleet pecked in silly gusts at my windows, like a man knocking at a door in a fairy tale. That lasted all day and all night. The next morning, I looked out and saw on the midtown buildings, in the polar light, glimmers that were the colors of birthday-cake icing: shiny white and pale yellow and pale rose and that dim blue no one likes to eat. The dawn air had almost a plywood cast to it, it looked so stiff.

When I went out into the cold, the air did seem to be stiff—locked. The visible apartment houses looked shut down or frozen up—as if the snowstorm had sealed them. On the street, it was your average shabby Atlantic-seacoast midwinter storm, with a pushy, grunting wind, an icy snuffling roar of a flu wind, a hacking ripper wind. A shoving wind. It didn't have a single moment (that I noticed) of a silencing fall of clumped, soft flakes—that white reward.

We had a good blizzard three years ago in New York—a beauty. The city entered a parenthesis and was so white and mute as to suggest that it and the air, the buildings, and the streets were like Japanese actors in heavy white makeup, motionless, performing a traditional pantomime of grave meaning against the whiteness and silence of a simplified city. And the day after the blizzard was bright with sun and truly cold, and the streets and parks were full of red-nosed people and kids, smiling, on sleds and skis. I went cross-country skiing in Riverside Park.

Both of this year's snowstorms were dimly lit. The first one was cold, gray, nearly lightless. Its unsympathetic nature was compounded by freezing, stinging rain and sleet. People were plunging and stomping and hopping, and yanking their feet from mucky suction in the gutters at intersections. Taxis slid in a clogged-tread way through red lights. No one was smiling. People moved collapsibly and warily. But obstinately. Making your way was complicated and uncomfortable. High-stepping it along an almost unwalkably broken-surfaced sidewalk, heeling and yawing in the sad passages of the streets—sad, poor, awkward streets—I got depressed: everything looked jerry-built, underarchitectured, temporary, disposable.

The night before the storm, as I said, was dramatically dark and seriously cold. Have you ever noticed when you're walking on a cold night that windows look tightly lit—without an ounce of extra light to spare? Does cold diminish the spread of light? Slow its speed? Do molecules and photons have an Arctic shyness? Maybe the tiny-fingered and practical part of science can tell us. The tightly lit windows on a cold night are also paler—not marigold-colored, as they are on autumn nights. You notice, too, how cold fits itself tightly to your face.

The morning after the storm, I saw footprints on the roofs of brownstones and some of the fewer-storied apartment buildings. I bet they were, most of them, those of young people new to New York and fascinated by the melodramatic way we have weather. Some, though, were assuredly those of superintendents checking for damage or blocked drains. Some were those of people who wanted to breathe the fresh air—city air is at its purest after a snowstorm.

Television tried to make a folk ceremony out of the snowstorm, informing people on Long Island, "Your loved ones will be three to four hours late tonight, so you don't have to worry," and interviewing countless people who were astounded to be interviewed—people stranded at the airport, and people standing in ticket lines for Broadway shows, and just barely civil drivers stuck at the entrance to the Holland Tunnel for a number of hours, and snow-removal drivers, and children, whose delight at facing the camera quickly faded as they came to suspect that they looked uninitiated or tongue-tied—feebly unlike stars-to-be.

One of the advantages of bad weather in New York is that it makes people peaceful toward each other. I can't imagine anyone stopping to fight with anyone in the cold, or anyone mugging anyone. A nipped, pinched, hurrying pacifism is what we get. That may be enough.

1987

THE SUBWAY AT
CHRISTMAS

The other day, in an ambitious wind that jostled shoppers on upper Broadway into little, unexpected steps to the side (itself like a shopper in Woolworth's, in Bloomingdale's, trying to get past), I gave up my idea of walking to midtown. This was in the afternoon, about two—often the warmest time now. I covered a couple of blocks and crossed wide Broadway toward the subway. The corners where last week fir trees had crowded the sidewalks and drowned the smells of the street in resinous odor were empty under an ugly, low-slung sky, and the unencouraging Christmas decorations were juddering ceaselessly in the wind. I went down into the subway, past maybe a Brearley senior tearing helplessly at a plastic package of tokens, and I put my token in the slot of the turnstile and squeezed my way through that guardian strait, with its ratchet bars—they are meant for what size people with what sort of hips and clothes, I wonder. And I entered the gloomy, heartbroken half-light in the cavern at the edge of the dry riverbed of tracks set in an unchanging forest of steel columns, which did afford the sight of some distant souls on the other side of that buried, unclean river. It was a daylight hour—as such things go in midwinter in New York—but it had been essentially gray on the street. Now I stood inside a square delimited by pieces of decoratively enameled, very yellow metal suspended from the ceiling: "OFF HOUR WAITING AREA," they said, and their yellow suggested sunlight.

Up and down the long platform (this was at Eighty-sixth Street), people sat on benches, leaned against pillars, stood at the edge of the concrete bank of the shadowy river. When the crowd builds to that size at that station, it generally means that the trains are late—there is a problem in the system. Seven or eight wide-eyed people stood in front of the news kiosk. Its light shone outward on their faces over a glossy multitude of figures waiting to be bought—a gaudy population of the acclaimed and enviable and scandalously in trouble on magazine covers and the front pages of newspapers. There they were, being stared at and considered, maybe sightlessly. And there we were, a speechless party of balked travelers. Yet not entirely speechless: in pairs, in some groups, people were talking to each other. But mostly the people at this landing were intent on their newspapers or (in a few cases) books, or on their thoughts, but not deeply, except two who looked deranged and penniless. "Not deeply" means that people glanced surreptitiously or quickly, and as if incuriously, at whoever passed them, at everyone who came onto the platform, or nearly everyone, depending on the looker's taste in glancing at people. We were a party, or were like a party in the sense of being a group of knowing people linked for a moment and enclosed with one another in a place that is not home and noticing one another but, of course, not smiling or addressing one another.

I think most of us there recognized the moment as a public one, an occasion not entirely successful, not exactly triumphant—not one of the triumphant occasions of American culture, or one of the great things about Manhattan, either. But in the general famine of light the faint glow of the urban glances (edgy and making a claim of being bored) had a Manhattan empathy, and maybe more, though maybe I imagined it: a warmth expressed with constraint but verging on a seasonal incaution, almost semi-brotherhood. Maybe it was just a public-transportation hidden hysteria in the grim tubes, welcoming something to look at and accepting the unnatural city kinship of random company, and doing it to a sophisticated degree—I mean welcoming the oddities here, and the sad general weirdness of a subway and of taking it in the middle of the afternoon, each of us being a me and here (a what-am-I-doing-here thing), and so on.

Actually, I am thinking mostly of the people here who were between the ages of twenty-one and forty, who were white and unbroken, who weren't limply or mutteringly or angrily hors de combat, and who were with no one, although some of the paired or grouped people also glanced around in this same key. I think it is difficult to describe the whole group, or crowd—an American group so momentary in its full contemporary splendor of pluralisms. I know of no other modern circumstance that can match the vocabulary-snapping pluralisms of a crowd, the populace, on certain Manhattan subways at certain pretty much accidental hours: the social and psychological and physical diversity, the diversity in age, in degrees of hope and kinds of style and moral and immoral intention (as a political and class and religious and metaphysical matter). I mean style across the board. What faces do while wearing earphones, for instance: public, unpublic, changeable, cautious, resolutely alert, bitterly lost. That's just one matter. Scarves and necks: turtlenecks, ties, open collars or bare necks even in this weather. Or a hidden matter: father-stepfather, economics and father complications. The age range is from a year old to seventy-something—that is my guess. The overall range is so broad as to seem senseless, but, of course, it must mean something. Even though this is so riotous a selection, it's probable that the group here still represents only a handful of the elements of the American social order. And then you might ask yourself how three social classes can possibly be enough to define us. Twenty-five would be too few to encompass just the financial variations visible here, let alone on the train once it gets here and goes from station to station, district to district in Manhattan. What an eerie community modern-day America has become. Weren't we supposed to be growing more and more homogenized? Of course, perhaps what we have become is a cultural anarchy in the dispersion and pervasiveness, the availability and lessening availability of money.

The souls gathered here, the jewelry they wore, their barbered hair, the eyeglasses, the postures—nothing was echoed or repeated enough to supply a category. Nothing you could call an East Side slouch or West Side intellectual hoo-haw or a West Point or Corn Belt look of outer rectitude. Here there was only variation. I would not have thought a slowing prosperity would do up so many so differently. The real and unreal noses. The skin colors. The colors and varieties of hair. Of the four or five insolently and cryptically (and, paradoxically, overtly) stylish people, Manhattan-cosmopolitan in their heavily encoded outfits, each, as time passed, openly, but without forwardness, somewhat pointedly acknowledged the others who were stylish in that fashion but stylish differently. One woman, maybe the richest, acknowledged no one; her coat was hiddenly spectacular. I was aware of this from having been told about that coat and shown a picture of it by a woman I know; otherwise, I wouldn't have penetrated the secret of its chic discretion. Everyone had some sort of style, good or bad. One guy, in metal-rimmed glasses and a kind of formal topcoat, very young—rosy-cheeked, actually—was reading *Barron's Weekly* and chewing gum (I think it was gum) and wearing somehow baggy lace-up black leather shoes, maybe very advanced and almost certainly cheap. A short, not thin young woman with what a fashion photographer might call an "important face" was wearing dark glasses and had truly improbable red-tasseled mittens. A tall madwoman had a dirty mink coat and a safari hat with a brim. A good-looking man, not young, had on cowboy boots and a lined denim jacket and a fur cap: he was not young but had very long hair.

Trains intermittently passed on the express track, with a shrill, hammeringly spasmodic, ear-tearing and mind-humiliating uproar extended mercilessly by the length of the train and amplified in the concrete sound chamber of the cavern: New York's special horror, that threatening uproar—often enough described as a dragon noise. While it lasted, people swayed or winced or stiffened or folded in on themselves, anemonelike, or seemed to tremble chatteringly and then reassemble themselves when the trains had gone, leaving behind echoes and squinting eyes—squinting with slow recovery from aural pain. Then those trains ceased. Meanwhile, people kept arriving, including some quite old people, one man aware of his presence as an image of strangeness in this adventure-laden and half-lit dark place, and looking alert and somehow naive and profound, and a woman, much poorer-looking and much more poorly dressed, seeming to be aware of little except the difficulties of what she was doing and the patience and fortitude and suspicion she needed to do it with.

Shaking a little from the noise and the tension of waiting, and knowing I would probably be late now for an appointment in midtown, I calmed or distracted myself by cataloging how many earringed people there were, and earringed so variously, from mere splinters of glitter, through a typesetter's store of dots, hoops, and Os, up to Ping-Pong-ball-size hoops, and up to plastic constructions the size of harmonicas (on a tall, longhaired, straight-haired woman with a heavily powdered face and no lipstick and rimless glasses and wearing a white leather hat with a blue plastic see-through visor). Then I cataloged the haircuts, the arrangements of hair: full and bushy, strict and skimpy, waves, curls, fluff, and dreadlocks, pompadours, bangs, straightforward falls, braided falls. The degrees of expense, so many degrees of expense, the signals—I wished I understood them. I couldn't think of the proper terms in which to catalog what I saw. What would the categories be—hair maniacs, proper hair maniacs, improper hair maniacs, hair ascetics, hair voluptuaries, expressive hair, dumb hair? Then I started trying to get an idea of the range of health, going by the visible degrees of health. Druggedness counted as ill health and rated as a forty on a scale of one to fifty, with fifty being in the grip of death—but no one was that skinny or damaged this day. A man in glasses, maybe late twenties, and wearing only a regular tweed jacket and a woolen shirt open at the neck and wearing no hat and no socks and only open sandals—bare toes—was a one minus, the minus for my thinking he was a fool. I soon gave up: it was too upsetting a subject, and I felt too pale and cold and too starved of light to rate myself with a number I could bear. I wondered if people's jobs had as much variety as people's styles. I decided no—that the variety arose in contradistinction to a widespread unvaryingness of economic fate, to a lack of variety in that area. I wondered what all-encompassing or archetypal platoon would be in a war movie now. What would the clichés be? Where have the old clichés gone? What if they had never existed? Would one have to rethink the past?

Then, without announcement or explanation, the wait ended; a stainless-steel train rocked and bumped and staggered into the station and bucked to a standstill and hissed, and maybe two dozen pairs of doors slid more or less apart in imperfect unison. So, the brightly lit alcoves of the cars opened to the gloomy jetty. People got off, and the crowd present got on. We moved into the brighter light of the cars and were locked in. Then we were in motion, rumbling along in the systole, diastole of track lights and darkness outside the windows. In the brighter light, I looked around and thought how sad everyone looked—but not everyone, not the teenagers, who looked mostly willful and nearly out of their minds with nervous and physical amazement at themselves. They were at sea on dry land. In this setting, the palely discursive eyes of the platform became sealed, like envelopes addressed to the proper-improper business of being on a subway among half strangers—blatantly messageless. Nothing was loose or apparent in terms of what someone thought: everyone was silent and withdrawn, potentially a witness. The differences in skin colors and national types and the incomprehensible range of variations in economic sophistication seemed even more strongly visible in this light, and more

so yet as people got on at the next station. No grouping—not even a pairing of two beggars hobbling through the car in opposite directions, both
of whom were one-legged—seemed plausible. No two people seemed sufficiently related to make a pairing likely. One of the beggars was good-
sized and fine-faced, clean and clear-eyed and long-suffering and likable,
and the other was crushed but angry and terrifying in the sorrow of all
that he had been excluded from and all that his life included. The mind
does make an envelope of itself and is purely in transit past the presence of
such sights.

The train, largely soundproof, traveled with its burden, a quietly
jouncing carload of uncategorizable fragments of the anarchic American
polity. Some clues, not unpredictable, to our social nature—the social
nature of some of us—emerged. The same people gave money to both
beggars, and the givers were mostly women and the young. Then, as the
car discharged passengers and refilled at Lincoln Center, more blanks
could be filled in, up to a point. Musicians. Music lovers. Ballet-ticket
buyers. Neighborhood people who liked opera. Foreign travelers sam-
pling our culture. Sensitive people, maybe. There were still some young
people on the train, but fewer—maybe only two of them. Then, at Fifti-
eth Street, seven adults and six children got on together, black and Hispanic, and black Hispanic; and all the adults, who were loaded down with
packages, had that quality—it's one you see sometimes—of being really
foreign to what was around them and at odds with what was foreign
to them, not with their own foreignness. I mean, if pathos can be self-
righteous, that's one brand of it. And they didn't look like good-humored
people; they weren't rich within the confines of their social whatever, or
passionate-looking, or greatly alive, or stylish in any of the New York bar-
rio or street or borough ways I knew of. They were strange-looking. Their
faces were partly backcountry faces, maybe—not happy. So the cultural
anarchy of the rest of us was not total: we were a specific group, an army
platoon, and here were some people who didn't fit in with us and made a
category of us after all.

I'm sorry to take so long, but I don't know a short way to describe
this thing. The children, all six of them, were everything their parents
were not: good-humored and rich-spirited within the confines of their
social whatever, half shy and half mannerly, at once wild and well tended:
interesting-looking and passionately childlike, American and released,

freed, without a lot of surface fear and rigidity, and at home in the day. The children had clearly entered on lives that were very unlike those of their parents. What sort of lives? What lives were being offered them? Familiar lives are what I mean the children had, I think—familiar to us. The subway, the country, the hidden American epic, the at-this-moment-in-time thing of being acculturated American children, middle-class in a way, honored travelers on the gravy train. The kids were stylishly dressed, were well dressed, were knowingly dressed—as their parents were not—and their faces showed comfort and intelligence and not a lot of foreignness, if any. I'm certain the grown-ups were their parents: the resemblances, for one thing, and the affection. And the kids had the look of being with their parents. The kids had that odd spiritual look that American kids get when they go shopping with their parents: they convert it into a kind of goodness and a matter of charity, a matter of the spirit.

I don't want to say that what happened next was a hopeful sign. I'm not sure what I think about what happened. The people in the subway car, the crowd, the anarchic and fairly random group, made an effort to clear a way for the children and the package-bearing adults. They hadn't done this for other people with kids, white or black, olive or yellow. Everyone, even the old, made way for them, I mean all the colors already present did this, and they did it with brief and simple mannerliness and with maybe American and maybe even tear-jerking sentiment. No one pompously stood up: people oozed to their feet; seats appeared. No one smiled obtrusively, but the atmosphere was formidably social, sort of here-is-something-we-like. Most of the people I could observe without craning my neck were deadpan but were sliding around making room on the seats or shifting themselves as they stood in order to make room, or merely looking on in a kind of joining-in way. The children had that faintly spoiled, slightly awed look of children being admired by a roomful, or carload, of people. The grown-ups, with their packages, seemed harassed, slightly worn, not particularly friendly or grateful or comprehending or surprised: they didn't expect this reaction; they didn't seem curious about it, either. They seemed foreign to it. Their voices were loud. Their faces, their voices, their manner emanated (I thought) a frazzled antagonism, rebelliousness, militance, a rough honesty within a foreign frame. And maybe exhaustion. Their children's bright politeness and superiority were a militance but also an early separation from their parents—a militance or unacceptance in that direction, too. The children did not, and would not, share their parents' moods. In silent agreement of a sort, hardly complete and utterly untested in terms of any strength of feeling or of serious regard, the crowd, as knowing, I think, as a crowd at a sports event, as instructed, as conversant, and as factional—here in the matter of social opinion—expressed a social opinion. The crowd in this matter of black-white or white-Hispanic interplay had its opinion ready, and it had decided that it admired these people who did not admire it except in the testimony of what the children were.

I don't want to judge the event. This time of the year, in this span of cold days, we, the most perverse of species, open in natural rebellion against the weather; we open to each other and to certain holidays. As the daylight hours shorten, we neither drowse nor flee but celebrate in widely disparate and kind of scarily separate ways. And we also join ourselves in truly strange ways on ski slopes and in shopping centers and on subways to our fellow-shelterers in the cave that the days have become. I swear to you that everyone in the car—even the madwoman down at the end—glanced around to see who was looking and who agreed and who disagreed about these people. It was the oddest, damnedest, most piercing event. For me, it was a stark or bare-bones display of what for want of a better term I'll call our onward-lurching, unsettled, old-and-new democracy in America, in New York at this time of the year, at this time in the history of the world.

1987

COMPANIONS IN
NEW YORK UNLIKELIHOOD

I f a survey should be made, it might turn out that I have one of the most envied lives in America. I work at home—freelance—in a fourteenth-floor apartment on upper Broadway, with a view the length of Manhattan, at sky level. It used to be that I could see any tall building west and south of the RCA Building; if it towered in that immense segment of the borough, I saw it. I had unobstructed views to the east and north, too. I remember the silence, and, one time, falcons—flying from their perch on top of the Waldorf-Astoria, I think—stalking pigeons in front of my windows. And the storms, the wind, and the rain. And the leaks. And the charity required when this was a declining neighborhood, and two welfare hotels were within a two-block radius. And derelicts sat in the doorways. And the girls worked Broadway in good weather and bad. And the restaurants were lousy.

Now, as the greedy world that reads real-estate pages knows, this neighborhood has become a get-rich zone for builders and owners, a magnet for magnates. We are experiencing a boom. At first, the boom was audible only to sharks, but then it became loud enough to startle the shoe-repair and dry-cleaning shops: they apparently took off, and while the dry-cleaning shops alighted again along the side streets the shoe-repair shops migrated to New Jersey or Palermo or into nostalgic memory. Meanwhile, the great splashing of money into hidden pockets has hardly been silent. The roar and boom of cement trucks, the rattle of cranes and scaffoldings, the explosions and drillings of foundations are like some immense mechanistic symphony that begins at 7:20 A.M. This has become a red-eyed, sour-mooded neighborhood. Young people, some very young, violently optimistic—active day and night—have changed the tempo of things, just as the influx of blonds in what had been a blond-shy district has changed the general color tone. The derelicts aren't gone—the homeless are unhoused and present—but some of the old ones have got dressier; one madwoman who lives on the street now wears makeup. And a group of elderly derelicts—five of them, two men and three women—have formed an alliance, and they panhandle together and talk in a way that suggests a kind of prosperity. The derelicts in general are better dressed than before: onetime expensive clothes are now self-consciously worn clownishly, as in Italian movies. And the girls who work the bridge traffic late at night and early in the morning talk differently. "Hey, you a Yuppie?" one asked a man in a Mercedes who had beckoned to her but was unwilling to smile when she got to his car window. The girls look less fierce and less drugged, more ironic and meaningful: a style. They are more talkative, less averse to stray dialogue.

Flights of mothers with collapsible-frame, silent-tired strollers block the wide sidewalks, which often narrow precipitously between new fruit stands and old gutters. The girls will address women, but they steer clear of the mothers. Some of us liberals, when we saw all the babies, like varicolored dandelions in the stone meadows, everywhere, in stores and elevators, lobbies and local parks, so many of them a Republican sort of baby, began wondering if President Reagan would try for some degree of nuclear disarmament.

A welfare hotel that once, ten years ago, bulged onto the street with endless vignettes of tragedy and violence (and brotherhood of a sort: all the better-housed kids on the block played with the welfare kids) is condos now, with a steady traffic of tennis-racquet- or attaché-case-carrying individuals in and out. Taxis and limos nuzzle like anxious piglets near the door of the place. In the video store, the pictures asked for are of a sophisticated order: *Repo Man, El Norte*. Everybody in the store is dizzily young. One said, "Hey, *Rambo* is stupid, but it's a movie-movie." I asked for the Nelson Eddy–Jeanette MacDonald *Naughty Marietta* the other week, and the kid behind the counter went right off to the dirty-movie section.

From my window in the early morning I can see white kids getting on crosstown buses for East Side schools and a flock of black kids heading for a local school. Earlier yet, I can see flocks of white-coated black hospital workers gathering on corners. Then, later in the morning, the doctors emerge from various buildings—or so I judge them to be, from their faces, the look on which I take to be medical seriousness. At any rate, their faces are graver and more open than the faces of the businessmen and lawyers, men and women, who have a look, on the whole, of imagined normality, calmly flexible: really a form of advertising, but reassuring in a way. There was a whole group of faces so oddly set in expression and style of self-presentation that I couldn't begin to guess at the profession that had given rise to such looks until my wife hazarded a new category: boutique owner. They seem younger than their contemporaries, and freer. And my wife pointed out that the faces we see on college campuses are less acquisitive than these. At a lecture at CCNY, she will look around and say, "See, there are some businesspeople on their best behavior," and there will be some stilled acquisitive faces. I tend to wonder about moneymakers. The figures that dance in their heads, I imagine, are juicy and plump with reality and zeros; and their mental anecdotes have a slot-machine melodrama of giant reward and easy loss that is missing from mine. When I think about money, it is limpingly unzeroed, just about, and it registers as a subject for anecdotes of literary pathos rather than active, world-harrowing greed.

The amount of construction going on is of some magnitude. First, let me say I did, when I was young, see corn grow, in victory gardens during the Second World War, and in actual cornfields, row upon row; so now I see the sprouting towers as immense corn plants, and the workers visible for long months as aphids—I do; I can't help it—and the whole damn city as a cornfield, hoed and manured and the rest of it. The gutters are filled with concrete dust. Construction workers sit in a row on the sidewalk in front of Charivari to have their lunch. You can tell the immediate weather from your window by seeing how the workers are dressed; they don't dress for the whole day, like office workers. The cranes, which fold up at night, open into very tall structures a little like leaning Eiffel Towers. And they move in slow comedy or parody of nature, as in monster movies. But the strangest thing to me is the way everything has risen into the air—the average life is higher up. At night, the apartment lights and the silhouetted figures on terraces and the blue windows of television watchers—at their new hearths—seem higher in the sky than is likely. It is science-fiction time, in a way: nearly the twenty-first century, fin de siècle. The highish air is full of noises, some of them clamorous, some of them domestic—it depends on the wind. In the day, here and there on the concrete and skeletal pseudocornstalks, sometimes almost at cloud height, the figures of workmen appear—a lot of them—some in bright clothes and hard hats, and some not. Different corps do different tasks. There they are, walking around in the middle of the sky—an odd population for the middle air—while the cranes hunt loads of pipes and buckets of concrete, which they lift in pretty drama and deposit with what, from a distance, appears to be fastidious, fantastic delicacy.

Outside my window, as I sit in front of a word processor—an advanced type, an end-of-the-century machine—I see, twenty yards away, workmen pinkwashing the newly laid, badly laid, badly stained, cheap-looking brick cladding of a newly built apartment house called—well, something ridiculous: Nepal, let's say. Its slogan is something like "West Side Living at the Summit." The apartment house has crooked columns and chipped concrete floors; and the way the pipes were hammered and bent into place makes me doubt their long-term usefulness. A foreman said to me, on the street, "I can't defend the way it's built." He pointed to two others and said, "They're better." He said, "This building is built without respect." The workmen wash, or pinkwash, with large brushes, long-handled; they sing, and yell at each other. Some of the yellers are good guys and some are bad guys, and I know which are which now. Sometimes I can concentrate. Sometimes I can't. In the next-to-last playoff game, when the Mets broke the tie, the men shouted. They shouted; and men inside the building, putting in flooring and ceilings, shouted. Workmen in other buildings shouted. I think boutique owners and lawyers at home for the day shouted, too. To put it in the present tense, invisible and scattered shouters, midair, we're all up here at the crème-fraîche level of the skyline, suspendees; we are, each of us, suspended in the sky, companions in New York unlikelihood.

1986

BAD STREETS

Two people were killed, one robber, one hostage. It was the morning of January 29. It began at the Chemical Bank at Broadway and Ninety-first Street and ended a short while later a few feet from Riverside Drive, in a fusillade. Police killed one of the robbers and the hostage he was holding, a woman named Aurea Bonnie Vargas; she was shot in the chest on the sidewalk in front of the building she lived in. The reactions of her neighbors are variable. "This neighborhood isn't so bad. The bank is three blocks from here. You're gonna rob something, you go to a bank—that's where the money is, a bank not a cigarette store," says a man who runs a cigarette store on Broadway. A doorman from Romania says, "It's terrible around here, worse than a war." (Neighborhood opinion has it that the doorman, though he is brave, is an alarmist.) Judy Malcom, executive director of the Catholic Big Sisters, says, "Oh, it's awful. They should have let the robber get away rather than shoot the innocent girl, the hostage. The police work so hard it's cruel to complain about them, but that's what I think." Mark Moradian, of Iranian extraction, who has lived in New York for the last seventeen years, works at Barzini's, a produce-and-grocery store catercorner to the pillaged bank, and he says, "It's bad around here lately. The liquor store next door has been robbed twice. The bingo parlor in the next block has been robbed. Ninety-second and Ninety-third are bad streets. The prostitutes hang out there. Sometimes you have trouble getting along the sidewalk; the guys standing there block you."

Moradian also says that people ran into his store to get off the street when the shooting started. He says he heard the shots; "I heard the bangs—they sounded like shots." He saw policemen approach, and saw transit policemen join them. The robbers split up. Four guys, only one gunman. Two ran toward Amsterdam and were caught. The gunman ran down Ninety-first toward Riverside Park and was killed. One eyewitness said the fourth man ran down Broadway and melted into the crowd; he had most of the money, over forty thousand dollars. One of the guys who was caught had twenty-one thousand dollars.

A man, who wants his anonymity, says that the gunman who was shot was big. "I saw him lying on the ground. He didn't have running shoes on." A man who works at the newsstand at Ninety-first and Broadway says, "I saw nuttin'." A woman says she was in the bank when the robbers entered, around ten o'clock. One vaulted the counter, which is slightly over four feet high, and began rifling the cash drawers. "He was some kinda athlete. I was scared. Nothing means anything to those people."

It seems probable that no alarm was sounded from inside the bank. The papers say a police car was flagged down; an eyewitness says the cops approached on foot. A corporate communications officer, Colleen Kelly, said, "We do not comment on bank robberies." She said no employee could talk about any aspect of the robbery.

Jay Pearsall owns Murder Ink, a bookstore in the next block that specializes in murder mysteries. He was opening his store when the robbery occurred. He heard the shots, six or eight, he says, and looked out and saw four or five people running for safety and one woman sprinting and pushing a stroller with a baby in it around the corner of his block. Then he heard more shots, from the direction of Riverside Park.

He says it wasn't on the whole as upsetting as coming to the store early one morning to open up and catching sight of what he knew at once was drying blood, a lot of it, blackish and bluish brown and stinking, spread over the sidewalk and splashed in a wide sweep across the front of his store and part of the metal gate. He learned later that some guy's throat had been cut there, accidentally or suicidally or in a murder, the police weren't sure. "No one cleaned it up and that upset me. My girlfriend and I had to scrub it off the sidewalk and the walls and the gate." Jay is from California. His father was a policeman in the Bay Area for twenty-five years. "I don't feel intimidated. That isn't it," he said. "But this stuff bothers me. I think it's getting worse."

Across from an OTB parlor and a bingo parlor, the bank is under observation all day long by men standing on the street in front of those places. Police, openly in patrol cars and perhaps working undercover in some of the stores—new faces—are staked out along Broadway all the time now. The prostitutes work the early-morning traffic at that corner. One of them said, "It's rough, man, and it's cold—that's all I got to say. You got a cigarette you don't want?"

1993

THE VIDEO VAULT

Those damn cassettes in the video store and the damn VCR and the hungry thirty-two-inch TV and the four speakers I bought to give me movie-theater sound in my own not very large apartment—the sheer bulk of my own home-entertainment center—are waiting for me. I had no idea what being *entertained* was really like. You have to know what you're seeing, did you know that? The names of the stars, the director, the supporting actors, the cameraman, the scriptwriter. You have to know the history of film and the history of each film you see—it's worse than going to the ballpark. For baseball and football, you have to know the names of the team owners and the general managers and the managers, but for film you have to know the studio heads, the major New York moneymen, and the personal quality and creative smarts of the studio's executive producers.

In what movie did Garbo wear Gable's pajamas and use a voice in a lower register than his? What movie first parodied Paul Henried's lighting two cigarettes at once—first parodied it in a genuinely funny way? What is *Casablanca* actually about? (True love means sending Ingrid Bergman away?) Is the line "Shane, come back" or just "Shane, Shane"? In two hundred words or less, indicate the differences between Capra, Sturges, Ophuls, Lubitsch, and Hawks in the making of world-famous, time-conquering comedies.

But you also have to know about now. Is Winona Ryder really good? Can Laura Dern do comedy? Is Tom Cruise a real star? Compare Scorsese with Kurosawa. Compare Scorsese with Kurosawa in the light of the movies each has made after he was forty. OK? Then, do you know how to position your television screen? Can you produce room-surround sound (is that term trademarked?), and how do you feel about panavision (should that be capitalized?) on the small screen?

OK, you come up out of the subway or you get off a bus or out of a taxi, or a car service drops you off, and you're carrying a briefcase or a book bag or an attaché case or a Sportsac—who the hell knows what you're carrying. You're weighted down, and you stop in at the video store for an hour of choosing what will divert, engross, soothe you, hold you breathless and helpless for ninety minutes or more. This reminds me: Why does advertising for entertainment always suggest bondage, captivity of mind, passivity? Can't the audience ever hold the cassette captive? The figures show, by the way, that after you have owned a VCR for three years your movie watching levels off or else falls off drastically. And we all know what happened to book reading, and to rock and roll—*live* rock and roll.

So you enter the video store and start contemplating your choice of the evening's visual and intellectual and emotional bondage: the stars, the plots, the costumes, the moods. And here is your neighbor—perhaps from your very own high-rise—mindlessly staring as well. Here are couples browsing the racks, and mothers with little kids in strollers, and adolescent kids sniffing at their future, trying to sense what's ahead for them. And you are immersed in very bright overhead light—*very* bright—and your head fills with the hyperventilated prose of the blurbs on the cassettes: all that knowingly wrought excitement, all of it proposing captivity to further excitement. If you don't make up your mind before you get there about what movie—or, at least, what sort of movie—you want to see, it can take a giant bite out of an evening to track your way through all the categories: horror films, comedies, opera and ballet, recent foreign films, classic foreign films, undubbed foreign films, and then adventure, mystery, children's, and X-rated, straight and "other."

Meanwhile, the television sets in the windows are playing, and two sets inside the store are showing movies with the sound turned very low. On the walls are offers for so many Disney movies at such-and-such a price—to silence the kids. Out on the sidewalk are little knots of people staring for a while at the movies on the sets in the windows while traffic passes feverishly behind them.

The store I'm speaking of was called the Video Vault. It has gone out of business, and its proprietors have opened separate stores—one a block away from the original, the other two blocks away. Near here, Woody Allen—in *Annie Hall*, was it?—pulled Marshall McLuhan from behind a poster in the lobby of the old New Yorker theater. Upper Broadway defines itself in terms of movie theaters. For instance, when you give someone directions you say, "A block north of the Metro Twin." Part of living in New York is keeping track of entertainment one way or another: arguing about it with a sort of New York expertise that may be slowly winding down, perhaps only for the moment, perhaps for good— arguments about whether it's better to see dance from the balcony or from the orchestra, or whether it's better to watch television in black-and-white or in color, or on a large set or a small one, and arguments over where to sit in Carnegie Hall to best hear the throb of the brass and of the violins, the squeak of piccolos.

The dreamlike hours inside the Video Vault remain vivid and weird to me. Discussions and thumbnail reviews of movies when two people were looking for a movie to rent: "Oh, that's not sexy enough." "I'm not sad enough for that one." "I can't take another faded Technicolor epic, Jack." "I'm mad for Carole Lombard. I think it's Carole Lombard—I get her mixed up with Jean Arthur." The intense cleverness of momentary moguls here, aficionados of the bondage of engrossment. The celluloid garden, maybe. For a while, the store had a number of volumes of reviews of movies on the checkout counters, along with catalogs, and people would quote the reviews and catalogs to each other.

"You know what X says about Minnelli's *Madame Bovary*? God, it's good!"

"The movie?"

"*No*, the *remark*."

On the walls, lists of movies soon to be released on video could be read mostly as lists of movies that had failed in the theaters. Movie posters on the walls were mostly for movies that hadn't come in yet—I mean as videos. This led to a little local corruption: hidden waiting lists for new releases and little bribes to get to the head of those lists.

I used to like overhearing questions from the people working there—

the staff—to customers asking for advice: "Do you like to be scared? That stuff is OK with you?" "You like dubbed or undubbed?" "You like the kind of satires with a lot of violence at the end?"

It was part of one's ordinary life, and then it was gone with the wind, sayonara. It was closed down. The windows were dark, the shelves empty. Someone from my building saw me pause in front of the dark windows of the defunct Video Vault and said, "Have you noticed how short eras are getting to be lately?" Of course, maybe he was talking about the collapse of the USSR. Or yesterday's real-estate boom.

Lately, an era of one kind or another seems to be ending daily. As I said, two smaller video stores, each of which looks like the old one, have appeared in the neighborhood. One is called Video To-Go, and the other—shades of Götterdämmerung—is called Sunset Video. The two owners, the former owners of the Vault, go up and down the sidewalk, often across the street from each other's new store, to study each other's window posters and to see what crowds are inside. I saw one of them stooping on the sidewalk at twilight and tying his shoe—it had been years since I'd seen anyone tie his shoe on the street—and watching the lights of the other store.

Once, in a fit of nostalgia, I asked a kid in the Video Vault for the now ancient M-G-M musical *Naughty Marietta*, with Nelson Eddy and Jeanette MacDonald, and he headed toward the X-rated section. This neighborhood is urban, and skewed in a lot of ways by being urban, and even if someone talks to you, you never know more than a little portion of any story. But movies pretend to have beginnings and middles and ends, and that is nice. Meanwhile, Souen, a health food restaurant, has become Mana. Charivari has closed its men's store and been replaced not by a grocery store but by a modern sort of—oh, food dealership, Broadway Farm. Broadway Farm!

1992

WHITE DUST AND
BLACK DUST

Some people were recently sitting in a room being nice to one another, here in New York, and someone said to the woman whose apartment it was that the room's dark rugs and light furniture were pretty; and she said she had discovered that now there was white dust and dark dust, and that the white dust went on dark things and the dark dust went on light things. I wanted to be clever and social and nice, and I said that when I was young, long, long ago, in Missouri, I had been told that if I had to be an artist I should be a writer, because writers were cleaner than painters were. Don't go to Europe if you can't stand dirt, I was told. Culture was less clean—dustier—than well-regulated ordinary life. Being patient with dirt was sophisticated and bohemian. My mother would say, "Picasso doesn't have to wash his hands, but you do." I said that household dirt seemed to me immediate evidence of entropy: a sad recognition. It often indicated personal tragedy, and it led to domestic melodrama when someone went after you for not picking up your clothes. And to comedy, too, of course. And to middle-class conversation, but more so in the old days, when you discussed servants, how they dealt with dirt. Men still didn't talk about it much except in relation to cars. One of the big social changes of the last forty years had been the disappearance of servants from most of the civilized world: the ebbing and dismantling of hierarchy and of the particular social distinctions that having servants led to. I could trace a lot of things to the disappearance of servants—the openness about sexuality, for instance: now you didn't have to impress the servants; you didn't have to worry about the example you set them.

The woman whose apartment it was, a grandmother, said she was old-fashioned—she still liked the word "meticulous." She said, "I don't think it's too much to aim for." Then she said, "I like people who aren't afraid to face dirt." Then she laughed, and said, "Many, many people are afraid to look dirt in the face and go after it. The ones who do are like a pianist—you praise him for his attack. I've seen people who go right down on their knees to scrape every piece of dirt off a kitchen floor."

"Scrape?" I said, surprised.

She said, "Oh, you, you're naive about dirt. Your head is in the clouds. I'll tell you: if you step on a raisin, it flattens, it hardens, it dries—it's hard to get up."

"Do you eat a lot of raisins?" I asked.

She said, "It's just an example."

One of her daughters, a woman not yet thirty, said, "No one has time for that nowadays."

"I know," her mother said. "I'm just being foolish."

I asked her daughter if dirt was a subject she tended not to think about.

She said, "I think about it as a nine-hundred-dollar washing machine I want. It dries, too."

Silence. A certain tension. She then said, "Oh, I don't mind talking about it. We're thinking of moving to the country—we want nicer dirt and less noise."

I looked blank, and her mother said, "Dust in the country is powdery gray, almost never dark." Then the mother said suddenly, "I don't know how dust is created: I don't think it is a particularly interesting subject. Well, of course, I know it's pollution—a lot of it. None of it is healthy anymore. I'm not sure there's such a thing as healthy dirt anywhere in the world, and it's hard for women, especially if they want to work, too." Then, also suddenly, she gave the following list of terms: "Dust, dirt, finger marks, grit, food particles, hair, and grease." She added, "Oily emission from diesels. Asbestos fragments. Acid particulates." Then she said, "I'm sorry."

Another daughter said, "Sand at the beach is all right. Who knows but if Chopin were alive he might write a mazurka against the tyranny of household dirt? Who knows what the music might be like?"

Another woman there, a young woman: "It's like starting over when something is clean, when it's clean at my house." And: "I think it comes from the sky, the household kind." She said, "Grease is food-oriented." She said she hated little carrot strips that stick to the floor, and she said that her name for an unpleasant degree of dirt was "nightmare." She said, "I had a nightmare last night. I got up and went to the kitchen and it was awful—sugar granules under my feet. I wanted to cry because of it." She said, "I have another word for dirt besides 'nightmare'—'revolting.' " She said, "I'm being sociable. I hate the dark topic."

Her husband, who works for a publishing company, said, "The stuff from pencil erasers is the worst thing—it's really gross. What are those things called? I suppose they're the unnamed." He said, "I feel that 'greasy' is the worst word ever invented." He said that when he was talking to himself the phrase he used instead was "really awful."

Is it always true that all subjects are intertwined? Had I been asleep and not noticing? I suppose not noticing allows you to get things done. That's called concentration. I guess everyone knows the importance of dirt ecologically and psychologically and economically and socially and militarily—the mud of Mother Russia, and the grit that grounded one of the helicopters that tried to rescue the hostages in Teheran a few years back. Women's stuff and health and class distinctions.

The man from the publishing company said, "If I were a soap manufacturer, I would call my soap Start Again. And I would advertise it this way: 'Wash your hands. Be clean and ready. For, and until, the end of time. Act Today. Big Savings. Free Trial Offer. Act Now. Do it.' "

1986

THE RETURN OF
THE NATIVE

I magine a couch reporter traveling. A flying couch, a miniature RV that allowed you to take your own life with you wherever you went, would be fine, but reality is cruel. Consider, I ask you, the postures and detailed discomfort of a tall couch potato on a medium-sized jet or even a jumbo, that flying slum. Then the return to New York after three months abroad, trying to relocate the walls of your apartment and to remember and set in place the intricate system of assertions and responses, the mental and physical aggressions, that are necessary in this city, that you don't use as a tourist passing through a place.

Each place my wife and I went to—Berlin, Venice, Rome—has its own inner systems of interlocking aggressions and violences, its famous culture of them. I became attuned to the gladiatorial spirit at Rome's Fiumicino airport and to the grim, order-giving xenophobia at Tegel, in Berlin. New York systems don't work in those towns—you get out of practice with New York systems, unless you stay in hotels that specialize in your class and nationality. Mostly, nationalities ghettoize themselves by choice when they travel. But if you've been a tourist immersed in other places for three months, the return to Manhattan, the home ghetto of choice—bitter cabdrivers, high-pressure face-lifted old ladies, mad landlords, and hard-edged homeless—it's like being dipped in hell, especially when you're jet-lagged.

The Nietzschean self-assertion of the locals is part of the mystic wonder of New York. And this begins in the overwhelmingly strange experience of using a New York airport. What do you suppose makes the
customs guards and the guides who indicate which window you go to
with your passport so sad? The aggressions of ethnic groups begin at
Kennedy. This time, a flying squad of WASP heroines pushed into the
line of people waiting for taxis and had to be chased off by a Russian
speaker in a golfing hat and Day-Glo wheelchair with a phenomenally
militant sense of justice. Earlier, Italians were taking over the best places
along the conveyor belt for luggage, elbowing you, looking at you
piteously. Or taking over vast sections of the airport for greeting, and
warmheartedly blocking all the exits from the luggage area into the daylight. And the silently angry French people in really good clothes were
cutting across your path with their luggage carts.

If your taxi driver is not aggressive, you will never get out of Kennedy
Airport, since people shamelessly block the crosswalks and ignore the
lights. No one cooperates. Kind liberals in cars who refuse to edge forward
into the shameless mass cause gridlock at the intersections.

The visual blight along the roads has behind it the great secret that a
glimpse of the incredible Manhattan skyline is coming, the towers under
a large sky, airplane-dotted, and with wheeling seabirds, and bustling
with clouds and light, including a glowing pale-yellow corona of pollution around the towers themselves.

In narrow side streets and at the lights occur traffic confrontations,
negotiations, bluster, and jockeying. Surely treeless Manhattan is the
home of the bald ego, the American national bird.

Different styles of aggression seem to be basic to gender. The virility
syndrome is different from the exoticism of the being-not-male-and-to-
be-looked-at syndrome that women labor under. New York women either
deny or exaggerate the exoticism element. Denial and exaggeration, and
male and female distrust of them, underlie much of New York's psycho-
analytic culture. But what is most striking on a return here after a long
absence is the extreme obviousness of male assertion, beginning with the
size and shape of the skyscrapers, the behavior of truck drivers, the partly
sly, half-mad swagger of some of the male homeless, and the often unconvincing humility of others.

A crisis of the virility thing is apparent everywhere in the world.
For instance, the reunification of Germany means for the more or less

unemployable men of the East a loss of their women to—let's say—capitalist practices. If the men then establish a style of violent virility, it is as comprehensible as is their fear of the rape of their women and contamination of them by foreigners, by Jews, when there are no Jews around—the term *Jew* in Austria and Germany and Italy, in France and England and Spain being taken by the right-wing movements to mean a new style of *successful* masculinity, unviolent, modern, and sophisticated and moneyed and sympathetic to women. The actual war between the old and the new specifically involves the standards for virility and relations—or, in a primitive sense, for access—to women. Italian television is lunatic about the escape of women from the old social controls.

In New York, male pretensions and female ones—women having their own exotic visual compromises and degrees of rebellion against being visual symbols—suffer particularly. It is almost impossible in New York to be rich enough for comfort in regard to your own gender. You have to be so rich—as in having your own plane or chauffeur, the lucky ones being whisked off by a retainer—that you are part of the general scene only in a small way, glancingly.

But those of us who are not that rich do not exactly return to New York. We return to a fortress segment of it, a willfully isolated, specialized part of it. And our exposure to the city's violence of spirit is determined by our style.

Drenched in momentary inadequacy and adrenaline, I arrived at my apartment house. The doorman on duty was the Hindu guy. The Guatemalan doorman of the earlier shift was just leaving, dressed in his helmet and quilted Tyvek jacket; he has a BMW motorcycle. The Romanian doorman, who has our mailbox key, wasn't there. The boiler was "half broken." Polish workmen were pounding on the roof. The Sunday *Times* when I bought it was missing the book-review and style sections, which I took as advice on what not to bother reading. The local macrobiotic restaurant was crowded with people dealing macrobiotically with the virility and exoticism factors. The wind was cold and aggressive. The lassitude, the listlessness of Manhattan, mark the era as one of waiting for a style, waiting for an economic direction to declare itself.

Anton, the Romanian doorman, is a genuinely competitive human being. He has about as much sense of social class as an elephant does. But he has an exceptionally alert sense of power, and he is very aware of menace. When I am jet-lagged, I can read my condition in how he acts—whether he is maternal or dodgy, amused or respectful.

He said when I saw him, "Well, are you ready for the madness here?"

1993

SPRING 1989

What is gone that was hardly here? Spring. And what kind of spring was it? A lousy spring, an adult spring for mature viewers, a typically nonexistent New York spring, six days of it—June 10, May 20, 19, 18, May 15, and April 23 (in reverse order)—and eighty-some days of a rotten April and an unfortunate, amnesiac May that mistook itself for September—then for March, August, and November in turn. It wasn't May-like. Grown-up attitudes, patience and forbearance aside, we had what I would call if it were offered for sale a contemptible and marked-down version of spring this year.

Our first crocus sighting this year was at the Sunflower Market, Thai Vegetables and Seeds, on Upper Broadway, in a snow flurry. Our first forsythia sighting was out our kitchen window across the blank courtyard of our apartment building, and in a neighbor's window in a rainstorm. It had the spindly look of wild forsythia, perhaps parkway-divider stuff, but where was it from? Perhaps it had been carried gamely back from somewhere on an airplane. On the plane we took to California in what was, to use a television title, *A Search for Spring,* a young girl, maybe twenty, wrestled an enormous pizza into the overhead luggage racks—a Ray's pizza from Third Avenue, a New York City version of traveler's forsythia, our spring export.

I've never thought spring was cute. But patience with a New York City spring has no happy outcome. It's dear of so serious and so financially intense a city to bother to have noticeable weather in the first place. But people here do not review or talk about the weather much if at all. They go elsewhere for the weather, as near as Connecticut, as far as the Seychelles. You can look on such traveling and the owning of surrogate houses as New Yorkers' marching resolutely to build a haphazard empire by purchase and, determined by weather, braving overcrowded and maze-like airports and hours of bad air and the screams and frets and pleas of babies and children, undeterred by untrue schedules. And food reinvented as malice and then the unspeakable movies (many of them in Day-Glo Cibachrome) and the broken earphones. Then the test of affection by crowded cars with often vomiting children on highways trembling under the weight of weekend traffic. And all this in pursuit not of profit but of the climate of their choice. The prettier parts of the world have been prosperously and domestically overrun by us—the Maine coast, Provence, the Greek islands, Aspen, Sun Valley, Bimini, and Umbria. This has influenced the rest of the world. I'm told half of France winters in the Caribbean, and a third of Israel is always in transit somewhere else. And the Germans are everywhere, from Spain to Wellfleet, and have been sighted recently shopping for house properties in Big Sur. The modern world is awhirl with the modern marvel of air travel, climate greed, and jet lag. Perhaps it is not television but the difference in travel from trains to planes that has undone the reading public's taste. Who would want to read a *good* book on a plane, one that makes life on the ground seem interesting, one that makes your homesickness for intelligence and good weather even more poignant? Who wants to mix the suspense and pleasure of reading a good book with the suspense and endurance of flying? Especially a long book you might never get to finish? We say trash soothes fear and makes air travel seem related to the rest of life and not a fiendish aberration in regard to it.

A scant five-point-two hours away, the San Francisco airport was balmy. It's a silly-looking airport, and flowers were blooming everywhere in it and around it, ornamenting and perfuming the jet lag. A van service took us to Palo Alto—"We call it Shallow Alto," an undergraduate at Stanford University, from New York, a Brearley girl, told us. The van drove past the flower-and-palm-tree-bordered approach to Stanford

University and its mud-colored Hoover Tower. Palo Alto contributes two springs a year to the gaiety of the nation (one in the fall when the rains come).

"Isn't it like being on the planet Mungo with its six moons?" we asked an anthropologist friend who lives there.

He said, "Oh, I knew when I came out here that it was good-bye to Persephone."

He and his wife travel east in spring when they can, to reenter the racial unconscious through the experience of slush.

It was very pretty in California in a raw way, and brilliantly sunlit. Everyone smiles a good deal. I saw one depressed-looking person on the streets: he was middle-aged, and walking an old terrier, and he and the dog were semi-fat. In California, any one of those three things—age, an aged pet, a pet's or one's own being fat—are recognized grounds for despair. A friend claimed to have seen a newspaper story about a murder in which one of the reasons given for the outburst of homicidal madness was "a tragic weight gain."

We went to a bar to have a drink. It was intensely dark—I mean so dark you couldn't see your drink. A pianist was playing cocktail piano and singing "New York, New York." The Brearley girl said, "So California. . . ." Indeed, you couldn't guess that sunlight had ever existed.

An hour and a half's drive north of San Francisco were small seaside parks, headlands and cliffs, covered with wild flowers, pink and white and yellow, purple, orange, and red, holding to their place in the soil and managing to remain undefoliated in sea winds so harsh that a gull riding the wind off the Pacific caught an updraft near us and rose straight up and very fast in a somewhat shocking way—not pleasantly. We saw a nearby sightseer's sunglasses blown off. The undeveloped coastline may be in part because it is an unusable coast. . . .

Loons, some already in their summer plumage, some still wintry—common loons and Arctic loons—rode in the cold water. We sighted three seals playing; they broke the surface and their muzzles shone in the sun like birds' plumage. A half-famous restaurant in Bodega Bay (a garbage spill closed the bay to swimming the next day) produced a heartbreakingly good salad out of leaves grown "hydroponically"—inland, in water tanks (hydroponically). Such greens do not have to be washed as much and they keep more of their flavor. (One of the salad greens is called Big Jim.) One California county is known for its large business in marijuana: some people argue that marijuana is America's second-largest cash crop, after corn. Articles written about it use the phrase "the hidden economy."

We saw joggers everywhere in the sun. And I spotted the largest, fattest hawk I ever saw, standing on a rock overlooking a road and staring downhill. It was an hour later before I thought that hawks in nature don't get fat. I got out the bird book and riffled through it. I had been too modest to realize I was seeing a golden eagle.

One bird book has, sensibly, ducks in the category "Ducklike Birds." In a bird sanctuary, among hundreds of birds, including a large number of very white swans, I watched for a while what may be the most sinister-looking feathered creatures I ever saw, western grebes: long black-and-white necks which they twist like malign, waterborne Odiles in a more than usually literal *Swan Lake.*

New York had the first of its six springlike days the day we returned. With wrecked circadian rhythm and stiff knees (from the plane seats), we set out on our first springtime jog late in the afternoon of the day we got back. No one in New York smiles as energetically as San Franciscans do; for one thing, it looks odd, and for another, someone here smiling with the West Coast lip spread would have leopard-spotted soot-bedraggled teeth. But it is touching how mild New York faces can be on a mild day. We ran past a girl with a mop of careful ringlets—a tall girl, probably a model; her hair went down to the middle of her back and looked like roan forsythia. It was a Sunday but she was dressed up—in New York, it's the opposite of small towns where people dress on Sundays. Here Sunday is a step down from workday dressing—or seven steps down—or a flight into madness. A corporate male in a purple velvet jumpsuit and gold jewelry of a Cecil B. DeMille sort can be said to be dressed up or dressed casually, as you choose. The model with the hair and some of the other people we— a little blurrily—jogged past had an air of gentle sadness, as if they wanted someone to save them. Metropolitan longing is febrile and wrenching. . . . Some fine-looking successful-looking people in a group had a droll look of affronted seriousness, as if they were being lured unwisely in the mild air into a truce with the rest of us. A tall man jogging toward us and young and in good condition and of the size and moving at the velocity that makes a tacitly effective claim to any route he might choose to take—who would thwart a behemoth—veered to let *us* puff past in a straight line.

In the park, on what was to be the last good day for three weeks, were all of New York's dispossessed, those without country places, working cars or reservations at the car-rental places, skaters, volleyball players, bikers, marchers, walkers, joggers, skateboarders—and babies in all the various new kinds of baby transportation, slings and buggies and collapsible doohickeys, strollers of far-fetched and of ordinary design (we saw two men running and pushing strollers, and both had sleeping babies who will have odd infantile memories surely). Everything that could be thrown into the air and caught was being thrown into the air and caught. Everything that could be ridden on, small, large, wheeled, legged—horse, or older brother or sister—was being ridden on.

Gulls at the reservoir uttered their sharp Eastern Seaboard cries. The Eastern Seaboard blue jays, milder-tempered than western jays, chattered from among the cherry blossoms. Smiling, overweight Chinese, seriously undepressed, were picnicking under the thick pink blossoms of cherry trees in bloom in a grove. We saw among the passing horses, as if to test our vocabulary, a bay, a dapple, a roan, a black mare, and a gray mare, not old, and a golden palomino gelding with a very, very long white tail and a long white mane. The riders were elaborately jodhpured and crash-helmeted and riding-cropped. Only one was in blue jeans; she had a long red ponytail and freckles and a baseball cap that said SNAKEVILLE.

It isn't that we guessed it would be the only really springlike day we would enjoy this year in New York. It was just seasonal restlessness. But we went walking, intensely looking at what spring there was, the couples, the clothes, the air, the light; the way, when you were warm from walking, the day was too cool in the shade and too warm in the light; and the way, as in perhaps no other American city, people read outdoors, good books often, serious ones, and the *Times* and the more earnest magazines. We saw a policewoman in lipstick that looked like a strong cyclamen pink. The lady cop was six feet tall and was standing in the shade, and she looked beautiful and strange.

At Lincoln Center we sat for a while on the black marble rim of the fountain and watched the brilliant-legged dancers stride into the State Theater. On Fifty-seventh Street we saw, as in a movie comedy, a runaway Sabrett's hot-dog stand. Its umbrella was open and dirty and flapping, and it came right at us on the sidewalk, barreling along and scattering pedestrians as if in a farce version of *Ben-Hur*. A high wind had sprung up, and this thing was careening along. It had a pantry part and then it had a bicycle part. The man pedaling had on his apron and the Sabrett's hat, and he looked as if he had cracked. Spring madness or too much New York. Or he'd taken something to make his hot-dog métier more prismatic, and it had badly misfired. He had a gray-looking pointed nose. I dodged and so did a young woman in a raincoat and a youngish man in a blue jacket and red pants that were tight at his ankles. The man in red pants had thin, blond hair over a large Peter Martins sort of face. The girl had long hair and tight-ankled pants and small earrings, and she laughed one of those untranslatable, charming European laughs. . . . Was it fear? Astonishment? Polite disapproval of New York's oddity? Untranslatable, as I said. But whatever it was, it was springlike.

The word *spring*, the name of the season, is essentially the same word as *jump*—or as in the compound word, *wellspring*—*welling up:* spring leaps into being. I saw it happen that way once. I had driven up to the Adirondacks for a meeting; and afterward, I drove farther into the mountains to a woods that is privately owned. A club owns it but allows people to walk through. It's primeval forest actually, never lumbered, I'm pretty sure, perhaps the only such stand in the Northeast. I think it's recuperative to walk there. The trees seem to emanate some quality of good sense that is suggested by such long-range survival. Bear tracks and bear pats make you a little nervous, which is wholly natural. The club has thrown bridges over the larger, noisier, rockier streams. Smaller streams have stones for fording, or you have to leap. At some moments, the woods are so full of walkers that it is as if an Indian confederation were passing through.

But this was April, and the woods were empty. No one was on the bridges or was visible from them. I passed two giant white trillium. The ground was patchily snowy. It was later morning. I walked too slowly to say I hiked—I walked as far as a place I know of where a stream has cut a bowl into the mountains, a natural amphitheater, perhaps a mile across, and lined with that haze of bare branches that seems to catch bits of sky and bits of shadow to make an effect of blue mist, the bare branches of seasonally bare naked deciduous trees, and the strong green serrations of intermittent firs.

The path travels in the woods and then touches a viewing point at the edge of the large cup of air. Thinly visible is a tenuous waterfall, a slender vaporous movement of trembling and tumbling threads of water with floating ghostly poufs of an accompanying white mist. It seems to fall hundreds and hundreds of feet. It also seems delicately, just fragilely able to manage to continue to fall, moment to moment, a shy, local waterfall, with its audience of trees and raccoons in a silence. (It's dramatic in autumn when the air in the bowl is full of red and yellow leaves like confetti and the walls of the bowl are butter yellow, red and bronze, and dark fir green.)

The little piece of ground I was on and its safety fence of bark-covered logs was unshaded, and I was resting and looking at the silent marvel, when all at once, and without warning, I felt the spring arrive: new, dumb air, like a blond calf, butting me. It was authoritatively unwintry air; it was air that had no feel of winter months in it.

Of course, in the mountains, weather shifts can be brief. After a while I turned and reentered the woods, and in the shade of the first trees came on a damp, sharp, cold smell, so sharp and stinging and cold that I stopped. I couldn't imagine what it was. Then I realized it was the smell of snow. There was no snow. There had been, ten, fifteen, twenty minutes before, when I got to the viewing point, but there was none now. The snow had melted perhaps only a few minutes earlier. I squatted and touched the ground. It was very cold and very wet. The last pocked spread of white had loosened itself and ebbed into the ground while my back was turned. I sniffed the brief, airborne, stinging memorial odor. Second by second it began to smell of wet earth and lost its quality of unearthly cold embedded in newly warm air.

I turned and went back to the sunlit open space of the viewing point. The silently shifting waterfall fell in quivering, new-struck light, palpably springlike and completely different from what it was a few moments before. To emphasize the newness and the precision of this moment, when temperature and climate pivoted between seasons as on a hinge, the sky was strikingly—and waitingly—empty of birds.

Then a single blue jay flew silently across the lower quadrant of the sky, and I sighed.

I don't think of lambs and darling buds and nestlings and England or the wisteria on the city walls of Rome on the Gianicolo or how girls look with blinking eyes in the restored sunlight when I think of spring. I think of that moment in the woods and that does me just fine.

1990

OCTOBER

October in school and in offices and on subway trains and at parties is one of the great months for falling in love. Have you noticed? Do you remember? Starting with when you are a kid, the infatuations and friendships and love-of-a-kind that spring gave rise to, have usually died by Labor Day.

And September was a kind of shopping and grand-reordering-of-your-life month, nostalgically and scarily so at times, especially when you're grown and working in the city and have a new job or a promotion and a new boss, but in college too, and high school, a sort of era of neutrality and enlightenment and major unease and maybe recklessness, really it's unattachment, for a month.

Unattachment and study: then your new life, this year's life, this season's life makes itself clear. You find out which teachers you like and which are monstrous, or whether your boss is reasonable or is a real crocodile, and which parent is in good shape and is more friendly to the kind of person you are, and which kids are the same size and have the same interests you have, and who among the people on your new level in the office care about Fay Vincent and corruption in sports, about the Democrats or about Republicans, and who among last year's friends don't mind your new income and which ones mind a lot or suddenly become borrowers.

Life reveals itself, reveals itself as life and not just a season. Summer dominates things with all that green and hot sun, or cool sun and mist, or rained-out weekends. Summer is relentless and relentlessly physical, sensual, and it's not just skin-deep, it's rooted.

But the first kiss of a new affair, a new infatuation in fall, is, well, almost political, or corrective. The pie graph of the self and its interests, that inner chart with its wedges of mind and property and sensuality and ambition, having restored itself bit by bit in September as the tan faded and summer clothes were replaced by stuff in fall fabrics with more body, more intrinsic formality, now makes itself into the political self.

What and who you think is "cute" or "cool" is less the question than are more sensible reasons for liking someone: propinquity, political alliance, and, very largely, a difference, a correction (you hope) of whatever turned out to be wrong or of whatever went wrong with the spring or the summer love. Or with spring or summer lovelessness.

A new sense of humor, a new body type, a new wardrobe do urge you on. Summer colors, having grown tiresome, seem, out of season, almost to have been no color; fall is the seasons of strong colors in much of America, trees and leaves, sky and clothes. Fresh winds tease the eye outdoors. Flirtatious walks have some of the serious of the ant world before winter. The grasshopper thing is rare, too reckless.

AIDS-caution and social wit add up to the return of good sense. On some levels of the active world, the employed, the successful, hardly bother with summer. When you're in your late thirties and forties, summer is partly work, entertaining and gardening and doing sports, and autumn for all its speeding up in the world is actually a slowing down, or, at least there's more time.

Strengthened and refreshed by summer, and newly freed from summer's chores, these people get a certain hazed look in the eyes sometimes or have a suddenly awakened direct stare, a sort of *you—will it be you?* kind of thing. *Will you do?*

Still-older people tend to make autumn even more firmly romantic in their own way, a firmer sense of the detonation of color and of physical ease and of excitement before winter.

Not a lot of the great loves began in autumn, not Antony and Cleopatra, not Héloïse and Abelard, not Romeo and Juliet, not Emma Hamilton and Lord Nelson, or Tatyana and Onegin, not Humbert Humbert for Lolita, or Rhett for Scarlett. Autumn loves are maybe too sensible, too functional for that. They're so political, so reboundlike, and then, too, one wants them to fit in with classes and with one's interests. Sometimes a book or a movie—*The Charterhouse of Parma,* or something maybe trashier, or some sentimental or half-comic or screwball movie, new or old—are shared and become the source of the code of what is said and done and liked by the two of you for a season.

Sometimes it's a sport, or sports, football and then ski-ing. In autumn loves, the guy often gives up watching sports if he's drawn to an "intelligent" woman who has other interests. The first drift into competition after the cool-eyed courtship, and the laughter echoes the football season and the pennant races; it's not as upsetting as it is in the summer when your paramour first shows his or her teeth, rides a better wave, or outruns you in a tennis match.

And greed—for companionship, for mutual ownership, for compliments, for nuzzling—has a pre-Thanksgiving air, a pre-harvest and then a harvest feeling: our reward, your reward.

But it's more likely to be a case of increasing irony and disillusion. The job comes first. Or you don't want to give up on your schooling. Sometimes you say things like, "Let's put it off until spring—I'm ambitious." Or, "There's more fire in the fireplace than in us." Or, "Fall, season of tweeds and winesaps—I had too much wine and we were both saps."

But just occasionally it works out. You get in step in being out of step. You hang on, almost clear-eyed, or, as if clear-eyed. Certain bits of connection continue. They catch on, they hook. It's partly a jolt, partly a matter of intelligence.

You say to a confidante, "I don't know why. I don't get it. But it's working in its own weird way."

Love, love of a kind, enough of that feeling that the days have meaning and you wake in medias res, part of a love story before winter.

One longs for something else. There ought really to be a Metropolitan Bureau of Longing to direct you to this or that attempt or to advise you to give up. But a certain class of people, or a group in each class, don't give up. The fear—of course, there's fear, fear and ordinary timidity—but the pressure to be alive and to experience what songs describe and what others have spoken of as happening to them or what is shown in steamy movies and music videos, the rhythmic recklessness and the self-divestment is irresistible.

Now I am not so eager for life to reveal itself; life reveals itself anyway.

It reveals itself as an appetite for love. The pie graph of the self and its interests, the chart with its wedges of mind and sensuality and property and ambition, bulges with this new consciousness of autumn exploration of tastes and your sexual powers of attraction now and your luck.

In October's walled sequences and its intrinsic formalism of stiffer clothes, in the carnal amethyst of New York twilight after a working day when the streets fill with employed daily travelers lost in the free hours of evening, it is mostly now the memory of appetite striking at my throat and abdomen. I remember the imagination and the actuality of the taste of lips with the faint fug of the office on them and an unfamiliar lipstick.

Was it pleasure? Was I caught up in it? The fall. Rich women in the stores are somehow like dangerous leaves, crisp and hued with smart color, and with that same quivering scutter of restlessness. Their social life, their autumn routines, their stingy husbands, have irritated them; and they eye men, checking out the neck and hands, the eyes, the clothes, with a quick eye-flick at the crotch that young women rarely do.

A flirtatious walk round and round the tie counter and then the handkerchief and wallet counter, glancing at each other at intervals, more and more admittedly amused. We're not clumsy children. We're not on fire either. Her look turns into another kind of look, another order of attention, one in the tone of fear of the serious feeding-problems-in-winter. The ant world is at work inside the topic of love.

The grasshopper thing is recklessly there as well, an ability to say no. One remembers all the false starts, all the conversations feeling out the situation. One's interest dying. One's suspicions rising faster than one's desire. One's reluctance. After all, disasters are in the streets.

But if she flirts in an ant's busy style in this season, I will engage with her for a while—why not? I am of that generation of men, old or older now, so buttoned into a kind of anti-rapism and sexual caution—toward becoming attached to someone that way—or perhaps it is always natural to be drawn by a certain fine-faced audacity.

In the old days, the very old days a hundred years ago, women died in childbirth or lost their social privileges. A trimly dressed good-looking woman who is sufficiently bold but small-voiced and who is not too sexually assured, not too insolent in her grin but who has that look of having known love, is still, like autumn itself for me, smart with death and scandal. Love, some love, a little love—and some upscale amorality—can grip the imagination. Games of command and of courtship exploration, the exploration of one's power here, one's power now, at this age, at this stage of one's life, have a distracting draw.

The other person's power—and the power of the possible story—knock against my legs. These feelings are like an ill-advised dose of cocaine, disordering but flattering one's sense of one's own ridiculous, real existence. A foolish depth of flirtation seems medically desirable, based on almost far-fetched good sense in matters of love.

What a tangle will ensue of sympathy for the inevitable catastrophes in the other's life with jealousy and longing and, often, rage—what would a Bureau of Metropolitan Longing say? The move across social classes or the mix-up of genders or the step across age barriers or the try at a platonic attachment seems too complicated to bother with.

It is not likely to work out.

At a party, in dressy clothes or sometimes in the office, a woman's arms and the little plat of flesh at the base of the neck haunt me with colored, shaded shapes, with the reality of possible touch, with the fineness of possible emotion. But it is a daydream. The reality might very well be a nightmare of drunkenness and torment. When you're in your late thirties and forties, the speeding up of the actual world has in its momentum a conviction that everyone is in some kind of trouble.

But now the game is not worth the candle, the sudden fire of interest, the special masking blankness, the daydreams and acts, the good and bad behavior. One has the humor maybe but not the actual will to attempt a piece of swagger, a bit of a strut, a mock-sullen, maybe an unironic, display of interest, of fitness, of readiness.

It can hinge, all of it, on a remark. Then another. And a stare. Then on a business of the eyes and the eyelids. The lips might produce a kinky, crazy, delicately would-be innocent smile, rehearsed and shocking or new and shocked, and some hook and eye are joined. Some initial mockery or sweetness is revealed as a surface manner. The sort of *you—will it be you?* thing in it. A *Will you do?*

The woman touches the clothed side of her own breast. The guy may lightly stroke his own thigh or knee, bending over to do it. The woman may grow very still. Or maybe she flutters a bit. Or becomes narrowly obscene in posture or puts on an insolently obscene expression of the mouth. Or he may do that.

Why not a narcissist? I want a narcissist? She/he can't be more selfish than— than the last one or the husband or the wife.

Touch is different without the air conditioner on. You discuss whether you like air conditioners or not. In New York, you use the air-conditioner fan late in the year because open windows let in too much noise and dirt. Still, sometimes you use the windows and let the gritty air blow in along with the street noises. Grit speckles the naked flesh, and buses whisperingly guffaw on the avenues. Geegaws and sexual games fit in more circumspectly when the temperature is between freeze-your-what-nots-off and hot-and-slimy. Weeping has a strange tang. The games with dirty videos—*All right, now let's try that one,* and the reply: *Oh, I can't, it's too creepy, it makes me feel creepy*—are rough equivalents of playground recess and lessons. Sometimes they are the death of everything.

Low screams, whistlings, rustlings, shouts and thumps, are the noises in a stadium brought down to one voice, to two in an immediate, not distant game. Afterward, the quick, hard talk about one's life happens alongside the bedraggled familiarity of digesting the reality of yet another body in your experience, those breasts, those untanned legs. Maybe it's office flesh. Or someone athletic and with an athlete's evasive and physical reality, a reality you've never known, perhaps.

The menu-playing. I knew a man, a pilot, who said nothing aroused as much fear in him as kissing an intelligent woman: *You never know what her mouth will do next or what is going on in that brain of hers.* Are you drawn to someone very short? A Southerner? A Russian?

Buying CDs for each other, other shared indulgences, a plane trip to Paris, a code between the two of you: the Eiffel Tower, the Arc de Triomphe, the rue des Anges.

Do you often give up watching sports on TV if you're drawn to an *intelligent* woman who is jealous and hates male habits? Do you actively invade each other's lives? That invasion is often the major sport for some people. The car phone, the beeper, add to the sport. Is it adultery in a mix of discretion and blatancy?

Everyone you work with is aware from the change of light in your face of what is going on. And of the start of open competition and struggle—the first real jealousy—your co-workers know. *Christ, I want to be let alone.*

The unspoken rules and limits and tastes of each bring on the backings off. But in some cases, neither one backs off. And you fall right through the gaudy surface into a glass landscape, black-and-white. The outer season disappears then. The temperature of your thoughts, the temper of your hopes, is the climate in which you live.

It is a world within a world, the thicket of breath, the bramble of secrets, the grove of phone calls and of moments together in cars. You can hardly breathe.

What if irony and disillusion don't set in? Something shows in your face, in the way your tie is never properly tied, in the way your hand jabs for emphasis when you talk. The pendulum aspect of an emotional tie, closer and bong and then apart and into outer coldness and then return or not, is not workable. It's tiresome. And too desirable and you're concussed by it.

You think *I'm ambitious, I guess,* and you plan to call it off, but it seems you're ambitious for this. Or you think, *Hell, there's more fire in the fireplace than there is in her.* But you know you're wrong.

Maybe you and she take on the masked stilled faces that hide the triumphant looks and hidden loyalties of a revolting couple who are *making it work:* you get in step at being out of step. You hang on, almost clear-eyed. Certain bits of connection take hold. Your days have this meaning, this point. The two of you complain about each other. She says, "This affair has a scorpio aspect." You say, "It's great but I'm an infant—I'd rather get outside and play football. I rather get tackled on the grass—know what I mean?"

Whether it collapses one-sidedly, or on both sides, or whether the thing works, you're pulled along more and more rapidly inside the falling temperature of the season.

That is, either way, failed or not, it becomes part of your memories of October.

1992

MY TIME
IN THE GARDEN

The memories of gardens, the green embodiments of the ideas that gardens carry out—ideas of happiness, toy vistas, sculpted light—are something I use to ease bad hours. I can recall happiness in a garden so strongly it fills me with a suffused delight, a blush of pleasure. The pleasures of gardens can be quite indecent and private.

My garden is my wife's garden now that I am ill. It wanders between stone walls that we built to guard a steep slope. Most of this garden is at eye level, and so it is like a living painting or series of pictures of plants but struck with active, not painted, light. One of the reasons for making such a garden is that someone my size can work in most of it without kneeling and without intruding on the plants. I have a green thumb but I am clumsy, and I have noticed that some plants when they bloom seem to have a Darwinian pride that needs space and, as it were, privacy in order to be at their best and most seductive to bees and humming birds (and even the wind) in the fat light, after the thin light of winter.

My wife is thin and adroit, and she works with a young gardener named Liza Macrae, who is as dextrous and who is also quite lovely and quite independent—it is in her posture, which is as fierce as that of any blooming plant using sunlight and sightlines and lifting its flowers to where they might be seen. She is fiercer than a plant, of course, but almost as quiet and nearly as silent. She is young. My wife is twice Liza's age but is beautiful, as beautiful as Liza, and is spindly-fierce in a similar style, but she is sadder than Liza and more overtly protective and a bit more lost in the vast spaces and corridors of fate and time, where Liza is pure defiance so far.

They are amazing creatures in the sunlight, neither ever admitting to tiredness or thirst, each one as fine-grained and as fine-nerved as the plants themselves; ruthless, quick, and deft, they dig and hoe and pluck and pinch. It seems to me they leave no footprints even in the softest soil, no footprints, no crushed leaves, no broken stalks.

Sometimes they take a break and talk to each other, one standing, one sitting, or both sitting, in their gardening hats. If they laugh, it is quiet and slightly distant, rather like the sounds the garden makes, or the sounds one imagines anemones when they conceive or roses might make, in the early summer air.

I am enraptured by the sight of women in a garden. . . .

I was always amused or struck by and fascinated with the controversies, as well as the rapture. Where I grew up, Saint Louis, there was a cultural rivalry in the 1930s between the old, rich French families and the newer English and Scotch-Irish families, and between them and the still-newer German families and the very new rich Irish-American families, who sometimes put shrines in their gardens. Women who showed you their gardens lectured on the superiority of an English rose garden to Italian or French geometry or the French use of salvia. Or they lectured you taking the other viewpoints, the superiority of French gardens, while bees buzzed and nuzzled the roses, and the wind pushed at the surrounding hedge and at the gardening hat of the lecturing woman.

In a simple hunt for pleasure—perhaps not so simple—I used to go from garden to garden, public and private, German-Italianate, English cottage-y, or rich man's topiary mostly just to look. In those days people had gardeners—or yardmen, sometimes quite a few of them. Luther Burbank and various seed companies had changed the nature of gardening, had given it a technological aspect, which did not please everyone. I remember a woman saying, "Why would anyone want a big chrysanthemum? We have dahlias." I was, you might say, a-*gape*. All the senses open in a garden, touch and sight and odors foremost, but taste and hearing too. It felt as if one heard the buzz of sunlight, a milder but more devilish sound than the buzz of bees. I chewed on grass blades, stroked petals—did you ever lick a rose petal? I ate nasturtiums long before anyone told me they were good to eat.

One of the things I noticed during the Second World War was the disappearance of the gardens. I suppose most of the gardeners were drafted or worked in war plants. I had my own victory garden of vegetables and marigolds (the stink of the marigolds was said to keep rabbits away). As I grew older and more sophisticated about the world, I saw the strange nature of American gardens, skimpier for a while than before the war, their degrees of eccentricity and freedom, wilderness and order. It was interesting how derivative they were or how original. And the extreme difference between very large, expensive gardens—separate worlds, really—inviting sexual blasphemy or laziness (if you were not the gardener) and very small, sometimes exquisite gardens in which the gaze and effort were focused, and it was clear one could not live even part-time in them but always entered them as a visitor, as someone there in passing.

I remember the house architecture and the leafy architecture of the nearby trees, and I remember seaside gardens and squinting. In a garden, I become a starer. I have tried to garden or just to help, but I like the look of weeds, and I become obsessed about the individuality of blossoms and of leaves. I become concerned with smaller and smaller sections of a garden. I understand that it is a matter of character and of limitation that I like the semi-austerity and minimalism of some American gardens and of some flower arrangements. A kind of Americanness.

I remember the first time I liked some people because of their garden. It wasn't even a real garden, but some flower beds and some flowering shrubs nicely set in front and behind a house made from an old coaching inn. This was in Massachusetts, and there was a very old tree just across what had been the coach road but was now private. The tree was richly branched and both ancient and secretive-looking and cast an immense amount of shade at the entrance to an old red barn. The house had a narrow lawn alongside the road, nothing fancy, just some nicely trimmed sun-bitten grass. Then, against the barn-red siding of the house, was an uneven, sometimes double, sometimes single, row of yellow tulips giving an effect of considerable beauty.

And in back of the house, set into a winding, rather long green plot of grass, was a terrace propped up by an old drystone wall overlooking a tiny valley. Here were flowering shrubs, white and purple lilac mostly, not very large. And alongside the house in back was a narrow bed of more tulips in a mix of colors. This bed was wider than the one in front and seemed almost sybaritic. In the distance, where the ground rose, massed conifers formed a dark, half-gloomy green wall.

Some years, above the drystone wall, a gardener put in flower beds, and there would be iris in the clear, pale air, and once, late in the summer— I think I remember this—zinnias. After three o'clock, in late spring, and through much of the summer and into the fall, this non-garden garden was actually beautiful, not pretty but beautiful. A woman and her architect husband had put it together. He was the pretentious one, but he had no taste and had given up architecture. She, of German extraction and tall and thin and bony, was the one with the money, and had the gifts of intelligence and of sensitivity to the realities of such matters as the pleasures of a not-elaborate garden. Earlier in her marriage and even in her childhood, she had lived among massive, show gardens, and she had decided that being impressed was boring in comparison to the fluctuations and gradations of pleasure in privacy among plants, each of which had life and color and eccentricity and each of which could be known individually.

Everything connected to the house that was outside it was beautiful in the way it took the New England light, which is a hard light, hard to work with, too. The front of the house and the back garden or yard were beautiful in their austere, even faintly comic, projection of what the Garden of Eden had come to in Protestant America. Or in their projection of what she had come to in terms of her sense of color and time. A plain woman and not charming, not even very impressive, but still a person with some quality, she looked gaunt indoors and, literally, became beautiful in a doorway stepping outside.

What she had done with her house outside was beautiful also because it dramatized or embodied, with rare subtlety, the stoniness of the soil and the importance of light and shade and the promise of straitlaced sweetness and ease and, to be vulgar, because of the shy, faintly angry way it indicated the presence of a lot of money, quite a lot of money, but also said to hell with the money. The simplicity was neither mathematical nor chic but was that of a limited personality creating beauty with an underlying acerbity or harshness, a harsh-ity, a tiredly self-protective, and a somewhat snobbish element, dignified-droll. It was a way of putting you onstage, of dramatizing what you added to or subtracted from the day, from the lobster lunch on the back lawn, or from drinking and getting sozzled. She said when she was dying that she had been destroyed by boredom. It really had been a setting for herself, something that amused her, at least a little.

After she died, her husband screwed it all up. It became all self-assertion, all ego and efficiency, not a stage, not an extraordinarily real, if fragile, capturing of light and color and intimacy and intimation, but merely a place, a rich man's place. I guess he felt he'd been kept prisoner here as she had. I suppose they imprisoned each other. The disappearance of beauty marked their escape.

The idea of a garden as a major part of a marriage in which the partners kept each other prisoner, the idea of an erotic prison (not necessarily full-time) returned in the gardens, at Sissinghurst, of Harold Nicolson and Vita Sackville-West. I think English gardens are wonderful but I find them pushy, anti-nature without admitting it, all those hypocritical masses of blossoms, compared to the perhaps wild discipline of French and Italian gardens.

I felt at home at once, soothed and peaceful, in the vast flair of gardens at Versailles, decrepit at the time I first went there in 1949, when I was nineteen. These are old gardens, centuries old, but visually still powerful. I fell asleep on the grass in front of the Grand Trianon, overlooking the canal. This was near some pink and white rose bushes, beautifully tended, individually, although it was clear the palace gardens were tended for not much money. There were gaps among the roses, and some of them, although trimmed and weeded, looked underfed. It hardly seemed a royal garden but was like the one in Massachusetts, more a we-do-what-we-can garden than anything one associates with Versailles.

The Grande Trianon itself is a one-story building, not large, made of a largely pinkish-red, scarletish-salmon-colored marble—really quite splendid, rich, richly flesh-colored, streaked marble—with some temporary repairs visible here and there, a cracked column, a cracked pavement in the small, open arcade. It was splendidly sensual and abandoned and clearly too much work. I am being inhibited. The marble is a clitoral or vaginal or inside-the-mouth or rouged-nipple and pale-white-thigh pink and white. The building is far off to one side of Versailles, on landfill, I think, and it kind of reeks of privacy and what-to-call-it? Naughtiness? Was it Malmaison that was famous for its roses? This Trianon escapes being laughably pornographic by the extreme elegance and restraint of the architecture and of the workmanship: the control is so tight that one cannot help thinking of the other, of uncontrol. It is an *elegant* discipline that is imposed.

Here there was the canal below the fairly high knoll (as I remember it); the slope had dandelions here and there. It and the canal looked run-down but still splendid and sunstruck, giving off the strangest sense of restless geometry, all straight lines and artifice, then the track of the breeze and the vibrations of the water, the beyond-geometry of the natural, a sense of nature and of the underpinnings of life *peeking* through.

But it was less cute than that. Then there were the birds, who seemed to know this was a pleasure ground, and who, as I lay on the grass, came hopping and peering near. Bees, of course, and for a long hour or two no other tourists. My God, how I wanted to be a king but one without a court and with not much money left. Of course, the Petite Trianon had been built to give some privacy, some human sense, and had not been meant as an extravagance. It must always have been partly a place of ruin-hinted-at and a place where one was refreshed but not in an idealistic way.

I spent three days at Versailles sleeping in a fleabag in town and returning to the almost unvisited palace merely to look at the various alternations of the natural and of the willed—well, the natural was willed. I soaked in the sights of the splendors of contrariety, or, if you like, of contraries opposed and linked: stone statues and untended, and often too-large trees and fountains (just a few working, but you could imagine the others). It was sky, earth, air (the immediate, odorous air of the garden), and water, and instead of fire, a few flowers. There were beds of salvia that seemed a bit last minute. The parterres were clipped and trim although in places bits of the low hedge were missing. It did seem like an erotic pen or prison.

But still more ruinous to my peaceful socialism was an extremely eccentric garden, four centuries old, actually a series of gardens forming one garden at the Villa Lante at Bagnaia, a small town set high in the mountains northwest of Rome.

Bagnaia is walled, dirty, cramped, and old, or was back then. And it was a very little town. Across the road from the town walls are the out-buildings and stables (I think) of the villa. I said these gardens were eccentric but they are also eclectic. Between and behind two more or less identical, inhabitable summer pavilions, painted and decorated, and with open arcades in front, is a variation of a Moorish water garden.

A lot of roses are spread aromatically on either side of a handsome, shallow watercourse, elaborately designed and rather steep. The pavilions are not overwhelming, but they are appealing. The joke has held up over the years, of one place for the in-laws or the grandchildren or the women and another for the men. At least I presume that is the point of matching *palazzetti*—heavy flirtation and control exerted over it all. The pavilions are the work of the architect Vignola.

In front of the pavilions is a small square formal garden, much more geometric and simple than any garden I had ever seen before, much more local in relation to the land and sky, much more overtly a garden, an act of will, than the parterres at Versailles. On reddish dirt, small hedges, six or eight inches tall, make patterns and curl and—you know—do those things such hedges do: round things and curving things. The dirt is tinted, I think. Then in the center, taking up what seems to be a third or more of the garden, is a very large four-part fountain with a white marble basin under another, smaller, basin, with water passing from basin to basin, and then on top, more-than-lifesize bronze male nudes by Giambologna holding up a thing with outstretched arms that spouts water over them and is, I guess, the emblem of the Lantes. The nudes are pressed against one another, and water runs over the bronze, and, well, the nudes are androgynous as well as wet, and the mass of them is, I would say, phallic, although if you are shy, you won't notice that for quite a while. And then you have the sounds of the water. It is pornographic and it is self-delighting but geometry wins: in spite of the movement of the water and the nudity of the figures, the suggestiveness is brought to stillness itself, is dreamed inside the four-centuries-old joke and the surviving beauty. The mind of the visitor to the garden, the mind and the nerve endings are not teased or drugged, but are set free—I suppose as in twenty generations of marriages and of flirtations.

The garden itself reflects this freedom although in an odd way. One side of the formal square around the fountain is an open balustrade, and past it and down some steps is a large lawn, somewhat like the New England one I mentioned, and then some deciduous woods begin, set a little lower on the slope and with a carriage path wandering through them. But the dominant element is a view, a blue-and-purple vista of distance, descending through mountains toward Rome with a double suggestion of freedom, as of conceited birds in this high, pretty nest, with recourse to one of the great cities of the world.

These woods, which used to be trimmed and raked and kept as an English park, were more tangle than parklike when I was there. They were messy and needed thinning and were intimate. And ordinary. The scale is small. But in them is the single most beautiful "garden" thing I have ever seen. As I said, this part of the gardens hadn't been kept up. They were not an Eden but offered a sense of profusion and of shade with a sense of difference from any other Italian landscape, and, then, because of the staggering, interlocking complexities of branches and tree trunks, they had an almost fairy-tale quality of grotesque crowdedness of vegetable incident, of biological life.

But at a certain point, near the carriage road, among the leaves and branches, among the profusions and tangles of leaves, is a broad-rimmed, square pool with oversized obelisks at each of the four corners. These obelisks are set on the rim of the pool in the deep shade. The sight, beautiful and unexpected, comic and amusing and sad and *reflective*, is startling at first sight: imagine finding such a construction in the woods.

If you sit on the rim, you see in the unmoving surface of the water the wild crisscrossing of branches reduced to two dimensions, and the woods-torn light reduced to a greenish bluish gray that sparkles dimly if the wind blows. Perhaps I make it too idea-ridden, the curious mixture of order and of disorder, of disorder reduced to a portrait-in-water; and it is so quiet in the woods; and the classical elements of the pool are so intrusive and unwoodslike and yet so *human* that it is like an idea, an image in a dream, but it is real and physical, the pleasure and geometry, the mockery, the assertion, the modesty. It has become an image in my dreams.

I had intended to describe my wife's garden but my neighbors in the country have made me too unhappy. Some of them are not behaving well—being right-wing and crypto-genteel and prejudiced and unethical and self-righteously greedy—and I will write about it at some point. For now, I would like to refer to those neighbors as examples of the unkind grotesque, trolls in the garden, and end with the memory of the pool in the woods at Bagnaia and of the complex and wonderful mood it evoked.

1995

LIFE,
LOVE, AND
SEX

FAMILY

I have one grandchild. The population explosion in my case has come down to one firecracker kid. But on a recent visit my only child's only child put her arm around my neck and asked me if I knew how many grandparents she had. I, of course, said she had four. Her proud correction was that she had fifteen.

Fifteen?

Her mother and father are not married to each other but are to other people, so that the basic parent count at the moment is four, which, since each of the four has two living parents, means an active grandparent population of eight. Active? Of those eight grandparents, two couples have divorced and each has remarried, adding four grandparents, making twelve—eight steppies and the primary quartet. Everybody's doin' it, so to speak. Then we have the child's then one surviving great-grandparent—a great-grandfather (my ex-father-in-law)—and his second wife: the thirteenth and the fourteenth. My grandchild's stepmother's mother has a sister she regards "as a twin," and my granddaughter seriously includes that step-great-aunt and will not put her in a lesser category. Fifteen.

Naturally, such a group is necessarily in flux: the child's great-grandfather died not long after she told me her grandparent count; but I have since heard that two in the child's line may be getting a divorce and marrying again, adding four and losing none, since the child surrenders no one and so far no one has surrendered her.

My granddaughter's family awes me—*Look at all the people.* Her family is a family in a wholly other dimension from anything I know. If I set up in my mind a genealogical chart on which a single horizontal line holds all fifteen grandparents, with the relatives by blood printed in red and the ones by marital increment in purple—well, how can I squeeze in all the *connections*, all the operative lines (lines?—wheels, spheres, starbursts) of family, the flung and whirling chains of family? It would require dozens of sheets of paper and elaborate cross-references and specially allocated colors for such details as particularly close exes and closely attached and affectionate steps, and it would need new kinds of signification for cousins by marriage when two or more marriages are concerned: A present wife's ex-husband's first cousin is what to you? And to your granddaughter? Such connections may mean more than silent blood does. And the charts should indicate this as well as what *type* of families are involved, Thanksgiving and High Holy Day get-together clans or close-knit or summer-property-sharing tribes or we-see-each-other-only-at-weddings-and-funerals units. The child's sprawling and far-flung and far-fetched family tree has in its branches such treasures as my present wife's first husband's mother's famous rabbinical father, a quite mystical rabbi. I have a lot of mystical rabbis through my real mother. (I am adopted.) Well, then, I can imagine my granddaughter, Elena—named after my present wife, Ellen (one of the steppies)—saying to her stepcousin, if that is the term for my stepgrandson (whose name is James Harper Willis), "My great-grandfather on my maternal grandfather's side was more mystical than your great-great-grandfather on your maternal grandfather's side." I don't think it will be in those words. Who knows in what sort of slang that social caste will be talking in five years? What social caste? My stepgrandson is through his father—my stepson-in-law—a descendant (father's father's mother's father) of Zachary Taylor, the twelfth president, one of whose daughters married Jefferson Davis, president of the Confederacy. And my granddaughter, through her stepmother's stepfather's father's second wife (I'd better check this: she might be the only wife, but I think she's a step; at any rate she wasn't on Elena's list of fifteen), may be descended from John Tyler, the tenth president, who became president on the death of William Henry Harrison, Old Tippecanoe (Zachary Taylor was Old Rough and Ready), and who was married twice, to a Letitia Christian and a Julia Gardiner. (This step-great-grandmother's maiden name was Tyler, and the young people in the family who mentioned the tie had heard that the Tyler connection was to someone famous. She herself says that she is an eleventh-generation descendant of Oliver Cromwell, through, the legend is, at least one illegitimate connection, which is what one expects in a Puritan line.) I suppose many modern families have such ties to various American presidents and vice presidents, but how many children have such ties to two presidents, maybe, one of whom was also a vice president and was disowned by both political parties? Since there is no money and no blood inheritance in common between the two children, maybe it shouldn't be called *family*—maybe it is a *joke*—but what if the children become close, and what if the joke becomes central to this new clan, or whatever it is if it is not a family: their ties to the history of the country through the presidency and vice presidency and presidency again of the United States?

But with such numbers of relations, such ties are inevitable; nearly everyone in the United States perhaps has such ties now if they look. Perhaps our money society is dying in certain ways, breaking down here and there, scatteredly, in just these ways: breaking down in matters of caste.

What *is* the social caste of a stepgrandmama who was a nightclub singer and of one who was a schoolteacher and of one who was an ex-softball semipro as well as an ex-rich woman and a novelist? Or of a grandmama of the blood who did public relations for Cartier—she hated having among her duties to wear, on occasion, a very great deal of good jewelry to lunch, in the line of getting publicity for the store—and who in the course of a contemporary grandmama's career acted on Broadway in a modern version of *Hamlet* set in southern California and written by Elmer Rice (it was called *Cue for Passion*: a smart-aleck remark was "It's about pool in LA")? She furthermore was the editor of a magazine called *New Ingénue*—surely one of the worst imaginable names for a magazine—and she was a vice president of a cosmetics house; and in the early 1950s, when she was pregnant with the mother of the child under discussion, she did commercials for a baking company in Tucson, Arizona, and was photographed sitting behind a table, holding a bag of cookies. She was known then as Miss Purity Biscuit. *What is her social caste?*

One problem here is that society—as a whole, and *society* society, or whatever the term should be—and what money means and what sums are involved and what is thought of as social position change so much and so often and so thoroughly in this nation of change that giving family names and jobs and listing marriages and describing summer houses and ascribing colleges won't tell my granddaughter or anyone in my granddaughter's generation much about what the families' social castes *were*.

After all, what social climbers and society bystanders and readers and social leaders now alive remember the social rank of the old *New York Tribune*? And its circulation? Its editorial clout? Or the plays and status of Elmer Rice? The *Tribune* (later the *Herald Tribune*) was my granddaughter Elena's great-great-grandfather Brown's paper: he was its managing editor and a force in the old Republican Party in the days when the most spiritually presentable, articulate Republican figure was the soul of the Industrial Age, post–Civil War WASP Ascendancy. The Union League Club was originally a bunch of antislavery radicals; he was one of them. That was Gaffer Brown's club, and he was also in the Century Club when it was raffish; but as the Gaffer's son, Larry Brown, said to me, "Unless you're trying to get into a country club, who *cares*?"

On the Democratic Party side, the onetime father-in-law of a brother-in-law of one of my first cousins was Henry Morgenthau, who was in Roosevelt's Cabinet during the Second World War, when I was old enough to notice. How many other people remember Henry Morgenthau? Is a connection to Henry Morgenthau a social haymaker or is it a dud now?

I suppose it depends on whom you are talking to. I have another cousin, an investment-fund manager, whose fund management was the best in the country for a year not too long ago. He told me that, or maybe he said "second-best," I don't remember. His name, for a year, had a strenuous effect on people on Wall Street: "*You're related to him!* What is he recommending? Nursing homes? Toy stores?" He once told me his first wife was a Hemingway, a granddaughter or a grandniece: I forget which. Sometimes he says Ernest Hemingway was the best man at his first wedding. Sometimes he says it's not something he wants to talk about. His sister is married to a man who owns a newspaper and whose mother gave money for a poetry prize; so they remain a good connection. These cousins are first cousins to me by adoption but by blood are third cousins (but they're not sure that's true). Are my granddaughter and I then related to Hemingway? Is this a valid concern?

Nor do my granddaughter's female ancestors' professions, college backgrounds, marriages, and charities describe the quality of the women, which is, or was, obvious enough in life. You can't mark on a chart *beauti-*

ful, or *grotesque*, *bad-tempered*, or *wonderful to know*, *brilliant talker*, or *famously snobbish*, or *awfully nice all in all*. And some of the connections that affect me won't affect her but are odder than you might think; for instance, the resemblance between my first mother and my first wife and my first nursemaid. One line of that nursemaid's family and one line of my first wife's mother's family came from what is described in the family's talk as *a small village near Stuttgart*. It might be the same village. Most of my real mother's relatives died in the war or in the camps. My ex-mother-in-law said she didn't want to know about her German ancestry, the collateral lines; she was snobbish toward her background. She wanted to be a WASP (by WASP I mean specifically Anglo-Saxon); she was anti-Semitic, but she was anti-Nazi, including Nazis related to her.

Her sister, my first wife's aunt—Elena's great-great-aunt—was a former (1930s) member of the Communist Party and married, first, the quite good Japanese-American painter Yasuo Kuniyoshi, one of whose self-portraits, this one in golf knickers, is reproduced in blurred yellow and black as half of a diptych by David Salle shown recently at the Whitney. This great-great-aunt said that Kuniyoshi was a descendant of a line of Japanese painters and that Kuniyoshi's pictures then, thirty-five years ago, were more valuable in Japan than here. One book says Kuniyoshi was the son of a dried-chestnut and cereals dealer who was later reduced to pulling a cart. He was highly regarded in the 1920s and 1930s. That great-great-aunt also said he was insufferably conceited and lonely. That aunt married a man named Shubert, an ex–labor lawyer, who became one of the founding figures of the Sheraton Hotel chain. I don't know how Elena will feel but I can't see a Sheraton Hotel sign without remembering Irvine. He had a cousin who was a critic for the *Times*, a man named Taubman, and that cousin's son is now a reporter on the *Times*. Elena's great-great-aunt was a painter, not one whose work I like, but she had a very interesting collection of paintings by her contemporaries (Marsh, Demuth, Stuart Davis, Pascin, Peggy Bacon, Julian Levi), some of which are now in the Whitney. I remember another self-portrait of Kuniyoshi in a golf outfit, but maybe it was a seated woman and a bowl of stuff on a table. We used to change my daughter's diapers on a couch under it.

So far as I know, that woman, Katherine Schmidt, is the only woman who was a painter in any of the family lines. She said she had much less of a chance to be recognized as an important painter because she was a woman. When I knew her she painted only pictures of crumpled paper bags. She also had a collection of the bloodier Audubons (ones with snakes menacing nests, ones with slain rabbits borne aloft by hawks or eagles); she explained that those were cheaper and "just as good as the sweet birdie ones."

The number of houses that have been in the family, and the number of apartments—that, too, is a difficult topic. The house I was born in still stands, in Staunton, Illinois (a small town: pop. four thousand and some)—a wooden house with wooden awnings over two second-floor windows. The house doesn't really have a second floor: the windows and their wooden awnings are small-town jeu d'esprit, or fake. That house is abandoned, or was the last time I saw it, three years ago, when I was doing a piece for the *Times* on the current state of small towns in Massachusetts and the farm belt. The piece was never finished. The house and the land were being used to store old Pabst beer trucks and discarded bar signs—the large kind that used to hang outside over the front doors of bars in the countryside: signs eight or nine inches thick, with red, white, and blue translucent glass with a lot of lightbulbs inside. Lit, they were visible at great distances in the flat landscape in the dark, a vivid element in night scenes in Illinois and Missouri in my youth. It was those signs that were stacked in what had been the living room. My daughter was born in the town of La Plata, Maryland, not far from Washington, where her maternal grandparents kept a country place, three hundred acres, and grew tobacco, and were weekend and summer gentry. Her first home was a 1717 house with large rooms, one of them dating from 1670, *maybe;* it was a funny-looking house, wooden and crooked on its knoll. My granddaughter was born in New Jersey; her mother was living in Frenchtown, which is on the Delaware River. My granddaughter's father was born in London; his parents lived in a semidetached house there. Her stepfather was born someplace in Wisconsin—maybe Oshkosh; I don't know in what sort of house he first lived as an infant. The child's great-great-grandmother and grandfather lived in the block of houses next to Saint Mark's In-the-Bouwerie, the block with a common garden hidden from the street; and then, when that neighborhood began to go bad, in a house on Hicks Street, in Brooklyn Heights—those buildings still stand, and I occasionally see them. Her great-grandfather, Larry Brown, dreamed of going to Annapolis—hence the place he later bought in Maryland: he was a gentleman farmer with a place not far from Annapolis, and he did some sailing on the Chesapeake. Larry said his bedroom on Hicks Street had a view of New York Harbor, and he looked at the ships every morning and every evening, when he woke and when he went to bed. In those days the boat and ship and ferry traffic in New York Harbor was immense, liners and tugs and coastal shipping and river vessels from the Hudson Valley. He said that in fog and drought the boats moved like blind men. He said that his family had insisted he go to Harvard, and he had, and then he'd led mostly a land-locked life, except he did buy a sixty-foot Nova Scotian fishing schooner when he was fifty, which he painted black and named the *Falcon* and sailed, as I said, on the Chesapeake, although not very far or very much or without mishap. But it looked very impressive, full-rigged, among all the powerboats and the sailing dinghies.

I lived as a child in a house in Alton, Illinois, which had a view of the Mississippi at a point where the river used to be sort of a mile wide (except in flood, when it covered the whole world), and I watched the boat and barge traffic when I was little. I wanted to be a river pilot before reading Mark Twain on the subject. I'm afraid that on first seeing the Bosporus I said, "It looks like the Mississippi." Some houses have been built blocking that childhood view, and that old house's lawn has been remodeled, straightened, like a nose. I suppose it's not like having a family that comes from one place. The child will probably not want to see all or most or perhaps any of the family's houses.

And family stories, biographies, photographs—the child might drown if she ever starts being interested in them. The terms will seem so strange to her: There is the great-great-aunt in my line who married a man because he tangoed well and "he had wavy hair that never got mussed, so I thought he wasn't vain, but it was just that his hair stayed combed." There is the great-grandfather who killed a Ku Klux Klansman, "shot his face off," when the guy came with a mob—a small mob; it was a small town—to hang a black man the great-grandfather had taken under his protection: he and the black man were ex-boxers, ring mates. Does this count as a murder in the family? There is the story of her mother's great-grandmother's brother who sold a recipe for making yeast to a man named Fleischmann. And the one who sold land on Thirty-fourth Street to a pig farmer, who unloaded it later to a fool who knew nothing about farming, named R. H. Macy. The cousin who is a fund manager tells how among the fortunes he didn't make is one when he sold his Xerox stock in 1959. (His voice changes pitch noticeably when he speaks of this.) And so on.

The child's present step-great-grandmother's first husband: among his businesses was the ownership of a swimming club in Philadelphia that had a pool several hundred yards by several hundred yards—a square lake with two islands in it. That woman was my granddaughter's real great-grandmother's—my ex-mother-in-law's—best friend: perhaps her only friend. I knew briefly one of my grandchild's great-great-grandmothers—that is to say, the mother of the mother of the mother of the mother of the child: I presume this is the line of descent that will interest the child most. So my ex-mother-in-law's mother is the farthest back in that line that I can go. Her name became my daughter's middle name, Emily. The primordial Emily grew up in Xenia, Ohio, and lived there until she came to New York with her husband to "have a good time": family legend. They must have been pretty sure of their looks and manners, their ability to joke, dance, entertain, and drink—their big-city merits. This was around the turn of the century. "They had been bored in Xenia and they wanted to meet Mrs. Astor." The family historians, over drinks, talked in this way that I am imitating. That great-great-grandfather was a partner in Consolidated Laundries until he was forced out, his son-in-law told me. A few years back, a building for the laundries still stood on the East Side, not far from the river. Their name was Schmidt—German for Smith. My granddaughter's mother's mother's mother, Anne, a very good-looking ex-Barnard girl turned modern dancer—comic dancer, a satirist—was described by nearly everyone as "difficult." ("Anne was difficult, you know," John O'Hara, the novelist, said to my first literary agent, who quoted him to me. "Edna St. Vincent Millay was the queen of the Village, and Nancy Hale was the wild card—she danced on tables at parties and was much admired—but the best-looking of them all was Annie Schmidt. But she was difficult. . . .")

My ex-father-in-law, my granddaughter's great-grandfather, and his sister-in-law Katherine, Elena's great-great-aunt, were the chief family historians for me. He believed style—real style, social American style—consisted of scaring you by how honest he could be; he said that that was "ruling class" style (Katherine when she did it said that it was a woman's clear-eyed realism plus her socialist realism). He said to me, "Annie's not

difficult. She's on the cold side, and she's dumb." He stayed married to
her; he said he found her too attractive to leave; she was a lousy cook and
when company came he did the cooking. Annie's mother, the primary
Emily, said to me that her daughter was "cold" and "not very smart." She
seemed amused. (She said her other daughter, Katherine, was a "red spi-
der.") She and the others warned me because they didn't want me to be
upset by her or her talking to herself or to her dogs and birds or by her
anti-Semitism and her politics. When drunk, after a few beers—she drank
beer—she would say, "Robert A. Taft is a great man, and a country that
doesn't appreciate him is on the road to hell." She always partly meant to
be funny. Taft was the leading conservative figure back then, before Barry
Goldwater, and he was from Ohio, as she was.

Annie's husband, Larry, was the only man *I* knew who talked about family
and was truly interested in it, except for one rather heavy boy I'd met at
Harvard, who had a dead great-uncle who had founded the American
Field Service and had known Isabella Gardner and Henry James. (He had
also known a man named Sleeper, who fell in love, my friend said, with
Tom Mix and gave him rubies. The same boy's grandmother told me that
T. S. Eliot, when he was twelve years old, spied on her and her husband-
to-be "when we were sparking. . . . In that family, we always thought his
sister Ada was the one with the talent.") These were people who had summer houses in places where the police kept the public from the beaches.
Larry was fearless and amiably, drunkenly mean about family. My pudgy
college friend boasted in a kind of high-flown way: "Mrs. Jack Gardner,
do you know what that means, *she was the most interesting woman of her time*!"
"Yeah? Prove it." I saw Annie a few times thirty years ago with her best
friend, who was to be her successor, a younger woman, a *nice* woman,
blond—Annie said of her, "She hasn't done anything interesting so she
hangs around me. . . . She's a social inferior but she is as sweet as the day is
long." With a straight face she called her "a social inferior."

Annie embarrassed everybody all the time. She was a terrific athlete
and remained good-looking up to her death, in her early seventies. She
used to say all the women in her family died in their early seventies. My
ex-wife said of her mother, "Well, she died on schedule: seventy-two."
Larry said all of Annie's family was good-looking, "but after seventy no

one's good-looking, so those women die." She looked good going off the diving board in her fifties, I will say. People were afraid to get into a conversation with her because she was so loony and made them feel so loony. She asked me on our way to the swimming club if she could introduce me without using my last name. "A lot of people are unhappy about Jews," she said, "and I want to be polite." "Are you going to make up a name for me?" No, she was just going to say, "And this is Harold," which she did, and I would murmur, "Harold Brodkey: a Jewish name." And she would say in front of these other people, "You don't have to do that!" I would say, "Yes, I do." No one seemed all that upset by the byplay, but I don't really know.

I said to my first wife, Annie's daughter, that I didn't think Annie and I had ever exchanged a single glance of human warmth or joint affection or even a look of mutual amusement. My first wife said, "She's like that; I never exchanged a glance like that with her, either." Larry said, "I warned you she was a cold woman." She was a great shock to me—an ex-comic (and romantic) performer with no humor and no sentiment. She and her sister, Katherine, the one who had been married to Kuniyoshi, used to fight over who had ruined whose clothes that the other borrowed when they were both adolescents, about the time of the First World War. They did this every Christmas when they got drunk. Larry and my then wife said that was a form of sarcastic family warmth. Everyone always said that Annie really had feelings even if you never saw them. Katherine said, "I never saw her show a minute's warmth, ever." Larry said, "But it's nice when she's happy." When she was amused or pleased, she did send off rays of light. But if she looked you in the eyes her eyes were still blank. Larry said of her, "I don't think anyone ever *liked* Annie."

But a number of people loved her. He said he did. Diana Trilling, in a conversation about beautiful women, said as the last word on the subject that the most genuinely beautiful woman she ever saw was someone she saw at summer camp when she was practically a child, a young woman who came to visit the counselors, a woman who became a comic dancer and then married *very socially*—some such phrasing as that—and I said, "I think that was my ex-mother-in-law. What was her name?" It was Annie, of course. Her daughter said that Annie's snobby mother-in-law—this would be one of Elena's grandmother's grandmothers, Gran-gran Brown—had said to Annie at dinner in front of the family (but family dinners in the summer house in Maine were twenty-five or thirty people) that if she couldn't talk sense she shouldn't try to talk to sensible people, and that Annie had cried then; but that, otherwise, her mother was impervious to any sorrow other than irritation and never cried in her daughter's lifetime, not once, only that time in Maine.

Annie's successor, that surviving nobody who is a quite marvelous somebody, has her own family line; and there is the one she married into the first time she married, all those ancestors and children. Those lines, added on to Annie's various lines, through Xenia and back to Stuttgart and on from there in the collateral lines, are not publicized as family lines but *are* family lines and must include several thousand people, all of them in my granddaughter's family trees, or family forest. Annie's successor's children from her first marriage have married and have children: those families, acquired by marriage—if they are added in, don't the lines of connection become continentally immense?

Larry told me that the woman who made Annie cry, his mother, was a greater snob than Annie, "in the days when being a snob in the U.S. meant something: we were on our way to having a class of gentleman." I imagine her a dowager. Larry said she was better born and was much, much richer than Annie, and "a determined woman," one who got away with looking down at the Rockefellers as nouveau-riche Baptists until the 1920s, when she had to give in: "The Rockefellers mattered to more people than she did—she cut her losses." She had five surviving children and two who died (the first, a boy, at age two; the seventh, a girl, at age seventeen): "Three of us married well, I married for fun. The fifth married a renegade Amishman." The Amishman, if, indeed, that is what he was, was shy and somewhat shame-faced and likable. Larry's brother married a woman I liked whose father ran a steel company: Allegheny Ludlum. I wasn't paying attention when Larry talked about the others. I liked the name Allegheny Ludlum and the phrase *steel company*.

Larry said that because of his upbringing under his rigid, ambitious, social mother he had never been able to be truly happy a day in his life, and his daughter—my first wife—said she had never enjoyed a moment with Gran-gran, her grandmother on Larry's side. She'd loved her maternal grandmother, Annie and Katherine's mother.

According to Larry-late-at-night—the two of us—the dowager had complained that her granddaughter's affections had been stolen by someone negligible and sentimental and middle-class. "We're not a good-looking family, and I married Annie to bring looks into the family! So, of course, we had the *only* attractive grandchild, and they fought over her." This is close to what he actually did say, I think. But it was a prejudiced account. About his mother, what Larry said was, "My mother was mean. . . . We had mean childhoods. I drink. I drink a lot; it's not a problem, but it is an expense. . . . I drink to forget that bitch." Ruling-class talk, maybe sincere, maybe half-sincere, maybe mostly style.

Larry *said* he was a member of the ruling class, "and we call a spade a spade." His siblings were scared of him. Larry said, "I can never write fiction—I'm not a liar." He considered his family line to have some American distinction "of a stupid kind: only a fool would want to be guided by it; and only the fools and failures in the family so far have been guided by it—look, we never had a secretary of state, or a really intelligent man, or one of the big fortunes, one of the great crooks. And we weren't ever good-looking. All we had was shrewdness. And luck in who we married." His mother was a Backus and (Larry said) a Noyes, a good Backus and in the second-best line of the Noyeses. (I knew a woman in the literary world who was a Noyes; she said her family was of the third-best line without my having said what my granddaughter's great-grandfather had said to me, so I presume this is a common way of talking about Noyeses.) Larry said, "The Noyeses aren't Mayflower—the Browns are Mayflower—but the Noyeses got here soon enough that it's no scandal. They know their place." He was drunk and maybe ironic and maybe not. Larry said those families were related to the Adamses, the Byrds, and the Crowninshields. He said, "None of that matters, if any of it is true: in the line I'm in, most of the family were poor ministers and teachers and small farmers—not *rustics* but educated—until the Civil War. Then we finally got a smart thief in the family. He believed in Lincoln's star, and he enlisted. He was a paymaster in an upstate New York regiment, and he came back with enough money to be a Republican and to start a newspaper. He wound up owning a piece of a feeder-line railroad that Commodore Vanderbilt had to have for the Central. He got a good price, and we entered the ruling class." "This country has no *ruling* class," I said. "The rulers are an accidental crew drawn from all over." He said, "Well, we started having advantages that we threw away over three generations."

About my family line with its claim of rabbis and scholars, he said, "Once language gets into a family it never gets out. Take my father and me. Take my grandfather who made the money—when the railroad got going, you notice he started a newspaper, in Rochester. Editorials are sermons. And my father and I went right back to being preachers in our way." His father, Larry said, had been the most famous editor of his time but is not remembered now. Incised in the stone of the outside walls of the Brooklyn Public Library are a number of deeply unimpressive poems of his. Larry wrote for the *National Review* and, before his politics changed, for the *Nation* and the *New Republic*, or so he said. I can't prove it. He said he started on the radical left and ended on the radical right. He wrote a fourteen-hundred-page-in-manuscript refutation of Oswald Spengler, denying that the decline of the West was inevitable. For a while he couldn't find a publisher, which he blamed on the decline of the West. Eventually he found a publisher and refuted Spengler in a shortened version. He wanted two things, he told me every time I saw him: to be secretary of state and a great thinker like Carlyle or Spengler. "It's little enough to ask," he said.

Life had promised him other princedoms, ones he did not want. He was, in general, in the late hours, after drinking all day, more his mother's son than he liked, rigid, ambitious, cold, and bitter. He said he had little affection, in retrospect, for the crooked paymaster in the Civil War who had established the family: "He was a lousy writer. What I would like to be is descended from a heterosexual Walt Whitman who married Abe Lincoln's daughter: now, Abe Lincoln was a nobody, but he could write."

Lincoln represented to Larry the actuality of an American great man. Larry said that Lincoln was, so far, the greatest American: "You want to get ambitious people to enlist, you form an Abraham Lincoln Brigade. Abe Lincoln is entwined with my family's history. Lincoln's election was the beginning of the greatness of the *Tribune*—see how the lines come together. Lincoln's best ally in New York State was Roscoe Conkling, the upstate Republican boss—do you know what my father's name was? Roscoe Conkling Ensign Brown—*inside, outside, upside down.* We used to tease him. You see how it all fits together? You see how I was cheated of my rightful heritage?"

"No." I never did see, either. These connections requiring asterisks on a chart and footnotes will perhaps be real presences to my granddaughter; she knew Larry, she liked him—he was one of the elements of her life, realer, maybe, than some of the images in color on the TV sets she watches when she is at any of her grandparents' houses.

My granddaughter's grandmother—my ex-wife—explained to me once, long ago, that in her view birth meant nothing, or very little: "You have to have held on to the money—the newspaper, the railroad—you have to still be close to Lincoln, and Lincoln still has to be president. Otherwise, it's just a waste of time. What you have is what you have." Larry tried to make it clear to me: "Stories about family aren't enough. Anglo-Saxons don't talk. They just assess your resources." Larry said, "It's not just having a newspaper—only a really powerful paper matters." His daughter tried to explain to me in what way she and Larry were poor: "The Rockefellers are rich, Harold. Only the richest are rich—everyone else feels overshadowed." Larry said, "If it's not the most money, it's not enough—people are proud. You know, socially the seven deadly sins are virtues. It's all reversed. Every last sin is a social virtue if you do it right. You have to be proud. You have to be good at being angry. Think about it. You better approve of gluttony if you want to dine out. If you won't be lazy, you get on everybody's nerves."

Some family letters survived from colonial days and the Revolution, including one from a man named Parley Brown, who was held by the British in a prison camp on Long Island. In sweet phrases, he wrote to his wife that he loved her and dreamed every night of the bread she made. Part of the letter was about what to name their son, who was Elena's grandparent ten generations back or so. Most of the early houses in that family have disappeared. The biggest one in any of the families was that of the Browns in Maine. Larry said, "We could sleep thirty, and did. My father put in a rose garden on the ocean rocks with walls to keep the dirt in. But all my brothers and sisters complained about how much it cost; they worried it was eating up the inheritance."

The rose garden, my ex-wife said, had been very fine in the sea light, and it had been wonderful to be small, she said, and to walk through a white gate into a space with walls around it higher than your head and to be out of the seacoast wind and among blossoming roses and their odors in the salt sea air. Gaffer—her grandfather—she'd liked. He was a good man, and it showed in the garden—it was pretty the way nothing else was in Seal Harbor, she said. Larry said the Rockefeller place next door to his mother's house was hideous, and the Ford place was worse. He said, "People made Gaffer sad." Elena's grandmother, during her days in the theater, said, "But I never had a good moment in that house, not one."

"Why not? Why do you and your father always say *not one?*"

"Well, my hair was dark, and all my cousins were blond, and they laughed at my mother because she was so good-looking and so stupid and mean; and they thought we were poor, although we were the smart ones and knew nicer people—famous people. We had a good time. I didn't like my grandmother at all. She was a bitch. And no one could have a good time around her."

"I don't believe you."

"But you don't know! No one wanted to have a good time! They wanted to be mean!"

All those family dinners? The guests? All of it? All the time?

"Yes. You don't understand. That's all they do. That's how they like it."

Larry said, "It's interesting but it's no fun to be from distinguished people."

How many pages would it take to chart the Backuses and the Noyeses and the Browns in their ramifications? A hundred, I think. The ancestry and the collateral lines. Then the five surviving children of the tough Bertha Backus Brown (I see where Henry James got his names), my ex-wife's father's generation and their marriages and their spouses' family lines, and their children, my ex-wife's cousins and their marriages and their children, and their children's marriages. Who do you suppose would not be connected to them by now? After all, as an example, everyone connected to me, a sizable number, from two distinct families, is connected to them now—through marriage.

"If you listed everyone you were connected to, you would see you were connected to a lot of people you wouldn't want to know. It's all boredom. And illnesses. And money—what else would it be?" Larry said. "Families are for the second-rate." Larry said, "I'm a fascist. But I would never be an anti-Semitic fascist. Jews add brains to the stew. I interviewed Trotsky—there's a man who could stir things up. You know what killed my mother? Boredom. She gave too many society dinners; she went to too many; she spent too many evenings in the company of society dullards; I swore I would never have a society dentist at my table, and I haven't. I know why my mother's mind went."

Gaffer had his ashes scattered in the rose garden, "but the wind was blowing, and most of them blew out into the water. I said to Annie, 'He finally got away from Mother.' "

Chains of relation: stepchains: we are *related by marriage* (for the time being)—modern circumstances dictate modern usage: we are *cousins of a sort,* and *You're from Mary's family from her second stepfather* and *Some people we're related to through my cousin's wife's mother, an aunt by marriage, an aunt three times removed*—we acknowledge some of this American reality. This is who many of us now are.

We simplify. My ex-wife, in her version of Larry's conversational style (and his style was a version of his mother's ruthlessness, probably), said, "The only part of a family I think of as family is the part with money and brains and power, if I like them." She practiced a kind of stylish ruthlessness. I think of her as a young person I knew once who is distinctly present again in Elena's manners and in Elena's voice.

Someone in one of the family's families when I told him about Elena and her ancestry remarked, "My family are all crooks—crooks and shopping centers." The man who said it didn't mean it; or, rather, he didn't apply it to the grandmothers. "I *loved* my grandmothers."

"Would you have shared them with a stepbrother?"

He paled. He shook his head.

"When I think of my family, I think of the ones who were the *good* lawyers," a lawyer said.

These networks of modern connection are embarrassing, partly because of the joke involved in the abundance of family branches compared with old family lines before 1900. And that is partly a matter of mortality—mortality rates and modern medicine and the germ theory. Virginia Woolf is often quoted as having said that human nature changed in 1910; that was about the time women and children had begun to survive in larger numbers, and everything did change then, obviously, or almost everything, as you would expect in the recession of death. Men lived longer, too. Death lost its central place as a family reality and was replaced by marriage and divorce as the grounds of the most common family grief, at least for a while, between wars.

What used to be "families" are oddly lost and blurred inside the constellations of the various new kinds of connection and relation; and no one yet knows what to make of these networks or of this new reality, except to live it. But how are you to stay informed or even begin to be informed about these family immensities? How are you to get and keep and file all the useful and necessary information? Few members of the family like to write letters. Letters used to be filled with family gossip. One falls back on long distance, or did before the "Reach Out and Touch Someone" campaign made the idea repugnant. I used to settle down on two or three Sundays a year and call around the country, but the emotional distances often had grown immeasurably since the last call. People I thought I knew well were inclined to tell me what their children were doing and omit themselves, as if to recede into embarrassed privacy about themselves as older people. But the news about their children was usually heavily edited. When the children answered the phone, they often complained darkly or spoke harshly of their lives and then were unknowingly contradicted when their parents gave me the more social or highly edited report they thought suited the social—telephone—moment. The most embarrassing moments occur when one is out-of-date about who is living and who is dead, and who has a brain tumor since you spoke last and who is well. A cousin I liked began by saying, "Hi. How are you? It's good to hear your voice." I said, "It's good to hear your voice. What's new in your neck of the woods?" "Well, I'll tell you: I have cancer of the liver and I'm terminal." A woman cousin said, "I'm getting a divorce. I'm crazy from it. You want to hear about it?" A lot of family gossip is about face-lifts. A lot of family talk is mockery of each other's lives. The cousin who was terminal said, "There's a lot of warm feeling in the family. Everyone's being good to me. There are a lot of good moments still. I'm trying to be strong." He was making social talk in the way talking on the telephone to relatives he hadn't seen for a while led him to. How much will telephone talk be part of my granddaughter's sense of family?

Not long ago, on a trip west, I had a drink with yet another relative, one with a beard, a purposefully Abraham Lincoln look-alike but short legged. I wonder what Larry would have thought of that. A right-wing nut, he runs a mail-order seed business, with the seeds supposedly from famous locations—Mount Vernon, for instance, Calvary, Valley Forge, Verdun. In one of my collateral lines is a man who teaches crossbow shooting. Homosexuality, lunacy, suicide, wig wearing—the usual things, we have those.

. . .

My first wife's aunt, who left her pictures to the Whitney, was one of those ex-Communists who live very well, as she pointed out; and she told me she had "bedded" *Bunny* Wilson and *Dos* Dos Passos and a number of painters from that era, and that she had turned Dreiser down. But you can't include lovers and spurned would-be lovers, I guess, in a family tree. That aunt snarled promptly at me when I was first published, "Don't get uppity! You don't look like Faulkner and you don't write like Dos." She was snobbish toward me because, with my background and my ambitions, I wasn't interested in being a Party member. She spent years waiting for her passport to be revoked. Someone on a plane once recognized me from a photograph in a magazine and told me she had seen my mother by adoption when, in her childhood, she had gone to visit an aunt in Alton, Illinois: "Doris Brodkey was the most beautiful girl I ever saw in my life, and if she lived there I thought there must be a good reason; so I always wanted to live there; and I do. I live two houses from where Doris Brodkey lived." "Why, you're almost a relative," I said.

I feel an irritable awe, awe and mockery, at this jumbled family that I never thought about until I started writing this, which was after Elena told me she had fifteen grandparents. A niece of Doris's told me of the daughter of yet one more relative, not a Brodkey, this one a kid in her twenties, caught at the airport smuggling "two million dollars' worth of cocaine. The dogs sniffed it out. They bribed the judge and the police with the cocaine and the child is on probation. Very contrite. Couldn't be sweeter. I don't think she meant any harm."

Family crime—crime in the family: no one will tell me much now because I might write a piece like this one. So I go light on crime here, not being up-to-date in the matter.

And the charitable ones, the saintly ones, the noble-souled ones—I have left those out, too. Actually, there aren't many of them now in the family lines I know about. My granddaughter cannot look back at a saintly group. Or, rather, not since child mortality fell, in the early 1900s. Before then, we had saints and mystics in all the branches, Gentile and Jewish, Amish and Japanese, and maybe in the rest. Larry said virtue was dull and that he never gave to charity and he hoped to go to hell for it: "I'd rather hear myself scream in hell and talk in words than sit in silence and stare at God."

No one in the family has kept a journal that I know about. We don't transcribe phone calls. The family history does not exist, I realize. I use some family history in what I write but not reliably.

I can't remember that it was ever mentioned to me when I was young that I was my second mother's second cousin. I was told I was of no blood relation but that may have been by my grandmother, who actually was not a blood relation of mine. I was related to her dead husband, Doris Brodkey's father, who, for some reason, took his wife's name when he married her, rather than the reverse. Perhaps he hadn't been very real to that grandmother.

My granddaughter's sense of family perhaps depends on fate—and who becomes famous and to what extent, and who has the money. Perhaps she will be like a countess I met once, who, having become poor, stopped using her title, saying, "I am in no position to boast." Perhaps it depends on what profession my granddaughter enters. My sense of the hugeness of her family is new to me, and perhaps it can't be a family—we don't all have the same name and we didn't go to the same schools and we won't be buried in the same graveyards; and so perhaps we won't exist for her in any way as a family used to exist for its descendants.

Well, we all know, or some of us do, that America is very strange. If I consider my friends, there is absolutely no social order to be discerned at all. One told me recently that in his family a distant cousin is now married to a woman reputed to be the richest in the world. He finds that an irritatingly bourgeois tie. Certainly my granddaughter, while not the inheritor of all the ages, is heiress to a mess of stories and a hundred discarded houses and the blood of many somewhat noted people. And of much sadness. And of many jokes. And of so much cultural oddity. Such a menu of nurture. Such human deprivation.

If she wants a family crest, I suggest this. Her great-grandfather Larry was the man who (but only a few people now alive will know what I am talking about) thought up the stunt (accredited to a circus promoter) in which the circus promoter put a midget on J. P. Morgan's lap at a congressional hearing into the stock-market crash of 1929. It was part of a move to discredit Hoover and the Republicans and Big Money and High Finance, in order, Larry said, to create the climate for economic reform. That is, the midget was part of a political stunt Larry thought up and carried out in his radical-left phase. That J. P. Morgan's grandson was at Harvard when I was, and I see him occasionally in New York; but I always forget to ask him if he knows about the midget. Larry claims he was the one who saw that the midget was necessary if the country was to trust Roosevelt and not J. P. Morgan. He had the savoir faire to be ruthless—"that's what being ruling class is for," he said. "You do what you have to do." When I was young, the event was still famous and often referred to; and the photographs of the midget on the lap of the great financier appeared often enough that it was part of my sense of the age. And there is Larry in some of the photographs, perhaps overseeing this demystification of the most powerful money figure of the time. What will this mean to my grandchild when she is twenty? J. P. Morgan is not a legendary financier anymore, is he? I could tell her he was someone like Ivan Boesky but honest, as such things go, couldn't I? But Elena will not have heard of Boesky. I could say an Episcopal-American Rothschild but that might not inform her, either. He was not actually the most famous J. P. Morgan; he was the son of the man who, when he died, having left a seventy-million-dollar estate, was eulogized by old Andrew Carnegie (who married at fifty-one and left one daughter), "And to think he was not a rich man." At any rate, I suggest that the scene with the midget be turned into a crest. It seems to me suitably American, bizarre and abstruse.

Larry became *a high-muck-a-muck*—Annie's term—in the Office of Price Administration during the Second World War, and a vice president of a fairly large chemical company after the war, a chemical company because he had overseen the prices of their chemicals in a way they'd liked: this is his account—he was a muckraking high-muck-a-muck. He said, "I am angry that I had to become a crook in order to survive." He said, "This is a country of shame." He wanted to reform it. Larry said he helped build the case against Alger Hiss, whose son is an acquaintance of mine now and says his father's trial was not a tragic event in his life, merely something that happened and that he became used to.

As my first wife said, "There's never anything to boast of if you tell the truth. If it's there, it shines in your face." Our marriages and our descent give us a French branch and two or three Scottish ones and an Israeli contingent and Italian and Russian ties as well as the ones mentioned earlier. We are overrepresented in law and journalism. We have two sitting judges, two sitting editors, and one accountant for the Mafia. That, I'm afraid, is hearsay. It's a matter of his guard dogs, maybe. He does not live in the same state as the one whose attorney general is someone we are related to.

It is a family only in relation to that one child. She has in her lineage people who died in the camps and people who killed them. She has people from both sides of most of the American wars. And people on both sides of most of the political movements here and in Europe in the last 150 years. She is descended from suffragettes and from reactionaries. Such a family as hers is not uncommon nowadays, is it? If it is common, what do you suppose it means for the psyche and for politics and belief? She has a great-uncle who, I think, is in the process of helping to found a new religious movement dedicated to world peace and mostly aimed at women; he claims to have seen the Virgin Mary in a vision while he was sleeping in a wooden pyramid in Denver, Colorado, and she told him that his line (which is also mine) was descended from her family. His religion has a program of pure water and famine relief in the Third World and faith in flying saucers and in the magic powers of pyramids. My granddaughter has a tie to the movie producer who did the 1930s Tarzan movies. We have in this tangle of families professors and CIA connections and two ex-FBI agents.

When I think of the lovers and ex-lovers, the friends and colleagues, the enemies and rivals of all the members of all the branches, I do, seriously, indeed believe we are the preponderant clan on the face of the earth. And if we are not that yet, a few more marriages will do it. I believe we are nearly everybody.

My granddaughter can boast someday, or, contrarily, she can be humble, that she is descended and connected as she is. Through her parents and stepparents she can find ready shelter in all fifty of the American constituent states and in at least five, and maybe seven, foreign countries.

Perhaps what we have done and are doing is trying a subtle adaptation in an era of massive danger to arrange for family survival. . . . Ah, I am quite mad with genealogy and the genealogical idea. It really is very difficult for me to imagine anyone in the world, except for some tribesmen, to whom she is not at some distance related or attached through friendship and then relation—the networks of relations of friends and acquaintances and people who work for you and whom you're close to. I feel so permeated by the world and by relationships in the world and by relationships enlivened and made fraught by this no doubt ridiculous structure I have thought I detected and have tried to describe here and helped create by marriage and example that I don't quite know what to do except to think, My God, how bitterly and deeply I want the world to go on.

1987

ON FRIENDSHIP

Some words apparently have always been confusing and hard to define. *Friend*, which is the word you have to start with if you want to look up the history of the word *friendship*, has a similar derivation to that of the word *fiend*—which does suggest childhood and Hollywood and tormenting adolescent friendships.

Anyway, *friend* is from the present participle of a word meaning love, so it comes from a root meaning *loving*. There was another word for love— love which was a form of *lubh* and was probably related more to desires. Love was a stronger feeling and maybe more outside public existence from quite early on.

The *Abridged Oxford English Dictionary*, edited by C. T. Onions— undoubtedly a proud and patient man and one with a sense of the comic—returns to the eighteenth century and Samuel Johnson for the lovely definition: *one joined to another in mutual benevolence and intimacy.* Onions adds, *not usually applied to lover or relatives.* But the *Oxford Dictionary of Etymologies* points out that in Old Norse—as early as that—*friend* meant lover, and today *friends*, plural, often is used to mean lovers: "They're friends." Of course, "They're friends," said with a different slant of the eyebrows and a different angle of the neck means you're-wrong-to-think-they're-sleeping-together. And some people are "friendly" with their families: *brotherhood* or *sisterhood* (actual or honorary) and *friendship* are fairly synonymous.

The Johnson definition is quite intense, and the dictionary has to take refuge in a subsidiary notion: a friend is one not hostile or is one who aids a cause. Friendships based on such things are not necessarily lightweight, temporary, or without emotion; one might say they apply to acts, one's actions, one's way of life rather than to one's self.

Liking, by the way, comes from a root meaning the body, so love or *lubb* and its attendant desires were probably more than physical, perhaps even pathological in some ways.

It seems to me most of these distinctions still exist although there is one mentioned by the dictionary that I would not use except ironically and that is the use of the word *friend* for addressing a stranger. Or maybe I would in any place except a large city: in a country setting, it wouldn't seem an absurd courtesy or misplaced.

In speaking of emotions, I find it a temptation to try for an epigram, on one hand, and a discussion of tribal culture and etiquette, on the other. In some eras, some social classes, there are various fixed classes of friendship—it is almost a formal thing; there are forms, anyway, such as the *tutoyer* in French or the *du* in German. A drinking buddy is, in some places in this country, a formal relationship involving money (held nearly in common) and girls (short of love or, rather, this side of love either held in common or mutually protected). Friendship as an alliance, or an alliance against loneliness, specifically, has its forms, its conventions, in the matter of confidences, for instance. One will tell a friend things about one's past and one's present that often one will not tell a lover, although psychoanalysis has changed some things for some people, and being lovers means telling each other everything: such love affairs flourish or can flourish. The thing is one doesn't have to tell a friend everything: one assumes understanding. And besides, there often isn't time; it's rare for a friendship to come first in one's life and to have the right of co-opting one's time. Friendships tend to be fitted in, except in an emergency, and even then, it depends on one's other responsibilities, obligations.

In fact—to put off for a moment talk about the pleasures of friendship—one of the most interesting parts of any friendship, professional, historical-in-one's-life (an old high-school friend or whatever), sexually confiding, social climbing, or relaxing with, is the setting of limits. A friendship pushed too far or withdrawn even slightly too much sud-

denly becomes questionable or unbearable—but not always: some friendships are strengthened by fighting, even by such invisible fighting, and
they take on a more permanent quality.

Permanence is slightly imaginary in human affairs: we change, our circumstances change—God knows, our moods change. Love alters moods.
So does one's family usually. Friendship often doesn't but seems to take us
as we are: this is not always easy and it does require limits. Some personal
friendships are out of place and unwelcome during business hours; some
business friendships, while pleasant off-hours, are never really separated
enough from business. Some friendships combine both and slide easily
back and forth and are in the way and arouse jealousy when one is in love.
There are amazing and circuslike acts of emotional balance—men and
women who have dozens of friends, none or few of whom are jealous of
each other; men and women who "make friends wherever they go." There
are odd forms of this latter: salesmen, bartenders, insurance agents, professional agents, some comedians, maîtres d'hôtel, some doctors, some
critics (they often form a brotherhood). There is still an odder form of this,
a condensed form, the stranger beside you on an airplane, a taxi driver, a
whore or gigolo. Then, coming back by an odd route, are "friendships"
with con artists (because they're amusing and one will pay a price to
escape boredom, one will be willingly conned up to a point), hurtful people (they test one's strength, and if one manages to survive, one feels
strong as a result of such people; or one may have a taste for certain types
of defeat), country-club people (where it is understood the "friendship" is
entirely without obligation, is purely for purposes of pleasure, let's say).

Some sins are sociable. Wife swappers, smugglers, practicing or overt
sexual sadists, are often good at friendships.

I myself would theorize that what separates friendship from other
emotions, despite its root (the related word *fiend* also means, in slang, a
fanatic partisan—a fiend for work or whatever), is that it is sensible—
sensible, often or nearly always rational, reasonable. When there is an
inequity—a very pretty, very bright girl and her dimmer, but still intelligent, and not as pretty friend, for example—something balances the
inequity, money on the side of the plainer, or some unspoken contract of
adoration short of sexual advances.

Perhaps one ought to digress for a moment and discuss the encroach-
ment of sexuality, androgyny or homo- or hetero-whatsits, on notions of
friendship: often, jealousy chooses this as a mode of criticism even when it

wouldn't criticize an openly sexual tie. If sexuality is present—and balked—in many or most friendships, it would make the path of friendship as rough as we know that of romantic love to be; but one of the ultimate charms of friendship—even the most crass and opportunistic—is that unless roughness is contracted for, as in horseplay or some emotional pattern of the partners, the path *is* smooth and eminently reasonable. If you are my friend, I expect, it's true, some favors from you (enough so that friends in politics, real friends, tend to be something of a liability in terms of public relations: one smells crookedness), but if I am a real friend, I would not expect you to compromise your honor. That, however, is perhaps a bit rarefied, part of finer friendships for finer people. But on whatever level I expect the favors, if I am a friend at all, I am reasonable; and so, too, corresponding to the level or rarification, is the one who does the favor giving at the moment.

Some friendships never quite solidify because there is a tacit or open argument about what level the reasonableness ought to be on. Still, friendship is a sane thing—transference or love for an analyst turns to friendship (or dislike), and when friendship arrives, so does the cure.

It is possible that friendship as I conceive it is a fantasy, and it is simply, in reality, a form of unexpressed or weak or diluted romance. One knows enough friendships and has experience some in which some powerful erotic element has entered—a friend and one's wife, a friend and another friend, a friend suddenly confessing love for one's self. I'm never sure how much that has to do with convenience—the middle class hasn't the range or patience to search over any great distance for its passions and so it discharges them on girls in the typing pool, a brother, or one's friend's husband or wife. Of course, that implies an element of reason in passion and thereby makes the passion suspect, but then friendship has to weather suspicions.

It is the gift element of friendship, separated from the erotic, plus an element of equality (or final equality or equity when all the factors are taken into the measure) that partly gives its high glow: a friend wants you to have a good time, will tell you of a piece of unspoiled coastline, and does not expect any sensational eroticism in return. This would imply that we are to some extent persecuted by the erotic, and that the wish to escape from it is strong enough to create a set of myths and of large and genuine pleasures that go to make up a relationship that is apparently unnecessary (for purposes of breeding or culture) yet is one that nearly everyone I know values—and to an astonishing extent. But not an unreasonable one.

The Great Passion of The Chief Friendships of one's life, then, if I am right, is with equals of some sort, equality with whom is flattering and yet reasonable—but may require labor. Shadows of competition are permitted but one is sensible about such things. A friend can be reasoned with, which means not only that conversation as opposed to chatter, reminiscence, confession, an exchange of information, is possible but so too are argument and an open effect on opinions—and one is not shanghaied or bullied erotically into this. Now the argument or discussion of opinions and principles, of one's profession, despair, hopes, and so on, leads to knowledge of the other, which can be construed as the basis for the possibility of the other acting as an equal, in the sense of being a substitute for oneself, an almost same self, as in being a trustee of one's estate or bringing up one's children if one is killed or for some other reason can't, or in more minor ways, representing one as an ambassador to one's children or to one's angry wife or lover. Trust and sameness, a balance, a reasonable and fortunate thing—think of the comfort, of the near painlessness.

Perhaps friendship is the least painful, the most painless, of those relationships in which we invest our lives, or more temporarily, our selves, our hearts, our secrets, our courtesies.

1979

LOVE SPEECHES

Some men, American men, men anywhere, claim not to love, claim they can outwit the thing, but I don't see how it's done; I think mostly they're lying for reasons of their own. Some men, the same American men, others, love frequently, to outwit the thing, and others love all the time: it keeps them busy, keeps them from loving one thing, one person, too greatly. They can love what they do, or love women in general, instead of one person. Some men say they feel nothing because they don't want to talk about it; and anyway they don't know how to talk about it; they can't talk about it well; if you can't do your feelings justice in speech or in gesture, why talk? Your feelings come out of your entire life—see Freud—and from lives before yours, dwindling or augmenting in force in you and differently at different times. Some men say love is in its realest part the wish to be loved by whoever you say you love, dog or child or woman.

Some men love some one thing at certain times, or only one time, so much more than they love other things that they say they love only once. Or only a few times and mean it. Men often, as it were, love romantically, and that is a great compliment to what is loved but what is loved may or may not enjoy the compliment. Few men can love a woman or a child (or anything) that does what it wants to do. Some men love fearfully and some love fancifully in the frequent range and in the infrequent one; some love differently each time they love. Some men love boldly. Some men love in all styles as they learn or in order not to learn. Some men have not much or no hope of learning anything. And I don't see how people can claim to know very much about love. It is not an easy subject.

Why should we expect people to know more about love than they do about their own long-term political self-interest? Aren't people fools? Sure, they are. Since they are, then what is it we hope for when we hope for love? That they will be fools in our favor?

See, you're never really on a desert island with just one other person. I mean most people aren't. They aren't ever caught in that limited silence. All stories, all love stories in reality involve your betraying one or two or half a dozen people who are involved, each of the lovers has things stacked up on both sides, people who usually know and care or mind, and enemies of course: people sometimes mind really a whole lot who you care about, who you care about most. The basic words or things such as time and moments, pain and pleasure, and stuff in between and mixed, ambition and betrayal, come into the realm of translatable active terms, love and money, for instance, and sexual life and death and *Death* itself, the big one, the collapse of biological identity and, for all we know, of every other aspect of identity.

Love is humiliation, we know that. Love is an expansive exaltation—we know that, too. But are we sure? Love is hard work. Love is jealousy. Men hate it if you're happier than they are.

Men make doctrines out of what they do more often than out of what they believe. They make doctrines of blame, doctrines of cunning, doctrines of hopelessness, doctrines of being cool about it, doctrines of being hot about it, doctrines about all possible degrees and slants of concupiscence or lechery or bodily or spiritual warmth in these matters. Most men have a doctrine about escaping from love. Mostly, maybe, men love if they can. Some men love wickedness and some love weakness in women and some love goodness and some love strength. However, except in old families and with strong men, most men are afraid to love what they love unless others love it too, unless it's the fashion.

American love talk says such things as *My feelings are real*. And: *I won't hurt you*. And: *We don't believe in love around here*, and: *I really like you*. I mean those last two things are often said as love speeches. What do those speeches mean? What does it mean if a woman says, *Everyone knows there is no such thing as love?* What does it mean if a man says it? How well do we have to know the man before we can be reasonably sure what he means? If love speeches are forgone in favor of meaningful breathing and fraught glances, does that mean the person is dishonest or only that that person doesn't feel adequate at negotiating matters of love?

How do you share power?

Is it love when you break the object? When you tend it carefully? How can you tend something when you are out of control? I suppose there are ways, but it gets odd. If you love someone as strong as yourself, does it become service, or servitude to love her, and does that love lack charity? Marital charity, aphrodisiac and intense, is a really big thing. If a man is someone who tends—a tender—and a woman is a freedom-seeking soul, what happens next, and what happens when a man who tends doesn't like tending long or steadily?

This is a subject that requires a lot of space and time, a lot of life and will, and much more style and wit.

1986

SEX AND LOOKS

Awoman I know, a woman seventy years old, asked me a few months ago to be with her when she was photographed for a book about someone she had known when she was young.

My friend does not like to be photographed. The photographer, a very interesting-looking woman of about forty who wore no makeup, said cajolingly to my friend, "You have a very good face."

"That does not mean I can be made to like being photographed," my friend said. And the photographer replied, "Your face stands for something—it means something."

My friend said, "Like old laundry—hanging on a clothesline—it means something, too."

The photographer said, "Why don't you like having your picture taken?"

"That was never the purpose of my face," my friend said, a bit snappishly. "My face is actually *personal*."

After the photographer left, my friend said to me, "I am not ready for cameraland. I would have gotten a lift—I only had my eyes done and a little bit on my neck. But tell me," she asked, "what is a 'very good' seventy-year-old face for? What was *she* talking about? Not a useful young face—she was talking about something for a photograph in a style useful to *her*. The purpose was a photograph." My friend sounded disgusted. Then she said, "The truth is, I am invisible now." She went on, "On the street, in my life, nothing happens the way it used to. I'm invisible. What are looks for? What are looks for when you're seventy years old? Historical photographs?"

Laughing wryly, she told me she had discussed this with her half sister, who let her ramble on but was silent until my friend asked her why she was so silent: "Oh," said the half sister, according to my friend, "I was always invisible . . . I was plain."

My friend said, "So I was ashamed of myself, but so what? I wasn't plain, and I miss what my life was like." She made herself a drink. "I'm ashamed that looks played such a role in my life, but they did and that's that," she said. "They were how I knew the world. They were fun. I was who I looked like. Of course, a lot of it was facade; I was there behind it, behind my looks. I *liked* the attention I got. Hell, sometimes it was like firing a gun into a room. Bang! *Who is that girl?* Guess what? It was me. The makeup, the hair, the no makeup, the hair a mess, the second looks— pardon me for living, but whoopee! I liked having people try to figure out where I was coming from. Now I'm wrinkled laundry. Well, I can live with it, but I don't know if I want to go on record about it with a *photograph*."

I made notes when I got home.

The role of looks in someone's life:

Looks inspire, attract, trigger attention in others—or damp it down.

The way looks indicate social class and character is partly under your control and partly not.

Also, the way looks indicate degrees of amiability or social difficulty is mostly under your control.

People are judged by looks, not just sexually and socially but in a variety of other ways.

We all know cases of new kids in school—or new people in the office, or in the neighborhood—the ways we judged them, the first sight we had of them, their looks and manner, their personal style, the cars they drove, and the first gossip about their economic or social background. We have a vast store of memories of occasions of judging and responding—in various ways, with various overtones—to people's *looks*. But we don't quite know what all this means: This isn't one of the things we're taught in school or that people talk about theoretically.

Terms of judgment:

OK.
A knockout.
Too much.
Much too much.
Ugly.
Yucky.
Too (pale, lurid, English, Italian, Jewish . . . whatever).
Awful.
Sexy.
Full of conceit.
Goody-goody.

I wrote, "Someone's looks make us jealous or curious, sometimes exclude us. How do we respond to this? Each of us responds differently to the stimulus—if I can call it that—and each of us responds in a distinctively individual way to the attention we receive, perhaps even to each individual bit of attention."

Looks of whatever sort someone has, plus the style and manner of dress and the presentation of the self, sloppy or willful, suggest certain categories of attentions that the person is accustomed to receiving or occasionally receives; or the whole represents a bluff.

Maybe there always is a bluff, an illusion, whether of romantic drama or of prim decency or of plump complacency; and some trouble always arises from this in that others want to test the illusion—and taste the reality.

Once, when I was in college, I went to the movies with a spectacularly good-looking young woman. Some guys hanging around the entrance to the movie theater made remarks. Two of them shoved me—not all that hard, but still it was a case of their starting a fight.

It was partly an example of masculine rivalry, of measuring someone else's nerve and rights and privileges. I'd already been in three fights over this young woman. Two of the fights were with guys at college, classmates. And one was with a tough young woman who mostly yelled.

I hadn't realized that spending time with this particular woman would lead to so many dramatic and half-violent and humiliating moments.

How do you manage your life? If someone is dressed modestly, is that person then acceptable without being particularly sexually attractive? The media—even the movies—show us largely an absence of sexual feeling, a world of events into which sexuality intrudes or erupts dramatically.

Freud tried to argue that sexuality is always present, but that is considerably harder to dramatize—the flickering ins and outs, the invitations and permissions, and the refusals and the disgusts.

We ignore sexuality often, but that does not mean it is not there. Or that everyone around us at that moment is ignoring it as we are, to the same extent and with similar notions of law or reason in these matters.

Before we use the words *harassment* and *abuse*, let's point out that a good deal of contemporary dress—jeans and sweatshirts, shorts, T-shirts, running shoes, as well as well-tailored suits on men and women—sends mixed signals: sexual/asexual, romantic/unromantic, attractive/businesslike.

Among the dramatic, or melodramatic, episodes of feelings in which everyone is involved sooner or later are some that are real trouble and that represent some actuality of abuse in semi or full horror. Vladimir Nabokov's novel *Lolita*, which has sold more than 10 million copies worldwide, is about this subject in regard to a child; and it is told from the point of view of the one who harms the child.

In the novel, the child gets revenge by running off with someone else who does such harm, and this drives the trespasser of the first instance to murder the trespasser of the second instance. The novel is a kind of feast about all sorts of signals and signs, and it profoundly sneers at the idea of innocence.

Considerable prettiness in childhood . . . curiosity about more-favored children . . . experiments in cruelty . . . in bossing each other around . . . and loneliness . . . and boredom . . . and the loneliness in grown-ups and the kinds of meaning a child carries . . . the looks and manners of Little Timmie or Little Sophie and their feistiness or tomboyishness or their safety in having *looks only a parent could love* . . . childhood passivity . . . childhood moods . . . childhood wars over attention . . . to be stared at, complimented, wrestled with, passed over and ignored—don't these things underlie what we know as adults of love and attraction?

I have an early memory of being passed around in a roomful of people, family members and neighbors in the living room, and being held and kissed and asked to give hugs. I hated it so much that I literally could not bear it at all, the smells and the thing of having no physical privacy, the strangeness of each person to me.

My family told stories of my rebellion. I particularly rebelled against my mother's mother, angering that grandmother who threatened me, more or less lightly at first but with a nervous edge, with no more kisses at all and no hugs or butter cookies or gifts of money. It was a joke.

Later, when I persisted, she grew more serious, more angry. She showed real dislike, even enmity (of a domestic, cutting-me-out-of-her-will sort), until I relented toward her. Part of what I looked forward to when I started school was wearing *tough* clothes and not being carefully combed and laundered all the time but being *ugly* and a boy and beyond this *other stuff*.

Is personal attention, whether the wanted or unwanted sort, *ever* easy to deal with? Don't movies and pop songs lie about this—as *Lolita* does not—and propose not only happy endings but truly happy endings and even happy beginnings (which are then interrupted by nightmares) and even actual paradise, perfection of moments, here on earth?

My seventy-year-old friend told me that when she was young she had an outfit she called "let sleeping dogs lie" and one she called "let's raise a little hell."

There were reactions in her husband's eyes and in the eyes of a number of males and in the eyes of women, effects of each dress and of her face without makeup and her posture slouched and so on. Anyone aroused is not all that easy to deal with.

To live in the middle of that is often felt to be interesting. And my friend missed that time in her life.

She said, "Of course, I can do all sorts of things now I couldn't do then—people take me seriously now. I'm not sure I like it."

What the senses and the mind, the nerves and mood apprehend of someone is what we know as that person's looks. And that sense of someone is never entirely fixed. I think we have private feelings about other people, and then we rely on group judgments.

The difficulty of interpreting these matters and the impossibility of guessing at or understanding the sexual motives and appetites of others without more experience than perhaps one wants, the wholly other scale of longing or of rejection of us in others—this is what we live with. We make up our minds what we will remember and what we will not be bothered by, what we will refuse to have in our lives, or, sometimes, what we will refuse to admit is there even though it is there most or all of the time. The way we ignore things is part of how we know ourselves, and it is part sometimes of how we tempt others. They want to wake us. I remember when I was a child hearing a girl I loved back then described as *a real little touch-me-not . . . a real little sleepwalker.*

I am not a permissive sort of person. I like people who follow rules. I like a reliable dryness of manner. But such preferences, real and variable and wholly individual, can rarely be accommodated in theory. Or discussed in the abstract. People want and don't want adventures and emotional and sexual dramas. They do and don't care about looks and venturings from one social class to another. Some people are refreshed by exploring ugliness as a valid thing to enjoy or to use as a tactic or as a shield (even while complaining about it). Some people can draw breath only in regard to the decencies possible for *colorlessness.* One can theorize endlessly, but you have to live this stuff if you want to comprehend it.

In adulthood, the things that form your basic personality and that are the foundation of the self are too much trouble to think about and take too long to unearth for it to be worth everyone's while to dig around and see what causes what in them. It's often an absurdity in terms of time and will to try to remember one's real history. While we are growing up, we are forced to learn to hide things—from ourselves and from others. I remember the wife of a colleague telling their son, *"You don't want a face like a television set. It's not smart to broadcast everything you feel."* We learn to do things indirectly and in steps, to be discreet—buttoned up—as part of manners and taste and part of our moral judgment and tactics of survival.

And a little blindness, a little carelessness on our part maybe adds up to some seduction on the side, a form of free will in these matters, at least to some extent. But can you choose the form that affection or appetite takes in some person who is involved with you? Even a child?

Well, then, what are looks for? They are part of our lives. They are partly under our control sometimes. They have power. Looks become stories that are comic or sad or romantic, but piercing. The derivations—the etymologies—of words having to do with looks are interesting: *Handsome* meant suitable for use, fitting the hand, a sword, a horse, fertile land, an easily defended site. It had to do with *function* in the real world. *Pretty* had to do with agility, quickness, dexterity. *Beauty* actually can have both those meanings—a movement or a suitability can be said to be *a beauty*—plus it has the more abstract meaning of creating awe, of impressing the senses and the mind and suggesting meaning. This has great value.

Looks are meant to have an effect. They show a degree of physical intelligence, *social* intelligence. Of course, there are degrees of strikingness, degrees of hurt and of winning out. When you are full-grown and you dress up, are you trying to silence ordinary life? Do you hope perhaps to enter the world of love and ceremony for a while? How much nerve and good humor, how much *strength*, how much cold-and-hot gambler's nerve (and defiance) does it take to be good-looking?

1993

THE SECOND SKIN

People in the city say now (and it is said of them) that they don't care about fashion, but that remark itself is fashionable. It may be the centrist, or most ordinary, position to take. But few of us want, even in a dream, to walk naked through a crowded ballroom. We do not want to be judged—or thought about—utterly bare-skinned and visible. We do not want to give out so much information about ourselves and to receive so little of the same kind in return. We want to be dressed, and we want others to be dressed somewhat similarly, partly for the democracy of it, and partly so that we are speaking a halfway common language—so that we are not isolated inside our own heads, trapped in the babble of madness or in fears of obesity or whatever, but are part of a dialogue about acceptable or exciting appearances.

In offices nowadays, there seems to have been a modification of this not-caring stance, in the form of clothes worn by both women and men who want to show off their bodies, and like to introduce a disconcertingly sexual note into the atmosphere of conferences, brainstorming, and plotting.

What is clear is that clothes and the city are married to each other. It is not really comfortable to go naked on the street in a modern city. Such nakedness isn't flattering, even for people who look good naked on a beach. I suppose that's because of city dirt and the ways that light caroms off the buildings and the unnatural patterns of wind and heat and cold in the city. Look at the people in tank tops on the street, look at runners in the park, partly stripped. Great beauty is out of the question. But in sunlight, near the ocean, everyone is strangely wonderful-looking. I am not talking about beauty in terms of bones and muscle but about a quality that bodies have at the beach, and, in the city, in clothes: they give off a sense of the moment, a sense of pleasure—and a suggestion of some potential satisfaction to be had in moments ahead.

Just a bit of history, a bit of sociology: in the 1920s and 1930s, few American magazines or American people spoke of "American style." In fact, the phrase was an oxymoron if your sense of style was highly developed. The reason for that was context: much of America then was small towns, and these places hadn't the architectural settings or the outdoor spaces—hadn't the culture—to support the idea of "high" style, let alone the necessary button shops, seamstresses, dry cleaners, hairdressers, and the like. I was born in the Midwest, in a town of five thousand inhabitants, which I left when I was two. I went back when I was thirty-two, and, on the basis of photographs and my earliest memory, it seemed the women were dressed in roughly the same way as when I had left. I'd like to say the hemlines had changed, but I think even the hemlines were the same.

Before small towns became dormitory suburbs, the female schoolteachers dressed differently from the other women, and so did the banker's wife. They experimented with *bits* of style. The banker himself dressed in an urban way, since he was not as local as the other businessmen; he was felt to have a broader and more sophisticated grasp of things.

For most of my early childhood, my family lived in an Illinois town of about thirty thousand, called Alton. Style there was overtly determined by money and by access to Saint Louis, which was across the river (the Mississippi). People in Alton were rich enough—at least one very large fortune arose in the town, the Olin fortune—so that women wore New York clothes or Paris clothes or Saint Louis clothes in order to show off. And hats. And gloves.

In those years, the great difference between small-town style, when it was actually stylish, and big-city or capital-city style was that the latter was aimed at the future, at something to come: it suggested romance, or a further step into cosmopolitan legend, into the next episode of a story about power. But small-town high style (as would later be true of suburban style) was not forward-looking; it was, just about absolutely, antifuture, or idyllic, which is to say anti-story, frozen, codified, utopian. Even if a woman got her hands on a Schiaparelli or a Mainbocher, it was a set piece, a final outfit—a sort of bossy version of the sweater set and pearls. This was because *real* style—the visual casting of yourself in the daring light of what you might wish for or be capable of doing—would, in the course of things, take you right out of town and into adventure, and very few women had that much nerve. Some did, and would be pointed out and whispered about. They were also the ones who talked well.

At the moment, haute couture is just starting to admit that it is dead—well, not dead but not of great interest. In its old-fashioned way, it still works. Haute couture, just as it has been from its beginnings, is concerned with rank, with dominating a room by the way you look. And it does say you have money. But money nowadays doesn't have the quality of romance it did once (and may have again). Power has more romance these days. And so does anti-power.

For the moment, something better—or, at least, more interesting—has come along: a much more fascinating set of rules, a much more delicious sense of contexts and how to dress for them, which is felt at street level and has nothing to do with the magazines and the designers. Rank now means that you can dress down if you like, in part as a signal that you are available to play. The extremely expensive designer dress or beaded blazer and the important jewels serve to announce that you are very rich and quite knowledgeable. But they also signal that you are out of the game at its liveliest. You are mostly a heavy presence, a small-town one—you are part of the small-town circle of important people, in the middle of the big city's whirl of erotica and self-invented eligibility.

Romance in dress is not so strictly class-centered anymore. It is defined by a freedom from being co-opted, by the possession of a strong will and a strong sense of risk—actually, I mean a sense of lust, and curiosity, and a willingness to be thrill-mad, a little. Sexuality and romance are part and parcel of a T-shirt and jeans or shorts, unfussed-with hair, no makeup—indicating a kind of sincerity of physical existence. (And a sense that all matters of taste, and all tastes, are a smidgen kinky.) Serious style—that of some older women, and some rich women—announces a certain dishonesty about immortality, about the word "classic." And it seems to me that a man's clothes, if they are too obvious in what they say about his rank and métier, tend to look like counterfeit statements except in very rare instances, when some vibration of truth about the man himself comes through all the fabric and buttons. Then male style is stunning, is a knockout. But male power expressed in the equivalent of old-line haute couture—in very expensive suits and shirts—usually seems to indicate a downturn in profits. Why should men of real power *bother*? The panache of great success is conveyed better by the intelligence of the look of the woman a man is with or by the expression on his face than by his clothes. (Maybe a kind of college-town professorial-male flirtatious chic is where men these days should start, using Turnbull & Asser rip-offs and tactfully updated classic shoes and belts; there's something witty about respectable shoes on a middle-aged man who jogs regularly and has a shot at a Nobel.)

Certain American upper-caste customs, such as heavy English suits in hot weather and thin coats in winter, have their touching side. Or very good, expensive long-worn tennis whites. These things do demonstrate strength and survivability. But they are too obvious as gestures. The person wearing these emblematic clothes is *the person making the gesture* and not a person with a full range of dialogue. That is, such gestures wipe out conversation. The person is busy mopping his or her forehead or pretending not to care about his or her tennis whites.

So, I think, the assertion of social class in dress is touching but not convincing. It is never convincing anymore without servants and great, great financial importance. It is ritual without substance. Claim without real privilege. But it is familiar to us—the claim of social rank in the not-so-rich—and dear, in its way. (Armani offers a comment on the notion of lineage, of inheritance in dress, since his clothes, with their elegant simplicities, their double meanings, seem to hint that one has a family past, of clothes and servants—a history of clothes, as it were.)

Does anyone want control of a room through clothes anymore? Social cooperation and *some* rank are what one wants. The categories of rich man's clothes, young man's clothes, intelligent woman's clothes, professional woman's clothes—the assertion of style as a function of intelligence or of stylelessness as a function of intelligence—have their specialized practitioners. And the depressives are always onstage. As are the underdressed narcissists. But a combination of some individuality in dress and some obscurity of personal intent, so that a riddle mechanism sets in (something paradoxically catches the eye and then can be ignored; the look is related to movement and to personality rather than to mood, and is suitable for half a dozen contexts), produces a jolt of response and amusement in city life. And the clothes required to achieve the effect, while costly to some degree, do not have as much to do with money as with the signaling of wit and perversity.

Once, in the 1930s, I saw my parents leave the house dressed for a costume party. There they were, outside on the suburban street in early-evening summer light, dressed to go to a dance, in real 1920s clothes. Movies and photographs and drawings can't convey the excitement generated by those clothes in real life, in real light: the short spangled dress with its low-cut, roundish neckline, the long pearls and the aigrette, the spats and vest and fedora, the spiffy jacket. The raw flash of such clothes seemed to radiate rebellion—a sheer, strange erotic extremism and a suggestion of unbridled motion.

I remember almost all the clothes I wore in my childhood. (My parents on their deathbeds remembered their clothes, back over their entire lifetimes.) I remember everything I ever wore that had been badly chosen for the context or that someone said was ugly or the wrong color, and I still tend to burst out laughing as I did then—from nerves and gall. When I was little, I had a sand-colored cashmere short-pants suit and a shirt with a Little Lord Fauntleroy frill at the neck and down the front, which made it impossible for me to button. My parents and my sister and my nurse used to take turns doing the buttons and brushing my hair curl by curl. (I had ringleted blond hair.) Like a lot of little boys, I had a Charles Lindbergh–style helmet with a chin strap, which I wore when I was playing outside. I loved dirt and anything resembling boots. I wanted to wear galoshes every day. My sister used to scoff, "He doesn't know *anything* about clothes!"

We were a good-looking family, and in the car, with all the windows open, the two children in the rumble seat, and all our different-colored hair blowing in the wind, we were a fine sight.

Style won't be interesting again until more people are willing to show off on the street. Suburbs don't have streets, and city streets are perilous—but nothing is as interesting as street clothes when the wind is blowing and the sun is out, or the rain is dramatic, and everyone you pass is playing the carnal game with you.

1994

IT IS ONE OF THE RULES
OF FOPPISHNESS

It is one of the ground rules of foppishness that no woman can determine how you dress. No woman understands men's clothes or men's lives or the power encapsulated in clothes, and the games and the signals of clothes; so, they mustn't interfere.

Very stylish women, similarly, make it clear they cannot dress to a man's taste; they cannot afford to; they would lose their reputation for *style*. It is a given among them that only women can understand the strategies and art in how women dress.

So, perhaps there is an element in high style which is intrinsically ungendered, almost asexual, or antisexual. Perhaps one chooses between high style and happiness of a different order. Or one becomes addicted to notions of style that are conductive to sexual restlessness, a kind of fateful independence. Do fops have a higher rate of failure in their affairs, their marriages? One suspects them of having trouble with women. One suspects high-styled women of having trouble with men.

Perhaps extreme style is inconveniently specialized—or is sexual display in a seemly but supremely unsexual way—at least according to some notions of sexuality. How can you be a sublime dandy, of either sex, if you are sexually happy?

Let us admit that the highest form of male dressing is to dress for your boss and your colleagues and your tailor. That's the major leagues. What room does that leave for a human attachment? The way you look shows how far down the list of important things in your life a woman is.

That would mean that real style was contrary to or decidedly opposed to or was thoroughly unrelated to sexual happiness, assuming that such a thing as sexual happiness exists. But, if such a thing as sexual happiness exists, then, of course, those who experience it, dress accordingly, in what must be mutual Pygmalionism, Higgins dropping his *h*s now and then and adopting the color blue since Eliza blooms when he is blue-tinted and has obviously softened. I tend to think when I see a well-dressed man—if part of the effect of how he's dressed is a certain oddity of color scheme—that something's off in the codedness of the signals, that his tailor and his colleagues and his boss are not the complete tyrants of his soul they are for other marvelously dressed men.

Let us say that one's boss, one's peers, one's women, are all influences on how we dress. One's boss can be defied but not reasoned with—so then that influence can be located in the unreasonable element in a man's dress. One's peers change if one's circumstances do—so that element can be located as the more directly faddish and social-class thing in a man's clothes.

But women's influence—ah, that is beyond codification. It is a negative influence, a war against the uniform, a censorship of the look of heroic isolation, a blurring, sometimes faint, of body outlines, concealing them from profane eyes. The matter of suitability to you as a man and not as an icon, a modesty, a backing down from being dressed in order to strut, these things emerge as a matter of course. A man's clothes are more likely to be apt than to be self-advertisement. A notification, instead, of a personal physical merit of a mysterious order creeps in; one suspects a prospering human tie.

Can a happy marriage (while it is happy)—or any other pleasing attachment—bring it about that you wind up wearing ugly clothes to suit a tasteless woman? Can Pygmalion be a fool? Socially, depending on how envious and brutal we are, we might judge that to be the case fairly often. In fact, it seems that men who are dressed partly in regard to their women tend to move in flocks excluded from other masculine flocks by reason of their heresy and others' envy.

But, really, can a woman who likes you have bad taste concerning the

colors and cut of your clothes? No. Her taste may be socially or professionally off at first but not for long since part of what a prospering human tie
is, is an education in the other person's reality.

Gigolos and young kids setting out live a storylike version of this.
Men growing plump through a clever woman's wish to fatten them out of
the sexual market have the worst part of it. Men marrying into different
social castes or into other societies have the most intellectual version of it.
Successful men, with well-defined styles, on which they have become
reliant, have the very worst of it since they can have no pleasure in an
unexpected cashmere scarf of a type they never liked but now ought to,
but can't, *und so weiter*.

I have seen the closets of men who have known happiness; and I must
say they are quite a historical mess. So I worry when I see men well dressed
in a pure fashion that they will be bad tempered.

I know only a few men who don't give in on sport socks and underwear
and swimming trunks. And kimonos.

One way out is to move to another climate or to the country. Some
couples switch social spheres. Actually, clothes are of unimaginable
importance to every couple.

But it is too late to go into that now. . . . It is too rich and too curious
a subject. . . .

1988

CARS AND LIFE

A good car, like a child, is an area of worry. The car is a problem and so is how one looks because of it. This reality is part of my emotional language, and I feel boring to myself and saintly and foreign when I manage to escape it.

In my professional world and among my friends—especially in the world of New York writing and, well, not thought but *thinkishness*—the number of people who don't drive or don't drive much, and who are not interested in driving, is nearly universal.

Cheever, Updike, Salinger, Oates, Sontag, Tyler, and best-seller writers and reporters, agents and editors, none that I knew or know, care about cars—except perhaps about who rents a limousine or who has access to one and who hasn't.

I mind this somewhat and don't mind it at all. I never tried psychoanalysis but I can't imagine a potent session for an American, male or female, in which cars didn't play a part, some part.

Anyway, years ago, I bought a BMW 320i.

I bought it for a number of reasons. It reminds me, indirectly, of my father's last car; my father became ill in 1938, and his last car, a step down from a 1932 green Buick sedan, was a 1935 Chevy, brown, two-door, cheap. The 1980 320i is a kind of sophisticated take-off on such practical cars.

I identified car grilles before I would speak. My Dad used to show me off by saying, "Do you see a new Plymouth?" and I would slowly pivot and survey the drowsy machines at curbside and pick out the distinctive gridwork that made up the grille of a Chevy or a Plymouth.

This was back when cars had running boards and headlights separate from the engine compartment, mysterious glass-fronted pomegranates, streamlined pears, that poured out light at certain times. And often rumble seats. Cars, car windows, radiator caps, car paint—I can still remember what year certain colors and kinds of paint were used for the first time—and car grilles, and the mirroring brilliances of chrome, these ideograms are essential to the graphics of my mind and interest me more than the shapes of typefaces or Jasper Johns's numbers.

I remember hugging and kissing parts of cars, inner and outer, steering wheels, gearshifts, door handles, tires. I used to like to taste things before I began to specialize in the use of my senses. Do you remember squatting and poking with a twig between the mesas of rubber in the tire treads?

We, my sister and I, used to have fights about the privilege of riding in a rumble seat. My father had a bachelor brother, a Jew who liked Shiksas, and so argued he couldn't marry while his mother, the terrible Faggai, was alive. He had first a convertible, then a coupe with a rumble seat. A rumble seat is where the trunk now is, and it opened up and there was a leather seat, cracked and odorous, windswept when the car was in motion, and it rumbled in a vaguely thrilling way partly because of the exhaust that throbbed remorselessly below it and partly because of the hinged back, its locks set for the upright position, which also rattled and clattered and, thirdly, because of the wind.

I remember punching my sister out—well, she was eleven years older and mean and liberated, sort of a Katharine Hepburn crossed with Lee Marvin playing a psychopath. She had mean eyes and mean, fat legs and the kind of self-righteousness that some lady novelists have, all lies and business and the hope that repetitions showed sincerity and soul: at ice-cream places, she would say, "I want vanilla, I only like vanilla, I think only vanilla is nice—"

And then, since she had no fear or sense of boredom, "Vanilla, vanilla, van*illa*—"

Or when we started to fight, "I'm NOT hitting you, I'm NOT hitting you." Sometimes, it was a direct lie, but sometimes she would say that while she pinched or kicked me, or even punched me, she having just learned at school this new and sophisticated treachery, this foul method for getting her way.

She argued that *hitting* covered *slapping* and *shoving* but not punching.

I used to scrunch down on my back and kick up toward her face.

"Not in the face, you terrible boy," she would say.

"I want you to have scars," I would say, desperate with unhappiness and vigor against the fact of defeat if I should falter in will or submit to pity at all.

The air streamed over us, over the squarish roof of the *coupe* (a word that's nearly vanished from use), and came rumbling and flapping like damp sheets on a clothesline. This was before clothes dryers, too; we didn't have any dryers except the sun and ovens, but we had all sorts of games among the hanging sheets, that desperately beautiful white light of the wet sheets. The air used to swing and batter and echo like ropes striking sandbags and sometimes like chains hitting a tar road or even a concrete one.

Fighting—kicking and pulling hair, and being pinched and shoved—while the wind rumbled, and my hateful sister's tiny breasts, really tiny, mean breasts, pushed around under her *blouse*—and her hateful pride and ferocity, and her passion for cars, her hate-filled jealousy of the male, her physical response of excitement and violence to cars, were displayed in her betrayal-and-tricky assault: we got hot and intense.

Whoever was driving couldn't see us because, in those days, the rear windows were tiny, about the size of half a place mat. In a convertible with a rumble seat, though, we were visible, and someone, Daddy, say, or Mom, would stop or order the car to stop, and they would get out and come back, or they would lean over the seat and say, "Stop it, stop it, you two—"

Threats were fewer in those days, punishments stiffer—the one that set up future problems in dieting (since freedom was shown by one's being able to eat whenever one wanted) was, "You'll be sent to bed at once without dinner—"

Cars: fatality, overexcitement, glamour, mobility, money, force, skill, getting away from home, showing off, wind, scenery, ice cream that drips. Motion and power.

The excited jiggle of riding in a car, and one's feelings, in one's bones and in one's legs in short pants, that group of feelings, if turned into a painting, would be a Jackson Pollock, layers and squiggles of color, aswirl and splattered.

I hear my voice saying back in childhood to one or another of my parents, "Get her out of here, I want to ride in the rumble seat ALONE."

Ownership is not a capitalist, or bourgeois, matter, even if borrowers and borrowing children angrily say so, but has an aspect of social intelligence to it, citizenship and judgment and folly, spiritual and financial, nuanced or flat-out folly, or canniness, and, of course, a sexual reality—which also has to do with father and mother figures. I mean shelter is sexual; one wants a solvent *and* sexual lover—or mother, or father.

One is revealed, nakedly, consumer-ingly, in one's degree and kind of *responsibility*—and one's sophistication, one's decency or indecency as a steward, as a host, here on the (maybe flagging) American gravy train, among the squandering of the world's resources. One's ability to arouse love shows, too, in ownership (of things, of traits, of one's self); shows anecdotally, lyrically, or as socialist realism. One time, when I was young, a young woman who'd been at Radcliffe, wrote a novel that became a bestseller: she introduced herself to me at a party as, "Hi, I'm Rona *'Best of Everything'* Jaffe, you're Harold, *'First Love and Other Sorrows.'* Right?" Now I'm Harold and his BMW among other names.

For a man is more allied with his car than with any other object.

For when a man buys a car, a lot of secret stuff gets thrown into the mixture and is revealed.

I don't think it's as direct as shopping for a phallus replacement or disguiser or enlarger or be-skiller—it's more like changing a context, the phallic context, too.

Much more is involved: investment stuff, as a measure of the mind, and what one looks like. Men are silent, or tacit, or secretive, or talkers of nonsense because much of what is involved in being a male and American is unspeakable. Decently or in any manner.

I have yet to see a fat man in a BMW. If one is on the cusp of being fat, and one doesn't intend to do anything about it, one has to think about going toward buying a nonentity-mobile, a male incognito-machine, a fudging-the-issue vehicle, *a bargain*, something old and sloppy, something old and marvelous, something incongruous. A Chariot of Modesty. Or one of Burning Gold—life being lived fully, flamingly—as in the finned killer-mobiles of the fifties that were also family cars. Now maybe the term would be "laid-back and fulfilled"—but not in a BMW, surely. The term might be right-wing, mean fascist old man, or whatever.

Discreet cars demand from observers that charity known as common sense, as *Don't pick on them, they're nice people—good citizens*—whatever. Sharp-wittedness-display, peacockery, money, or person pimping as a branch of self-pimping one way or another—or Bogart-like scarred vehicles—are other routes. Maroon sedans seem to me shameful and to show a crookedness of disposition. Whenever a man says, "It's practical," or "It's got a great overhead-cam design, carelessly manufactured, I'll admit, but easily serviced, know what I mean? And I can get a full load into it—" I feel superior—and pitying. As toward a two-VW family. The ecology-bicycle route is better. In the 1930s, when my father stepped down from a Buick to a Chevy, it hurt him a lot. He said it wasn't just the difference in the way women acted toward him, it was the damned boringness of the car. A lot of what I do, I do to see if I can do better than my dad in those areas in which he is in me, in which he is most of what I know still. It's not *exactly* competition—it's just a matter of ownership, of wanting the trait to be mine and not simply an adaptation or steal from him or something taken over but not lived or examined.

It's hard to admit sometimes how much of one's life is not covered by art or theory very well.

One stays in one's lane in a reasonably well-washed car and one not painted in a way suggesting tattoos and a wanton longing for a biker's virility, but someone can guess at a lot about you anyway and be accurate enough to make this whole business uncomfortable.

A motorcycle is actually an adventure, the danger is real, and the lack of safety is aphrodisiac, as aphrodisiac as marital charity.

The pornography of persistent and dominating and abruptly changeable rhythms, the sharply defined noises of acceleration and deceleration, the air in one's face, and one's vulnerability—making one conscious of flesh and escape—and the near sentience of the machine's movements and angles of lean make a motorcycle unmistakeably direct as an indication of some aspects of sensual and perhaps nutty masculinity. Or perhaps just a flat out indication of sexual competitiveness beyond all bounds of good sense and suggesting a serious deficiency in the practitioner, but made up for, romantically, intensely.

Similarly, a car—which may be a boast or an exercise or a compensation—or all three in sequence, over a period of time. An automobile pretending to a state of mechanical nature like that of a motorcycle is a fake, a compromised machine. I had a Honda Accord before the BMW—both companies make motorcycles. Under circumstances of age—I'm fifty-one now—some fakery and compromise and combinations and dilutions of virtue are more than OK: they're advisable. The world being as it is (too much for me, and too much with me, lately), as one comes around the bend as either Man O'War (my dad's favorite horse) or as a tiring middle-aged male dressed in horse costume, being a horse's ass, and not exactly a winner and not exactly a loser, the half-real thing begins to look good if the half-real thing is socially evolved and available and less ripe with immanent fatality than the real thing apparently or really is.

A car is an evolved, a diluted image—I'm talking about the idea in the mind when one sees a car and is away from cars and the word *car* comes up and about the feeling one has when one is in one or is dealing with one. Image includes one's physical sense of it, the pleasures and convenience and inconvenience and discomforts, and then the meaning of the vehicle. Meaning includes the Romance of the Car and money (money is deeply romantic: affluent eras are usually romantic, and affluent and money-mad cities have an aura of romance; one reason is that one rewards oneself for having made money; I've yet to know a male writer who didn't reward himself for a successful book with an affair that was somewhat over his head, or a female writer, either, come to think of it), and meaning includes what is signified, one's dexterity, one's reflexes, one's common sense (literally: with what group do you share ideas of social common sense), one's social class—or one's social pretensions, plus all the stuff about cars in general, mobility, suburban living, travel of a sort, always modified by specific experiences with specific cars as well as car-rental agencies, for instance.

I would like to say that a car simply is too weak and too complex to be a good *symbol*, since neither does it plow, and it does not weep either. It is not warlike or a mounting or a frame the way a horse is (but a horse is philosophically null, too). Plato, Spinoza, Kant, and Hume do not discuss the horse or animal slavery; philosophical notions of meaning—and freedom—changed when the machine civilization began; philosophy became more mathematical for one thing, and people largely disappear from philosophy. People become the subject of novels but then they disappear from novels and become the subject of movies. Now they are disappearing from movies and becoming the subject of television.

A horse was *necessary* only in a sense, and so, too, a car is and is not a *necessity*. There is no valid, private, individual, and personal view of a car. One can't pity a car or pity its owner, and one's admiration for a car, a whore-mobile, has in it the seeds of future ownership—of whoring and advertisement. By being general and easily transferable, a car—like money, like a whore—moves out of meaning, which is primarily capitalist and private, with public centers in which meaning is traded and can become a social necessity, but meaningless except in certain limited and really private ways.

I married a woman I liked and I, thereupon, bought a BMW.

I had been working on a book for a long time and had grown reclusive and out of touch. I took a teaching job in upstate New York and bought a Honda for it but the Honda was inflexible, it was like trying to deal with a stubborn, power-mad, middle-class Japanese woman who was very short. Its insistence that it was not a whore made it seem like a kiddy wagon or scooter with a roof and a team of squirrels in it. You drove it its way and you didn't deviate, and you couldn't find new or interesting ways to deal with it. It was not interesting. I fell asleep in it on any trip longer than half an hour—and this in a car with a stick shift, I might add, and with me competing with other cars on the road and using dexamine, an amphetamine, to stay awake.

The idea of the BMW was that one might begin to live more fully physically, in terms of getting around. It cost less than a country house or than two trips to Europe for two of us. It issued a challenge, more than one: Learn to drive, have a complicated mechanical experience, talk to your new wife in this extraordinary and as if picture-windowed mobile setting. Take your place in the whore-society of your time (I'm not sure civilization is anything ever but a whore-society—Athens, Rome, Paris, old Jerusalem, and the angry prophets).

Actually, one can't talk much and drive a 320i well. The car is light, precise, too responsive to ignore even for half a second. Being on automatic pilot or half-attentive won't do. Attention is lured, is necessary, or one drives in zigzags and looks like a fool, like the first really fat man with a BMW.

I liked the car so much that I ran it into the tail end of a Pontiac the first day I had it. I was reluctant to jam on the brakes before they were broken in—that sometimes ruins new brakes—and I was only going five miles an hour and the car sort of awed me, it was mechanically so sophisticated, so neat, so precisely honed, and so much better at what it did than I was in what I did to it, that I thought it would stop, it would somehow negotiate part of its own safety. But the car, my darling BMW, is a very passive whore, angry and masochistic and then vengeful. The brakes had not been roughened or broken in, and the car slowly and remorselessly glided into the backside of a bent and rusted ten-year-old Pontiac driven by a stubbled and drunken old man with bushel baskets full of what looked like canteloupe rinds in the backseat. This was on Long Island, and Long Island is exotic, but not nearly so exotic as I, a long-time recluse and man ignorant of things, picture that wanton tongue of Real Estate to be. From Coney Island through Brooklyn Heights to the startlingly ugly remnants of the last world's fair or the absolute weirdness of the architecture at La Guardia Airport or at Hofstra University, Long Island as an expression of mind and social reality is much, much stranger than Los Angeles.

At any rate, I never found out what the bushel baskets actually held, and I never even found out the stubble-chinned man's name—he spoke no known tongue, he was ethnically unidentifiable. My feeling is he was an underground and sullen WASP, and he practiced a mode of temper that mixed suspicion and threat that I associate only with American WASPs in certain areas—and social classes (such as Appalachia or LA and Orange County), and Italian-Americans *who are very thin* (i.e., clearly mad and exiled from their mothers and from any dining community)—and resignation and slyness that I associate only with Long Island, with being sly and rural in such an urban conglomeration.

I told my wife, Ellen, that I was glad in a way the BMW had been marked up because now it was mine and I would be less afraid of it. She is accustomed to men's tactics. Her first husband once lost control of a bank through a lawsuit but he managed to claim it as a victory. He claims everything is a victory for him: it is always V-J Day in his heart.

My wife has a small face. Salinger, in a story the title of which I can't remember, says of a character, Booboo Tannenbaum, something like, in the category or area of small faces, hers was a stunner. I feel reproached often by the smallness of my wife's bones.

I said, "No, no, I'm not claiming this as victory, I'm not looking at the brighter side—I'm being honest, I'm relieved the thing has a defect now." Finally I said, "OK, I'm lying. I'm heartsick."

The brakes had worked well enough that the nose of the BMW had lowered itself—as if it were the forward shoulder of a charging left tackle—but it was only a nose and a frail one.

I like car fronts to come to a point or center. My favorite automobile in American painting is a Loewy-designed Studebaker in a Richard Estes oil, a picture of a seamy part of Forty-second Street. It's the model Studebaker that has a Cessna-type nose as if for a propeller. I never liked *that* car but I like car grilles that have bowsprit or prow characteristics or nose ones; as I said, I like cars to be boatlike or human.

The BMW of my year has a double oval, like nostrils, nares, buttocks, I don't know what—these are aluminum and set into black carbidelike plastic lateral fins. Plastic. Frailer than checkers in the game of checkers, a little stronger than a plastic hair comb. I dented the buttock-or-nostril front of the BMW and part of the hood that for safety, opens in reverse.

My first car, which I bought in college (or which I bought part of—I had a rich roommate who bought most of it) was a 1941 Lincoln Continental with a boat prow. A long hood came to a point or vertical line and the chrome grille was like a bow wave splash.

The Lincoln Continental had been made of very thick metal, maybe four times as thick as that used for postwar American cars.

This guy, the rich roommate—he'd had his own sixteen-thousand-dollar-a-year trust fund since he was fifteen ("It's supposed to teach me how to handle money before I come into any of my real trust funds but all it does is make me be a fool before I'm ready to live with knowing what a fool I am." "Yeah? Oh. Lissen, Henry, *I* don't hate you—")—wanted a car, and I said, "Let's find an old Continental." In those days, old-car collecting wasn't common, and we found a '41 for sale for six hundred dollars in New Hampshire. I paid one hundred of the six but I didn't take a sixth ownership. Henry was deeply concerned about being swindled and I hadn't been close enough to my father and he hadn't lived long enough for me to have been told or to be ready to see that someone who is afraid of being swindled will swindle you in order to see to it he isn't swindled. Between Henry and me, I was the dominant one, the pursued one, but I didn't give a goddamn for money, and so he sort of glimmered with self-satisfaction and superiority looking forward to the long run when money would speak, would cheer and roar for him.

At any rate, I had no legal title to any of the Continental.

We put it in his parents' barn, and we took it apart and we sanded off all the rust, using his parents' tools.

Henry explained to me that I was no good as a workman and so my labor was worthless. "Yeah, I see that," I said.

It took a couple of months, and we painted the car a metallic shade of gray. Metallic paint was new that year or was recent. It consists of a mixture of paint and, I believe, metallic particles, that keep the paint from being a single shade. The paint has variations and brightness so that the painted surface has a kind of depth that, like old-fashioned lacquering, suggests expense and makes outlines, or lines, clearer. The car was so large and had so many surfaces that we had to walk back and forth, back and forth, holding spray guns. I was told I was a lousy walker and my painting was worth nothing either.

I thought Henry was merely swindling his way to thinking better of himself. It really hadn't occurred to me that property was so important. I thought when you liked or needed people, you shared things with them to a considerable extent in order to forestall their hatred and their lying to you and leaving you. And I was so startled by the degree of competition among students I found at Harvard, where Henry and I were seniors, that I wasn't ready to believe, yet, in the common or garden-variety thing of social swindling, money and money gouging, in which you weren't supposed to take personally the ways in which you were exploited.

But then I didn't think Henry should take personally the ways in which he was inferior as an athlete or in looks or, more specifically, in mind. Henry was very, very dumb. But not when it came to money.

And while he was ungenerous in most ways, he was generous in talking about money and lawyers and rich girls' talking about money to rich boys, and I was willing to *pay* for that stuff.

He was in analysis. He'd been suicidal when I met him, but we'd straightened that out, and now he wanted to live and triumph. (At his most suicidal, he hung on to his money, however. But he picked up the check from time to time.) At any rate, the analyst was supposed to wean him from his dependence on his mother—who had the money ("Dad married Mom or the bucks")—and from me; I'd said, "I don't like you hanging around the way you do and scowling at my friends and calling me late at night and dumping on me, OK?"

Henry was tall and slack-bodied and slack-eyed but good-looking in a somewhat large or hairless-horse way—sort of sad like a horse about to be sent to the knackers.

But, so far, anytime I really insisted on something, he would give in. If I'd insisted on part ownership he would have given in, and if I'd demanded full ownership, he might very well have given in. It's hard to know since I never tested him about money except once when his mother offered me a small trust fund for what I'd done in rescuing him and getting him to study and to become less hysterical and *messy* and *shaming*— her words—*sloppy* and *shameful* would be mine. And I turned her down, saying I could only take it if she promised not to hold him in such contempt from now on and promised to prevent her self-important and sly husband from castrating my friend, Henry, every chance he got. (The idea, on Dad's part, was to stay as the favorite of the moneyed woman.) Well, you don't say things like that to rich, psychologically frail, aging women—and you don't do things like that, either. She blew up, and I was embarrassed, but I said, "Look, you give me the trust fund the way things are now, and Henry will *always* feel like a jerk: the money is evidence. I want the money but I don't want to do that to Henry."

She didn't stop yelling; the offer was withdrawn; and I got heartsick. I went looking for Henry, who was out in the woods behind his mother's house doing a watercolor.

I said his mother had sort of offered me a trust fund because she thought I was bright and ought to be given some kind of support in my work, but I had apparently blown it.

He said, "She'd never offer you money, you're crazy—"

He said, "You're dreaming things—"

And suchlike.

Well, after that, it was touch and go between us, with my mostly despising him but being nostalgic about the college years, and his dramatizing everything as his being dependent on me and having to get free, which I saw as his using me but trying to do nothing in return.

But when I wanted to drive the Continental, I did. I gave the orders, and he could go shove it.

Unfortunately, I wasn't nearly as good a driver as he was, and when things went wrong with the car, I'd get mad, even lunatic. The car had two electric motors that raised the convertible top. One night, I was driving, and only one motor worked, and as the top lurched up crazily yawing and whining, I couldn't think of what to do or think or feel except to feel lament and madness, which I knew was not culturally right.

Anyway, early on, I was driving the car; Henry was in it, indulging me in this one mode of payoff; and two other guys and one girl, maybe, were in the car. We were at a stoplight near the North Station. The light changed, and without signaling, a taxi on my right cut to the left. It crossed in front of me, it's motor roaring, the driver looking both sneaky and victorious as he cut off the blocklong Continental, with the college men, boys, whatever, in it. And I'd bought a yachting cap with visor and gold braid, which I wore when I drove the damn thing, which made it worse for him.

Henry was a great shouter. I mean on the spur of the moment. He had a kind of wit that came out as abrupt exclamation or shout. Ignored by a guy ladling out fruit cup at Hayes-Bickford's, then on Mass Ave, Henry shouted, "I could buy and sell you, you creep." I know it sounds merely stupid, and it was stupid basically, but Henry was so slack and so rich, and he was sort of stamping his foot, and he did add, "Give me my fruit cup, you Communist," that it seemed funny at the time.

Well, here's a better one. In Manhattan, once, having driven down from Cambridge—I think it was to see Kirsten Flagstad's final opera performance in America; I'd never seen an opera—we were waiting at a light to cross Times Square, and Henry got rattled: he was an amazing reproduction of his mother and her fantastic systems of blowing up, of finding things to be too hard or too common, but, anyway, too much one way or another, and she would sort of blunder ahead. Well, Henry was that way about stoplights and New York. He figured wrong, and some of us in the car were slouching well down and trying not to make a really big issue of his lack of cool when the cop came over.

Henry and the cop discussed things, New York, and traffic lights and the necessity to read signs.

Finally, the cop let him off with a warning.

The cop walked off, and Henry started up the car, and suddenly he shouted, "Don't talk mean to me, we grow your food where I come from."

I knew Henry wasn't talented, but, believe me, in the ordinary give-and-take at a college, he wasn't the worst wit. A lot of people who knew he was rich, thought him witty.

So, when the taxi was crossing in front of us, Henry shouted at him, "Death-hound! Killer!"

Now the Lincoln was a heavy car. Its lines, those curves and such, couldn't be done by machine tools but had to be leaded in by hand. And the brakes, while reliable enough, couldn't stop that metal land-yacht quickly once you were in gear and had started to release the clutch. The engine was a twelve-cylinder number ("Count them, twelve," was one of Henry's routines). We sailed, semimajestically, into the taxi, while Henry shouted, or muttered, terms of Freudian and college and rich-kid liberal abuse at the taxi driver—"child molester" was one: Henry had gotten that from a guy who's now a curator at a New York museum.

The right front fender hit the taxi's left front fender. We were doing about five miles an hour. The taxi for all its roaring was doing maybe fifteen.

We shoved it an inch or two—or a foot or two.

I felt that sickness in my stomach of having done something really stupid and damaging.

Henry had taught me to drive on his parents' Lincoln—that year's model—and, one time, we had a race, him driving one of his parents' Jeeps across a field while I hurtled his parents' newish Lincoln along a backcountry Massachusetts two-lane road. Henry was pulling ahead by cutting diagonally across a field, and I looked at him and threw the Lincoln too fast into one of those right-angled country turns when one road ends in the crossbar of another road T-ing its way, and I skidded down and up across a shallow ditch and into a bona fide New England stone wall.

This felt like that.

But we all got out of the car; we were all six-footers; one guy stayed in the car—he was drunk, and not as tall, and he was a coward, he said. Three of us converged on a small Lebanese taxi driver who began to tremble.

I said, "Look, I don't want to see the damage, everyone back in the car—except Henry."

Henry had little dignity and often resembled a sheepish horse.

He came back to the car and said, "This car is built like a tank—we got only a scratch. The taxi is smashed to hell—"

When the Lebanese had driven off, I got out to look. There was barely a scratch. And I'd seen the damage to the taxi when it lurched off on its illegal turn. We hadn't summoned a cop, and none had turned up because the taxi driver seemed to have been punished enough. We discussed the ins and outs of the justice of this event, and social justice, in general.

Had I expected the BMW to be as invulnerable? Yeah.

It cost seven hundred dollars to fix, and a slight gulf still shows between the hood and the body more on the right side than the left. I tend to notice on other BMWs if they have undergone this, and a surprising number of times, they have.

I was rather humble toward the bodywork shop that fixed it for me. In fact, I asked the owner, an Italian with a slight swagger, to tell me what he knew about BMWs. "Treat 'em rough," he said. "Enjoy it."

A friend of mine said, when I told him I wanted to write about the BMW, that cars were secrets and I would inevitably be secretive about the BMW, too—he said oracularly, "Words don't have fenders."

He meant that what I know has to do with language and not with something as unlanguaged as a car.

Books—novels, I mean, or books of essays or stories in groups or singly—aren't much good, it's true, about cars. But television and movies feast on the automobile—but not BMWs, it's true.

Many movie rhythms *are* car rhythms. We are in the child's seat again, the screen is so big. Those figures up there reduce us, comparatively, to the size of children—perhaps in one of those cradlelike seats—facing a windshield looking onto a world in which everything is in grown-up scale.

But television has an eavesdropped-on quality plus that feeling of board games and toys. Television makes us feel as if we were stowaways and spying, like kids spying from underneath a couch on matchbox models come alive—the nutcracker coming out of the matchbox.

I can't imagine television as tragic.

The paucity of cultural terms for everything, not just for dealing with a car and one's feelings about a car and about cars in general, is strangling us. My present wife's ex-husband refused to own a car although he lived as a rich man. He didn't like to be humiliated gratuitously by garages. He didn't want his children to have the freedom of having access to a car. He didn't like his inability to haggle over the prices of things automotive.

My first father-in-law owned two or three cars at a time and a couple of Jeeps and tractors but he more or less brutalized them in order not to be dominated by them. I was told by a salesman for word processors that most men prefer to buy small computers that require more knowledge of how to operate them and are somewhat difficult and less adroit, and that is so because men want feelings of mastery and of control (whereas women prefer the more *transparent* machines). Men don't want to feel inferior to anything, death or machinery; they want to feel superior and that they have to compensate with added skill for the defects in the second-rate machines they buy—and perhaps, too, for defects in their children and in their women.

As I said, my acquaintances in Manhattan, on magazines or in publishing houses, and writers and poets, are without exception mechanically and automotively illiterate. Whether that represents a kind of snobbery or a kind of culture war or a kind of defeat varies in each case. My feeling is that the failure of certain sorts of movies about cars (*The Betsey*); the adolescent tone of such novels as *The Green Hat* (which has a Hispano-Suiza in it) and *The Great Gatsby*; the absence of cars in Eliot, Auden, Hemingway, and from the cover of the *New Yorker*; and the lack of a good travel book using a car have made the car look socially unacceptable; it's not apparently a good subject. This pressures the upper demographic group and sours it on the subject of cars, making the subject odd and oddly unpalatable.

Detroit's power in the old days has something to do with this. It was assumed anyone talking about cars had been corrupted by Detroit or by hysterical resistance. Everything concerned with cars in public discourse was a lie for a long time. And social class influences this stuff: it is the lower echelons that bother with demolition derbies and jazzed-up machines, with the beautification, testing, and sacrifice of cars.

Movies, though, as I started to say earlier, have been good to cars, have been fixated on them, one might say, on motion and power, privacy and plot—as on women's breasts and bellies, motion and power, privacy and plot.

Movies devote a lot of attention to cars—although rarely to a single machine, obsessively and faithfully regarded. The movies treat the promiscuous and promiscuously disposable and subject-to-men aspect of cars in the way they do not let themselves treat women. Relationships to women in the popular arts are fantastically idealized in relation to fidelity and then dismissed, or thereby dismissed, by the idealization in the first place.

Just as movie background music comes from Wagner and Tchaikovsky—but Wagner more so—much of the movies' attitude toward women comes from Hemingway—Lady Brett, who is racy and fine (and whose body has the lines of a racing yacht, I believe: I always picture her as coming to a single long point like a bowsprit in front instead of having breasts); and Catharine in *A Farewell to Arms*, who dies, but oh, is she nice to men. Just as Garbo is really from fin-de-siecle writing, such as Wilde's.

But *beyond* that is a similarity in the way movies use cars and use women. For both subjects, at least when the women are young and in very good trim, movies use an uncosmopolitan, satanic, satiric-farcical drive. The idea is male excitement—and male hope. Like having a car magically strong that demolishes ugly and ill-meaning taxicabs. Burt Reynolds's Trans-Am is like Barrymore's or Powell's Carole Lombard. Any good car chase in a movie, the car is like Clara Bow or Claudette Colbert or Louise Brooks when she was being a good sport.

The bulge of the hood over the motor is the bulge of buttock over—never mind. The speed of a car represents the tough masculinity of the man driving it—this is comic or a matter of competence or it becomes overtly sexual if the car is attractive, if it is the equivalent of those movie women such as Ava Gardner, Bacall when she was brand new, Sternberg's Dietrich, the woman without a family, the sort of promiscuous wanderer, the woman who is terrific and has some mileage on her and some speed in her, the woman who really wants to fuck and knows what that means.

She has to be young. The same attitude in an older woman is demeaning, castrating to the man, usually fearsome but often comic, or even wildly farcical.

So, too, with a rattletrap car.

1981

MEDITATIONS ON
AN ATHLETE

The stillness of an empty playing field in early morning is an unstillness of mist floating over the grass inside the rough fence of the surrounding trees. An empty classroom is unstill, the desks, the smell of chalk and of textbooks, the dim light when the electric light is not turned on, with inhabiting ideas and shades or ghosts of restlessness—what is seated is errant, the errant flitters of mind, the notes passed, the wads moist with spittle thrown. The very sight of an empty classroom, like the experience of entering one, has no unstillness and no sensory solidity. A classroom is a place where time is strange between the ringing of bells that mark the hours, strange because of the movements of mind and because of the oddity of language that, even as it occurs, word by word, syllable by syllable, in a train or procession, strains at being gists and nubs, synopses and conclusions, summaries and immortal (and vastly important) formulas.

That pseudo-timelessness of classrooms includes imaginary eternities and infinities—infinitudes—and the insignia of lesser time, clocks and wristwatches and the bells marking the end of a class, of a session of geometry or of American history, and real time, bureaucratic and mindly.

But a playing field is still or unstill with motion in a direct sense, and the field itself is alive whether it is empty or not, as space and grass and light, while a classroom is abstract. An abstract envelope, geometrical and unpretty, for the bodies are seated at each desk in imagination or in reality, shoulders and necks bent over work set out on the desk, eyes fixed on the blackboard, buttocks plunked on wooden seats.

And then there is the difference in subject matter. Classroom matters deal in what someone knows, what I know, what I need to know, what I have to know.

And the playing field is vaguely heroic and ordinary and real; it is concerned with what I do, what I want to do, what I *have* to do.

But the chief difference has to do with the relation of each to time and to a sense of time; the long school corridors, me walking down them, tall and thin, and in the classrooms in the glare of school light, and then in the gym and in the locker room, the change in one's sense of time was great. It always seemed to me that real time began in the locker room along with real breath in the flare of undressing, in the brief, odd, boyish nudity, and the nearness of violence, of roughhousing or of competition, and of embarrassment, an embarrassed or an unembarrassed ferocity about it, sometimes a fake ferocity, a deep involvement in the gestures and maneuvers of a sport that so far as I know always occurs in real time, continuous time, the real thing, almost as if inside the heartbeat of an enormous bird.

The real time of the real world begins for boys, at least, or did when I was a child, in the minutes at recess on the playing field and then in the locker room minutes, and in the figures and bodies, so temporary, so startling in the juvenile brevity of existence, of the boys I knew.

One could write about women, the athletic women at school. And since. I have married two women who were athletic. You can discuss or give a discourse or write an essay on health and suppleness, on strength and identity, on bullfighters and ballplayers, on swimmers and secret images of immersion and submersion. Posture and carriage, and a quality of the face—the muscular nature of the face—and a quality of movement mark the athlete, the stance of muscularly thickened dexterity, the supple stiffness of the neck: the athlete unseen by himself, or herself, a prisoner of bodily condition and of time but, of course, not quite; for a while, freer inside real time than the rhythmless observer, freer from the exigencies of speech, with a wider and more controlled repertoire of bodily movements, with an odd tie to the rhythmic reoccurrences of patterns and tactics in the intricacies of sport.

Sweaty and thoughtful but with oddly physical thoughts—*you move to your left, count ten and turn, I'll track you*—that's football, shoulder pads, jersey, cleated shoes, the athlete enters a period of reality. Here is the flat green plain of the field, here is the air around the moving figures, here is the light. It's easier to remember the warm-up than it is to remember the game. The pressure of the game is pretty much beyond language, beyond respectable language: *fuck, oh fuck, let's kill 'em, come on, let's go.* The score is 29–14. Line up, shift to the right. The extraordinary chemical distortion of the body, the adrenaline, the strain of acting and moving well beyond your limits—or being paced in a four-hundred-meter run and mindful of heartbeat and of the stopwatch, while everything else is subtracted for a while, until it's time to sprint, to go all out; and then you mustn't think, or improvise more than physically; the mind is set and sparking; the chemicals feed in you until you are pretty much an openly animal self, somewhat anesthetized and sensually and sensorially enlarged. Vision and drive, play after play, utilizing the strengths of your teammates, or your own, heartbeat, muscle, speed, matters of spirit and morale, nothing is separate from time or is made of anything timeless, including the elements of being thrilled, the long, aching wait for a pass or for a fly ball. The cells churn, the nerves hum, the skin burns, all of you maybe tingles and aches; one's breath stings but the identity of human substance as clocklike or as time in these other forms of muscle and nerves—our being compacted of elements that themselves are forms of time—the permeability and dependence of the self and everything about it on time—indeed, the awful significance that nothing in us is *timeless*—a truth, this truth, shows itself in sports more strongly than anywhere else. Modern sports are derived from the English revelation that the real is the real. The athlete moves in time as much as he moves in air. Time and space are inseparable. Muscle is an extraordinary human substance reflecting hours and days more clearly than trim and agile sentences do or can. An athlete's carriage, when she or he is in condition, represents a labor-intensive ripening. An as if corn-fed dimensionality. Corny muscle mass. A mass of quick-reflex tissue. Nothing else in culture is as direct an image of life as we live it.

Character exemplified in public performance and detached from most other considerations—such as spiritual morality, as in oratory or social display—character tied to the body and to will and to form, to a wholeness of the body, and the very long periods of training in which theories of diet and of organizing the nerves and muscles and of how to get results are experimentally followed, all this is set, is encoded in language of a particular order of topical and short-term or unlasting chatter, professional chatter: an intellectual silence.

Few characters in English and American fiction who are sympathetic or important are athletes. Dickens and Austen are, in their way, antagonistic, as is Henry James, to athleticism—as too worldly, too unnuanced.

Shakespeare is odd about the matter. I would hazard the remark that a certain sort of athleticism in a character in Shakespeare and in Sir Walter Scott indicates a quality welcomed for breeding purposes, worthwhile, a sign of character and a mode of sexual validity, a courtship trait.

No great athletes have risen to posts of political power in England. In the United States, we have a former basketball star named Bill Bradley who is a senator; and certain corporation heads and exalted figures in finance and the military. No one in journalism.

This may have to do with silence or with the kinds of cunning and of decency in sports and in politics and in journalism.

Studies of how much and what people in the United States read (and watch) seem to indicate the obvious, which is that books are not in rivalry with television so much as they are with life—running errands and traveling—and with sports.

The attractiveness of athletes, the attractions of athletics, both to watch and to take part in, hasn't always a directly sexual underpinning or overlay or core. One falls back on Darwin and the words *fit* and *fitness*. And one mentions that traits conducive to success in nature (so to speak), such as obstinacy verging on monomania, a purposeful stupidity and clearing of the mind, physical dexterity (or prettiness) and physical usefulness (or handsomeness) are the traits that sports and athleticism are maniacally concerned with.

But, actually, the chief trait is one of concentration attached to abilities, a demonstrated power of concentration on physical and measurable reality. And the mental focus or editing that goes with that, the mental focus that a strong and even murderous sense of competition gives rise to, and the control of that and of all the possible sources of diffusion of effort and confusion of principle—while these are transferable to sexual events, they are not directly sexual.

One has to imagine them transformed, translated. I think the strongest sources of sexual interest in athletics come from the control and the rhythms or, if you prefer, from the discipline and the sense of time.

After all, sports are public and the demonstration of athletic will (and command) is public and even exhibitionist—more for daydreams and movies than for actual bed, perhaps. The exhibitionism is an antidote to the other and yet more traditional local and flaunting and dangerous exhibitionism of politicians and journalists.

Let me propose an idea: that memory and all our sense of pastness, near and far, represent not just intelligence but the raw material of intelligence. And that prediction and our sense of the future represent character, which would include useful intelligence in action measured and rewarded.

But the present tense, which is reality, after all, is where the elements of what we are find themselves tested in actions. Sexuality is an embarrassingly present-tense action, neither ironic nor nostalgic and there it is like sport but it is more forgiving and less focused than sport. To whatever extent sexuality is physical—and it is not entirely physical ever—a well-tended body has its sexual merits; it might enter into the picture as actually desirable although often it is intimidating and elicits odd desires and not straightforward ones.

But the mind-set behind, or above, a well-tended body is of interest, although not in the usual way that a mind-set is of interest sexually, but rather like a gravy boat filled with gravy. We see this, I think, in dancers, and Nabokov pictures this in the nymphet Lolita. This gravy sweetens sex, which is a difficult sort of thing for the mind to live through, actually. It is this, I believe, that in athletes most fascinates, the chattering but actually largely silent mind-set that has guided them and goaded them and constrained them into a degree of education in present-tense performance that promises a degree of actual, lived, and immediate life impossible for some of the rest of us.

1992

AIDS AND LOSS IN A
CITY OF GHOSTS

Ohere of the rotten things about returning to Manhattan this time of year, jet-lagged and not young, is the immediate visibility of decay and loss in the city.

Manhattan is not a great town for history or even for memory. It's always been right up there and right out front, a place that was happening and that was shamelessly immediate. It had no real history of plague and exile or of siege and bombardment. Its confidence—glass towers a fifth of a mile tall and huge street crowds—were like a locally universal foolishness.

It was pretty much a town of certain kinds of greedy optimism verging on delusion and of individual despairs. To someone returning after being away for months, that seems to have been reversed. And individual will in a great many people seems to be carrying the town's continuance against the weight of the spirit of the place.

Is it an exaggeration to speak of the gloom of Manhattan? Is it only midwinter gloom, the old, hovering lightlessness, the old frigid semi-hibernation of February? Is it the changeover in politics, the convergence of rebellions bringing on a momentary collapse of style?

The town seems to be carried now by individuals' optimism and will, which show fairly brightly—two cops grinning and talking to each other and patrolling on foot among the street neutralities—people who aren't so sure of themselves.

The decay is so obvious that it hurts the mind as well as the eye. This is a recession-hued, cautious town now, with empty stores with papered-over windows and a strangely lackluster street life. Nothing, or nothing much, glitters and bustles. Dowdy store displays and unexpectedly de-energized and mostly dreary placards outside and in—a kind of demoralization of the nutty, high-flying huckstering that used to be a major part of Manhattan's somewhat nervously cheesy pursuit of class and glamour—drain the liveliness away from what was, five years ago, the flashiest and most hypnotic street-and-store theater in the world.

Some of this has to do with mind and perception, with lowered expectations, scandals, firings—a loss of morale combined with a sense of change in the era itself as we head toward the end of the century. It has to do with money and salaries having changed in nature. If the homeless, their plight, their visible suffering, now trumps whatever else is visible, it might be because they aren't intruders at a party anymore but are symbols and warnings. You know the street vendors aren't going to make a good living and move to the suburbs. They're not going to be new members, beginners, in the bourgeoisie. You can't figure even that the beggars and panhandlers have a private world like the one in *Threepenny Opera*. You figure Brecht was wrong and that the private world of these guys and of bag-women is more intense and strange than Brecht would have it, not a parody of middle-class life and greed.

Or if it's not them, it's something else, because there's a notable absence of whatever created the sense of a bustling metropolis that the city had even two years ago. New York was never a city of ghosts. But it is now. It is haunted by ghosts of itself, earlier incarnations of New York and early institutions and local rites. It's haunted and plagued by the ghosts of all those who have died of AIDS here, for instance.

Part of what is most wrong with the city now is the absence of homosexual street life, the obvious stuff. Nearly everyone is haunted by the deaths of individual friends and acquaintances, but the city itself has a black hole in it. What used to be the homosexual presence in Manhattan, the swagger, the challenge, the human color, the style and electricity, is gone.

Certain dull phrases such as *alternative lifestyle* refer to things that aren't dull. It used to be the case that a largely or even greatly alternative world was present visibly, daylong and nightlong on the streets and in the subways and in the stores. You can define it any which way you like, and polemically and as a danger, but it was a counterculture with some of the eerie quality of an exploding circus, a world of a life unlike ordinary bourgeois existence, and it was part of a terrific duality.

It is more than cosmopolitanism; it is merely common sense to want variety in a city, or, if you prefer, to come to terms with the natural variety of things and the need for structures to represent dualities and rivalries, temptations and repulsions.

The old homosexual world in New York had its faults and drawbacks; but with its wit, its occasional obscenity, its intelligence, it was an island of escape from mindlessness and silence.

On that island, people talked—often nonsense but often not. The presence of the community colored New York in a thousand ways. One was tied to it through friendship, acquaintance, envy, curiosity, intellectual need, and sexual vanity and close attachment, and through simple pleasures of the eye and ear and the more complex pleasures of shock and dismay and intelligence.

AIDS is a tremendous curse. I don't know what rhetorical device to use to curse it in return. The Great Rottenness. The vile maw. But the subject here is not the disease but what seems to me to be a silent winter.

The partial otherness of the homosexual community—*otherness* is a lousy term—meant that one's perception of what-was-possible, one's perception of *the average* as the center point of the overall community changed drastically upward when these other kinds of lives and minds and sensibilities were factored in, were thoroughly present and on display.

New York as a place where people talked, for instance. New York and homosexuality seemed to form a separate kingdom of *Linguistia*. Homosexuality is the only American lifestyle in which men talk.

The shocking alertness and aliveness, the secrecy, the rebellion and rebelliousness of intellect-and-will brightened everything so that it literally seems now that the very air and sky have lost color. It's grief, of course. It's not only grief. Everyone is partly homosexual; so a part of oneself is silenced. The outward manifestations and dark allurements and minor-league flirtations acceded to or refused and one's being hectored and lectured are part of what is necessary. They exist, anyway—even in small towns and farms and in the military in various forms. But a world capital of it, an openness of it, was part of the working of the mind. Perceptions, like emotions, like ideas, like language itself, acquire shape by comparison and competition and by association. The bright faces and quick eyes of the earlier version of the housed-but-yet-in-a-way-homeless reflected the sky and echoed the colors of lightlessness of the air and gleamed with different electricities of mind.

No one is a solitary sensorium, even someone who has been as much of a recluse as I've been. One lives among invasions and signs and signals from other people. Political rage and gallows jokes, art talk and gossip and argument about movements and schools, sloppy polemic and nifty malice, odd bits of media poetry, and a great magnificence, a splendor, a rage of hospitality toward language, toward words and gesture—for the moment, they're gone.

I'm not writing about the people who are gone—the voices, the actual voices, the presence of minds and hearts and moods and ambitions and kindnesses. I'm not writing about the individual souls who are absent.

I'm writing about the city, and what we've lost.

God, it's awful.

1993

HURRY UP, IT'S TIME

One of the problems concerning time is that the mathematics so far developed to deal with it are unidimensional, and language-and-anecdote are better for a number of purposes if you are concerned with ideas about time in reality.

But language, unlike mathematical notation, has a somewhat slick surface, and the degree of slickness is not measurable. For instance, Einstein, verbally the most talented of the physicists who have used language formulations, in one anecdotal proposition asked us to picture a spaceship traveling at nearly the speed of light at a distance observable from some surface like the surface of the earth, where we have to place a stationary observer. Such an observer is an imaginary proposition, since, of course, she or he cannot be stationary but is in motion planetarily. The solar system is in motion as well, as is the galaxy among the lights and fires and dark out there, the anomalies and starry freakishness.

He, or she, is relatively stationary, and is assumed to have no velocity for the purposes of the anecdote, for the verbal experiment.

Then a flash of light travels from the spaceship to a mirror near the stationary observer and to the eyes of the stationary observer, and Einstein uses some term in German like *instantaneously*. The light is reflected back in such a way that it intersects with the path of the spaceship to which a large mirror is attached and which then shines, and that flash is visible to the stationary observer.

Einstein said that the two flashes of light seen by the stationary observer and the one flash of light seen by the people in the spaceship occurred in the same instant. He needed simultaneity to define a unit of time. Clock measurements are ours and are arbitrary and represent our perception of the passage of time rather than the movement of time (if one can call it a movement).

Anyway, he wanted to argue and did argue that a clock on the spaceship measuring the passage of time would be measuring time passing more slowly than would a clock beside the stationary observer on the surface of the earth, in that only one flash of light occurred on the clock in the spaceship in the same instant that two occurred for the stationary observer.

But you see in the *nearly the speed of light* and in *the same as instantaneously* he is blurring the issue of speed, not to be tricky, but in order to make sense. He established theoretically that the speed of light was an absolute (and was unchanging). The distances he is proposing in the anecdote are infinitesimal so that the percentage of error he is proposing is very small mathematically.

And he was careful to say *it would seem* that the passage or flash of light for the stationary observer is longer in distance and therefore represents more or faster time within simultaneity.

The Heisenberg principle of uncertainty is a mathematical observation, and one is using the phrase metaphorically in saying the blur in Einstein's terms is more likely to be a blur in mine. But isn't his notion of simultaneity suspect? Or, doesn't it require thought and elaboration?

A single flash of light even at a short distance is not emitted and received simultaneously; it is merely perceived that way.

The actual nature of simultaneity over distance in the universe is mathematically unexplored, or rather, has not been discussed in any popularized fashion. Theoretically one would think simultaneity was exact and that ideas of it and measurements of it would vary. Wouldn't it be interesting to conceive of simultaneity as, so far, an unmeasurable absolute?

Einstein's theory that links time to space in a time-space continuum is one of the great discoveries—as we all know. But the verbal expression of the theory has some oddities. If space is inseparable from time, is time inseparable from space? If so, how? I'll come back to this. But if we have a time-space continuum, there *seems* to be no reason not to say that time is the universe and that one can say it not as synecdoche (using a part to represent a whole, as in willing hands at work) but simply because space and matter are the mediums of time's existence, its skin or body or, if that is too anthropomorphic, its defining element, the border of its identity.

That is to say, to make time the first element rather than an accompaniment or medium for matter and physical distance might prove interesting for discussion. The differentiation of one moment from another supposes the existence of identity—otherwise, time would not be a motion, although time, by definition, is a motion, a motion so far undefinable but which does not stand still.

And it is possible that this "motion" requires space, that it has a physical identity, like particles or quanta, except not like them either.

Well, don't mind me. But play with me with this stuff. To put it another way, the identity of particles of matter requires time as an obstacle (and as disproof) for any sense of fixity or limited or absolutely defined identity and you have to use time as an element in defining what is a kind of time-ridden absolute of identity-in-real-time.

Identity, like simultaneity, tends to be conceived of in absolute terms, to be separated from the actions of actual time. Does simultaneity have motion in it? Can it be defined so sharply and narrowly that the motion of time can be conceived of as not mattering in the contemplation of the undoubtedly real phenomenon of simultaneity? If simultaneity has motion, then are we talking of a kind of unison? And while it sounds strange, it might be that the identity of the motion-of-the-time presupposes matter and space or even creates it.

That might sound nonsensical. Or gassy. But the implication of the Einsteinian formulations is that it is likely that logic cannot be separated from time. The identity of what we call particles is a peculiar construct since particles are also waves; so, then, identity has to include transformations but only a limited number of them, or, to be really confusing, a limitless number although still within a limit. Let me propose here, as a bystander, that quantum mechanics seems to illustrate operations or particles, or an existence for small pieces of matter that resembles operations of our consciousness. We are theoretically capable of an infinite number of thoughts, not the entire infinity or true universe of thoughts but only that of our own thoughts.

Particles are said to undergo all permutations of possibility but not all these permutations have consequences in our universe. This too sounds like what the mind is capable of and of the ways in which it is limited.

Now look at Feynman's formulations in words of some of his experiments. Accused in his lifetime of hoking up his language to get attention, he is now taken seriously since a great many scientists are now hoking up their language in order to get public attention, prizes, and grants.

But Feynman was guilty of just that. His terms, for instance, about the reversal of time for some subatomic particles is hype—is hyper-science fiction. It is not clear if he was proposing that the particle moves against the flow of time or if he was proposing that the flow of time was reversed in a patchy way.

But the question is, when did space and time get the divorce that would permit such a physical movement? In Feynman's formulation, the space of this event is our space.

Feynman was describing and naming conclusions to be drawn from a brilliant experiment he performed, mostly photographs of collisions, and he made mathematical allowances for the Heisenberg principle, but perhaps insufficiently. In a grander sense that principle interferes with all the verbal formulations of quantum mechanics since, to repeat myself, they seem to illustrate that the operations of particles resemble operations of consciousness, our consciousness.

There is no good reason to deny up front that matter in its subatomic reality might not have or even be a form of what we call consciousness, and that the physical and perceptible macroworld is made of elements possessing this consciousness—this consciousness of identity and of time. Or that it is made of these expressions of it. Philosophically and logically, that seems more likely than not, if only because identity presupposes a memory and a consciousness of self, although not necessarily memory as we feel it. But when the wave re-forms as a particle and has the same, i.e., continuing, identity, it is displaying "memory" plus inanimate—if you like—judgment in re-forming itself.

Feynman proposed that particles seem to do everything possible, to make every movement possible in a given sequence of units of time, but that only a few of those movements seem to have consequences in this universe, in time, our time. One notion is to spin off alternate universes of consequences immeasurable and unperceivable to us so that all those "movements" have consequences somewhere.

But another notion would be to suppose that a form of memory and a form of contemplation of possibility was inherent in everything and anything conceived of as having an identity. In terms of a particle, an alternative path in a given sequence would be that the sequence, the event, did not take place. This shudder of a previous state continuing or reappearing and divorced from the consequences of some other paths that do have consequences is what Feynman described in the verbal—and hyper—formulation that the particle had traveled backward in time on one of its paths.

The evidence is a photograph interpreted in relation to other photographs: that is, there is data but no evidence-in-motion. From the fixed data, the motion was inferred, and the verbal formulation is a public-relations hypothesis.

It's also conceivable that subatomic identity has a memory that can register on film. The issue would be clearer if we knew what the consequences were in this universe of that so-called motion, how symmetry operated then.

So I am asking two simple questions: is the resemblance to consciousness of what we are told are the behavior and identity of particles a *fault* in the observation, in the entire procedure (as Einstein seems to have felt about the earlier work in the field), or do we need to consider the ineluctable nature of identity in a universe permeated by the motion-or-the-motions-of-time?

1992

LANGUAGE
AND
LITERATURE

JANE AUSTEN VS.
HENRY JAMES

Let us start with a joke, not mine, but Jane Austen's; not a joke exactly: more an exercise of wit. A not very famous, not very rigorous exercise of wit. It is from *Mansfield Park*, its opening sentence:

> About thirty years ago, Miss Maria Ward of Huntingdon, with only seven thousand pounds, had the good luck to captivate Sir Thomas Bertram, of Mansfield Park, in the county of Northampton, and to be thereby raised to the rank of a baronet's lady, with all the comforts and consequences of an handsome house and large income.

Now a more famous sentence:

> It is a truth universally acknowledged, that a single man in possession of a good fortune, must be in want of a wife.

Because these are merely sentences, it is somewhat easier to keep them in mind than it is to keep entire novels and groups of novels in mind. But these are not merely single sentences but opening sentences, and it is a little like meeting a single Frenchman, say, one chosen as an ambassador and meant to represent and introduce a large number of sentences, a population. That is to say, a sentence in a book is not only itself but is one of the general case: one of the elements of a text that is particularly expansionary (something written has always an explosively expansive element in the mind: it grows to the proportions of a stage or landscape or one's experience of one's own life). One way a novel functions is to generate its own generalities intelligibly; this is part of what makes novels didactic and instructive, willy-nilly. (Modern music of the past age attempted to mimic this.) So that, in a good book, an opening sentence is seen, or read, doubly: as itself, and as the first of a category of sentences, a category with a great deal of variety to it; and that first sentence functions like a Rosetta Stone, translating one's knowledge of speech and of other books into knowledge of the language games and systems here in this book.

Novels are the largest chunks of continuous structured language that we have. Criticism directed toward them tends to stretch toward being book length—toward literary theory—in order to deal with them. I will try not to do that. Both the Austen sentences—the jokes—have, if you want to look at them, historically reminiscent qualities; you can, if you want, hear Gibbon and Congreve, Swift, Pope, and Cowper, the ironic historical, actual epic (of the Roman Empire) and mock-epic in various forms; and one can hear Defoe and his notion of prose fact. I would assume the young Miss Austen was as well-read as the young Virginia Stephen, who became Virginia Woolf. In writing of a certain quality, the ambition is often present as a driving force of correction of earlier books; and in Austen there is a good deal of internal evidence that she was both trivially and importantly well-read.

The two opening sentences I quoted are literate and impatient, quite complex in their relation to time: we have the generality, or comment; we have the moment in which we read what is written, the real time involved in the act of reading (which is usually swifter than speech); we have an onward momentum of some moment; and we have, in this act of speech and of listening, the time mentioned or referred to (or, in the second example, present by inference) in the story itself—the characters immersed in their time, their age, and in the passages of their speeches and stories. We have, in the onward plunge of our two sentences, a gathering or accumulating of meaning. The rather pronounced hard and soft stresses give a rocking gait, which functions as tempo and which gives mnemonic and structural (or grammatical) aid, imparting a great deal of regularity to the operations of the wit, which concerns itself with human blundering, our sublunary lunacies and realisms and realities. These are accepted in an oddly broad tone and set within the cantering or galloping speed of the sentences.

The irregularity, then, of human things is offered us in relation to rhythm verging on meter, and with a suggestion of absolutes in the tone of aperçu, almost epigram. The generality of the statements—Tolstoy does something similar in the opening sentences of *Anna Karenina*—confers a hint of a conviction of meaning in human affairs. There is something Platonically Luminous about the whole shebang, but which is meant to be Christian rather than Platonist.

The penumbral music of the wit—the sense of greed and of the lives and minds of women as relating to greed—and the rhythms of propriety and impropriety in such outspokenness, in such formality and informality, was new in prose. If you read Voltaire—the most successful writer of his time—and then if you read Goethe, *The Sorrows of Young Werther,* for comparison, or *Tom Jones,* you can see or feel what it is Austen did in not being Goethean or Voltairean or Fieldingesque or like Smollett. There are lines of history for novels of other sorts than her sort; but it is from under her cloak that some of Flaubert and some of Tolstoy emerge, and much else besides.

I would attempt to characterize both sentences I quoted earlier as citizens of the novels they introduce and as conquistadores in literature, in which they proceed to occupy and colonize a large tract; and, new in their time, they remain new and conquering still. They propose a kind of speech requiring a kind of attention that is new, which we can never entirely succeed in giving. In a novel, the world happens syllable by syllable. And the author has had some time with the syllables, time which we can never mimic, since the syllables now do not border on real nonexistence as they did for her. In her sentences, evidence of the world is given in a tone which is meaning; the persistent success and half-success of her wit extend throughout the entire verbal and syntactical regions of the sentence and even into the blank space, the silence, the zone of implication at the end, past the end of the sentence. The roller-coaster ride—or rather, the canter; it is a pre–roller-coaster era—its directness and its kind of focus are English, and pragmatic. We are English and provincial here: this is not urban wit; this is not writing from a capital city. But it is provincial in a new way: we are in no way inferior to folk from the capital; we are not without extreme sophistication and vision and a true knowledge of things—even of complex, complicatedly expressive, and partly formal language. The social-class placement, the placement in art as well, the modesty and yet the directness, the local Platonism with a claim to a continental or universal Platonism—the ambition—this is new. The truth of statement and the human dexterity of the music indicate that we are in the presence of a voice at a level of artistry within a proclaimed degree of inventiveness so noticeable that it seems (to me, anyway) to be inflected by the spirit of the industrial age. Chapter by chapter, paragraph by paragraph, sentence by sentence, phrase by phrase, she is one of the most inventive writers—inventive structurally and verbally—in prose history. There is little or no cant phrasing and few clichés of any sort in any of her books. She embodies the spirit, if you like, of the factories of England at the time. It is imperialist, such inventiveness and truth, almost military—imperialist toward *art*; it colonizes art; it is in an English way revolutionary, this voice, this ability, in what it does to art. It is one of the greatest and most important voices in world literature.

If you compare the tone she has to the somewhat pleading tone of *Tom Jones*—its *please read me*—or to the youthfully intellectual, pre-Rilkean, lachrymose tone of *The Sorrows of Young Werther*—its *let us cry over a sad tale*—those worthwhile tones of other created traditions of subsequent lines of descent in the novel—you may, like me, see something particularly central in the Austen, and not simply the switch to a heroine from a hero or to tales of courtship and marriage from tales of masculine education and picaresque adventure, but to social analysis, an analysis focused and steady and dramatic.

And it is done in a tone, a manner, at once healthy and headlong, even reckless, and yet well regulated in a sunlit humanness of quite extraordinarily unreconciled coldness and acuity—accuracy—of vision. The bitter, *financial, financially romantic* truth, the apparent correctness of the politicosexual-psychosexual observations, is oddly well-grounded, is so couched as to be unarguable, or positivistically sayable; and yet it is quite broadly applicable—it opens toward quite a wide audience.

Her attitude toward the reader is not that of someone trained as a courtier. Fielding and Goethe were courtiers in life and carried that sophistication over into the novel. The great creators in prose and poetry had for centuries largely been court poets and writers and writers in capital cities, aware of and partly educated in court matters, who were trained in the highest contemporary use of language—i.e., at a court or near it.

Here the remarks summon a daily truth like that of *That day the marquise went out at five,* or like the one Wittgenstein has in mind when he asks, "What do we say when we say 'RED'?"

The music of the technique—the words, the rhythm, the enclosing music of the effectiveness—amounts to something in an English form, a semi-Platonic tone of pragmatic anti-fable, real and practical in an Anglo-Saxon manner, with an ungreat Anglo-Saxon greatness to it, literary greatness in a democratic-imperial tone: democratic within its class and immodest in its claim to its rights and imperial in its snobbery (of a kind), in its mastery and control of subject and motion of narrative—and self-willed in the extreme in its inventiveness.

But, notice, she is not using a private tone. It is not the tone of a letter written from the provinces; it is not the tone of religious reflection; it is not a woman's tone of parlor uses, or a woman's boastfulness, as in Lady Mary Montague and Madame de Sévigné. It is a woman's tone, but oddly and not wholly. It doesn't have a particularly indoor sound, as purpose-fully, the voice does, in a grim drawing room, of *Wuthering Heights.* This is a public tone, but not of political address or outdoor storytelling; and it is not the tone of the coffeehouse or of the Houses of Parliament or of the court. One doesn't *talk* like this. It is bookish but it is not the tone of letters or of diaries or of newspapers or of military reports. It is not fanciful; it is very factual.

It is a woman's imagined or invented public speech and it takes place in an imagined public space. It is a little like the imaginary halls and stagelike and theatrical recital spaces where poets combat with their predecessors, but it is more imaginary: it has no sense of a street corner or of a recital hall. I consider it one of the greatest inventions of literary space ever. It becomes the space of the art novel. It is the governing space of *Madame Bovary*—which may be taken as a considerable revision of *Pride and Prejudice,* say, and which could be subtitled *Actual Provincial Erotic Pride, Actual Human Cruel Prejudice.* It is the governing space for most of Henry James, for Dickinson, and for Whitman. It is the governing space of much postmodernist work. And it is central to modernism—in painting, too. In a visual form, such an invented, provincial-and-central space is the determining element in Picasso. There are other spaces, other traditions as important. But Austen invented this reactive mental space with its discourse held within limits—the limits of the feminine world, so to speak—and these limits supply something like the Aristotelian unities for a nervous century. The whole thing is arbitrary and yet naturalistic and formal both. A version of it, very pure, is to be found in T. S. Eliot's work, especially in *The Wasteland* as it was edited by Ezra Pound. The social world is dominant. The mental space is constricted—and this is part of the drama—but is acknowledged as where the voice is coming from within a naturalistically perceived world that is limited in range, as a woman's is held to be. The unities of place are inexact: a variety of settings are used within a certain limitation and well inside a frame of sticking to the subject. Nothing widens out into the heroic, or descends to picaresque or into farce, or moves into the *bildungsroman*.

In the nineteenth and twentieth centuries, after Austen, we had more women writers of extreme excellence than is true in any other European language—the two Brontës, George Eliot, Emily Dickinson, Christina Rossetti, Virginia Woolf, Elizabeth Bishop. This may well have been cultural, something peculiarly Anglo-Saxon as well; but it almost certainly had more to do with Austen's invention.

There is the presence in European art, after Austen, of images of women in invented spaces—and of women persecuted by invented spaces in their own mind, by their own inventiveness and brilliance. This is partly because she showed how artfully such things could be done: she established the blueprints, the recipes for such characters. And such characters command more brilliant language of presentation and speak more intensely—and brilliantly—than others; and the limits of space and possibility around them consequently enlarge the importance of the mental possibilities of the narrative. Other factors certainly entered in; but let us remember that change begins at one point, and that change initiates further change at once, for which the original impetus is hardly responsible and yet is entirely responsible.

I think that perhaps Austen broke open the sexual harem, but I am not a scholar, merely a writer having a go at this subject. I think the representations of women changed because of Austen, and that women as subject matter and the subject matter of painting passes from the portraits of Reynolds and David through the battle scenes of Delacroix to the Austen-like worlds of the later nineteenth-century artists, the Impressionists and the Postimpressionists, and on to Picasso and Matisse.

Her invention—her inventions—particularly, her invented public space, the space in which she cast the voice of her novels—is, in my view, the first great democratic use of consciousness, a construction of consciousness local and yet literary, Platonically nearly absolute, and, through the literary descent, worldwide in a sense.

Austen's invention—for all I know, her intense appropriation of how her sister Cassandra saw things, or of what some writer unknown to me but of her acquaintance, perhaps a letter writer, may have invented— allowed for a separation of truth from a notion of language experience as limited by precedent. She invented a proper mode of revolution, of innovation, which is sustained in the great writing of the next two centuries: it may be unfairly summarized as *we go to a party* (or do something social and involving a number of voices) *and then we rethink what meaning is and what literature is.* And we need the limitation of parochialism, and the parochialism of middle-class (or upper-middle-class) individuality, for this. Baudelaire's and Eliot's wit and spleen, and inventiveness and careful brilliance of workmanship, and Austen's wit and spleen, and inventiveness and careful brilliance of workmanship, seem to me to be as related as Flaubert's and Austen's (Flaubert's in *Madame Bovary*, that is).

One way to attempt to define, amateurishly, what she did is to say that she elevates honesty—almost as in a Baconian experiment—above literary precedent and artifice. Dickens is truthful but not honest. Dickens mostly emerges from writers other than Austen. The positivism of the novel— the need for a novel to be *right* (usually, or mostly, or entirely depending on the genre of the novel)—requires that most of the events of the novel be taken as true or right or as unarguable; and that the statements made are as often as possible unarguable, either on the grounds of fancy and of comedy, or on the grounds of being acceptable as description. Very good novelists enclose their statements in qualifications and in dialogue; and they use dramatic contradiction and modifications that come about in plot movements as corrections of knowledge. When this is done well, the skill and power with which it is done does tie the art to a precedent, to a kind of truth one associates with art since the Greeks. But part of Greek dramatic and epic art was fated and folkloric and magical; and much art has remained tied to that precedent. Or prefers that precedent. If you compare Austen to Fielding and Congreve—or to *Les Liaisons Dangereuses* and *The Princess of Cleves* and to *Adolphe*—you can see how greatly she is the inventor of the first great commonsense *social* novel; and you can see how her invention of imaginary space frees her to invent dramatic forms of great width of reference, so that the movements of the characters relative to each other embody truth in a new way—a way unknown to the others, who, rather consistently, must rely on notions of fate and damnation and redemption, of magical intervention. I do not say you will prefer her to the others: that is a matter of taste. But she is a much greater dramatist, a much greater novelist technically. With Austen, you have a well-founded sense of the good sense of the statements you are reading and a sense of the profound wonderfulness of the responsibility of her observation and invention, responsibility of the sort that occurs in the work of Shakespeare and Aeschylus.

Of course, I may be wrong. And I may be exaggerating in the heat of argument. You will have to investigate on your own to find out.

Now I am going to ask you to consider the similarities of tone and of approach to the drama of an opening sentence, and the similarity of the wit or joke—and by that, I mean the tone of unarguability on a secular level—in this compound opening sentence of *The Golden Bowl*:

> The prince had always liked his London, when it had come to him; he was one of the modern Romans who find by the Thames a more convincing image of the truth of the ancient state than any they have left by the Tiber.

The rhythms, the gait are familiar if weaker. The tone of polite and yet presumptuous truthfulness in the Austen has taken on a shabbier aspect of gossip and personalities, an overelaboration of tone around an arguable observation—certain truths of the ancient state were still more convincing in Rome. And the Catholic Church was there. James was writing, perhaps, in a burst of British patriotism, a bit of propaganda. The idiom or usage of *London, when it had come to him* is a reversal of *when he came to London* to suggest that his feeling happened to him when he was popular, *when London came to him,* when the thought came to him—the hint is that he was busy and lazy both; provincial; occasionally social. It is a kind of patois, a social jackasserie elevated to something or other. James is certainly a marvelous writer, but this sentence is simply not as good in either of its clauses or in both together as Jane Austen's two, given earlier. His is not as good English; it is not as solid a piece of observation; it is not of the same order of workmanship. Nor is the meaning it is invoking central thematically to the book that follows it. That said, one can still find it delicious—it is the work, after all, of a master, in his last and most enormous phase. It is not well-founded as observation, but it is wonderful in a certain sad spite it has, which may be central to human nature, and which is a very great thing to portray; and what James does that is so daring and shows such mastery, such sociability, is that he is not superior to it: in fact, it is his—the spite, I mean. There is no generality and no generosity in it and there is no God—this is partly what T. S. Eliot means when he says James's mind was so fine no idea could violate it.

Everything in the sentence is askew, as in a bombed building. The empire we will be dealing with is Verver's and American, not English, not related to London. London is proposed as the center of power here, and later in the book as the center of amusement, rather than Paris. The prince's notions of Roman or English power are not central to the book. James grants the prince no determinative power in the narrative. It would have been better for James to have begun with Maggie, or with the prince in relation to her rather than to London—better, I mean, for the projection of a dramatic context and for establishing meanings. This is an unusually oblique beginning. James usually grants no substantive existence and no potency to men in his fiction, except in their feminine mode—Osmond in *The Portrait of a Lady* as sophisticated malice or Verver, as Lady Bountiful, in this novel. The prince is an impotent figure. I believe that *all* men are impotent in James. James's self-portraits (in that sense), or his predilections in subject matter, do, in the course of each piece of work, give way, and the fictions take on independent life. But they do not retain it to the end in the mind afterward. The endings tend to be overdetermined and cruel in the reattributions of *real* impotence to the men: the male characters are granted their success, if they are allowed any, by women—often caryatidlike, androgynous women, or an angelic one here and there—and by their own efforts never, except their efforts of understanding the monsters, the sphinxes and angels, that James posits.

Here James is seeing through a princeling; this is different from Austen's sarcasm, which is general and outward and not so personal and so inward. Both halves of the Jamesian compound sentence have weak endings. The sentence as a whole works by reference and the boastfulness of condescending to a prince and the evidence then that we—the Londoners of the book and we present admirers of James—are tigers and the prince is not, but is ahistorical, a luxury, something to be not only bought but *entirely* bought: a rarity, I believe, in the titled-husband market.

A dry, dull version of James's sentence such as "The prince needed a world capital and found it in London; Rome, being provincial, would not serve his purposes" would not do for James's purposes. The center of the book is not a fact or clear attitude but is a tone suggesting—as if politely—the prince's impotence. The *tone* of James's sentence and not its substance is central to James's pursuits, and that is what some readers in their subtlety find ravishing. Is this a cruel and worldly love letter to the princeling, this book? Tone governing substance is ravishing; it is an act of will and of fantasy; it is usually considered feminine; and it is also, at times (not always), one of the forms—one of the chief forms—that intellectual and emotional swindles take: to give you tone and no substance, and judgments that are not worth much and which will not get you into any trouble, which will not diminish your flexibility in the world.

James here, as so often, is not quite the real thing as a writer: he talks about it so much, about being the real thing, that we know it is a savage issue with him. He is aware. And tone governing substance to the extent that it does in James is usually held to be decadent or "poetic." The prince went shopping for a life; Maggie went shopping for *him*. The struggle between prince and heiress over what and who is to rule their life together is not given us. Such a story has substance apart from its tone. Its implications are of a different order from getting the point of James's tone. When you alter or pass over James's tone, you allow the prince some dignity, and not by rewriting or perverting the actions of the book but by returning to the fact. James, here, does not want the fact. The tone does not permit a physical sense of reality; the lifelikeness here is not part of what might be called a full-blooded characterization, but lies in the truth of making everything personal and biased and insiderish and secretive and spiteful and affectionate. The tone, the tone of gossip, is the center of the action, is the central fact, is the objective world here. The music of spiteful gossip is the background as well as the heart of the book, which is about a triumph over such things. James is writing a book with a happy ending (of a kind), and he is writing in very elaborate narrative patterns. His voice originates less sociably and more socially than Austen's, in a smallish, secretive space, a place for urban gossip—he pretends to want an audience, but his voice is not pitched for an audience as hers is. And the extraordinary condescension, the tricks of presentation, that make the prince minor and lazy even while he is meant to be the most attractive character in the book—these tricks, which are also a wisdom of a kind, are not for a wide audience. And, as I have been trying to say, they cause the opening sentence to be not even particularly, or essentially, true.

The prince *is* the one the others want—everyone wants him; and his glamor and the life in him enliven the others' lives. He is sneered at and presented in this way to show us that he is nothing much as a prince in the world: he is not the prince that Verver is. This derogation is at once sentimental and a misstatement on James's part. A prince is a specialized creature, as in Tolstoy's and Proust's representations of princes. I think James would be on solid ground if the prince and Verver were in the same field of endeavor—if the prince were a princely young American, an artist of some kind, and Verver and the author were parallel, were novelists. If the prince is not a prince, but a handsome young artist with a fine manner and no real talent—or real talent, but no real reason to deform himself to mine it—and if Verver is a great artist, and Maggie is the emotionally longing daughter aspect of such an artist self, then the book coheres: tones, notions, scenes, opening, and closing; otherwise, not.

That is, I suspect James of being personal in a particular, encoded way in this sentence and in this book. One wonders, then, if beginning the book with a classical reference is an attempt psychologically and aesthetically to deny the claustrophobic privacy of the Jamesian tone and to claim, not the imaginary public space that Austen invented and which is in use here, but a descent from classical art—a claim of descent that Austen circumvented any need for, but which serves to protect James, in his own mind or in ours, from imputations of portraying himself.

James, a sexless man—he mentions in a letter *an obscure hurt*—is talking here (I think he is) about love and sex, and masculine marriage on a field of common endeavor, between two artists, both male; and Austen is talking about love and sex and marriage on a field of common social endeavor, common social reality. And James's book is fairly open on its own terms about the masculine marriage between Verver and Amerigo, the prince. The secrecies, the encodedness, are very fine—but are, on the face of it, supererogatory. After all, James was—to use a title of my own—telling a story in an almost classical mode: patient Griselda, or Cinderella. In him the classic story is highly modified Austenian rather than Vergilian or Horatian or Shakespearean or French. And James is not

Christian, not Dantesque. This is Eliza Bennett and Darcy, but now Eliza Bennett has the fortune, and Darcy lacks sexual probity and is entangled with Mr. Bennett, who marries an old girlfriend of the prince's. . . . One of the problems for James is that he cannot do desirable characters except as sinister beings. He refuses to desire them, or he cannot, and so we have trouble doing so, and we lose track, then, of the issues of the tale. To judge him on this is to say, yet again, his story is immured in, anchored in, consists mostly of, *tone*. We can ask: is James's *tone* wise and knowing or petty and self-loving? I think it is both, and that this is flirtatious and offers us an alternative to living the story or identifying with it: we can watch him being an artist instead. But we cannot relax and accept his mysterious story—we cannot *watch* it happen.

James's subject matter is always, I think, sexual nonexistence, sexlessness, in a sexual universe but in a social world that he suggests is mostly sexless. He cannot do the reality of people who are not sexless, who desire and are desired. He does sexlessness observing or being victimized or triumphing over sexual people. In James, it is sexlessness judging the world—it is sexlessness at large in a universe that has meaning only for the sexual soul. Some readers find that James cannot be read when their lives are boiling along with feelings and serious event. Do you have to be in a deadish state to appreciate the master? Some say you can't be young and you can't be old: the young need more life and the old require more heat, and more evidence, and are short of sympathy for someone who never threw his life away.

James, in a very particular sense, is the master for those in the middle of their lives who are working hard and who are trapped and perhaps not very alive—he is the careerist's master in an admirable sense. And no matter how invidious I become, he is a very, very great observer of human beings. It is just that that observation is off and on, and is not part of the narrative structures of his novels, his données and his course of events.

Well, but he is a master. Granted, that in James there is no war of voices, no ventriloquism; granted that his arguments seem solipsistic and dismissible, past their aesthetic dimensions, as mere remarks by an opportunist; granted that the alternations within his repertoire—avuncular tones, hasty tones, orotund tones, exact tones, dramatic tones, comic tones—remain unlike Austen's, within the limits of the one overarching tone of a storytelling (and inspired) gossip. (Here let us point out that Pound—a despicable man, but the greatest judge of talent of his time—said that a novel is gossip that stays interesting; and let us point out that Faulkner is Jamesian, by the by.) Let us still celebrate him as a master, and let us then admit that part of Austen's great invention was in the portrayal and even perhaps the further invention of a kind of sexlessness for the sake of one's well-being, not for a spiritual reason but for the sake of reward—at least, a form of sexlessness, a self-control, perhaps even self-deformation.

Now, by sexless, I don't exactly mean sexless. Words are damned odd and skittery. I mean something comparative, something like unsexed or desexed—the sort of thing Lawrence and Forster (and a number of others) attacked as life-denying. A form of what I mean lies in the *sexual terror* and sexual distaste mapped by Eliot and treated with amazingly simultaneous obscurity and clarity by Hemingway (and treated pictorially by Picasso). A religious—or religious-old—version of it is in Tolstoy's self-castigating diaries. Dostoyevsky has brilliant versions of it often perversely set in his soft-focus portraits of whores. But he and Tolstoy—and Picasso—do not propose sexlessness or sexual defeat and sexual terror in the English fashion.

James's is an invented female voice, extremely intelligent, entirely self-involved in a disguised way. Austen manages to be everyone. Austen's tones are greatly varied, like Tolstoy's—a party tone, a quiet tone, a tone of longing—and other voices constantly intermesh with and interrupt hers, and the intruding voices are genuine. She does not suffer technically in comparison to Tolstoy. That she doesn't, and the fact that she does voices and James does not (and that T. S. Eliot commented in a way on this matter of voices), need not be a ground for final judgment. Let us compare her sexlessness to James's. She posits it as choice, spinsterishly, or as semi-choice, or as morality or as good sense; and she places it in conflict with, or versus, sexuality openly. Her sexlessness is at war with the immoral universe, and is a (she says or implies) Christian device—that is, she proposes it, not as fate, but as self-control and faith.

I think it is this in Austen that often frightens people. She is a rather great pre-Tolstoyan prophet. She does insist that most of what happens to you is your fault. Hers is a different sexlessness from James's, more like that of a child or an adolescent than like that of a wounded and frighteningly social man who has no sex, who is sexually damaged, who is, perhaps, sexually deranged. Certainly his rhetoric is more androgynous than hers. Austen's novels, truthfully or not, give us a set of self-controlled heroines, damaged by problems in their minds and by social realities; but these women are not sexually cowardly or defensive or, seemingly, sexually inexistent. They are as sexless as they are, she seems to say, because they are so responsive once they start to respond. Independence of mind and fineness and a release from ordinary destiny depend on their sexlessness. We never quite know, but we can suspect that they have feelings other than distaste or rage toward the sexual act.

Austen lived at a time when childbirth was dangerous, and families failed if the women did not manage to live, if there was no maternal continuity or presence. I believe that she is the first to explore the subject of sexlessness as not martyrdom but its opposite. In *Tom Jones* and *Clarissa* everyone is more or less sexual. I also think the subject as Austen presented it to us, and which became so important in English, is not as determinative in other languages as it is and has been in English since Austen. Consider how few of the great women writers in English, in the last century and in this, were married, how few were not lesbian or partly so—and that none of them had children. I, of course, omit living writers from this consideration.

Then I ask you to consider the forms this subject takes in Dickinson, Whitman, Lawrence, and Woolf. Baudelaire and Tolstoy assume a sexual existence, as do Flaubert and Chekhov. As does Proust. Thomas Mann, however, treats sexlessness in various forms, more often as innocence and fragility than not. But *Death in Venice* is his, in a way, most English novella, is his most pronounced Austen-James meditation on the subject.

In *Mansfield Park* Austen begins by introducing a character she despises for having never been more than sexual. Is she as rude as James is in his introduction of his princeling? Austen deals with the facts of the matter—a Jamesian phrase—and the contempt she feels toward the woman who was once sexual but had no other worth is balanced against the woman's standing and power now: and the events of the book, and Lady Bertram's voice and actions, bear Jane Austen out about the woman's life and mind. James's characters surprise but they have no inner laws of being—they have tone and perversity instead. In *Mansfield Park*, as in *The Golden Bowl*, some very attractive people are counterset to some less attractive people; but where in Austen the glamorous young are intent on throwing away their lives, in James they are construed only as sources of pain to the sexless. Austen places against her various sexually temperamental characters a serious heroine, Fanny Price, whom few readers like until the end of the book, if then—but she is a heroine and she is rarely wrong: if she were not long-suffering she would not be so right. It really is a quite frightening book. And Miss Price is sexless. Her apotheosis comes through her being morally and politically apt and stubborn and untouchable.

Maggie Verver's triumph comes through the power of love backed by a very large fortune. It would seem Austen is more adroit, more interesting, than James here, at least if James means us to take his story seriously. And he may not. He may be intent on parable or allegory and codification. I said earlier, and I repeat, that James is not artist enough to give us *a* prince—or *the* prince—in dialogue and actions, socially or sexually. Again I say: see the princes and princelings in Tolstoy and Proust for comparison. James's prince is dealt with in terms of gossip about him, which is clever but lifeless and, in the end, irresponsible. The essence of art is that it does not ever consist of a single voice without some evidence beyond that voice: art involves at least one convincing voice plus at least one other genuinely existent thing. Not to be able to create the personal reality of the prince is a suffocating aesthetic flaw. James does not love enough to be able to picture the object of love—and we are not given a monstrous love in Maggie for the decadent prince as we are given a monstrous affection in Charlus for Morel. Because of the misdrawn figure of the prince, we do not believe in Maggie's love—or in the prince's villainy.

And James is so smart that he does not want us to, except as a transcendent thing, as a matter of social sympathy on our part. Something in him wants this love to be read as a fictional act—an act of an artist, just as Austen wants us to read her books and accept the acts of her women as commonsense acts when actually her women are quite visionary and are nearly martyred in most cases and are artists in their intelligence and obstinacy and readiness and their opinionatedness. I would like to propose, not entirely mischievously, that James's novels *The Ambassadors*, *The Wings of the Dove*, and *The Golden Bowl* can be read as relating indirectly James's history of sexual romance and attachment at the end of his life. In the first novel, a sexless bystander comes to accept the idea and romance of sexuality—if it has sufficient style. In the second novel, the sexless person is embroiled in and is the center of the tale, the self-sacrificial victim of the others, but the ultimate victor in terms of the imagination and of moral eminence—as a writer might be said to be. In the last book, a complete personal and sexual triumph is presented to the sexless over the sexual. Well, why not?

Austen's suspicions of sexuality are better founded than James's. The right of women to live a mental existence is not quite the same as the right of the hardworking and sublimely talented sexless to rule over the sexual. Austen is full of emotional violence—one critic speaks of her "well-regulated hatred"—but she is not a bully and James is. Sexuality is very hard to define—whether it is a bullying thing or isn't, for instance: *if a man does not bully you, he doesn't love you,* is an aphorism in a dozen languages; certainly bullying has something to do with desire. But sexuality has to do with the validity of this world as we find it. One might say that sexuality represents a successful bribe on the part of nature—and so Tolstoy presents it. Flaubert and Proust are excessively bitter about it but they accept it. Certainly the bribe is not successful with all of us to the same extent, or equally from week to week or year to year. It can also be defined as the mode, other than parental or blood-similarity, by which we are attached to each other past the point of being able to perform casual betrayals—although perhaps spiritual or congregational bonds are sufficient for that in some of us.

Both James and Austen in their last books—*The Golden Bowl* and *Persuasion*—are at their warmest, whereas earlier they deal chiefly in notions of betrayal and insult. If we add a quantifying clause to our notion of sexuality, we might say: to the extent that we prefer to die rather than see the other seriously harmed—or some sliding scale related to that value of the other person—we love. The definition of sexlessness might be that it prefers death, its own or that of the beloved. Of course, these feelings might be familial. Austen deals directly with the lines of self-sacrifice and when to deny them. James is utterly melodramatic—and unreal—on the subject. The nonsexual attachment he says is sacrificial I believe is not: he is obviously lying (see *The Wings of the Dove* and see what you think). Austen accepts this sacrificial quality to love, but she argues we can control ourselves and love intelligently—we need not sacrifice ourselves to fools. Flaubert and Tolstoy are considerably harsher, Flaubert harsher than Tolstoy. James finds a great many substitutes for love. He is like someone who substitutes money for everything else, except he substitutes artfulness, cleverness, social genius. It is almost enough. After all, Proust does it successfully. The greatest of all novels so far is loveless and sexless—in a way. There is a general love and a general sexuality.

I think Proust shows the major techniques of the novel to be both relativistic and positivistic in combination—grotesque and subjective and
factual and sunlit. James cannot qualify as a master of the major techniques, and Austen can. James cannot establish the positivistic frame or
justify the relativistic grotesqueries and fantasies he proposes, but he does
not entirely need to: his claims and his sense of others proceed often
enough in the realm of fable or of art that he escapes any arraignment of
real failure on his part. But it is interesting that only in these last books of
his, these last hiddenly romantic books, does he become interestingly
inventive syntactically. If you glance through Austen you will see the pro-
totypes for most of the various kinds of Jamesian sentences except for
some of the sentences of wonderfully high rhetoric in his last three books.
That is, Austen's mental grounding, her notions, did allow her to inno-
vate from the beginning, while James, great as he was, does seem to be
limited to stirring the ashes.

Why does newness matter? Newness matters because why not otherwise read only the old books? If you compare Molly Bloom to Elizabeth
Bennet and Fanny Price and Anne Eliot, you will see that the imaginary
space from which Molly's thoughts emerge into speech via Joyce is
Austenian, I think, although it is very sexual. And James cannot adapt in
that way; he is an observer of *that*, too, a bystander toward literature as
well as to life—and that is *his* greatness.

Proust, a voyeur and bystander openly, is, in his sociomoral notion,
and in such devices as the little train, Austenian. And Proust is never successfully sexual in his book (he is probably, on the evidence of *Contre Saint-
Beuve*, too ashamed). But the wake and traces left by sexuality in the
Proustian novel are accurate or don't matter—that is, sexuality is not central to his claims. Shame makes him dishonest to his life, but he is honest
within the frame of his novel: honest bystanderhood and honest suffering
are central to his claims. And that is precisely what James, in his disguis-
edly autobiographical late fictions—or fables—will not settle for. He
claims a romantic knowledge and a personal power he has no right to. It is
self-indulgent of him. It is not James's doctrines or his life or his tone as
an artist or his degree of artfulness that I object to but merely the plotting
and the working out of his meanings as he sets them forth in his art.
His references to things, his depictions, his alterations of geographical
reality, of psychological and social topographies and sequences, are marred
by too many lies for such a yet very good book. Liars do not make the

greatest novelists. They may be the best people and the most truthful in real life, where truth is so often cruel and a lie is a truth of affection in the moment; and they may be the best friends—but they are not the best novelists. Novel writing is a truth-telling proposition with (highly) relative dimensions: the grotesque realities of people and of mental space *and* a shattering factuality are at the heart of the novel. The novel is an enterprise having truth as its starting point and with truth as its ending; and in between it is a truthful journey. It is a study in truth about people, about moments, actions, feelings, and ideas and ideals.

Now what is it in the tones and music of Austen's narrative procedure and intelligent comment that is unusually unarguable—so seemingly truthful to such a degree? Why aren't her wit and certainty merely didacticism—or a mannerism of the age? Furthermore, how can it be truth in "an imaginary space" and in an invented voice and in formal structures that have no truthful or complete origin, only a willful, aesthetic origin? What makes her omissive omniscience acceptable? We know that she knows what she is talking about; part of the acceptability in Austen of what is so omissive an omniscience comes from the consistency of emotional topography that she presents and the convincing consequences she invents: we suspect reality *is* there. In a recent novel a character, a woman, was said to be "disadvantaged," to have never been looked at with love although she had slept with a number of men and often. But in real life, if that were true, it would mean that here was a woman who was very unpleasant sexually, who was even sexually appalling and unable to learn from sexual experience, or who refused sexual existence—or how could such a statement be true of her? Another novel postulated a woman who mistook the lifelessness of a dying raccoon for affection, for a desirable friendliness. If the ebbing of vitality in death is what you want as animal friendliness and peaceful regard, then it is not surprising, as in the book, that the man she said she loved avoided her. We do not necessarily reason about these literary "facts" that are offered us as we read, so much as we have a sense of untruth, of special pleading and denial of the truth, somewhat in the Jamesian mode but far more extreme. Or we have a sense of psychological estrangement from art, a sense of the disqualifications of the author, which may please us by releasing us from any need to take her or her art seriously as a conduit of truth.

In Austen we are never, so far as I can recall, given such unacceptable facts and asked to accept them. James does it frequently (although never to the extent of entire disqualification): in *The Golden Bowl*, old Verver is presented to us as a good, kind, self-made billionaire. James is nicely obscure about it but it still won't do. In Austen, Knightley is good to his tenants. Who is Verver good to? Maggie and Verver are presented to us without their egos, and the prince and Charlotte are presented to us without their virtues. It's amusing and it is sophisticated but it is not pure souled with the truthful corruption of the best stuff, of the best art. It is the stuff of fairy tale, a fable with naturalistic elements. Austen is attached to a kind of novelistic and formal optimism that might be fablelike. Her early death and her last book undercut some of the merit of what she argues in the earlier books. Where James is ambiguous and his narrative power too often rests on a sense of fable—of advertising—Austen is clear and open-ended. By open-ended, I mean Austen is shrewd and clear-eyed and always gives us an open-endedness in events. Her tales are not made of events cast in iron as if by folkloric retelling; her stories are not known in advance, and her people and marriages are not fated or destined; everything can blow up in an instant. Everything rests on character and sacrifice but is subject to surprise and accident—and to the operations of will and futurity in what might be said to be, or to seem, a normal way. Will and heroism in James are highly melodramatic and are portrayed as fabulous. His system of representation lies a bit about the unknown thing that rests at one edge of real minutes and which the real minutes spill and upend on us as they proceed, whereas Austen accepts the unknowability and accidental and contingent nature of things in a rather pragmatic way, rather like Tolstoy—who got it from her, perhaps. The degree of the reality of the time sequences, the way the events seem to happen in real time, is interestingly similar in Austen and Tolstoy.

Austen is extremely difficult to write about. She is the first and most direct of the unfated or freewill writers of the industrial era; and who wants to argue about free will or the industrial era? She is among the elect, among the writers of surprise and of real-time amatory events. Her lovers make their own fates. They are active and dramatic entities. Tolstoy steals a scene from her, from *Persuasion*, to represent realistic and actual love in *Anna Karenina*: the proposal scene between Kitty and Levin is taken in great detail from that of Anne Elliot and Wentworth.

For many years in this century, *Pride and Prejudice* was the best-selling book in England after the Bible. We might expect that Austen's influence would not be much studied, since she is a woman and we are chary of ennobling women in certain ways (while we ridicule them with exaggerated ennobling in other ways); and she is a largely sexless moralist, so that only a moralist would be comfortable studying her; and she is very good, which is very daunting. In the mid-nineteenth century Macaulay said that in terms of the convincing creation of numbers of characters—the honorable and aesthetically effective portrayal of human beings, persons—she was second in English only to Shakespeare. That is likely to be the case still. I take her to be in the line of Homer and Tolstoy, and Shakespeare—considerably more limited, but not to the extent you might expect—a maker of sunlit epics in which people are pictured with a wholeness of effect remarkable for the power of representation. This is a strange, rare talent. Words do not automatically represent things and do not automatically suggest human presence. Firstly, words are not exact quantities of sound or meaning; they are areas of attention that we scan, often racingly, in context, and always only in a context of some sort. And it is very difficult to describe how words function as what they are *not* in order to be slidingly what they are. The difficulty in any boundary of definition is the inherent suggestion of what is not being said: to make a comparison as I have here is also to argue that comparisons are foolish and not useful, for instance. Deconstruction follows on definition. The creation of characters has a highly dramatic element of the loss or dissolution of those creations. Words such as *great* and *greater* mean what they do slidingly, in context. What they purport to represent, what they falsely claim, or do successfully represent, is very odd. Austen's tone of anti-fable is a claim of reality paradoxically supported by the rigor of her formal classicism, sometimes false, sometimes true. But she is very clearly one of the very great heroes of the novel, one of

> Fame's Boys and Girls, who never die
> And are too seldom born—

1988

READING, THE MOST
DANGEROUS GAME

Reading is an intimate act, perhaps more intimate than any other human act. I say that because of the prolonged (or intense) exposure of one mind to another that is involved in it, and because it is the level of mind at which feelings and hopes are dealt in by consciousness and words.

Reading a good book is not much different from a love affair, from love, complete with shyness and odd assertions of power and of independence and with many sorts of incompleteness in the experience. One can marry the book: reread it, add it to one's life, live with it. Or it might be compared to pregnancy—serious reading even if you're reading trash: one is inside the experience and is about to be born; and one is carrying something, a sort of self inside oneself that one is about to give birth to, perhaps a monster. Of course, for men this is always verging on something else (part of which is a primitive rage with being masculine, a dismay felt toward women and the world, a reader's odd sense of women).

The act of reading as it really occurs is obscure: the decision to read a book in a real minute, how one selects the book, how one flirts with the choice, how one dawdles on the odd path of getting it read and then reread, the oddities of rereading, the extreme oddities of the procedures of continuing with or without interruptions to read, getting ready to read a middle chapter in its turn after going off for a while, then getting hold of the book physically, having it in one's hand, letting one's mind fill with thoughts in a sort of warm-up for the exercise of mind to come—one riffles through remembered scenes from this and other books, one diddles with half-memories of other pleasures and usefulnesses, one wonders if one can afford to read, one considers the limitations and possibilities of this book, one is humiliated in anticipation or superior or thrilled in anticipation, or nauseated in retrospect or as one reads. One has a sense of talk and of reviews and essays and of anticipation or dread and the will to be affected by the thing of reading, affected lightly or seriously. One settles one's body to some varying degree, and then one enters on the altered tempos of reading, the subjection to being played upon, one passes through phases, starting with reacting to or ignoring the cover of the book and the opening lines.

The piercing things, the stabbingly emotional stuff involved in reading, leads to envy, worse even than in sibling or neighborhood rivalry, and it leads to jealousy and possessiveness. If a book is not religious or trashy, the problem of salesmanship, always partly a con, arises in relation to it, to all the problems it presents. A good reader of Proust complains constantly as a man might complain of a wife or a woman of her husband. And Proust perhaps had such a marriage in mind with the reader. A good book, like pregnancy or a woman known to arouse love, or a man, is something you praise in the light of a general reluctance to risk the experience; and the quality of praise warns people against the book, warns them to take it seriously; you warn them about it, not wanting to be evangelical, a matchmaker or a malicious pimp for a troubled and troubling view of the world.

I can't imagine how a real text can be taught in a school. Even minor masterpieces, *Huckleberry Finn* or *The Catcher in the Rye*, are too much for a classroom, too real an experience. No one *likes* a good book if they have actually read it. One is fanatically attached, restlessly attached, criminally attached, violently and criminally opposed, sickened, unable to bear it. In Europe, reading is known to be dangerous. Reading always leads to personal metamorphosis, sometimes irreversible, sometimes temporary, sometimes large-scale, sometimes less than that. A good book leads to alterations in one's sensibility and often becomes a premise in one's beliefs. One associates truth with texts, with impressive texts anyway; and when trashy books vanish from sight, it is because they lie too much and too badly and are not worth one's intimacy with them. Print has so much authority, however, that sometimes it is only at the beginning of an attempt at a second reading or at the end of it, and only then, if one is self-assured, that one can see whether a book was not really worth reading the first time; one tells by how alterable the truth in it seems in this more familiar light and how effective the book remains or, contrarily, how amazingly empty of meaning it now shows itself to be. It is a strange feeling to be a practiced enough reader and writer to see in some books that there is nothing there. It is eerie: why did the writer bother? What reward is there in being a fraud in one's language and in one's ideas? To believe they just didn't know is more unsettling than to doubt oneself or to claim to be superficial or prejudiced or to give up reading entirely, at least for a while.

Or, in our country, we deny what we see of this and even reverse it: fraud is presented as happiness; an empty book is said to be well constructed, a foolish argument is called innovative. This is a kind of bliss; but lying of that sort, when it is nearly universal, wrecks the possibility of our having a literary culture or even of our talking about books with each other with any real pleasure. It is like being phony yachtsmen who only know smooth water and who use their motors whenever they can. This guarantees an immense personal wretchedness, actually.

Of course, in Europe, cultural patterns exist that slow the rate of change in you as a reader (as well as supplying evidence to use in comprehending what happens and will happen to you if you change because of a book). Of course, such change is never entirely good or wise. In our country, we have nothing to hold us back from responding to any sort of idea. With us everything is for sale—everything is up for grabs, including ourselves—and we have very little tradition worth hanging onto except the antic.

The country is organized not by religion or political machinery but by what are seen as economic realities but which are fashions in making money and spending money. We are an army marching in the largest conceivable mass so entirely within cultural immediacy that it can be said this is new in the history of the world, emotionally new in that while this has been true of other cultures for brief periods in the past, it was never true as completely or for such a large part of the population or so continuously, with so few periods of stasis. We pretend to tradition but, really, nothing prevents our changing.

·   ·   ·

And we do change. Divorce, born-again Christianity, the computer revolution, a return to the farm, a move to the city. In Boston, at college at Harvard, I first knew people who claimed to be cultivated to the degree they remained unchanged not only in spite of the reading they claimed to have done but with the help of it. They did not realize what an imbecile and provincial notion that was—it was simply untrue: you could see it, the untruth of it. A rule of thumb about culture is that personal or public yearning for a better time to come or one in the past and nostalgia of any sort are reliable signs of the counterfeit. The past is there to be studied in its reality, moment by moment, and the future can be discussed in its reality to come, which will be a reality moment by moment; but doing that means being honest just as doing it makes you too busy to yearn; and doing it shows you that nostalgia is a swindler's trick. A sense of the real is what is meant by good sense. And because of the nature of time and because of how relentlessly change occurs, good sense has to contain a good deal of the visionary as well as of ironic apology to cover the inevitable mistakes. And this is doubly so with us, in the United States. Reality here is special. And part of reality here or elsewhere is that novels, plays, essays, fact pieces, poems, through conversion or in the process of argument with them, change you or else—to use an idiom—you haven't listened.

If the reader is not at risk, he is not reading. And if the writer is not at risk, he is not writing. As a rule, a writer and a book or a poem are no good if the writer is essentially unchanged morally after having written it. If the work is really a holding operation, this will show in a closed or flat quality in the prose and in the scheme of the thing, a logiclessness, if you will pardon the neologism, in the writing. Writing always tends toward a kind of moral stance—this is because of the weight of logic and of truth in it—but judging the ways in which it is moral is hard for people who are not cultivated. Profoundly educated persons make the best judges.

The general risk in being a man or woman of cultivation is then very high and this is so in any culture, and perhaps requires too much strength for even a small group to practice in ours. But should such a guerrilla group arise, it will have to say that cultivation and judgment issue from the mouths of books and can come from no other source. Over a period of centuries, ignorance has come, justifiably, to mean a state of booklessness. Movie-educated people are strained; they are decontextualized; they are cultivated in a lesser way. Television and contemporary music are haunted by the search for messiahs; the usual sign of mass inauthenticity is a false prophet (which usually means a war will shortly break out and be lost). The absence of good sense signals the decline of a people and of a civilization. Shrewdness without good sense is hell unleashed.

I would propose as a social cure that in fourth grade and in the first year at college, this society mandate that we undergo a year of reading with or without argument as the soul can bear, including argument with teachers and parents and local philosophers if there are any. Of course something like this happens anyway but we probably ought to institutionalize it in our faddish way.

After all, if you don't know what's in good books, how can your life not be utterly miserable all in all? Won't it fall apart with fearsome frequency? The best of what this species knows is in books. Without their help, how can you manage?

If I intend for my life to matter to me, I had better read seriously, starting with newspapers and working up to philosophy and novels. And a book in what it teaches, and in what it does in comforting and amusing us, in what it does in granting asylum to us for a while, had better be roughly equivalent to, or greater in worth than, an event involving other people in reality that teaches us or that grants us asylum for a while in some similar way, or there is no reason to bother with it. And I am careful toward books that offer refuge to my ego or my bad conscience. A writer who is opposed to notions of value and instruction is telling you he or she does not want to have to display loyalty or insight or sensitivity—to prose or to people: that would limit his or her maneuverability; and someone who does not believe that loyalty or insight or sensitivity or meaning has any meaning is hardly worth knowing in books or on the page although such people are unavoidable in an active life.

The procedures of real reading, if I may call it that, are not essentially shrewd, although certain writers, Twain and Proust, for instance, often do play to the practice of shrewdness in their readers.

But the disappearance from the immediate world of one's attention, that infidelity to one's alertness toward outside attack, and then the gullibility required for a prolonged act of attention to something not directly inferior to one's own methods and experiences, something that emanates from someone else, that and the risk of conversion, the certainty that if the book is good, one will take on ideas and theories, a sense of style, a sense of things different from those one had before—if you think of those, you can see the elements of middle-class leisure and freedom, or upper-class insolence and power, or lower-class rebelliousness and hiddenness and disloyalty to one's surroundings, that are required for real reading.

And you can also see what the real nature of literature is—it is a matter of one's attention being removed from the real world and regarding nature and the world verbally: it is a messy mathematics in its way; it is a kind of science dealing in images and language, and it has to be right in the things it says; it has to be right about things.

I learned very early that when you were infatuated with someone, you read the same books the other person read or you read the books that had shaped the other person or you committed an infidelity and read for yourself and it was the beginning of trouble. I think reading and writing are the most dangerous human things because they operate on and from that part of the mind in which judgments of reality are made; and because of the authority language has from when we learn to speak and use its power as a family matter, as an immediate matter, and from when we learn to read and see its modern, middle-class power as a public matter establishing our rank in the world.

When a book is technically uninteresting, when such a book is not a kind of comically enraged protest against the pretensions of false technique and ludicrously misconceived subject matter, it is bound to be a phony. The democratic subversion of objects, of techniques, can never without real dishonesty stray far from its ostensible purpose, which is the democratic necessity of making our lives interesting to us. Folk art is, inevitably, a kind of baby talk in relation to high art—and this is shaming, but so is much in life, including one's odor giving one's secrets away (showing one's nervousness or one's lechery), but it is better to do that than live messageless and without nerves or desire. The moral extravagance of reading—its spiritual element and its class element—is bound to reflect both an absence of humility and a new kind of humility and both in odd ways. Two of our most conceited writers, Gertrude Stein and Ernest Hemingway, overtly wrote baby talk. Nowadays the young like financial reporting as a window on the world, and television and the interview. They are pursuing fact in the plethora of baby talk, and they are trying to exercise judgment in the middle of the overenthusiastic marketing of trash.

American colleges have taught our intellectuals to read politically in order to enter and stay in a group or on a track. One reads skimmingly then, and one keeps placing the authority for what one reads outside oneself. But actually people cannot read in a two-souled way, shrewdly, and with a capacity to feel and learn. Learning involves fear and sometimes awe and just plain factually is not shrewd—it is supershrewd if you like, it is a very grand speculation indeed; and graduate school stuff won't open out into awe and discovery or recognition or personal knowledge of events but only onto academic hustling. I mean when you stop theorizing and think about what is really there. Do I need to go on? One of the primary rules of language is that there must be a good reason for the listener to attend to a second sentence after the first one; to supply a good reason is called "being interesting." Not to attend to the second sentence is called "not listening." The reasons to listen are always selfish, but that does not mean they are only selfish.

It is hard to listen. It is also hard to write well and to think. These ought not to be unfamiliar statements. This ought not to be news.

1985

THE ONE WHO WRITES

I am too delicate to have had a life. I am too easily interrupted. I have
never had a real or outward life, never had anything to do with living
or walking or seeing outwardly. I analyze those things—they fill me
with wonder. I am suspended between eyes and hands and mind and paper
among alphabetical squiggles and syllables—the hands are the hands of a
robot. I am not a robot; I don't mean that. But when I work, the outside
shell, that person is an automaton.

I am entirely suspended among a sense of sounds as heard in the head,
not real sounds, but as if whispered, but very fast, a short-hand, short-ear,
short-tongue. I have rarely, maybe only once or twice, if that, ever spoken
to anyone, ever emerged in speech—at least, I have no sense of its having
happened except at quiet eery moments when I was, in a way, sleepwalking. I did not know what I was doing.

A sense of sounds but not real sound, a sense of thoughts, but actual
thinking is something some other self does, and while it is going on, it
can't be written down. Usually, the outward self talks to someone or to
himself. And whatever was thought moves blunderingly toward language
and being written.

My playing field, my landscape, my entire reality is words, words in
sequence, very rapid and aimed all ways, clustered and smoothed out,
aimed at readers, and then, transcription, which is slow, and I am like a

single held breath. Imagined events, imagined readers, imagined processes of work, of writing—I imagine myself finishing this paragraph before I begin it—are a real landscape if I am not ill or interrupted. I lose my real ears; they are useless. And my sense of taste doesn't register whatever the outer automaton chews on including his own lip. I have no sense of the touch of the pen or the pencil or the keys of the machine or the color of the screen.

I have nearby selves who are aware if I wake to them, if I am dispersed, and one of them takes over. But me, I have only a startled sense of other people—I mean, entirely real, bodied people. Or of my outer self, or selves, the athletic one, the newspaper-reading one, the one who learns to use machines. My awareness or awakening or their self-assertion, either one, is like a silent burst of fireworks or of some sort of artillery but the burst is sensory. Anyway, it murders me, disperses me, and this is so absolute that my separation from life is more than a haremlike imprisonment, more than is easily imagined: I cannot talk to people or run or see, and yet I am not a mole or a cripple. . . . I have means of inner locomotion.

I have tried to lessen the separation. I have tried to stay concentrated and to live alongside or inside a living self. I have tried not to be dispersed, but it has never once worked. It seems large. It seems likely that the split between the privacy and the isolation is nearly absolute in the shadowy limbo of chutes and tunnels, perspectives and unreal woods in which I live. It is shadowy only in part. It lights up where I am. It lights up quite a lot if I imagine a general outdoor light.

My outer self, or selves in committee, that congress of worldly selves, creates me like a special counsel. Sometimes I tug at those outward powers, apply a faint or a choking tidal pull, but I have no power. My outer self is reluctant—afraid. Sometimes, like an older brother, it imitates me. It manifests a kind of choking half-dark will to be alone, to sleep alone, to have his dreams to himself—I mean it pursues an isolation that is parallel or analogous to mine. Sometimes it writes—and talks—in imitation. It is very strange, my dependent existence. I can pull away from the outer self with its wealth of attitudes into an eyeless daydreaming, but after just a second or two that outer congress has to allow this, has to be entertained. I am alone but enslaved, capable of all sorts of shadow feats, forced to work and yet I can really only work at my own volition. I am much weaker than a child. I have never really met or seen anyone's outer self, only an in-here version. I share memories and information with my outer selves, but only partially, very imperfectly, in both directions. I have no power except that of curiosity—and, to some extent, the power to amuse. Oh yes, pride. I have the power of pride. I am very largely a forbidden manifestation and unwise and unlikable when I work, someone to be teased. . . . My outer self has to indulge me, warm me, protect me, has to let me live and adjourn or kill itself for a while. Muscular restlessness or muscular wretchedness, the need to piss, almost any state other than hibernation and a certain degree of automatism in the surrounding congress disperses me, and I am done for until I am summoned, re-created, and then agree to work.

I can describe him in moonlight, relieved not to have to imagine the moonlight, not to have to phrase it, the silly moonlight, not to have to imagine the city street, the tight row of town houses, the windows, but to have it all be there, solidly there to the senses—he likes to be free of me. The unimagined world intoxicates that realer self, and I am—it is clear—a twist that his life has taken that he often dislikes.

I am dispersed by movement, by focusing my outer eyes. I am easily dispersed. My world is imagined, but it is the only one I live in. I have around me a gulf of silence, a second or two of blankness—a distance—to wholeness. Everything in me is fractured and incomplete, is in small pieces that sometimes coalesce or that expand. In this citizenship, all is amusement and shape. Everything has a point, a clear purpose. Opinions are important, are final—for a while. Meaning is never absent; even meaninglessness is full of meaning here. I am, and I am in, some sort of simultaneous city of vistas of attention—ideas, words, and sentences in motion—oh, so many motions. I suppose not a million sentences but a million shadows of words, of syllables, whole New Yorks of half-written statements pour through me. . . . At times it seems I have a complete citizenship, an entire world, that the whole world is here in an unembodied way.

But that is an illusion. Gaps of absence, of omission, quickly appear if I look for logical connections. It is all very stylized . . . very Manhattan, very Venetian. Something abrasive and nervous in this, some rebellious and unwise quality in this, rubs against the rest of me and erodes my outer self. My outer life often feels that the dramas and exertions of order, the emergencies and efforts of imagination of this inner Manhattan are shortening that outer life. And have ruined it and are ruining it more. For me to work seems reckless and lonely, peninsular.

Now that my outer self is ill and tires easily, I am a respite from that. But I am weaker, too, and when I begin to come to the end of what I can do for the day, the outer world bursts on me more gently than it used to. It begins to announce itself as daytime or nighttime brightness of colors, of objects, and of sounds—tangible, all of it so that the word *place* as it springs up reflects forward and back, reflects the inhabited word—the word inhabited by what is visible, not to me, but to my outer self—I merely remember this—and reflects itself, *place* and desk and lamp burning and stereo playing, colors and surfaces, reality, nothing silly and illogical like the paragraphs I have been writing. Nothing like moonlight. Merely a room.

But I am almost present in it, almost present alongside my outer self. I have never had a life in any usual sense, but I will have a death.

1994

FRANK AND HAROLD

To love books is not necessarily to love writers. Anyway, I don't actually love books; I love some books, and I am uncomfortably addicted to reading. This addiction extends to the genre of literary reminiscence and to the literary interview, but the Golden Age rhetoric—how happy we were, how profound we were, how depressed and ambitious and important we were—oh, the loveliness, oh the dark happiness—the self-love by profession makes my queasy.

The genre of literary reminiscence has produced only one masterpiece in English, Boswell's *Life of Johnson*. And it is the greatness of Samuel Johnson's talk and the magnificence of his character—a noble Christian fat man, a depressed Falstaff worried about the sublime—supposedly pictured in the book which makes it a masterpiece. That and a sort of lovingness that the character possesses and a lust for parties. This has influenced almost all literary self-representation since. As well as stand-up comedy. For a long time, readers and scholars believed the reproduction of Johnson's speeches in the book because they believed Boswell was too stupid to have invented them. Boswell presents himself as naive and shallow—as young, uncalculating and inept, incapable of counterfeit, which, considering the artistry of the book, seems hardly likely.

Boswell's papers were found in a country house in Ireland (after the Second World War) and these papers, now at Yale, led to a new view that

Boswell was a smart, twisty, syphilitic, gonorrheic, depressed, alcoholic literary adventurer, quite capable of inventing the lovable Johnson he put on paper.

I met Frank O'Hara when I was seventeen. I don't think he ever presented himself to me as a person but as a writer, a veiling of glory over a defective young man. He did not want to have much to do with anyone. Conversation with him was like making a documentary about greatness and fame, good poems, good paintings, immortality. It was his role in life as an ex-Catholic to prepare this other salvation for himself. And for the people around him.

There was no *real Frank* that peeped through the veil of glory—that was part of what made him effectual and, by paradox, made him honest, through the depth and honesty of the pretense, of the attempt. He was not human; he was great, greatly monstrous. But monsters are forms of humanity often of inestimable value. I was younger by five or six years, but was no realer. I was barely past a terrifying childhood, and my role, my persona, was normalcy, ersatz M-G-M.

Frank was, of course, startlingly smart, and he moved easily from the literal to the symbolic, to a fantasy-metaphor of salesmanship or daydream. It was part of what he offered, part of the excitement. But he set the rules for that. So sometimes I was real in my role; he made it real. One time, when he was living with Joe LeSueur, and for some reason Joe and Frank and I were talking about or had referred to Joe's sitting in Auden's lap, Frank, jealous of Joe, switched the talk to the arena of metaphor and literary criticism by saying, "Ashbery sits on Auden's lap." That is, he implied that Ashbery was a ventriloquist's dummy. Of course, memory being what it is, he might have said, "Ashbery shits on Auden's lap." We were drunk.

Peter Schjeldahl, Frank's first biographer, came to see me fifteen years or so ago to ask me about an affair Frank had told his friends he and I had had at Harvard—he told them even while I was still in college. A few years after Schjeldahl, Brad Gooch, the second of Frank's biographers, asked me about the college affair. "It isn't bloody likely, is it?" I said. I said something like that. Gooch said with a wry smile, "I don't KNOW—that's what I am trying to find out. . . ." (He spoke in an imitation of Frank's inflection.)

I knew Frank almost entirely through conversation. In conversation, one had a sense that Frank never had a real affair—certainly not as real as the fantasy ones he projected: "I have experienced *perfect love* with Bill [Berkson]." He was too busy to be logical. Or consistent. But this fantasy projection of love was part of his *thing*—part of his sense of the world carried over into talk, part of the best talk of his time.

The best talk of his time? Well, that, too, is a Golden Age category. Frank was good, and Sontag and Renata Adler and Mary McCarthy and the Bernsteins, a lot of people were good talkers, Theodora Codman and Mendy Wager and William Shawn and Marc Blitzstein and J. J. Mitchell and Sam Barlow and an English teacher I had named Margot Johnson, who took me to have tea, by God, with T. S. Eliot's mother. A lot of the good talk came from talkers who were drunk, who were pretty much drunks. Good talk is disposable wit in passing, a hidden art. It is practiced with a certain careless salt in regard to honesty, a certain brio in regard to fact, to lying and to demolishing the lies. It mixes discretion with indiscretion both coolly and breathlessly. It is never coy, rarely ungenerous, and it never happens under oath.

I met Frank, at Harvard, through a cousin of mine from Saint Louis. My cousin admired Frank's bravura, fund of knowledge, and publicly outrageous brilliance—there was nothing sotto voce about Frank. My cousin said, "I want you to meet this guy—he'll make you feel dumb." Frank had a straight manner then—U.S. Navy and Harvard—that he used when he was sober and in public, and a flauntingly gorgeous manner (supposedly ripped off from Edward Gorey) that he used when he was drunk or angry. It was literary, semi-inspired, infinitely interesting in how it made language and voice and implication come alive. It was something useful when he wanted to govern a room. By the time I was a senior, Frank spoke almost entirely in what had become the O'Hara mode; he spoke as emphatically as if he had been born gurgling with those inflections. He was sure of his style: his veil of glory was pure New York, and nervy, terrific. And it involved taking possession of the language and of speech and of ideas of propriety. . . . It involved perpetual social triumph on the order of Samuel Johnson's, as Boswell presented it. Or invented it. (It doesn't much matter.)

In New York one lives in the moment rather more than Socrates advised so that at a party or alone in your room it is difficult to guess at the long-term worth of anything. Artists tend to have the carefully frightened faces of the inmates of dictatorships. Judgments are everywhere, are constant. . . . Your haircut, your forearms get reviewed, sometimes in print. Would-be writers whisper to one another out of fear of drawing down on themselves the wrath of some American or Aussie or Brit critic practicing *savage indignation.*

Frank and John Ashbery (who met Frank two years after I did) were David figures who confronted with their slingshots the incipient wrath of the generation before and the envy and mockery of their contemporaries; they did this bearing their messages of new art, new American art. John became politic and more recessive and elegant—and much more famous and widely agreed on and recognized—but Frank was obnoxiously saucy until he died. The insolence went so deep that he insisted for a long time that he knew the truth, that he knew what truth was.

New York literary friendship is strange. Most contacts go in and out of courtship of one kind or another and combat of one kind or another. Changes of idea, of status. It is New York professionalism and ambition, the hunt for ideas and experiences. What made Frank different was the quality of the new experiences he offered: A Beckett play, Balanchine, the homosexual world, up and down, mostly down; the first two times I entered a gay bar everyone there grew silent. Frank said, "They think you're a cop." Later he said, "You made a good entrance."

He gave me a part of New York I was too shy and stupid to find for myself. I am kind of catatonic; I needed someone who knew things and talked: *Show me, show me, show me.* . . . I suppose I thought I was too freakish to trust my thoughts. I thought I had no validity. I am a kind of inwardly frozen curatorial Jew. So New York was scary for a while for a hick like me.

I told Frank this while I was in college, and the year he met Ashbery and Larry Rivers, Frank asked me down—to see "the real" New York with him—and I said I would come with Bradley Philips, my roommate.

This was New York six years after the end of the Second World War. New York didn't glitter then; there were no glass buildings with reflections on them. The stone buildings looked stiff-sided and had smallish windows that caught sunrays and glittered at twilight; rows of corseted, sequined buildings. Driving through its streets in a convertible owned by Bradley's very rich mother, one was presented with a series of towering perspectives leaping up and fleeing backward like some very high stone-and-brick wake of the passage of your head. Past advertising everywhere: billboards and neon and window signs: New York was raunchy with words. Words of salesmanship. And it was menacing and lovely—the foursquare perspectives trailing down the fat, endless avenues, which were transformed in the dimming blue light of the dissolving workday. The neon signs came on in a form of invitation to an end to loneliness. Everywhere you were offered the treats of self-destruction. Overwhelming beauty and carelessness, the city then, one of the wonders of the world.

I was a junior in college at that point. We entered the Village like the Jews into Canaan. Frank and Ashbery and Larry Rivers *greeted* us. As I said, Frank had met them that year (I got that fact from Gooch's book) but I thought back then they had known each other a long time. I was the youngest of the five of us. All of us were nobodies except Bradley Philips, who in headlines would have been "HEIR TO UPSTATE UTILITIES FORTUNE." Frank wasn't a nobody, quite. And Larry Rivers had been praised by Clement Greenberg (I don't remember this either; I read it in Gooch's book). John Ashbery had already been praised by Auden; he had been the most admired young poet at Harvard. Everyone thought well of Ashbery. He was a superb compromise if you cared about art and distrusted artists.

Frank hadn't yet become so clearly embattled but he was glamorously angry and obscene. And sure of himself. His outrageousness rested on the hard evidence that he was one of the smartest people you would ever meet. And he was an interesting poet. I hadn't much liked his poetry in the literary magazine, the *Advocate*, which John and Bradley and I had worked on; I liked Ashbery's. But I was sure Frank's was the real thing too.

I kept laughing with pleasure, even at his tragic remarks. Ashbery, as always, was damned hard to talk to. He dressed in suits and vests, and he had a tightly furled foreign umbrella and a derby. It was a vague parody of T. S. Eliot with a touch of upstate New York elegance thrown in; very funny and impressive. But he was rarely overt, and many of his references were obscure and daunting, while Frank was directly, addictedly conversational. Frank was, after all, *Irish*.

I knew Frank was going to try to seduce me, and that was OK, since he was offering me New York. New York is worth a pass. Frank was amazingly confident; this was his part of New York—I learned later he was shy and easily silenced uptown. Frank asked if I wanted to see artists, the real people of the real New York (that was the way he put it). We went to the

San Remo. If I work at it, I can remember the old San Remo bar, the windows and the light outside and inside, and the crowd, the smells of lye soap and turpentine and sweat and beer. The light in the bar wasn't bar lighting or anything like modern lighting: it was a very bright not-darkness. Frank moved around talking to a lot of people, including a drunken and angry—was it Rothko? Kline? Pollock? I don't remember. None of them was famous then, either.

In the midst of the noise, Frank and Ashbery showed off for us. Frank shouted that surrealism was dead. John or Frank shouted that the entire surface of the canvas mattered. John, I think, said that Auden had loosened the girdle of form. Frank announced the death of the well-made. The shouting was necessary although we were standing very close together.

I kept bending over to hear better and to see their faces, and then I would stumble and start to fall. (I did remark once I was too tall to be a postsurrealist.) Someone would stiff-arm or pull me upright, Bradley usually. I was not good at being drunk.

I believe we also talked surrealism, the real thing, the manifestos and Breton's statements while he was in New York. I think I remember Frank saying, "But Larry looks like Duchamp," awarding a medal, a destiny. . . . I hadn't enough acquaintance with the slogans of New York art hunger, of *I want to be an artist*, to follow the threads. Bradley was more experienced socially and acted as the translator for me at times. I said, "What?" and he told me what the words had been in the last speech. He was good at the *music* of the voices in a kind of sarcastic way. But I could tell that while he knew what was being said, he wasn't listening, either.

Then we went to the Cedar or to dinner, and then we were walking in the streets. I don't really remember the sequence; I don't really remember clearly who said what where. It seems likely it happened like this: Frank did a riff about the era, a section of time that he said we would define and in which we would star. Frank said that he, Frank, was the chief literary intelligence in America, the chief aesthetic intelligence, and at some point, when I responded to this by saying, "Cut it out," he said haughtily, in his new manner, "Well, I am."

My unreliable memory says they were talking about *immediacy* in art, but they didn't use that word. They talked, not about the automatic writing of the sort Yeats did, using his wife as a source, or that the surrealists advocated, but about the escape from the self into the realer self through a direct gesture, a direct attack by a painter on a canvas or something very like automatic writing for a writer: they were sponsoring an idea of immediacy of creation to get away from the stale and overworked and on to freshness—and greatness. You did not cover up the traces of the act's being actual.

It was a kind of anti-illusionism, anti-wartime-propaganda, truth-at-last thing that you can see in Larry Rivers's work and notice in the work of all of us, the surface of direct immediacy, sometimes cool, sometimes comedic, sometimes impassioned, and depending on the use of the present tense of the verb and on present-tense actuality—a *now* radiant with feelings (terror, for instance) and poked at by the past and mounted on fishhooks of whatever-was-coming-next, the future. It was a little like Zen and satori before those became big-time New York ideas.

We talked about sex, of course. New York was the capital of American sexuality, the one place in America where you could get laid with some degree of sophistication, and so Peggy Guggenheim and André Breton had come here during the war, whereas Thomas Mann, who was shy, and Igor Stravinsky, who was pious, went to Los Angeles, which is the best place for voyeurs.

And everyone knew that New York was good for fucking your way into a career—especially good for writers. The rule of thumb for anyone who wanted to be celebrated was that they had to sleep with anyone and everyone who wanted them, critics, grant givers, editors, older writers . . . who otherwise would become enemies. If you were sexually recessive, you were marked as someone not actually serious about discarding the body and being *intellectual*.

The sex talk involved the mixing of races and social classes and of homosexuals and lesbians and heterosexuals in the Village—Frank believed that the bohemian Village housed almost the entire truth quotient in American life. The trouble with the sexual-and-careerist invitation the Village offered was that you were aware you might not be able to manage: you might drown, you might fall off the train, the horse, whatever metaphor you preferred, *before* you did anything interesting. You would have wasted your life without having created good work or entering legend.

In a flittering, fragile memory, I see someone walking in the street, in the gutter, and gesticulating. That was probably Larry. He was a New York hotshot—a boxer, a saxophonist, kind of a sex fiend, he said (or Frank said), and he knew about drugs; he has written that he would fuck anything, with anything: he was cheerful and smart-ass and not bored or boring: he had a sly, nervously active, *friendly* smile: every mother's nightmare, really: amoral in style, a forerunner of the underground guy-heroes, a precursor of the Beats and of Quentin Tarantino, and about to be a world-famous painter and cultural influence on everyone. . . .

Rivers and I were Jews, ex-Jews, obstinately still Jews—one of the questions of the time was about old modes of piety and new ones. But Rivers had a social scope to him that I never had. He and Frank had a famous friendship, and he was much tougher than I was, and still is; he had the limitless self-daring and the restlessness and ennui that Jerzy Kosinski had. He was ready for everything and I was ready for nothing (Frank may have said that). I felt overshadowed and consequently and perversely safe.

All of them had manners and styles for various stages of drunkenness—or whatever it was we were. Ashbery, all stylishness and depths withheld, carried his umbrella and slid often into French. Bradley, who was very tall and dark-haired—who was very rich and very handsome and not relatively, not as a metaphor but absolutely—kept slipping into his Eastern-seaboard rich boy's faintly nasal tones. (His mother when Bradley asked for something would think and then say, "Yes, of course. That's what the money is *for*.")

Frank has been so often described that it seems foolhardy to try to add anything, but I'll mention these things: he rarely, if ever, gestured. His head was rather large, and his features were large, but he always struck me as being a small person, or like a boy. The most lasting impression was contradictory, of parochial-school rigidity of posture and then humor— well, humor and grief. And then the boyishness was contradicted by an effect of densely compacted weight, as if he were a statue given life, a short *commandatore* come to take you to hell at the end of *Don Giovanni*.

Also, in life, on two feet, Frank was the important one, the master of ceremonies. This was not a given; he was a scene-stealer, a diva. Everyone I knew over the years who knew him wanted to be present at one of his abrasive, temperamental performances. Perhaps not two of them. He overshadowed most occasions and most people. Frank didn't always hog the floor, but he did a lot. And so did Larry. You would think neither of them had a gift for growing old, but Larry actually did, whereas Frank, even when he was young, was visibly raddled with temper, blistered with impatience, with the black bliss of rage and the insidious moodiness of being a star—always as if he was on the edge of being tired of it. He was wonderful, and he was the opposite of the life of the party—the shadow of the death of pleasure. That is just my opinion, not a literary fact. It is a fact, however, that Frank was jealous and punitive about power.

Perhaps we were all youthful monsters, five incipient *Tyrannosaurus rexes*. Well, Frank and John were the most interesting in speech. That night, Ashbery said (I think), "The forms are broken," in the very light but severe way he had. And Frank, jealous of John and ruthlessly competitive with him, cut him off and said, "They have mussed Lana Turner's hair, and Merle Oberon has gone bald." (He practiced a Hollywood-Paris surrealism in talk and argument.) And Larry said, "Joe DiMaggio ought to dance for Balanchine." And started to go on, but Frank exclaimed, "Larry, that's *brilliant!*" and shut him up.

I said, "The genres are gone?" Bradley was shaking his head no at me, don't listen to these arty types, but I thought Ashbery was right. "I agree," I said. And my life was changed then and there (toward failure, Frank might say). It is wonderful, perhaps tragic what is brilliant or useful for you when you are young.

That night, Frank O'Hara, John Ashbery, Larry Rivers, Bradley Schoellkopf Phillips, and I spent the night together in one bed.

I don't think I had an opinion about homosexuality, and none about what I was. It seemed natural to me for anyone to have an interest in militant and specialized and showy homosexuality. I had seen two or three transvestite shows in Europe and been impressed by their curious splendor. . . . Ah, sophisticated Harold . . . And it seemed natural for people, on the defensive or the make, to make a big deal about their sexual normalcy. I don't think I had a preference, exactly; I didn't think the two modes of sexual self-presentation were similar or mutually excluding, but, of course, I wasn't sure of my own judgment. I was aware that I was resentful of women for the emotional range they allowed themselves and resentful of the power they had to make me respond. I was scared of obligations. I thought the fifties were phoney and that the eternal verities of the time wouldn't last.

On the other hand, with Frank and his friends I was scared of art and physically very quickly bored. Broke and lazy, I had a mania for brave talk and some flirtation or sense of possibility—and then I wanted to lie down and think about it. (Bernard Malamud said not long before his death that I had talked away a dozen books I might have written. I never told him how much time I spent lying down and staring at nothing.) With men I had more autonomy. Guys could share horror and vile drunkenness and their search for power, or at least reveal it. Guys could get drunk and melodramatic in the bedroom (which was boring), and you could throw them out or walk out, without getting a knife in your ribs, although not always, while if you did that with a woman, walked out on the melodrama, there was a hell of a storm. Vengeance is mine, saith short, angry women. Regular guys did all sorts of homosexual things, and did them overtly, but as if unself-consciously—took off their clothes in each other's presence, and received in the bathtub, and made out with each other when drunk, and mimicked women's walks. It didn't count, first because everyone concerned insisted that it didn't count and second because these people were concerned to not be members of the homosexual category. There was a line you crossed: the third time you got blown you were no longer quite straight. But you weren't queer either. I went to bed with Frank twice in college—does that constitute an affair? I had been to bed with Bradley more often but never *thoroughly*. . . . And with an ex-RAF pilot and a French colonel and an Italian actor-whore. I had been to bed with more women, mostly whores. . . . Things were different because of the war. I was startled to see that saying I was everything (sexually) was the same as saying I was nothing much. A woman came along who was better looking than Frank and more aggressive and more interesting about her aggression, and I did love her, with reservations. She and I had an arrangement that we would not talk about the past or be faithful to one another but we wouldn't be too public about it. She said she was jealous—I mean it was a trait of hers. I had no gift for jealousy, and I never liked talking about someone's life or sexual predilections. Anyway, the young woman, somewhat older than I was, suggested that we get married or her father would separate us.

So we married, and Frank hated her, and, for that matter, he hated me, but we met for a meal from time to time. I did not ask him for aesthetic support or favors, only to show me pictures. And to cut out the romance shit. My first wife and I met a lot of people and had a pretty good time, and some of the people were famous. But I clung to the acquaintance with

Frank—he was like a dance partner who followed your lead, reading your mind (and stealing the scene with his cute sense of what would work in New York in the world of art). He only a few times asked me for something other than romance, and then it was for money, not very much, and not for himself. He did this even in years when I made a tenth of what he did.

What Frank mostly did was to hold in focus the imbecile and avid energies of New York; he invented an idealized version of New York. The longing to find an actual ideal present in life is very strong. Frank had it—how could he not as an ex-Catholic? His exaggerations, his fantasies, his lies, suggested that the nearly ideal existed close by. He usually credited High Art but he saw the ideal in borderline art, and in popular art and its self-promotion. He had no interest in the middlebrow, and he was anti-English, but everyone was in those years.

He was street-smart long before that word was in use. It was said of him that the work he advocated lacked classical restraint and certainly lacked perfection, that it was hard on the viewer or reader, impenetrable, a hoax. Well, it was new. Frank's embrace of the greatness of imperfection was a spiel. But he was right that perfection is never an issue in the best work, that the idea of perfection is in fact insulting to such work. A Pollock painting, one of the drip canvases, doesn't even pose the question. It is an impoverished abundance and it is beyond criticism and propaganda because of the sheer generosity, the size, of the pleasures it offers.

Everybody I knew was always yacking on about *perfection*. Avedon's word in those years was "impeccable." Irene Selznick would say quietly and with finality, "It's beyond criticism. It's *beyond* . . ."

Of course, one problem was that we, the young—I was young for a while—were not part of any single, complete culture and could not find a complete culture anywhere in this country to make art for. Nowadays some people even speak of niche art. When I say Frank invented part of the background, part of the ground of a pure, non-elitist American modernism, I am also saying he thought up revolutionary modes of success for a lot of people. For us. Irene said of Beckett, "Well, he's slow." Avedon and William Maxwell thought Beckett was far-out. Frank's sense of art was to consider it a party here and now. He said, "Beckett is better than Milton Berle." Frank believed that the past deserved to be regarded coldly. The party starts now. With us.

And he believed that American art, despite its efforts to be public or traditional, was neither, that it was more like a struck match, angry at its own inspiration. (Frank was very dogmatic—have I said that?)

The night we all wound up in one bed, Frank and Larry and John began talking about art-for-now. Of course, I don't really remember who said what; I was very drunk. I might have said art-for-now had to do with swiftness and money and the automobile, but I think it was Frank. I think it had been my idea and Frank took it over and made something of it.

Frank was quite intense about automobiles having changed everything in art—he saw history as, first, horses and guys standing there, then horses-and-buggies, then as all of us being overtaken by cars. He said someone ought to write about the effect of cars and trains on Billie Holiday, Jackson Pollock—the rhythms in Holiday like the trembling of a car motor, the element of luminous surprise in Pollock's work as being like the headlights and tree shadows, the tangle of tree branches, the glimpse as a speeding-past in a car turned into a near-stillness of a vibrating glimpse. Or that at least is what I understood.

Maybe I said it. Maybe I'm saying it now. Frank's goadedly festive extremism is part of my sense of the art of that decade. I mean, he was right, which, in the end, in the financial world as in the art world, is how you judge intelligence. When Frank said Pollock was a towering figure, he was right. It took me a while to believe him, and what a shock it was to get it, to see just how towering.

Of course you couldn't *believe* Frank right off the bat. He was imperfect and often wrong. And for another thing, he talked too much. But Frank was someone who generally knew (in a serious sense) what was happening. And he was one of the best intellectual dance partners of all time.

Frank programmatically propagandized with full energy for women painters, a liberal idea then—Joan Mitchell, Grace Hartigan, Elaine de Kooning, Jane Freilicher. Besides Larry and Rothko and Pollock and Kline and Philip Guston, he campaigned for Alex Katz and Milton Avery and Bob Rauschenberg and Jasper Johns. And John Button and—I don't remember. He worked to get attention for a number of poets, including Ashbery: Kenneth Koch and James Schuyler and Bunny Lang. And dancers and dance critics and choreographers. Frank did a spiel about Edward Denby that was pure love—well, it was nasty and bile-splattered, but you know what I mean. And Beckett. Nobody else in Frank's lifetime did this, not with the same method or madness-tinged clout, not with the same breadth. Frank huckstered intellect, instruction and originality and pleasure, vast amusement. And he pointed out that you might make money in the long haul if you listened to him.

No one did this for him. No one propagandized for him. His own poetry was largely ignored. In a sense, he had almost no recompense except the excitement as he went along. His poetry matters now—people read it aloud to one another. (This was one of the measures of good poetry that Pound proposed.) Frank's poems are swiftness itself: their escape from absolute meanings into catch-as-catch-can ones, raunchy and provincial, army-and-cowboy-boot territory, is pretty wonderful.

I did try to get them into The *New Yorker*, but Howard Moss, the poetry editor, was obdurate. He was pissed with a lot of people, Moss was, and with me, too, when I was young, but he became friendlier when I was older. Anyway, Frank arranged his own publicity, his own poetic career. The poems I like best are the ones of surface immediacy, chiefly the *I did this, then I did that* ones. The ones that rely on time and Frank's private sense of fact.

One time, talking in the cafeteria at the Museum of Modern Art, Frank did a riff about colors, à la Rimbaud: "What do you think of orange? Isn't it a swell color?" Then he quoted John: "Ashes said it was about the same as olive green. . . . Larry said orange was hot. . . . I would like orange neon. Underwear is never orange."

He wasn't really talking, he was writing, he was sketching in extinguishable talk what might or might not prove, on paper, to be a stanza or a line that would be inextinguishable, at least for a while, that would outlive us. I accused Frank more than once of not caring enough about his poetry, and he answered, "I am working at immortality. I don't know what *you* are doing."

Nearly everybody interferes with the surface of a painting, as it were, cleaning it, lighting it pretentiously, touching it up, repairing it, brushing against it. Around this time, Clement Greenberg repainted a David Smith sculpture because he didn't like the color Smith had used. What Frank did—he took me to the places where the canvases, the ideas, the idea of painting itself, had not yet been tampered with. It was the same with Balanchine and with Beckett. Frank got me there before the hideous falsifications of media recognition and intellectual essays had set in. The jokes were still pure; the grief more visible; the colors literally glittered with individuality and inventive madness and expressiveness—with power.

O'Hara, in speaking of Willem de Kooning's work and his beauty as a soul and as a metaphysician, talked of the suffocation in Catholicism, the long-term asthma of belief. So Frank was a loon for *freshness*. He yattered about de Kooning and then, hearing himself talk, veered into a riff about the beauty in Arshile Gorky's paintings. Frank was and is a character in much of what I enjoy and in the memory of enjoyment. I mean that the praise he gave canvases and texts, even when he was being a salesman or doing a rehash of some earlier speech of his—it all still seems to me to have been mostly correct. The integrity of the surface holds even if my memory tampers with it.

When I was given the Prix de Rome, in 1959, I got depressed, and I called Frank. We met for lunch at Larré's. I was depressed because the prize marked me as not a leftist and as someone whose work was *sensitive*. I thought that was unfair. My stories were more than that. The prize signaled failure.

Frank said life was shit and, in his generosity, praised the stories, spoke about the honor of even the silliest prizes, and then began to bawl me out for having snubbed him sexually. He mixed this with weaving an entire mythology about my being young and going to Rome and divorcing my first wife, which I hadn't yet done.

A drink or two more and he was calling me a glamorous and lying faggot. He cried out to the young Breton waiter that I wanted to fuck him, Frank, on the table.

At first, I was impressed by the insouciant wretchedness and lunacy, but then I grew bored and returned to my very considerable unhappiness, my suicidal state of unreason. I said to the waiter that Frank was pure merde; Frank said that decent people did not act like me. I began to laugh at him.

Frank launched into invective mixed with praise: ". . . a Jewish genius . . . a suppressed homosexual . . . a spiritual fake . . . a hypocrite . . ."

"Well, I am a Jew," I said, and I muttered something like, "I can't bear your tiresome innocence. . . . You have no sense of the criminal nature of the world."

He said, "You're too logical—you *are* a Jew."

His dejection was much deeper than mine, and mine was bad. I said, "Frank, we're friends. . . ."

He said, "No, we're not—we're lovers. . . ."

It occurred to me years later that he was probably right. He thought I was snobbish toward his version of homosexuality. I was. I *hated* his suicidal onrush. I see the generosity now in his insistence on my role in his life. He was obsessive about being known—recorded and known, portrayed and known. Perhaps Frank saw me as a recording device; I was someone who bore a registry of him.

"If this is the way you are a *lover*, why would I want you near me?" I asked.

"Don't be logical! It's too Jewish to be so logical," he said, half-sneering.

"I irritate people. No one ever worries about *my* being irritated. . . ."

Frank said, "That's not true. That's autobiographical bullshit."

I had forgotten the episode of the night the five of us spent in bed—I hadn't thought of it for years—when one night at dinner in New York, maybe fifteen years ago, Ashbery produced the names and said that in the oversized bed we had all fucked one another, except that I had fucked with Larry and Frank and not with him. I said, "I didn't fuck with anybody that night." John said, "I know what you did." "Well, you're wrong," I said. The exchange went on for quite a few minutes in a kind of hapless fashion, and then John did a kind of melodramatic crumpling, flinging out his arm, and crashing to the floor, and his glasses went flying.

Do sexual histories matter? What I remember of that long-ago evening with the five of us in bed is that we came to a building, and I don't remember where it was. I remember a narrow hallway, one that looked like the tenement hallways in movies. Larry's room (which may have been John's) was pretty big, and yet I remember only one window, and one chair and a couple of mattresses laid on trestles and plywood. On the wall was an unpromising (I thought) painting, very large, a dark green and brown and orange variation on Bonnard. It was less mental or hazy than a Bonnard—not at all a painting of consciousness or of feeling or of unstill light, but really a painting of a painting, a painting about itself. The complicity with such wit and ego was like being in a car with someone who wanted to be a painter. The blurred way objects were represented had more to do with a suggestion of the speed of the glance, of life's hurrying by, than with the complex ways one is conscious of a garden one is familiar with.

Once we were in the room, the intimacy quotient shot way up but nothing intimate was said. I had thought I could manage this but I couldn't—well, hell, think of the complexity of those people. I would manage by detaching myself and thinking it was funny, and by being mannerly.

I think Larry, with Frank's help, was trying to sell a picture to Bradley. I remember Larry saying, "I am broke." No one undressed past their underwear. Cautiously, I took off my shirt but kept my undershirt and my trousers on. Or so I think. I didn't say I didn't want to have sex, but something dumber like, "Leave me out." The lights at some point were turned off. The room was quiet. Then things started to happen in the dark, mostly under the sheet but not to me. I had a pillow over my lap.

In the dark, one had a confused sense of erotic activities but it was more like stagehands shifting furniture on a lightless stage than like reading a dirty book. If I'd had real style and confidence I would have turned on a light. I remember in the dark the squeaking and rustling and the moist sounds of affection that force one to be tactful. Even when I sat up, I couldn't see anything. The gigantic bed was set in a corner, flush with two walls, and I had taken the corner for myself. I didn't have my glasses. They were across the room on a bureau. I was not going to get up and walk across the bed to get my glasses although now I wish I had. Here the paradigm is that no memory is fully translatable into clarity or provable as intelligent fact.

Professional calculation and personal vanity and unhappiness and embarrassment as well as aberrations of memory and wish add up to falsified confession; falsified confession is what fiction and painting are. Sexual reality (or truth) is lost. . . . Most literary reminiscences are wildly dishonest, and no one applies commonsense logic to them. Admired writers in English tend to be presented as sexless or as sexually unhappy, not just T. S. Eliot or the very plain Auden. After all, no one has written about Pound's sexual nature. I have a faint, foolish idea that I might have whisperingly sung, "Anchors aweigh, my boys, anchors aweigh." I am not trying to hide my sexual past. Would the reader like a list of the men I have had? And the women? The parties I attended in the sixties? Would such lists be any use without a description of feelings and actions? The history of the world is in part a history of disbelief in the sexual statements of others.

Did anyone sleep? I did, briefly, incuriously. And I remember waking up and the pessimistic vigor with which we began, one by one, to creep around, gathering our belongings in the early morning. It was a couple of years before it was quite clear to me that no one was really sure what had happened in Larry's room (which may have been John's). Bradley changed his story; he said he had made out with John, and then a year or so later, he said he had made it with Frank. Maybe he made it with both of them. Bradley was very self-assured but had a lousy memory.

So, many years after this, John and I could bicker over who did what, who liked whom. I always thought of John as honest but it is never clear to what degree anyone is honest in a given moment. At any rate, a writer or painter dealing in autobiographical anecdote and in resentment is like a mechanic getting used to oil and rust, to the dirt of the engines he works on. That night was a gnawing festivity, without loneliness or sense. I will never forget it. But I forgot it. Bisexual, omnisexual, we stagger on. (And, anyway, attachment is clearer when you don't love than when you do—when you feel emotion, you are caught up in a punishing blur.) Bradley, dying, said, "Frank never liked me." And, "I never got the money." He never inherited, never had more, he said, than sixty thousand a year. He knew I had never had an income, and he said that at least I couldn't complain about how love had treated me: "You have always been lucky in that field." How would he know that? We weren't close after I began to publish.

Ah well, it is unbearable to know people. It is unbearable to lose them. It is unbearable to go on seeing them. There are other things to worry about besides people: The graveyard sense of the presence of dead artists—not the fear of them, but rather the sense of them as family, and the pressure of not yet having done work you really liked, trademark work, breakthrough work, all of this makes you nutty. Or the thing that Larry did, he kept listening for phrases in other people's talk—that hunt for ideas which is, sometimes, like picking up dead birds or bits of trash, that ragpicking for ideas.

American art for me is hardly separable from the vigor and moods and anger and aggression of Frank and Larry as well as the discretions of Ashbery. Their interest in popular art, the dishonesty in the invention of their personae as artists, the overt or deadpan levels of mockery—Frank was so deadpan that it was a temptation to try to get his face to be active, to break up, to be innocently torn by laughter—were terrific. Their irony comes from a different tradition of revolution, one not known in Europe and one not easily studiable, and from a different sort of society.

Of course, I am prejudiced but all art talk still, forty some years later, seems to me to spring from Frank and John and Larry. Of course, I don't know where their talk sprang from. But the violent processes of undoing—call it deconstruction—was like the stuff in American movies, as in the Marx Brothers, movies that have a New York quality, or like the ruthlessness of real-estate people here in reshaping everything. New York is, in its inextinguishable folly, a kind of poem anyway. It is gratingly dadaesque. One day my second wife, Ellen, shaking a bit, came into my study and said she thought she was having some sort of seizure but she had just had the impression that she had seen King Kong climbing up the side of the Empire State Building. (We can see it from windows in three of the rooms.) I went to look and, of course, it was real; it was a publicity stunt for a remake of *King Kong*. A very large, let's say eight-story-tall, rubber Kong, inflated, was being pulled aloft. Something went wrong and fairly soon the creature deflated, and we saw it flapping in the wind.

Later, running in Central Park, we saw an enormous brown pile of something; it looked like an enormous shit pile. We went to look, and it was the rubber King Kong half-inflated, partly repaired. This was O'Hara territory—*the day King Kong deflated near the top of the Empire State Building.*

The patterns of awareness in New York are all crazed anyway. Larry said at Frank's funeral that everyone close to Frank knew he would be the first one of us to die. The city of art forces on you a tropism toward the greater and lesser suicides of the mind, as when a dreamer wakes up and the world of the dream and its people disappear, and then the real thing, the abrupt end of that other population, the morning is there after the massacre. And you are the king of dreams. Well, the opposite is true as well: the dream beckons, and the massacre may be only of oneself.

Then you have as well the pattern, the violence of will with which we all work. In the last four or five years of his life, before he was run over by a beach taxi on Fire Island, Frank had weird rages and was inconsolable. But why? He was known and felt as a power. He was highly regarded at

MOMA. He had a lover, a dancer, and the paintings he owned had become valuable; he was rich, or nearly rich.

His rages were so dark and anguished, they seemed so clinical and final, and Frank sneered so, that it seemed impossible that he could live. But then rage does appear to be inextricable from ambition. It is the reverse of glamour. It is not a joke, the great clang of pain in New York. It is the sound of brassy people at the party—at all the parties. Literary talk in New York often announced itself as the best talk in America. People said, "Harold, you are hearing the best in America tonight." But it was cutthroat monologues mostly, delivered by the highest-ranking sufferer in the room.

It is not only the human losses. It is the concern for what is in the diaries, for the light one casts or doesn't cast, for the role one is given. But the point is that truth was not the issue, and it almost never is in New York. Frank made a scene once at Ned Rorem's, in front of Aaron Copeland and Virgil Thompson and James Leo Herlihy and Edward Albee and Stella Adler and a great many others. Herlihy was showing me he could swallow fire; he had brought his fire equipment, when Frank arrived and accused me of having an affair with Rorem. But I hadn't had an affair with Rorem; I didn't *like* Rorem. And I was talking to Herlihy. Frank said Rorem had told *everyone* that he—Rorem—and I were lovers. Frank said the party was to announce our engagement, Ned's and mine—then Frank went on in front of Rorem to invent an erotic history for him and me, in front of Rorem and that audience. He wasn't placated by anything I said or frightened. No one quite believed him or disbelieved. Frank, I suppose, liked it—it was part of what he did. This creation of tissues and veils.

To speak with an old man's rage for a moment: at the Central Park Zoo— I used to go there a lot, and Frank would meet me there occasionally— Frank would say that the hippos were farting in dirty water like the rest of us. Renata Adler said that you could get anyone to be disliked in New York merely by praising that person to someone nervous and competitive. You could assassinate by means of sharp praise. (Everyone is jealous.) Diana Trilling said of someone, "She was such a good friend that I could tell her my good news." The beasts of influence and power farting in dirty water, the crocodiles waiting in the water hole: literary social life in New York—madmen and madwomen at parties pimping and lying and doing favors, making gassy public statements and being modest, blackmailing and threatening, giving blurbs, having dinner and going on later. Expert and important and *meaningful* name-dropping—we lived among name-dropping as if in a fusillade of pigeon shit. I have done it in this piece.

In this madness, it takes a special ability to get work done, to be generous . . . I don't know. Frank's importance wasn't only that he was mostly right about work and people's talent. He wasn't entirely honest—I would never say that of anyone. But he had the audacity to accept the voltage of the supreme work of the moment. It choked him and scarred him and made him difficult and unsociable as he aged. His work was fine, but it wasn't enough. It wasn't Pollock or Gorky, but their work hadn't been enough for them, either.

Gorky was overtly a suicide, and Pollock was close. But I guess what I mean is that Frank did the work, he helped establish New York and the definition of American art; he admired the work. And that is what matters. This city, culturally, was (and is) an Oedipal dream for men and women—fame without fathers and at your own will if you can organize the beasties around you.

It is more fun to cheat than to attempt the real thing. But I think the truth is that excellence in work remains a hard fact. There the lying stops. The biographies written about Frank so far offer varied theories for his rages. But possibly his moods at the end had to do with all the echoes, mistaken versions, of himself that were returned to him and some sense of work not done, of life unlived. I think he was disturbed by the unrewarding echo of his own voice in others; it was as if he had been wrapped in paper and could not stop being a *present* offered to artists and voyeurs. You can choke on your own agilities if they are public agilities. To be stuck in the terms of earlier success can be hell as you age. The pleasures of talk were lost to him. He did not know which of his poems were good and which were less than OK. Everything he did was semiofficial: he would say, *I am Frank O'Hara and I say it is so* or *not so*. I suppose that in the middle of his life, which turned out to be the end, his drunkenness and accusations were pursuits of the ordinary, were perhaps recurrent wishes to be hurt by it as in being pinched to see if he was awake or dreaming a grotty and wonderful and semi-awful dream. His cruising, his *Bovarysme*, had a terrifying Everyone Will Die quality, was a Catholic sense of apocalypse. He was apparently in search of men and boys whose names had no neon aspect. It was an anguished, American desire to be in the world merely as another person, to hear voices other than his own, to be fed and refreshed by the existence of people not like him and who did not require anything of him. Perhaps he wanted to start over. The question of awareness becomes quite terrifying when you have a *famous awareness*.

I was crazy about New York, dependent on it, and scared of it—well it is dangerous as hell. I have always been cowardly. Frank was an Irish lion and snake, braver than Galahad. He could be dull. Frank was promiscuous toward places—as if in failed self-protection. He loved the Hamptons, and Maine, and Paris. He kind of made Grand Progresses. (Bradley and John both lived in Paris for years, which made me envious.) Me, my literary reputation is mostly abroad, but I am *anchored* here.

Anyway, my sense of the beauty and importance and usefulness (to the mind) of this city is inextricably entwined with Frank's poems—let's call them Frank's paintings.

One time, he said how he wanted to die: if he couldn't die in Cézanne's arms, he wanted to fall off a girder a mile high with the prick of a steel-walker in his mouth. He wanted to look at New York as he fell. . . . He wanted to come and go in the same instant.

I can't think of any other place I'd rather die than here, but I would like to do it in bed, looking out my window. I would prefer not to have the falling sensation that Frank thought would be *great*.

One time, I took Frank to see *The Polish Rider*, the nowadays disputed Rembrandt, at the Frick. It was so long ago, it wasn't even a famous picture then.

The rider is a young man with a Slavic face, mounted on a very, very large, gray warhorse. One of his elbows is cocked toward the viewer and his hand, a fist, is on his waist. The picture has been cleaned and now the fist sort of floats. He is clearly on a quest, but not a mythological one. He is looking for a job out in the life-and-death world. He is young and utterly defiant. His face is dumber now, since the painting has been restored, but then he was clearly not a fool. Not entirely.

Frank said—without any archness—"That's me, that's a picture of me."

I said, "He looks more like me—you don't have a face like a Slavic pie plate."

But he did. Frank did—a tight-skinned Irish version of it.

The figure in the painting, Frank pointed out with malicious seriousness, was *jaunty* and *dapper* . . . was *cruising us. Summoning our souls.* The picture really does look like Frank. "He wants me to admire him, and I *do*. . . . You're not like that. . . ." Not evangelical he meant. Not a mad leader.

I never showed the painting to anyone—including women—who did not feel it was them, the young off to serve in the wars of the mind, the heart, the eye in their time.

1995

FICTION IS FICTIONAL

A story in a magazine or a book, a fiction, a lie, a fantasy is an odd thing, not quite part of the world, but it doesn't seem to exist only in one's head. It is an odd thing that seems to exist in reality only trickily. Nabokov (and a great many others, including Poe) said a story was a riddle and a collection of riddles—the story itself and its suspense element—in the characters and their qualities of virtue and in their destinies or in what they might or might not do. But part of the riddling is always about what is real, what is true, and what is silly and just a game and does not matter.

It is not rare to tell a *story*: Children do it early often as an invocation of reality, sometimes as reporting, as describing reality. One of my earliest memories is seeing on the faces of my parents that I had failed to tell what happened. I wasn't making sense. Telling the story again, perhaps improving it, but telling it to children or to a teacher—and they might have been lying politely—the account seemed coherent. And comprehensible.

When I tried again with my parents to relate the same event, the earlier thing happened: I failed with them. Certainly we fought, in various ways, my parents and I, other children and I, over what happened in games, or what happened in an argument or fight, or about promises kept and unkept. Some children go the way of law. Others are more like detectives and become hooked on the nature of truth and the possibility of being clear some day, of telling the definitive version of what happened—of winning out in that fashion. Others go to lies, charm, gestures, and art.

It is less odd to watch a story being enacted than to hear one extemporized, and to hear one is less odd than to read one, although we may prefer to read in order to escape the presence of other people. Among people, we live among actual stories. We do that diagnostically; we watch each other, watch things happen, nosily or out of caution or in sympathy or by necessity in real life. We have to figure them out, have to make stories of events. It is a privilege to ignore people and events—if you're not punished for it.

Culture, including religion, helps you determine what is and is not a satisfactory story. *An eagle bit me.* Or *dropped a snake.* Or *stole a neighbor's kid and took him to heaven.* Or *is a rare sight around here but is breeding again.* Culture, the ways we have been educated, and individual taste help us decide what is *worth* knowing in stories—this is where form gets mixed with content. Our culture—the modern, technological, media-centered one—tries for a retelling that covers everything really, but we have no time for that, for everything. So stories, even in movies, deal in representative moments. Those moments represent everything the way Congress is supposed to represent all of us (ha-ha).

This brings us crudely to the issue of idealism versus realism. The mind snips off trailing ends and rounds off numbers and generally simplifies. Simplifying something and getting the point are the same thing. The simpler thing should have overtones of complication. But put that aside. The simple thing is the ideal thing. The more ideal—or the more simple—the more melodrama is required in a story. The mind has no persistent common sense (except in some people who shouldn't be writers except of comedy). Simplification, getting the point, the ideal thing, and winning the argument—having the last word—are roughly related. The mind can extend anything to an idea of absolute, final, unchanging perfection or to conclusion, can do this as physical description or in relation to action or in regard to ideas or conditions such as peace or love or war.

Fiction, modern fiction, is a form of story in which the mind is prevented from moving toward a hazy total: perfect peace, perfect love, perfect happiness, perfect or ultimate argument. But, of course, the mind can play around. This perfection thing is said by some philosophers to define us as human. It's like a pull of gravity for the will. Willfully we gravitate toward a really happy, absolutely terrific ending, or toward total suspense, a totality of horror—but that doesn't really work in prose fiction. The characters must have flaws; the events must have some limits, or the piece, the story, is not fiction but theology. Or hogwash. But they don't have to have a lot of flaws. Old, pagan stories are more boastful even than modern trash, but they put failed perfection right up there at the center. It is weird, failed perfection as the human thing, rather than a mess and an attempt to do better.

A Christian story has an attempt to do better with a lot of suffering in it and with transformation or reversal: the truth is not what it seems, the real heir is so-and-so, not such-and-such, that kind of thing. And it has a lot of scraping along in horror—the worst conceivable is where the hero winds up; this is like the earliest novels in ancient times, Hellenistic tales. The worst conceivable has to involve common humanity, prisoners and mad pedants and murderers and the falsely accused and innocent thieves. In medieval tales and in the allegories and writings just before modern prose fiction came into existence, you descended and then you rose. The chief characters did, and you went along with them. The Christian reversal of the ancient definition of heroes (and of perfection) and the Christian takeover of timelessness and eternity particularly did away with the old ideas of *Fate*.

You get the real world as realer than before, but you get a lot of the ideal as well, knights and pilgrims and visions and kings' daughters. Part of the Jewish inheritance of Christianity consists of elements of Jewish story, the Bible story, with its mixture of history and legend and its very queer, very potent realisms of characterization and voice but with the admixture of God and angels in direct touch—perfection, transcendence for the reluctant or bald or stammering prophet or the murderous old father. There is also the Talmudic story; it is usually without individual characterization and is parable or allegory. It is rather like Byzantine art. It represents a social or cultural level of religious government.

Years ago, millennia ago, daily life, the real world, the real, was called secular or sublunar and was said, disapprovingly, to be in *flux* and to be, therefore, inferior because nothing lasted, and that seemed wrong and disappointing. In practice, nearly everything (including stories) had a snobbish or upside having to do with being long-lasting, eternal, whatever. In practice, military reports, political oratory, legal argument, served as precedent or as model and, naturally, in stories, took on the cast of immortality.

News and anecdote and religious knowledge relied on narrative, and no matter how fanciful those narratives were, they were actually intended as reports. Or swindles. What a photograph of a riot does—indicates that a riot happened—is pretty much what so-called factual reports did. Something was there and left visible, describable traces.

The old two-tiered sense of meaning, time ridden and plot-and-story-filled, and then the significance or point, with the significance guarded by a churchly setup (or a rabbinical one) gave way to modern capitalism and its more or less orderly information. But really more like Prometheus stealing fire from the gods or like Caesar doing his *Veni, vidi, vinci* number, it was a takeover, a theft, a rivalry, a conquest. The churchly role as guardian and mediator was largely done away with.

The change that capitalism brought was very boastful. That-which-is-timeless and beyond reach was now considered graspable by one's will and was held to be present in all objects at all times. Ruskin, who complained about the changeover from the Gothic to the neoclassical, was complaining about this.

With capitalism, the middle class seizes transcendence and makes it daily and accessible to everyone without one's having to depend on a priest or minister or rabbi. That is, capitalism presents a one-tier, pretty-much-omnipotence-and-omniscience-ruled world with the claim that people, women and men, share in that omnipotence-and-omniscience. This is when modern prose fiction originated.

A version of that is the feeling (or argument) that we were transcendent or in touch with transcendance and were omnipotent and omniscient in that fashion when we were young. Modern disappointment and despair—drug taking, alcoholism, modern art—and modern politics display this democratically immodest grief or sense of a problem.

Prose fiction in its modern form is inordinately ideal (sometimes as blasphemy) or, let's say, papal or rabbinical. Art and rebellion—against the past, against the old-fashioned sense of the difficulties of transcendence—art as rebellion offers omniscience and omnipotence and control, a realer timelessness. And it does this with things unseen—a kind of pragmatic transcendence. I know it sounds tendentious but you can't ever turn a piece of fiction into a movie, just as you can't photograph it. As was said at the beginning, a story exists in words and in someone's head but not in the outwardly visible world. The visible world doesn't have the same connections between cause and effect or the same degree of focus. And the initial lie, the made-up names and made-up people, can't be translated into anything merely physical such as an actor's claiming to be Huckleberry Finn.

They are different kinds of study of power, of winning the argument, and each claims to be final. It's possible that a new visual cinematic-television form will evolve that actually peers into a story or a novel rather than claiming it or retelling it.

The unreality of prose fiction, the lie, means it cannot be photographed or filmed, although ideas for visible stories can be drawn from it. And at the same time, no evidence from the past can prove or disprove the story, the fiction, or add to it factually: the damn thing was never true in that sense. It was, or is, true (or not) in another sense, but this other sense is grander and has to do with final meaning, laws of behavior and theories about them worked out as destiny in the story, moral or amoral principles both personal and of the universe.

Of course, aesthetic strategies, supposedly immortal patterns and rhythms, enter in, and these are always conceited even when in a kind of reversal—nationalistic or ethnic or by social class or by sexual practice—the fiction claims to be literature—not *literature*. This stuff has to do with style and social usefulness and does not always fall into disuse but lives on, a sort of interim Bible, history *and* fiction for a newly enfranchised group, since a newly enfranchised group needs the lie, the boastfulness, the perhaps indirect truth, the maybe forced and vaunting truth.

The changeover two centuries or so back to modern prose fiction occurs in poetry as well: the notion of story, of fiction, changes as well in long narrative poems, and the notion of the short poem with or without story changes. And "modern" opera comes into existence at the same time. Opera stories and fictions are the predecessors of those in movies and on television (and in some books).

It's easy enough to see that in this country what are called fiction stories (to use a vulgarism from the 1920s and 1930s in suburban America) were, in a sense, anti-English and democratic. The short-story form wasn't considered big-time, and so we specialized in it. Our stories were modest in certain ways, but that very modesty was extremely self-important; it was a special modesty, a trick modesty, the best modesty, a final modesty; and it offered a counter-transcendence, a correction, a final rightness.

But what is this final rightness or winning-the-argument? What is the A.Q., the quotient of art, in fiction? Remember, the story cannot exist or have existed. It is not a documentary or an historical fact except as a fiction. There is no reality that can be studied or dug up or dug out to add to what is said in the story—you can only get stuff about the writer or about the success or failure of the fiction in its own time. A *fiction story* has no physical counterpart: if you could reproduce the Battle of Borodino and study it, you would not find Prince André or Pierre there or Tolstoy's Napoleon. Visual representations (which can only illustrate the story, which then must be familiar in advance) can form pictures in the mind of considerable power—perhaps these are lies or sales talk, but they form a context for the mind. They are double photographs in a ghostly sense, involving the past, but actually attempting to picture the future, actions in the future, and the way the mind sees things in the future. A photograph or a movie or a series of drawings is *real* in a way that is historical and actual and continues physically as a piece of prose fiction does not.

The point here perhaps is that many aspects of our species are invisible in the way a prose fiction is—thought, dream, memory, feelings, acts of thought, a dream episode, acts of memory. The portrayal of things unseen (and unseeable) is sort of the heart of the whole project. Invisible activities of the mind seem to be the models for fictions or, if you like, unphysical, unbodied tales. A tentative conclusion would be that only a mind cut off from the world and escaped from doctrine (a discipline for the mind) and rebellious toward it can make fiction, can narrate a prose fiction. Thought, dream, and memory become experientially available (to study, to look at, to draw on) only in states and fairly long-term situations of mental freedom. In unfree situations, those acts of consciousness as models are constrained by revelation, by decree.

The way the mind makes stories for itself is very odd—look at actual memories or dreams or thoughts. They flit, they juxtapose, they get names wrong; they are peculiar. The mind is very peculiar. The bloody fucker doesn't have an outward animal shape or the limits of an animal anatomy. It moves faster, goes further. It doesn't have to obey the sequences of actual time. It can leap around, leap ahead, leap sideways in chronology, as clocks cannot. In the middle of so much strangeness, the mind might prefer ritualized narration and often does. Besides, the reality of inward words, words and images inside your head, is peculiar to each person's uses and associations as well as education. We learn to *read* stories, and sometimes that requires quite a broad education. We might prefer stories that are close to what we had learned before we were educated culturally, so to speak. We might prefer fictions of socially pleasant behavior. Or despise them.

But prose fictions, fiction stories, are mental flags for real or imaginary social groups, or movements: invisible nations of certain casts of mind. Most churches and some philosophies, and closely bound groups in general, tightly control or forbid fiction stories. A special and privileged group—not exactly deracinated but enlightened and complicatedly open—is drawn by fiction as education; as travel; as extension of the self, of one's own memories and thoughts. By the novelty quotient, the newness. This tends to have a revolutionary aspect, a quality of overturning what is out there, and moving toward utopia—and superiority.

Some prose fictions play on this and have an encoded quality and suggest they are for initiates. Some fictions rely on uncertainty, mystery—having been trained by dreams and memories and thoughts or having been irritated by false clarities or simply by finding that to be a more realistic way to portray events and characters and to present meanings.

But fiction stories offer a conscious control of mystery even when they are very dark and obscure. A mind, a consciousness, is a fretfully crippled force-field of a thing: it is a monster-thing. As long as it remains inward, it cannot be argued with. It is all thoughtlight and assertion, a great drifting of ambition often without logic, an eerie king or an equivalent, a royal mad *thing*, maybe a prophet, maybe a demon, maybe doomed.

The mind can accept almost any image of people or gods or ships or animals or monsters—things in dreams and mishearing one another train us. In life itself shadows cast by real light or by artificial light suggest shapes. Ideas and notions have a strange parentage. Mindlight, thoughtlight, the filtered light of other minds, then filtered into ours through stories, through prose fictions—in the light of what is seen by the mind, a story, a lie, a prose fiction is uncaptured by the need to be a factual report, and it is true, let us say, more in the light of consciousness, more in regard to consciousness, than in the light of navigation or an actual day.

Consciousness is not a particularly big deal. Some people keep theirs very narrow. Often it is unbearable inside dreams, inside one's sleep. In fiction as in dreams it is a quality of conspiracy and of conspiracy denied in aery credibility. The sexual illusion and the pleasures of illogic form a world the attention rests in and believes to be real. A piece of fiction cannot be all imaginary—a rock must have some resemblance to rocks one has seen (or has seen pictured). And this is not a matter of philosophical essences but of whole objects, including their appearance. But fiction can jumble and combine and steal from other fictions. A mind has no conceivable nakedness of the sort a body does except in terms of will—this is why scholars fall back on biography and a study of writers' lives.

When you are reading a prose fiction, emotion and response are distorted by the mind's more or less conscious interference. In life, many writers have fictional qualities—it is a convention, a form of dress and speech. Biography undoes that disguise. But since a mind is clothed in a life, in someone's life, you could learn more by studying the lies in life—the made-up, the element of makeup.

Anyway, a mind (or consciousness) is by its nature and purposes Promethean, rebellious, Luciferian—what else can it be? It is an independent bustle inside the skull disciplined only by its failures to be superhuman outwardly, unless it ignores its failures and goes sort of mad or really mad. Where failure lessens, the hues of brisk manias arise, as in dreams. Prose fiction is a mania, of theory and explanation, and of the exercise of intellectual will. Some writers feel that editors consequently hate fiction. They alter that will and impose another.

An individual story is a memory waiting to exist, like a child hiding before springing out at you. It affects the conscious or mindful sense of reality. Perhaps what seems virtuous here is the degree of coherence. When we read fiction, we are in a theater of story, among attributes of reality that are really the aroused and re-aroused and surprised qualities of mind, and that can be scattered by a loud noise. Sensible people often dislike this, but a kind of civilized, perhaps electrical touch occurs, so proper that it is hard for others not to love the experience. No matter how close to journalism (and the journalistic) the fiction story is, it is subject to will and exaggeration, to repicturing.

The writer's command is fictional, is the chief part of the lie. The mind is inevitably a story. The infant's initial story might go, *I was hungry and hurt and I was fed and that was good and now I am hungry and I hurt but I will be fed.* If you have a sense of revelation, that is final, and you don't like any more stories.

The complication here is that originality and ritual are two very divergent goods. The moral dimension of fiction is sometimes its modesty, sometimes its being revolutionary. This has been taken over by magazine news stories, which use photographs and verifiable facts. All stories hurt in their self-concern. The pain of suspense is rarely obeyed by readers—

what other pattern does pain have? The structure of suspense is that the fictional reality (like life) is actually open-ended. The fiction story dives into black unknowability. Or it cheats and generates the suspense of a very minor act, a nickel tossed into the air between a door and a sidewalk, say, an act in which the universe, or the social universe, is reflected. You never know if you will survive a piece of fiction. Fiction is dangerous.

Poets can speak of eyes, eyelids, and the day, Eden and being alive and the absent Adam and the trees decked out in flowers. But prose fictions are not often allowed to be interesting in that way, since they have to deal with the dances of ideas and feelings and sensations and with actions: prose fictions are really theories of behavior, are news stories or feature pieces complicated by the will of the writer. You read and have to answer the phone, perhaps, and you wince and feel yourself a stillness, like that of a child or a tree, but interrupted. People are desperately sane—a social matter. Nowadays we reinvent sanity each year. There are trends in sanity, in the pale ceremonies of sanity.

The elements of storytelling limit the sense of nuttiness. Reading a *piece of fiction* is marred by suspiciousness, by holding back, by a kind of peering ahead to see what happens so that you aren't too susceptible to the intimate wrenching and unlatching of nerves and then the incredible spread and variety of lateral distances into the details of feeling and of rivalry with the characters and into curiosity. Such a response is inherently private, which is to say domestic, but the story itself, the prose fiction, may have a public quality.

Maybe the soul is humble, but the world is not. The world is a hellish peacock festivity (with a good deal of sweetness thrown in), and the world tends to celebrate certainties, pieties, new ones. In a story, fish, air, cries, waves, fires, ideas, affections, and actions are quite certain and are shown with style.

How has this happened, this kingdom of unactual sights and feelings? The fiction-moment represents the mind's calibrated thuggishness of self-assertion, an unreal degree of knowledge, and an astounding escape from argument. The calculating, frail dandelion-gone-to-seed head, and half thoughts deny this when they read most fiction and see reality or see an argument and what-is-real. The skull and the young weight of hair are thrilled to be in agreement with the story. The speed of the transfer of attention as one reads suggests one's power, not one's terror. And this soothes the sore, quick mind and its ghosts and hallucinations, which hang around its windless, inner moments.

A life's moment, everything mad with significance as in poetry and dreams and music, usually, though, a bleak significance, fills a story that seems to be about the reader and her or his will to some degree. It is as if the reader writes the story—or his or her misapprehension of the story. How delicious.

1994

THE ROAR
OF THE CANON

Considering the noise that writers make about it in this world, it would seem that, after movie stardom and the presidency, immortality through writing a book is the most widely desired American destiny. But literary immortality is a curious notion. Some pieces of writing are good that are not lastingly good or enduringly wonderful, and it is not always clear that disposable work is not preferable to work that tiresomely and toweringly imposes itself on us. Some books of merit—*Ulysses*, for one—are actively hated: "So great I want to throw up," I have heard a critic remark of that book.

Nor are the immortals endlessly praised. Dickens and Jane Austen are frequently condescended to, as is Whitman. Novels and short stories are, as established genres, not even three hundred years old—a long time, but a bit short of immortality. Then, you have cultural accident, wars, and famine. That Palestrina and the poet of the Lusiads are less popular with us than Mozart and Hemingway is not a matter of intrinsic or overall merit, or even a matter of what we think we like. We are not given a wide range of choices, and cultural and social accident determines much of what we get to choose.

The best stuff, if it could be defined simply, would probably be said to be the writing that has the strongest force as good advice—on how to live, on what to do about your feelings, on what to value. In a sense, immortality is the odd if explicable reward for good advice and good information presented in some amusing form and combined with a whisper of beatitude. But the people who give this advice, these paramount instructors, are usually not especially homey or comfortable figures, or even decent exemplars of their own counsel. In some cases, they boast about their work and despise it while despising a good many other things and living miserably.

We have fewer "immortals" than Europe does. Such European writers as Chekhov, Tolstoy, and Goethe seem, at the end of their lives, not to have cared about their own assured possession of the interest of future readers, their imminent death and their own works having educated them, and their intelligence having allowed them to predict the inevitable thrust of the talented and the untalented young to overturn all literary reputations. Proust seems to have cared more about it; in his marvelous book he boasts of having given literary immortality to some of the people whom he modeled his characters on and who were, in the march of generations, already forgotten. So there is the pleasure of having the last word about the people one knows. It's possible that Proust warmed himself from time to time in the last two years of his life with the thought that the unhappy writers around him who had considered him a fool were now consigned to oblivion and despair, while he was not. He triumphed over unpleasant neighbors, disloyal servants, and unfaithful lovers as well. It's possible that the glory waiting for him after death appealed to him because he believed in the Catholic heaven. But dying—to put it impolitely, he choked to death on asthma and literary strain—he seems to have been in a different mood.

The great literary voices of America, hoarse with the resonance of their likely literary immortality, upon getting a foretaste of what it actually means, were not, apparently, greatly thrilled or consoled. James and Hemingway and Eliot—expatriates all—seem at the end of their lives to have been unhappy with their fates and disgusted by the unteachable world and concerned mostly with death, with a sense of their own failure, with a sense of their own approaching release from indignity, rather than with a sense of their own glory.

John O'Hara did not in his lifetime enjoy the accolade of high-level critical interest or of extensive classroom attention, but he seems to have felt literary immortality to be the only thing that mattered. He was known in his lifetime for his sensitivity to slights, his drinking, his intemperate rages, and his prolific output. He published 402 stores and 14 novels, produced dialogue for an unknown number of screenplays, wrote at least 5 plays, turned out a weekly column for *Newsweek* for a while, and supplied the book of a successful Broadway musical, *Pal Joey*.

Now a slight but discernible movement to reexamine John O'Hara's claims has emerged, in the form of *Gibbsville, PA*, a collection of fifty-three of O'Hara's stories, chosen by Matthew J. Bruccoli, of the University of South Carolina. Bruccoli has done a biography of O'Hara and a bibliography of his work, and wrote the entry for O'Hara in the *Dictionary of American Biography*. Bruccoli and George V. Higgins, of Boston University, have supplied (respectively) an introduction and a preface, both calling for immortality for the work and, of course, for the man.

The candidate was born in 1905, in Pottsville, Pennsylvania, a part of the world then given over to coal mines, small manufacturing of various kinds, and the harvesting of chestnuts used in turkey stuffing, candy, and horse mash. Irish Catholics had not yet been absorbed or assimilated into that culture; many people considered them less assimilable than African-Americans. The Irish had, in effect, their own religion—a form of Catholicism not widely admired, or even accepted, by sophisticated non-Irish Catholics—and their own criminal organizations, like the Molly Maguires, a secret society that killed and terrorized, and defended its own. Mineowners and mine supervisors—Welsh Methodist, in O'Hara's stories—lived in fear. Shebeens, protection money, and the like were part of gossip and local folklore about the Irish as late as the 1930s, when I was growing up at the edge of the coal-mining country in Illinois. Stories were common about the supposedly unredeemable peasant nature of Irish Catholics, about their ineducability and inferiority. They had emigrated from an oppressed society, the oppressors being the Anglo-Irish ascendancy in Ireland; and the Irish relation to America's populist capitalism and its Protestant ascendancy was antagonistic.

O'Hara's father, an able doctor, reasonably prosperous, is pictured in bits and pieces, in stories like "The Doctor's Son," as a brainy John Wayne: two-fisted; smart; incorruptible; with worldly, cynical judgment, and a mastery of unsentimental kindness. In short, ideal and dominant in the world, a man of local power and of sterling personal effect—an Irish ideal, a local great man who was never humiliated.

In stories and interviews O'Hara has led us to believe that his father was well able to handle the loose tongues and slurs of the small-town

Protestant gentry around him. O'Hara himself, a strong, handsome kid in his stories, was, in life, difficult (half a throwback to tougher, earthier ancestors) and oversensitive and talented (half a throw forward into another generation and another predicament). He seems to have been vulnerable to and seduced and goaded by upper-class WASP pretensions. He began to drink too much early in adolescence. Drinking to a savage extent was something the Irish were widely accused of—although how they could have drunk more than the local WASPs is unclear. Their *style* of drinking was different, though. O'Hara was quarrelsome and undisciplinable, and he was expelled from three prep schools.

While he was trying to rescue his chances to go to college—to Yale (his desire)—his father died. The doctor did not leave much in the way of an estate. O'Hara had been working as a journeyman reporter, and he soon moved to New York, where he worked for the *Herald Tribune*. He was fired for his drinking, as he was fired from most of the jobs he held; he was a falling-down, no-holds-barred, contentious drunk. He wrote stories on the side, and he was first published in this magazine in 1928, when he was twenty-three years old. (John Cheever, who also had problems with alcohol, who did not go to college, and whose family also had come down in the world, was first published in this magazine when he was twenty-two. John Updike, who, like O'Hara, comes from a small town in Pennsylvania, and whose father was a schoolteacher, did go to college—to Harvard—and was first published here when he was twenty-two. Success as a writer often seems to rectify an anomaly in social class. Or the reverse: an anomaly in social class often leads to the concentrated effort that brings early success as a writer.)

In 1934, O'Hara gained literary celebrity with his first novel, *Appointment in Samarra,* and quit being a reporter, and to the end of his life, through three marriages and no famous love affairs, he seems chiefly to have written. In 1953, after a hemorrhage, according to Bruccoli, he stopped drinking. (Bruccoli uses the word "permanently.") In the seventeen years from then to his death, he made a direct, self-conscious, and focused attempt to be an important literary presence. He did this largely by writing stories of almost Chekhovian emotional pretension, and by issuing collections of such stories, and by angrily claiming his due in letters and interviews. And by writing two very long novels—*From the Terrace* and *Ten North Frederick*.

His novels tended to be commercially successful. He worked within contemporary notions of the well-crafted novel, in the prize-winning mode of the generation of English novelists before him: Huxley, Galsworthy, Arnold Bennett. He did not work in the form in the ways that Fitzgerald and Hemingway did. He did not pursue any would-be essential social truth or analysis of community in his novels, as Dreiser and Faulkner did in theirs. Perhaps O'Hara knew his own fragility: Hemingway ended a suicide, after all. Perhaps O'Hara gambled ineptly but not suicidally: he stayed in the popular-serious mainstream.

Appointment in Samarra is an exception among his novels. It is written in the Ivy League literary manner of the time—the manner of, say, Thornton Wilder. It is akin to *The Sun Also Rises*, too, but not in technique, merely in feeling: the doomed or ruined man, the hero no longer heroic, a figure of the Lost Generation. O'Hara hadn't served in the First World War, and his lost hero is an alcoholic WASP Cadillac dealer in Pennsylvania, a man named Julian English, whose bitter fate is to be crushed not by the evils and horrors of battle but by the terrestrial crap of Pennsylvania. He commits suicide. The book is short, strong-fibered, with short chapters. It is a bit sentimental about doom, and very knowing. It is more male than Wilder's *The Bridge of San Luis Rey* and rougher in asserting itself; and it is less shapely and much sourer than *The Great Gatsby*. But it has a restraint, a nervous elegance that O'Hara never attempted again, perhaps because literary taste changed so greatly in the 1930s, becoming steadily more centered on social questions and discarding most of the terms and forms of artistry developed in the 1920s.

In *Butterfield 8*, O'Hara's second novel, he attempts the new tone of social realism in relation to a stylish woman: life is hell, everything is going down the tubes. He is dealing with high life in New York, sort of, and the woman, later portrayed by Elizabeth Taylor, is sensitive and feisty. *Butterfield 8* is pre–*Bonfire of the Vanities*, an odd mixture of a socially upgraded proletarian novel (almost but not quite a cautionary tale) and a society novel, a novel of local manner. Not, though, a novel of manners— rather, one of attitudes, of carrying things off, of getting away with things or not. The book's ambition as Balzacian social portraiture of rough, corrupt life in a big city didn't arouse highbrow enthusiasm. The book is more dilute and less impressive than *Appointment in Samarra*, more in the grip of what used to be called "magazine fiction." After *Butterfield 8*, O'Hara was increasingly and with more and more finality relegated to the second rank.

O'Hara wrote steadily, nearly always with some commercial and middle-level critical success. Of the two long novels he turned out in his sober period, *From the Terrace* aroused more interest in its own time. It appeared in 1958 and had two printings in hardcover and thirteen printings in paperback. The cover of the paperback says, "John O'Hara's MASTERPIECE!" (*Chicago Sun-Times.*) Inside, in the opening pages, are these quotes: "More than any other American novelist O'Hara has both reflected his times and captured the unique individual for generations to come. . . . Magnificent . . . Deserves the Nobel Prize!" (*Los Angeles Times.*) "John O'Hara's greatest novel . . ." (*Berkeley Gazette.*) The last pages list other writers the paperback house prints whose work readers might enjoy: Leon Uris, Taylor Caldwell, Roger Vailland, Dale Van Every, Graham Greene, Harold Livingston, Hollis Alpert, Amanda Vail. This list is, for us, a comment on newspaper fame and middle-level status: these writers are no longer famous, except for Greene and Uris, and in England Greene is considered a not too serious popular entertainer. *From the Terrace* was made into a movie, with Paul Newman and Joanne Woodward. Fame has a number of aspects, and it doesn't do to complain if one kind doesn't translate into every kind. Literary status is a relative matter. Fame of a more direct journalistic sort is often a substitute for it, but such fame does seem irritating at times to those who are accorded it.

Cold sober, O'Hara was too cold to be stirred by any actuality. He day-dreamed of epics, but the last novels have an extremely limited emotional range. His dialogue habitually ends with a dying fall, partly as a matter of taste—to avoid the baroque—and partly so that he can write flatly and refuse the discipline of treating the events he is narrating as genuinely influencing the characters and the story. The flat style is reasonably skilled, but it is loose and wandering and is not closely tied to narrative purpose. It is profoundly expository. The toughness and naive narrative egoism of his storytelling in his more trenchant work are gone, and they have not been succeeded by anything large or "deep"—or despairing. The books are very long tics of professionalism. (They do arouse a reader's interest in O'Hara's sexual knowledgeability, and his knowledgeability about social details, and his scabrously scandalous anecdotes—about a sophisticated woman's reaction to a particular man's genital, for instance. This was in *A Rage to Live*.) The last novels did not help his literary reputation in his lifetime and have aroused no enthusiasm since. He died in 1970, a famous writer but not a seriously admired one.

.   .   .

Bruccoli writes, "John O'Hara is a leading contender for the title as Best American Short Story Writer. This truth has few adherents." There are reasons for that. First, American short-story writers are almost never seen as being in contention. The title of Best American Short Story Writer doesn't exist among critics or in legend. The American short story is not a boastful form. Who cares whether Thurber or O. Henry is better? And, second, in any case the proposed rank is obviously not possible for O'Hara. O'Hara has never been and cannot be in contention with Hemingway, James, Sherwood Anderson, Poe, O. Henry, Twain, Salinger, or Nabokov in the story form.

O'Hara still holds the record for the most short stories published in this magazine, his nearest competitor being John Updike. He was its most famous social commentator until Cheever, in his married, more prosperous incarnation, became the laureate of the suburbs, of his own corner of WASPdom. Nabokov and Updike and William Maxwell, differently from one another and differently from O'Hara, covered some of the lower, more melodramatic terrain that O'Hara dealt with in some of his stories: small American towns and interlopers and soulful or future exiles, below the country-club level.

At the stage in O'Hara's life when another generation of writers was taking over his territory, he wrote "Mrs. Allanson." The story is from 1964. More direct than his earlier stories, it hints at wisdom, and is in many ways admirable. It did not appear in the *New Yorker* and seems largely unedited. O'Hara's faults of diction and the flatness of his style— his technical inadequacies—are raw:

> The simple facts of the problem were that Marjorie had practically overnight developed a figure that was voluptuous enough to compensate for the beauty that Nature had withheld from her face, and that boys were hanging around the Allanson house.

The stylistic fault has to do with time: the three elements—the new figure, the plain face, the boys—are not set clearly in sequence. O'Hara works with what in manufacturing would be called loose tolerances: the parts don't fit closely or relate carefully. So he doesn't define Marjorie with any clarity. For what he is going to tell, he needs Marjorie to be two girls:

one is a mess, and one is charming, a *jolie laide* unappreciated in the town or by her mother, which is to say a girl and woman worth knowing. But he doesn't have the technical resources to make the changes in her occur because of the events of the story, and he leaves the circumstances of her promiscuity vague. This means that the promiscuous and victimized Marjorie and the triumphant-in-her-humiliation Marjorie are not the center of this elaborate story so much as the scandalous reason for reading it.

Marjorie's snobbish, small-town-socialite mother, a large-waisted woman of great pride and complete asexuality, is talking to herself when her troubling, promiscuous daughter has disappeared for the night after a quarrel. O'Hara says the woman "listened to this report from herself to herself":

> The ecstatic shudders of a kindly man, the water break, the cries in the night and the soiled diapers and the second teeth and the simulated pride and the secret appraisals were all lies, all equally spurious and unexperienced.

This cannot be the woman reporting to herself. It is O'Hara in an editorializing vein, trying for emotion, for passion. Neither the "ecstatic" nor the "kindly" in the description of her dead husband's sexual style and manner is supported: the dead husband never appears, and the words are kitsch, cheap terms in this frame of reference. This is (O'Hara has told us) a rich woman who has servants and is concerned with her one child as a reflection of her position—as a possession. If, for once, she were to consider physical reality, she wouldn't do it in this fashion; she'd use different terms, and she would move in and out of what she might call "coarseness"—cold, harsh realism—and temper, grief, and pain. And she might go further into feminine and maternal realism than this.

The strength of "Mrs. Allanson" is O'Hara's truly extraordinary sense of private story, private event: a quite rich, small-minded widow, very small-town la-di-da asexual, and her town-scandal daughter. (Raymond Chandler and others used a similar idea melodramatically, usually in relation to a father.) In various small, peripheral scenes O'Hara presents the actuality of such a situation as a human destiny. His particular kind of realism—the sniggering and hotly interested boys—gives a *frisson*. If the story were as good as some of its bits, it would be a great story. O'Hara's gift of observation, combined with his sense of how Americans talk (and attempt to talk), hints at the tragedy of humiliation, his special province. But he hints at it without portraying it.

O'Hara has the girl appear at the end of her mother's report to herself:

> "Mother?"
>
> Sara Allanson did not turn. "Yes?"
>
> "I'm sorry I was rude."
>
> "Well, I should think you would be. Where did you sleep?"
>
> "In the attic."
>
> "In the *attic?*"
>
> "In the old playroom."
>
> "Why? What did you sleep *on?* There's no bed made up."
>
> "I know. I'm stiff. I slept on the floor."
>
> "Why? What made you do that?"
>
> "I don't know. I just did."
>
> "Well, you'd better get yourself a hot bath or you'll be stiff the rest of the day. I see you haven't changed your dress."
>
> "I know."
>
> "I was just going down to breakfast. What do you want? And rumple your bed. I don't want Agnes to think you stayed out all night."
>
> "Mother, I don't *care* what Agnes thinks."
>
> "I'm sure you don't, but I do."
>
> "But I wish you didn't."
>
> "You have to care what people think in this world."
>
> "I don't."
>
> "Well, you'd better start."
>
> "It's too late for me to start."
>
> "Oh, ridiculous. What shall I tell Bertha you want for breakfast?"
>
> "Two soft-boiled eggs."

The scene goes on to be concerned with social strategies, with the mother's wish that the daughter avoid being seen alone with a certain boy. A lot is said. O'Hara, however, sums up the scene with "The things that were to be said were not said." That is, he is telling us that the scene hasn't happened; it is a throwaway. It is good dialogue, a Great Idea, and an Untold Story.

I think the scene and the dialogue are best understood as an attempt on O'Hara's part to rise above magazine fiction to greatness and immortality. The scene as idea is outrageous and archetypal, and embarrassing: proper mother, sexually scandalous child. But O'Hara does some odd things: he excuses the daughter from mannerism in speech—something he does frequently with favored characters. The daughter sleeps on the floor, she sleeps around, but in the scene, as in all the scenes in the tale, she is excused from any imputation of misjudgment or nuttiness. She is not slavish and guilty, or troll-like and dirtied, or defiant. She is lonely but considerate; she has no moods or tics. She is in command of herself. It is a signal of animal-like sluttishness—or, at least, of guilt and penance—that she slept on the floor in the attic, but she says it calmly enough. She has no original attitude toward her mother, no animus or demands or near madness. And the mother's responses don't affect the child's mood. They merely fail her, the child; they fail both of them, child and mother.

O'Hara means to attack puritanism and cold hearts and the Protestant Ascendancy; he means to charge it with soul-death. But he fails to understand the Protestant utopianism of the mother—how the Protestant ethic leads to the claim of Eden, of temporal grace, and how that blackmails its devotees. The Protestant sense of grace in terms of possessions and of behavior, in terms of country clubs and country-club matters, has a realism about it which is hard for some Catholics—with their sense of the dismissibility of this world in favor of the next one, with their sense of how awful this world is—to understand.

O'Hara's difficulty in portraying WASPs recurs in story after story— "Zero," "The Locomobile," "The Hardware Man." WASPs are hard. Mostly, the vivid characters in English prose are working class. Or stylized fools. Or pagans. (The great exceptions are in Henry James.) In "The Locomobile" O'Hara makes his Protestants stylish, and he gives them good manners and a high degree of nervous, social honor, but he laughs at them, and they do not come alive; he makes them fearful and petty and dull, inane.

O'Hara can't do the childishness or the effectuality or the cleverness of WASPs. In the end, the scene in "Mrs. Allanson" that is pretty good as dialogue, whether or not it suits the story, is almost purely about the mother's embarrassment and the daughter's living with humiliation; that is to say, the psychology is Catholic. The mother would be more comprehensible as an Irishwoman of the Rose Kennedy sort but less rich, less overshadowed. And the daughter would be a much clearer figure if she were an Irish *he*, an Irish alcoholic son, hung over and showing off his power of digestion to his pious, emotionally deaf mother—a son obstinate about his own guilt, and obstinate in his refusal to obey his mother's wishes for him. The chief action in this, as in almost all O'Hara's dialogues, is confession: indirect confession, half-confession, confession balked—not priestly confession but human and sociable.

The chronicle form, a compressed soap opera, covering twenty-five or thirty years, is what O'Hara uses in "Imagine Kissing Pete" (1960), perhaps his most widely praised story. It is technically a lot smoother than "Mrs. Allanson":

> To those who knew the bride and groom, the marriage of Bobbie Hammersmith and Pete McCrea was the surprise of the year. . . . I was working in New York and Pete wrote to ask me to be an usher.

The narrative voice is civilized, and, if it seems minor, it yet offers pleasure in the company of the sort of sophistication that one ascribes to the influence of such *New Yorker* editors as Katharine White and Gus Lobrano and William Maxwell. Pete McCrea is a fool—Ichabod McCrea—who marries the town's prettiest girl, prettiest *rich* girl; she wanted another man (one from Greenwich) and couldn't get him. So a failure as a temptress, a humiliated girl. The boastful smallness of the story attempt, part of the old *New Yorker* style, is made clear in the phrase "the surprise of the year": the size of the theme is set by the measure of a year's talk in a small town. This smallness of scale conflicts electrically and rather ironically with one's sizable sense of embarrassment and one's gauzy sense of black comedy at the thought of the prettiest girl grabbing the set's fool out of humiliation and marrying him in front of everybody.

It's one of those psychological story conceits that don't actually make psychological sense. The girl would most likely have married a fool from out of town if she was going to marry a fool. She isn't pregnant. Perhaps in the untold story she was. Social contempt moves on to sexual contempt for the characters, for their not marrying sensibly, for Ichabod's being a sexual nothing. The wedding appears—and disappears—in one sentence only, before we divagate into a long, long passage on Bobbie's looks and her rank as a beauty and her erotic history: she is "hectic," and too much for most men to handle.

We see Bobbie and Pete together in a scene with the narrator several months after the wedding, and it's clear that Pete is jealous of the narrator: "He kept a silly grin on his face while saying the ugly things, but the grin was not genuine and the ugly things were." One of the ugly things Pete says is "No funny business while I'm gone. I remember you two." That might be ugly, depending on how he said it, but it seems to me to have more pathos than ugliness.

O'Hara is operating here on a middlebrow, voyeuristic level; the truth he wants us to chase is a gossip version of the truth. The relationships—the real story—are hidden from us. The elements of truth come from gossip and from confession. When O'Hara does a scene head-on, it's poor—an obligation met. His indirectness, his slyness are better: he is writing about things out of his range but tricks them into being in range by these means. If I imagine him at his desk, amid his treasure trove of inner refusals—a refusal to be oversensitive or drunk (from 1953 on), a refusal to be anonymous, a refusal to tell a story in a direct or simple way—I imagine the ambition in his head like a slalom skier among those refusals.

Pete undergoes a farcical metamorphosis after marriage, rather like the male figure in the Updike stories of marriage, "Too Far to Go: The Maples Stories," or like the liberated Piet Hanema in Updike's *Couples*, but more comically and violently. After Pete tries to "rape" Phyllis (he "tore her bathing suit and slapped her and did other things") and behaves similarly with other women, the local people stop finding him silly, and while they think he's unpleasant, they "forget" to call him Ichabod. Bobbie is not aroused; she is disgusted. She can't stand him, but she doesn't divorce him. And O'Hara doesn't say why. To me, there is something eerie in the paganism—almost an absence of conscience—in Cheever's characters and in William Maxwell's. In O'Hara, by contrast, it is not paganism but, rather, a conviction that conscience doesn't exist; pride does, and social class. This is how he understood the decadent modern age.

Bobbie's story is that she has a hell of a life, and longs for the O'Hara alter ego: someone who would know everything and be strong, someone who would be beyond psychology and would know how to drink and how to let her live or to help her live. This story is more contemptible than the rougher "Mrs. Allanson." And, in the end, it isn't a story; it is an allegory of redemption through Bobbie's having, finally, a successful son, who graduates well from Princeton.

O'Hara is resoundingly secular, entirely untranscendent. His manner is one of intelligent burlesque. One reads, thrilled, uneasy, aware—as one is not in the troubled Fitzgerald's better stories—that what is at issue is whether the story is working or not, whether O'Hara is really a good writer or not. Some of the time, it seems clear that he is. But there is a steady series of misjudgments on O'Hara's part that undermine his authority:

> Mary Morgan Lander was the third generation of a family that had always been in the grocery business, the only store in the county that sold caviar and English biscuits and Sportsmen's Bracer chocolate, as well as the most expensive domestic items of fruit, vegetables, and tinned goods.

You can't really romanticize money and groceries in that way and not look like a fool, ironically or not. To some extent, if you list John Updike's virtues—the long descriptions of places, things, and people; the American literacy; the vague but present humor; the absence of rawness—you list some of what is missing in O'Hara. (It would not be surprising to discover that at some point Updike corrected O'Hara consciously in the course of finding his own voice.)

"The Doctor's Son," which O'Hara published in 1935, is, like "Imagine Kissing Pete" and "Mrs. Allanson," a long piece in which the story is not well told and finally doesn't matter. It is a horizontal chronicle, a survey of the whole county during the flu epidemic of 1918. O'Hara was a good reporter, though not as good as Hemingway, and the story he hints at and half tells, with its central idea of humiliation—cuckoldry here—and its sense of social existence and sexuality, suffers by comparison with the weight of the reporting on the social milieu and all the deaths in the influenza plague. Here, when he is just thirty, all his later traits are present: dialogue as confession, the dying fall of the scenes, indirection, getting the people and emotions wrong. And there is a lot to praise: the sense of embarrassment at being young, especially around the ill; the concern for one's father's reputation; the honest reporting on the callousness with which lives and honor are treated by the world. One can say, having moved backward in time, that O'Hara did not learn much technically or change much in the course of a long career; he learned almost nothing. But what a talent he began with.

I have heard it argued that the conspiracy notions of American Catholic writers were formed in their childhoods by the very real rivalries between parochial and public schools, when certain assertions and claims of theirs, of their group, of their families, were blocked—plotted against, if you like—and that that set of obstructions was struggled against, often with rage. This has led in many such writers to a mechanistic (not a human) sense of conspiracy—as in Don DeLillo and Robert Stone. In O'Hara, it leads to a mechanistic sense of retribution and rivalry, and that is given expression in a superior tone, rather like that of a former Communist Party member writing about political events; that is, the tone of someone who has spent time in possession of absolute truth, time he assumes the reader hasn't spent.

When the voice in which a writer's narratives and letters and nonfiction are couched has become a voice drenched somehow with language and with concern for capturing the not yet captured in literature, we might speak of a man or a woman aestheticized. O'Hara refused that transformation. His persona, his voice, and even the public forum in which the voice of the stories speaks, are to be understood as real. He addressed his stories to readers as a fellow citizen, a regular guy, not as an artist or a sufferer or a singer of some sort or a priest of literature or a sacrificial lamb. There is no gulf of magic between him and us. His first sentences announce not a theme or a mood or an idea but the fact that they are professionally interesting opening sentences. He is going to relate a story in a magazine—or in a story collection. The connection to the actual, secular world is very strong.

In his guise as a man-who-writes, he was like another writer, a woman, Mary McCarthy—prolific, Catholic in background, and a person of notable temper, of green grudges expressed with brio. No matter how famous she became, she remained a woman-who-writes; she kept the persona of someone undamaged, which is to say, untransformed, except in her degree of fame, into a *writer*. She was not like Willa Cather or Virginia Woolf. This role, this persona—is it just to call it a safe, upper-level mediocrity?

We are all, in part, mediocre. Extreme ability, like extreme work, tends to be singular—and isolating. Humiliation and a subsequent sense of self-protection, a well-guarded quality of alertness, might make such isolation not only unappealing, even to an ambitious writer, but psychologically repellent. O'Hara and McCarthy substitute their sense of rightness—and of social and public success—for any genuine sense of the aesthetic. Their version of being aestheticized merely by being right and having good public judgment in their day and age, and their sense of being people-who-wrote and triumphant, and their sense of material opened a door that a number of writers have walked through. One thinks of Updike, Joyce Carol Oates, Philip Roth, Alice Munro, and Robert Stone, not as disciples of O'Hara—they have tried to avoid his limitations—but as writers who seem to have been influenced, consciously or unconsciously, by his notion of a more strenuously real representation of life in America at the citizen's level and by his sense of a conscienceless era.

Isn't O'Hara's work valid enough on its level, and in relation to the achievements of these other writers, for continuing interest? Doesn't O'Hara finish high enough in the scramble to get *some* immortality?

O'Hara reduced everything to what he could do—to what he was able to do—throughout his career. He was too busy, too successful, and perhaps too nerveless to polish his work. He kept pushing toward narrative greatness without making a leap, just by being shrewdly flat-footed. And this is interesting and touching. But I think that an unhappy aspect of O'Hara's refusal to be other than a man-who-writes is that we become aware, on the wrong level, of the drama in his *trying* to write. And his trying to write is not, as a drama, as absorbing as the stories he claims he will tell us and then does not tell us.

Is he, then, an interesting figure historically? O'Hara was the last of the journalistic short-story writers to become famous. The short story originated as a feature in newspapers, as a more orderly and more detailed—and more haunted and folkish—news story. Poe perhaps invented it, and the form's relation to news stories was clear as late as Chekhov. In England and France, and here in the 1920s, the short story was a variant of a feuilleton, lyrical and full of nature, or lyrical and dramatic and stark, as in Hemingway. O'Hara worked with small-town news and gossip. Doesn't that make him a social historian?

Well, the other realists are more convincing. And O'Hara was suc-

ceeded by short-story writers of considerably more complication of surface: Cheever, Nabokov, Salinger, and Barthelme, whose portraits of
reality seem more valid if only because they claim to be true as impres-
sions or mistakes, because the issue of factual truth is not the paramount
issue for those who admire their stories. These writers did become aestheticized. O'Hara is more rawly the journalist telling you what he thinks
is the real story. But no writer has yet found a *journalistic* way to know the
real story of anything. The real *story*, when it is told, rests on art and an
artist's perception. O'Hara's use of clichés and other not very clever clap-
trap to extend the revelations he offers in dialogue, in overheard talk, in
the frame of a gloomy sense of life—to extend those moments of powerful
writing to a length and to dimensions where his claims would make
sense—does him in. Over time, the realer thing wins out; it emerges as
being more worth one's time. That the two realities, of reading and of
knowing about reputations, don't match is sad but inevitable. Because of
the needs of classes that teach writing, O'Hara might emerge as "a master" of the self-consciously masculine story on a much simpler and more
straightforward level. He might be useful in writing classes for a while.

More than a dozen years ago, at a restaurant on the Upper West Side,
before Raymond Carver had appeared in the *New Yorker*, he told me he
owed everything to John Gardner, who wrote *Grendel* and *The Sunlight
Dialogues* and *Nickel Mountain*. Carver said that Gardner, then the most
highly regarded teacher of writing in the United States, had taught him
to write, had led him over the line from aspirant to public practice, and
to his voice, to the techniques later enshrined in the doctrine of literary
minimalism.

Carver said he wanted to thank Gardner, but felt that Gardner was
avoiding him. Ellen Schwamm, my wife, had studied with Gardner, and
they were friends. Gardner was teaching at Binghamton and Carver at
Syracuse, and I was at Cornell. Ellen said she would arrange something.
Gardner and Carver came to our house in Ithaca. Whenever Carver tried
to talk to Gardner, Gardner changed the subject or moved across the room
or addressed me or went into another room even when Carver was in mid-
speech to him about what it meant to have studied with him. Have I said
that Carver was beginning to be famous?

Not long afterward, Gardner, drunk, telephoned me late one night in New York and said he had to come by. In the living room of our apartment, he sat on the floor, unable to manage sitting in a chair, and red faced and stricken, said he had made a list of our contemporaries he thought had a shot at literary immortality. Gardner said that Ray was on his list although he hated Ray's stories, but that he, who'd taught Ray, was not— that he couldn't put himself on his own list. Gardner's suffering was so great and seemed so unnecessary: look, he had quite a life, and he'd survived and made a living—why couldn't he just let time and luck decide?

Gardner was a generous man, but he wasn't generous to himself that night. He had other things bothering him besides literary immortality, but his misery on this particular subject was too apparent for me ever to deny to myself that it very likely played a part in the subsequent, anomalous motorcycle accident that killed him.

Does fame really matter enough culturally and morally that anyone ought to suffer over it? Or cause suffering because of it? Gardner said it was time for America—and for him—to grow up. He said it did no good to pretend the game was not a killer's baseball. John Cheever, when he was close to dying, told me he had been reared to face the ruthlessness of nature and that he put the matter of final reputation in the same category as the cruelty of age and death. He said we have to face those cruelties unless we can skip one of them by dying young. Why add to the burden? John Gardner said that aspiring to immortality was like motorcycle racing: you did it for the thrill; if you did it wrong, you were killed. Eugenio Montale said once that the practice of literature was like carving a secret amulet to placate the world and the dark gods. Cheever explained himself in this way: "We short men have to make ourselves noticed." He said, "I want my work to live. . . . I think some of it will live." He talked to me about what would become of his journals, about the merits of his stories compared with his novels. He spoke of his contemporaries, old men now dead, and the living. He gave his judgment. And when he came to John O'Hara he said, "I'm not as badly off as that son of a bitch. At least, I have a chance."

I think anyone who spends his life working to become eligible for literary immortality is a fool.

1993

STANLEY ELKIN,
THE STORY MAN

(Afterword to *Criers and Kibitzers,*
Kibitzers and Criers)

This is about Stanley Elkin and a book of *stories*.

The story—well, the long story, the novella, the short story, and the very short story—constitute a genre troubling and difficult to write, troubling and difficult to write about; difficult to analyze and review, difficult to get a grip on in terms of teaching or learning, a problem technically.

The genre of short prose fictions of a certain length (the definition proposed by Henry James) has puzzled critics since its inception. Writing courses in this country have made it the genre of entry into the profession of writing. And the ways it is taught—as a form of confession, as a form of emotional philosophizing, as diary-keeping-cum-joke-telling (American autobiography plus attitude) or as a branch of letter writing (in terms of a more sophisticated recounting of what are essentially anecdotes)—make the reality of the genre still more puzzling. Writing courses teach kinds of prose—kinds varying from course to course—that have as much to do with learning to think, while keeping a record of that thinking, as they have to do with propitiating some god or goddess who bestows inspiration, or with literary merit.

The modern story, or novella, is *not* book length. It lacks some principle of independence as a publishing unit—a principle that has to do with meaning, I think—and so it remains a journalistic genre largely identified as *not* being a journalistic (or biographical) anecdote, while existing under the constraint of always having to be considered as something more suited to publication in a periodical than to publication as itself alone, as a pamphlet or a book.

Meaning and length. The matter of *length* is probably the most important element in the genre technically, and in such important other ways as the length of time it takes to read it and the length of time it takes to write it and then the amount of actual time it purports to represent. So that someone who writes passable stories, and passably good stories, and very good stories, and very very very good ones (the category Stanley Elkin is in) can be discussed in terms of his or her regard for and intelligent use of length in this genre—length and scale, length and duration; the kind of attention that is asked for, the kinds of characterization of places, people, actions, that are used in the account.

This is not the place to discuss the relation of journalism to art, that is to say, the relation of journalistic accounts to amusement, instruction, catharsis, and significance. Or the roles that story and character play (and don't play) in various cultures.

One might mention, however, that in a journalistic account of an event, two stories are automatically present, that of the event and that of how the information was gotten, written, and presented—and that in journalism, any extensive study of either of the two stories is called *news analysis*. News story and journalistic history and commentary are like text and biographical study and critical analysis.

So far, in the history of the modern story, stories that are too journalistic have not done well in the course of time in terms of popular and critical judgment. Journalism is perhaps a horrendous but essential and valid and *moral* (sometimes) simplification of life—useful within reason and, of course, very dangerous, as a basis for immediate judgment—while *art*, to use a maddening term, when it is capable of holding the attention of an audience over long stretches of historical time, is not a simplification of any significance: it does not philosophically or morally simplify.

In a story, the formal resources of ancient emphasis—soliloquy, interlocking accounts, dramatic revelations—interrupt it, usually. Perhaps it can be said a story is a study in the simplification of emphases and in uninterrupted, or steady, attention. When you read a good story, you mostly don't rest your attention until you finish. Generally, in its apparent invention of a sort of narrative time (and of a public time and public place of auctorial speech to a reader), the story uses techniques and devices (tricks) to convey ideas and to generate feelings. It's probably all right to call this *significance*: the reason for reading it, the reason for writing it. The pattern of significance in a story of any length is unlike that of a news story and is unlike that of events in actual time. It usually gives to readers a sense of conclusion and of concision but not of complete conclusion, not of completeness, not of true finality.

The presence of often stale significance is taken as simplification, but, except in terms of study time, staleness is not simplification: it is emptiness. Concision is a matter of the weight of meaning per word, phrase, sentence, paragraph, and piece: How much padding is there? How much dubious or pseudo meaning is present? How much dubious maundering?

Concision has nothing to do with simplicity. It relates to something often called *density*. Density is not often praised, particularly by readers who want to feel emptiness is concision. Anyway, in *art*, concision is a complex matter. It is partly a matter of courtesy toward time—but not in terms of the time it may take to absorb what is concisely said when what is said is worth saying. It asks something of a reader: it asks for sophisticated comprehension.

But here is where biography enters in: for a long period of time after something is written, it can ask for comprehension only as sophisticated as that of the author.

It can be argued that a novel should be more accessible than a story of any length because the novel is less concise, less driven by considerations of concision, and of codification, and so is more accessible than a story. There is more time to learn the writer's language. The writer gives more evidence for his opinions. One has more time to use what one learns about comprehending the procedures of significance in the course of reading so many pages by one author. Strenuous forms of emphasis can be used. It should be taken for granted that the reader's attention will vary; the reader's mind will wander; her or his attention will even stop at times.

On the whole, the greater the significance for us, the less we notice the concision as we read. And the harder it is to define the concision. And the less the significance, the easier it is to discuss concision, and even to see it.

After all, on one level, concision is a convenient trick having to do with publicity—with journalism. *Veni, vidi, vici* is showy fun that has stayed amusing for two thousand years in its concision, but it is not of the same order of meaning as *ripeness is all*, although it uses the same number of words.

Elkin is of the *ripeness is all* school of writers.

Journalism, because of its nature, must be self-righteously conventional. It deals in clichés because of the constraint it is under to be current and to be read with appropriate quickness. It informs a reader: it does not train her or him in the use of the language of description of feeling and of event and in the actuality of character.

It deals in changeable clichés of no great age.

A news story—a newsy account of a love affair as part of a murder scandal, say—is a shrewdly worded account that deals in quick responses and in a quick transparency of *apparent* comprehension. And it is meant for large numbers of people, an audience larger than any single congregation addressed by a single voice, than any audience limited in size by considerations of any actually physical architecture, than any audience for traditional art.

Good stories, I think, very often correct journalism. Thus, the stories in this collection.

If these stories of Stanley Elkin's are art—and it is more than merely likely that they are—then they convey significance that is not simple; and they are not journalistic or familiar in form (or in intent), and we must approach them—and here is the paradox of the genres—in a spirit entirely unlike that in which we open the magazine or journal in which they might appear.

And this is a problem. . . . Where does one find the context in oneself? It is easy to say that a good story is worth six or sixteen or six hundred bad novels, but reading sixteen bad novels—and six hundred news stories—is a preparation for reading that is not much like the act of reading these stories.

What is our experience in reading *good* stories? If one is an absolute-absolutist, one says that doesn't matter. Truth is truth. Excellence is excellence. And so on.

But if one is a sensible relativist, one says that one ought to know a bit about postmodernism, about Guy Davenport and William Gass and John Barth, and, also, about Saul Bellow and J. S. Bach; but it is also true that nowadays education is more diverse than it used to be. Reality—not the reality of the realists but the reality of the philosophers and the scientists and of some writers—reality invites pluralism in discourses, in approach, and in perceptions: reality rests on diversity.

Old-fashioned flat remarks are not very useful: they never were, really.

I say the presence of art means a greater degree of truth than is possible with journalistic simplifications, and that one approaches good stories like these as one approaches a semi-secret assignation with someone, one's tie to whom is a correction of one's ordinary attitudes, habits, self-denial, hiddenness.

But the modern short story and the onset of mass literacy (or nearly mass literacy) go hand in hand. And many of the attributes of the story have to do with mass literacy and not with privacy and some semi-illicit nakedness or secrecy of response. The attributes of modern literacy that fathered what turned into the popular novel and the popular movie—whether that fathering is stylistically disguised or not—inevitably play with the idea and reality of media fame as if fame were the princess in a legend or the happy ending that replaced the happy endings of the large-scale chronicle novels of the last century.

And famous stories exist—there are stories that have a mass media existence.

But I would still want to argue (even if a figure of speech is not quite an argument) that good stories mostly exist in people's talk and in individual minds, and that in settling down to read them one is as if going to a rendezvous.

Two writers in the past, great and journalistic (and in English), are Defoe and Dickens; and much of their work can be broken into units of linked stories. And their sense of diction at a rendezvous has stayed modern.

A writer has a great many ancestors and a great many sources for his or her work; in Elkin's case, rightly or wrongly, I see a line of descent from Defoe and Dickens.

Some people equate Jews with mass literacy but let's not discuss that here except to say that elements of that question inflect Elkin's work. His literacy is enormous—verging on enormity. The literacy of the Jews in his stories, the verbal dexterity, is rarely less than extreme. His characters are not victims, like Wozzeck, because of ignorance or verbal inadequacy. And moral questions for them are not hovering and inexpressible—are not implied—but are present, expressible—and expressed. This is a form of clarity, not of simplicity.

And it comes as something of a shock, the extent and ways they are articulate. And then, too, American writing this articulate is rare.

Some people associate Jews with the death of Christian social classes (mass literacy and mass moralism destroy the distinctions between the old social classes that were set by differences in literacy and illiteracy and by consequent differences in moral outlook), and Jewish literate classlessness happens to be an element in Elkin's writing as well. The absence of social distinctions of the usual Christian social sort found in the canonical novels and the stories written by famous novelists may obscure the accuracy in these tales of the sense of actual predicament and of actual character, shown by linguistic means here, and the degree of "realistic" but more often "stylized" social observation.

The short and long story, as we know it, took shape in the nineteenth century as a result and concomitant of revolutions: the American, the French, the industrial, and then the Decembrists, 1848, the Paris Commune, on and on. . . . The creation of a large, monied middle class—the *responsible* class in modern times (*pace* Marx), but new, ill-informed, untraditional, with no great moral claim except as *responsible*—changed our sense of language. In fact, in one sense the new class deconstructed all prior uses of language and all later deconstructions unwittingly mimic that and are, I think, willy-nilly middle-class movements no matter how disguised as radicalism.

Part of what grew up in that deconstruction was a new hierarchy of *literacy*, which, tendentiously, I would like to describe as consisting of rich men's and protected women's art novels, and of the popular novel (and drama), and of the quite low-ranked but extremely important journalistic story. These three ranks of the New Literacy are highly aware of one another. Some of the effect of beauty in Elkin's work (as in Chekhov's) is the combination—the conflation—of elements of the three ranks.

The new class needed daily or weekly or monthly information because the newly formed industrial world moved rapidly and, also, partly because the new class did not have methods and systems and traditions of its own and was improvising as it went along and needed quick, up-to-date advice about a great many things.

Such mass information (and the consequent social arrangements and social organisms or *mechanisms* perhaps) formed the spine of its existence, and the grounds of its superiority to the lower classes and to the hereditary aristocracy, and was the grounds of its power, its efficiency, its efficacy, its ugliness, and its many obvious failures.

The line between this as a search for a sort of Baconian truth of daily existence and the corruption of this information as *propaganda* was always, in actual practice, uncertain.

And that moves over into art where it becomes a question in the works of Wagner and in nineteenth-century philosophy and early-twentieth-century philosophy, in general; and in our country, it becomes a central issue in Thoreau, Melville, Dickinson, and the rest—and, currently, Elkin, Gass, Davenport, and others. . . . I mean the refusal to accept mass information is overtly central in their work.

The games, the strength and dexterity of language, and the sometimes appalling truthfulness of these stories of Elkin's—their having a very large truth-element as art, not journalism—makes them important; but it is not an importance that can be dealt with by the reviewers, academic or popular, who deal with such matters, unless they are willing to be students of his and to recognize their own defects—their thinness of conventional response in the light of the largeness of *his* response, the depth of technique, the subversive game of new emphases that he plays and the games with length, speed of narration, concision (and unconcision), and so on.

Conventionalized discourse and false and true revolutions lie at the center of what I think of as the melodrama of the spread of a form that depends on length of attention and subdued emphasis as the main elements in its formal arrangements. I think you can see this in these stories—a war with conventionalized discourse and a recurring surrender to it—and the characters caught up in false and true revolutions of attitude, of outlook.

Chekhov began by writing for a newspaper, as did Dickens, and as did George Eliot (in a somewhat different form). The movement into book length by the latter two is more than roughly equivalent to Chekhov's movement into longer sentences, longer tales, and, generally, more complex forms of concision and less-simplified significance as he grew older (and more famous).

In his case, one guesses, he did not intend to write in the shadow of Tolstoy. He avoided the genres Tolstoy had exploited. One can see in Nabokov's silliness and frequent absence of significance how crippling Tolstoy's shadow was. One can also see in a number of Nabokov's novels the presence of long stories, which are more truly what they are if they are considered separately as stories than if they are considered to be parts of novels. Often, excerpts from those books are considerably better, are more artful, are more matters of art, than are the books themselves.

Elkin bathes these matters of inherited forms and of commonly held information and banal but also real revolutionariness (if I can say that) with a kind of bottom-of-the-heap Jewish lyrical snottiness and direct and inverted skepticism that has amazing reverberations (I don't mean Elkin personally, but the persona that stands behind the voice of many of these stories).

Length, not requirements of narrative, determines the scale of things in a story. The reader supplies much of the story. If you consider that Poe and Sir Walter Scott and Lord Byron are roughly coeval, you can see that Poe expected his readers to know that other sort of adventurous narrative with its usually happy ending. Maupassant expected his readers to be familiar with nineteenth-century French narrative, Hugo and Balzac. But Henry James and Chekhov seem to me to rely much more on readers knowing journalism, not novels.

They are opposed to and yet derived from journalism.

The blowsiness of novelists is no accident nor is the marvelous use of not going on at length by story writers of merit.

Chekhov, now taken to be the greatest master of the form, wrote paragraphs and sections of stories that are clearly *novelistic* in their use of length; but he and other short-story writers of the (currently) highest rank have been so far more clearly artful and restrained in form than their novel-writing counterparts have been.

Not Maupassant, who was trained by, and who was considerably less artful than, Flaubert. And sometimes a coeval short-story writer and novelist are nearly equal in their sense of formal restraint, as in the cases of Katherine Mansfield and Virginia Woolf (but the latter includes more and has emerged as the writer of greater formal interest). Chekhov did, ably, place a great many novelistic paragraphs in sequence—he did it with care and usually with some punctuation of unnovelistic paragraphs. The more novelistic a story writer is, the sloppier in matters of length and shape and in matters of characterization; but these ace writers make it work.

The matters of length and shape should be paramount in any study of stories, long or short. But that is lousy work—hard, vague, unvocabular-ied, really bad work for beginners.

In our century, which now is ending, the line of good and very good short-story writers can be said to split into three categories. One is public and very popular: O. Henry and Damon Runyan. (And some novelists chose to do similar work in popular and not so popular novels: one thinks of Jack London and of Nathanael West.)

A second category is of the intense and rather odd. This category includes Katherine Mansfield and Saki and W. W. Jacobs. And Sherwood Anderson. Borges. Kafka. Babel.

But the third category is that of the quite serious and effective and valid but not actually short works, not actually stories. This category is occupied by able novelists such as Lawrence, Joyce, Faulkner, Mann.

So far as I know and judge, no writer has written with equal success in two of the categories; so far, it has always been one or the other.

None of the three categories can be taught—and none is reducible to formula. One can say the chief difference, if one thinks of the symptomol-ogy of stories, is in the nature of significance: there is no real significance in a story of the first sort, merely a sensation of pleasure, and perhaps a sentiment.

The significance in the stories of the second type is primarily solipsis-tic: it is rarely, if ever, a matter of character, no matter the pretenses of the story. Good stories of this sort, as of the first sort, match one of the Bahk-tinian categories—that of subversion of official language—but cannot produce a plurality of voices.

The significance of the third sort of stories has not been written about much. The assumption has been that the writers did it better in their nov-els. But one can notice that the stories in this category are subversive and do, usually, offer more than one valid voice.

Stanley Elkin, but not with great firmness, is in the last category; but it would seem that at moments he tries to be a writer of stories in the second category.

Good for him.

One notices the rhythms of the opening of a story—the rhythms of individual sentences and the successive rhythms of the first five sentences, say, including the rhythms of the presentation of the emergency, of the reason for writing this story, for relating it (two different things), and of what is offered you as an inducement to read the story. The density of the concision, of ideas and of events—indeed, if you will permit me, the presence of the absence of no-meaning—is at once recognizable as the context for the rest of the story.

And the matter of length, the length of time devoted to a character, to an action, to an idea, is apparent in every sentence, every phrase, every reference. This is why good stories of the first and second type, and many of the very best stories of the third type, suggest they are a form of poetry and of poetic drama, and do not seem to be directly related to novelistic prose or to the prose of memoirs and of letters.

The length of a sentence, of a paragraph, of a scene in a story, is a showy matter as it is in popular music. As it is in classical music in concert halls. It should not be a matter of such importance in a novel—and in the good ones, it isn't.

The history of length, if I can say it like this, is partly the history of seriousness; and in every public and popular form it is something an audience knows about. Art of this sort, a public sort, widely known about, is always microhistorical—as are sports.

But melody and orchestral color and mood in a piece of music are all subsumed under length or are aspects of length in a short story and in a long short story and in a very long story and in a novella. The length of a riff, of a speech, of a scene, is the melody, the orchestration, the public mood, in the stories in this collection. The matter of length can be so showy a matter that one might say it can supply a basis for dealing with the question of significance—the brevity or extension of a moment, a scene, a phrase, a sentence, an observation, a joke.

That is, as the central element, length (and its opposite, extreme quickness) can supply a beginning and provable (or almost provable)

ground for one's efforts at interpretation and analysis of "The Dead" or
of "Criers and Kibitzers, Kibitzers and Criers" or of Kafka's parables or of
Chekhov's tales.

For instance, in the title story of this book, it is the presence and portrayal of the workday that underlies almost all the uses of length and concision. Or, rather, the effect of Elkin's uses of length and concision portray
the day so that it might be the case that it is the workday that is the hero,
and the hero is simply the human creature whose workday it is. Here is a
workday gone through despite grief—grief not simplified, not lied about,
not sentimentalized.

Oh, it's art.

And one can see various things then. One can see how the use of length
(rather than emphasis or storytelling) gives stories of this third sort their
human dimension, their humane music.

But one can also see that as the chief formal determinant, this sort of
gardening of attention imposes an almost impossible strain of meaning
and presence on the language used—almost an inhuman strain. One can
see how a very very good story is always in competition, oddly, with
poetry in this regard. One can see how the language must carry meaning
at all times, and must not be stale language used sentimentally and
trashily and popularly—except as a joke or as an expression of pain. That
is to say, the language of the thing, like the language of a review or of a
news story, carries the burden of displaying the morality of workmanship,
while the overall meaning or significance of the story carries a more public
burden of topical meaning and significance—which, however, it can't
convey without the help of language, unlike the novel, which can function in regard to meaning without disciplined language (cf. Dreiser, Zola,
early Solzhenitsyn, many current Americans).

So, you have two kinds of dexterity going at once in good story such as
Elkin's, one having to do with the duration and nature of attention and its
extension or its rhythmic curtness, and the other having to do with language similarly attached to duration and the nature of attention and used
with considerable extension or with considerable rhythmic curtness.

It's a juggling act. It's W. C. Fields doing ballet, sort of. Once you get
on this horrible-wonderful treadmill or merry-go-round of the length-
determined modern forms, not only must the sentences interrelate in

terms of event and of technique, but the tone must be sequential, and the narrative or progression of meaning must be consequential. And in a country devoted to shrewdness and to confidence tricks, to a steady middling sort of decent lying you're supposed to be sharp-witted about—in a country of mass-produced cars and nearly universal considerations of the prices of real estate—this means producing a piece of work that is like a hand-produced sports car that a limited number of people can afford and a limited number of people can drive well, can deal with, can be unintimidated by with regard to the significance and excellence of the thing.

The great historical switch to the political preponderance of the middle class has in it a double element—a defense of the merits and abilities of ordinary people, but also of the rights of the mediocre. When ancient states were wrecked by the mediocrity of their rulers, it was not always considered mediocrity, but fate—which may or may not be considered tactful.

Elkin's central thematic preoccupations have to do with ordinariness, with mediocrity, but with human merit as well, and fate; but these are considered in the light of the fatal injustice, and of individual merit and individual feelings, and of individuals and their actions as good or evil.

Elkin is primarily known as a novelist, but notice that his preoccupations as a short-story writer seem to match the form, and the history of the form as well. He is a novelist who seems to have been born partly to write stories.

In the nineteenth century, mediocrity took on its modern meaning and was named as the enemy, but not in the best stories (Chekhov's, for instance), and mediocrity was praised in socialism and in lousy stories and was courted by the media.

One can see the literary history of the century as a Napoleonic one, a recurrent attempt by artists to enlist mediocrity or to come to terms with it or to embody it as part of a campaign for the conquest of history.

Echoes of this survive in Elkin but he is more than modern; he is postmodern, and was even before he knew it. The bitter skepticism and newness of attitude in these stories matches something that was happening historically among writers.

Elkin was born during the same era in which Kafka did not publish much in his lifetime. Babel was silenced once it became apparent just how good a writer he was. Joyce was considered difficult. An existing great translation of Proust into English was held to require simplification—and was ruined.

That is to say, the truest art, or some of it anyway, is felt to be anti-Napoleonic, honorably unseductive, and perhaps not recognizably art at all.

Art becomes recessive, inverted, teasing—it becomes incoherent in regard to mediocrity and fate.

More than a good novel, a good, or very good, or very very good story challenges mediocrity, our marvelously vicious and successful emperor, but it does so in a sort of privacy of unmedia-overseen intimacy.

That means, given democracy or socialism, given any dictatorship, a good story challenges the social world.

Stanley Elkin, being a very good writer, does just that, paragraph after paragraph in his books and stories, but he is also a practical man. In him is the longing to be a popular writer of the cliché-ridden, calculating sort; the solipsistic, trashy, self-loving sort. It is almost part of his aesthetic—almost a love affair. Each of Stanley Elkin's stories here shows a tendency now and then to escape from itself and enter another category, often at a lower level. Modesty and greed peek out, but meanwhile, almost ferociously, the story resumes its own wayward grace, which is to say that Stanley Elkin, the poor tortured creature, gets on with producing his art.

Most of his characters—perhaps all—are Jews. In the story form, if even a single phrase has an obvious flabbiness of meaning, that absence of significance tends to signal the unimportance of the story—the writer doesn't care. It often takes the form of shtick or of romanticizing the reader's experience as the reader knows it in whatever verbal form he knows it; that is, in its use of kitsch and shtick as elements of a display of social virtuousness: he's a good guy, one of us, and so on.

You can study this in translations of Chekhov when the translation is no good. You can tell it's no good because even Chekhov is no good if the translation is flabby, no matter its claims of accuracy—if it lacks a certain energy of progression and a certain deep cleverness about the uses of length as a formal element, and a certain sense, a certainty of significance being present. Those elements determine which translations of Chekhov are acceptable.

The presence of the openly journalistic (the journalistically formulaic) means, flatly, that the story is not worth one's time. One might enjoy that, however. The feeling of superiority to the writer is one of the democratic pleasures.

It is impossible, I think, to find much that is journalistic in these stories. For the moment, let us call that a flaw. But I don't think it is a flaw at all. It is impossible to feel superior to Elkin. He is too good a writer. He thinks and feels too profoundly. He is modest and human and down-to-earth and all that, but he is too good at what he does: he's a little scary.

Some stories that appear in print and win prizes are quite wonderful on first reading. They may be a high form of journalism, and of a quality that keeps them readable for a decade—but not two. One ought not to make time to return to them.

And many stories are useful as training devices: to train one's attention, give one experience at decoding narrative progressions; and they ought not awe the reader too much, or she or he will be too awed to learn. It is like tennis: one should play with people not too greatly superior to oneself.

But such stories are not really of enough merit to read with one's full attention. They are good for purposes that have little to do with actual reading. Reading is a dangerous act. One mustn't be misled by the usefulness of teachable stories into thinking they are any good. They have the same relation to merit (and the real thing) that examples of business letters given in textbooks written a decade or two decades earlier than one's time have to raw business letters in a time of economic emergency— letters that affect your destiny and that of others, lying letters, truthful letters, letters in the real world.

Elkin-on-the-page is too immediate, too large, too good to try to learn from. One tends to be a bystander—except humanly, except as a man, say; then one is a student always, I suppose. But as a writer Elkin is not imitable, which means he is not for classroom teaching except of an elevated sort. These are good stories.

Elkin is often a marvel. His language is often splendid, often low, always supple, dextrous, frequently inspired. It is never without meaning. It is true his use of length is a bit uncertain, but that is true of all the writers in the third category when they write stories. They know too much. They are too experienced in other forms which don't use length in that way. So they are all unreliable, no matter how good they are.

As an American, Elkin is a bit shy about being an artist. He clearly is one, but he is too playful and he puts in things to show he is a good guy. He dilutes effects. He has the self-sufficiency, the sense of order, the near madness of a major figure. He plays with the Chekhovian sufficiency notion that in a story everything must be part of the story, must be usefully part of the creation of the overall effect, the meaning—but then he plays with that by going too far, by being too much. (May I use those idioms here?) He is a bit like a dolphin playing in an aquarium pool. He stands comedy and meaning, pain and compassion, Jewish realities, and terror on his dolphinlike nose—so to speak—and on *their* noses, and he sets them dancing, often upside down. And then he says or implies that the things he is playing with are logical and not at all playful in themselves, and that their obstinacy as fate in reality wins out. And often, then, my heart is broken.

At moments he is as good a stylist as Bellow and at times he is as funny as Roth—funnier and more passionate sometimes. He has never written a short piece as magical as Bellow's translation of Singer's "Gimpel the Fool," and is never as seductive as Salinger or ever as brilliant at farce or at editorializing as Roth. But he is wider and wilder in attitude and in subject matter than all of them, and far more reliable in moral judgment than Ozick. He is unlike anyone else; and in certain ways, he is superior to all of us—I mean, in his unremitting seriousness (even when he's trying to sell out), and in his concentration and the consequent energy, and in the wit of his narrations in relation to significance. He is much bitterer than we are, and a better delineator of character and of the consequences of specific actions on human affairs (and feelings). He is more serious than anyone now alive, which may mean he is at times a better writer than anyone. Time will judge these matters for us. Later readers playing with the danger inherent in reading anything will have their turn at voting and judging all of us now alive.

But what I want to say is that he is never a journalist, and that his stories curl your hair, inform your mind, instruct and terrify your heart, and make you laugh and make you wish you knew him and that he would live forever and write more and more and more and more.

1990

THE ABILITY TO
BE ORDINARY

Max Frisch, the Swiss writer, represented to me something very curious—a literary figure partly unmarked by the shame, or to use a more difficult word, the *guilt*, the complicity in abomination that made so much European writing after the war not merely strange but often (not always) meretricious. The nihilism, the criminal praise of the god-awful in Genet, in Beckett, the awful leftism of a Grass, the boredom, the boredom, the despairs, essentially the lies (and brilliance) that so wearied all of us, that so prepared the way for American writing to be fundamental for decades for Europeans, this was not present in Frisch. He escaped. He was the man in the background of the newsreel—an ordinary man of more than ordinary judgment, the wrestler who survived the slaughter in the arena.

One could not fail to find in him something of the ordinary man who was, all in all, at worst an only minor murderer. . . . I do not mean to sound so melodramatic, but European history was and has been and continues to be so melodramatic as to defy all attempts at restraint. Frisch, whom I found to be corrupt and opportunist, and whose writing showed those traits, was also a man of profound feeling and of profound comprehension of what it meant to be an individual separated from the melodrama by his own moral restraint or incapacity. He did not think clearly, but he wrote clearly. He was derivative as an artist but he was, as an artist, more honest than all but a very few of his contemporaries. He managed to express some of what it actually did mean to be alive in this era. A thousand more famous writers pale in comparison to him. Perhaps more than any other Continental writer of his time he kept alive the image of being, in the end and foremost, merely human, ordinarily alive no matter how melodramatic the circumstances were that surrounded his being human in that way. . . . This was, no matter how it sounds, a very great achievement. . . . His tone, his metaphysics influenced me very much.

1991

THE RUSTLE OF LANGUAGE:
ROLAND BARTHES

One reads Roland Barthes for the music of his rebellion and for phrases and insights, aphorisms, aperçus, and for the portrait of Barthes, and for one's own memories of the era. One does not read him "seriously."

A professor of literary semiology at the Collège de France, Barthes began publishing in 1964 when he was already nearly fifty. In the next fifteen years he published 152 articles, 55 prefaces and contributions to miscellanies, and 11 books (the figures are from his French editor's brief preface). That body of work amounts to an unofficial history of Sixties-*isme*, installments in a curious life text documenting the most enthusiastic and profound (and most consequential) of all movements of thought and of feeling since the end of World War II.

It is Barthes's relation to Sixties-*isme* which is important. No critical book, none of his phrases, famous for a while or still, survive as authoritative or of real interest in current literary controversies. But while it would be wrong to separate his reputation from the idea of fashion and from the conduct of fashion, it would be wrong to limit his worth to that or to think of his career as merely a reflection of fashion.

. . .

To define an immediate moment in history is difficult, but it is tempting to name the present one as colored by a desolation following the collapse of those motions of history that erupted in the 1960s with such force of disorder and hope—and with such overwhelming cultural success, at first.

Barthes, who died in 1980, was a leader, a speechmaker, a figure on the barricades in that enormous and somewhat hollow event. His book, *The Rustle of Language,* is a posthumous collection of forty-four pieces, some quite short—there are radio talks, newspaper pieces, papers given at colloquiums—that deal with "language and with literary writing," (the phrase is the French editor's, as Richard Howard has conveyed it in his amazingly adroit translation) and that chart with surprising completeness the arc of initial enthusiasm, the days of wild Jacobin excess (and success) and the subsequent collapse.

In the book's first essay, "From Science to Literature," printed in 1967 in the *Times Literary Supplement*, in the first paragraph, Barthes announces the revolution: deferring to "all the social and human sciences," he proclaims that "what defines *science* . . . [is] its *status*. . . . In a word, science is what is taught." This is not criticism or creation, it is not either particularly true or untrue. It is carelessly worded and incomplete; it is too accurately observed of certain colleges and certain journalistic usages to be entirely dismissed. It is a shot fired in insurrection against largely academic interests.

At the time that it was said, it might have proved to have been importantly true if what Barthes calls "language" or what he calls "literature" had later turned out to be what he said they could be. He said of literature, for instance, that its "contents are precisely those of science . . . the world of the work is a total world, in which all (social, psychological, historical) knowledge takes place, so that for us literature has that grand cosmogonic unity which so delighted the ancient Greeks. . . . Like science, literature has its morality . . . and consequently [it can be said to submit] its enterprises to a certain absolute spirit [of truth]."

That is not quite the case. Literature deals in truth but hardly in an *absolute* spirit, no matter what the professors say. Barthes means, it seems, that there is no human truth outside of language: "Confronting [the] integral truth of writing, the 'human sciences,' belatedly constituted in the wake of bourgeois positivism" (the use of experiment, habits of research, the keeping of records, statistics), "appear as the technical alibis our society uses to maintain the fiction of a theological truth, superbly—abusively—disengaged from language."

In effect he transfers what was granted by the old theology, a sense of absolute truth in relation to human doings, to a not yet existent *science* of language and to a literature seen as an absolute total of the human. He proclaimed it—he proclaimed literature as an absolute. Then a year or two later he proclaimed writing about it to be an absolute. "The death of the writer," one of the famous phrases of the era, marked the death of the "Author-God" but it also marked the deification of the writer-critic: "writing" in the light of the still newer knowledge that Barthes proposes became an *absolute* act. This meant you could "supplicate" language itself to grant you freedom and strength and meaning. To change language was the equivalent of what piety had hoped to achieve: language in a certain educated form became a way of bringing grace and affluence into life, God's favor in a new and more universal way.

Sixties-*isme* played itself out from the *intentions* of Marx, Freud, and Wittgenstein—the three overseers of twentieth-century thought—rather than from the substance of their arguments. Barthes attempts a quasi-Marxist, pseudo-Freudian, trebly secular deification of language in order to outflank the strictures of the new thought against certain kinds of generalization. And it is here that he makes language God—specifically academic language (discourse). This is a particularly dangerous thing to do. Barthes was, in French terms, one of the *saints* or *demons* of this movement, of post-Holocaust Euromodernism and its permissiveness: an idealism of self-indulgence in a world in the nuclear shadow. A term such as *late* modernism has a certain terror in it. Parisian late modernism was fixated on the media and on notions of success and of self-promotion. It popularized the perversity of language, observation, and pronouncement as being a necessary and general rule of intellect and *freedom*. The programs proposed in such quick succession, structuralism and then semiotics and then deconstruction, each claimed to be remaking history and to be freeing us from history now. Each is referred to in this book. Each was a mode of rebelliousness, a method by which the outs control a conversation. Barthes points to this device and its nature as a device of control in a number of books, twice in the present volume. Barthes and these movements operated within a French frame of the scandalous. His charm is scandalous. His power to be interesting is too, if you know something in advance of what he is talking about.

The elements of Barthes's style rest on a finicky and purposeful effrontery, which devastates the subject and which gives pleasure, in the Sadean or orgiastic sense, of satisfying one ultimately, not in terms of intellect but in terms of burning the hut down. One no longer feels left out of whatever society of fellows was holding a meeting inside the hut. Sade, Genet, and Gide with his wicked schoolboys in "The Counterfeiters" have helped create this fifty-year-old and very well educated street boy, this vicarious street boy of the classroom.

There is far more of hysteria and of political-theological hysteria and of feeling in what Barthes does than there is of intellectually grounded argument. But his writing is accurately placed at the points of most severe strain, intellectual and personal, of the period. What Sixties-*isme* did primarily was that it refused to wait for proper arguments or great men. It not only demanded change, it instituted it without authority.

In his 1976 essay "On Reading" Barthes writes this extraordinarily opaque (and, I think, foolish) passage: "Reading, in short, is the permanent hemorrhage by which structure—patiently and usefully described by Structural Analysis [which he was to abandon within several years]—collapses, opens, is lost, [is] thereby consonant with any logical system which *ultimately* nothing can close—leaving intact what we must call the movement of the subject and of history: reading is the site where structure is made hysterical." He *liked* hysteria. He permitted it as the quintessential human imprint, the point where theory and specialization became a kind of wholeness in opposition to education and the past.

Barthes proceeds, often, in a closed system of hysteria in this sense, in a series of jargon-ridden generalizations. His greatness lay precisely in his desperation, in his public willingness to display his desperate hysteria, and to proclaim it logical and necessary. His work, sprightly and convoluted and popular as it was, was intellectually of the second rank. He persisted in his "hysterical mode" until the mid-1970s, making his life meaningful (if I may put it like this) by his own proclamation, movingly and with great international success.

What led him to his proclamations was never as vital as the proclamation, or as useful. Reasoning was not his strong point. Yet the age did not mind his unreason but praised it. The notion of what an idea was was radically changed: ideas became not ideas in the old sense, apparently neutral and involving life and words and pessimism and form; but since Marx and Freud and Wittgenstein had successfully argued that ideas could not be neutral, Barthes and a number of others decreed that ideas must become instruments of the avowedly optimistic intention to change the world, to make it utopian, for the sake of amorous happiness, for the sake of freedom.

This was more plausibly a French extension and purification (or corruption) of American movie-and-advertisement notions—Eden as sexual and personal happiness and glamour. (Barthes is a little like Jimmy Stewart in an old comedy proclaiming the triumph of the common man. The common man does not look like or speak like Jimmy Stewart and is not so ferociously clever and so deeply well educated as Roland Barthes.) The intentions of American commercialized romanticism became a field of thought like nuclear physics, or Freudian psychology, or Marxist studies—not quite practical, not quite honestly theoretical. But this particular part of the cultural landscape was dominated by movies of mood and motion and by rock music—by activities close to languagelessness. Barthes became a star of a major sort on the grounds of creating a god in language itself and in encouraging attempts at creating a new society almost solely through proposed corrections of language. It is a vision, and it is of great value. He was an essayist of some stature, but he was not much of a critic.

Barthes said that his were "intimate" essays, but their democracy and intimacy rest on too great an amount of culture for that quite to be the case. French probably is no longer the world language of culture—and probably American English is—but French remains the language for world trade in ideas. One example of a Barthesian aphorism is about Culture as "a bizarre toy that history cannot break"—it survives a nation's wars and its defeats. He means just such trading in culture as he does. But how sincere he can have been is unclear considering the often unnecessary difficulty of his writing.

Barthes says often that what art or even what language is, is an assertion of will that alters reality and that it is nothing else. Later in his life, he distanced himself from that and began to admit he wanted to write a journal or a novel of worth—i.e., with some human material in it. He is a professionally "revolutionary" figure, a traditional role in Paris, like that of Pierrot.

He names the "Utopic" (his term for Utopian) as something not only hoped for but immanent: this is the tactic of ads promising happiness in relation to your buying and using the right soap. Such writing is narcissistic and proposes narcissism as the primary critical, intellectual, literary—and political—reality, the preferred state for individual consciousness. He will propose—he does propose—a Sadean orgy as an example of a properly functioning group activity. A bit of thought would show the impossibility of that proposition. An orgy would be a riot of trespass that cannot be coordinated, and Sade says as much.

Barthes, at times in his career, proposed a *totalitarianism of pleasure*. He was not a Michelet or a Montaigne. He was exemplary, somewhat infantile. To use his terms, we should not look for an Irene Dunne to possess the qualities of a Garbo. His style is larded with words it is not much pleasure to learn: *imbrication, enthymemes, acratic*. Still, it is wonderful to have this terrible and yet very interesting book in this marvelous translation at the moment when it is time to discuss literary and social theories and which ones are of merit and which ones are not. The failure of Sixties-*isme* as a way to live or govern or think leaves us in a general wreckage of language (and doctrine). It is time to do something about a revolution that changed everything and accomplished nothing.

1985

LANGUAGE IS
ARTICULATED CONSCIOUSNESS

Let me begin with the notion that language is articulated consciousness. Articulated how? Articulated for purposes of comprehension in real time among the physical laws of breath and hearing or eyes and comprehension.

The spiritual and physical properties of speech operate in a set of procedures that takes place in a sequence of seconds and minutes in actual time. Part of that procedure, speech, or language is definitely not consciousness and does not operate at all in the ways that consciousness does.

It operates without simultaneity, for instance, and without immediately determinative association.

But before then and after then, speech, or language, is mixed with the properties of consciousness as consciousness exists in the mind, and here, at last, words become difficult, because one is using words to say consciousness-beyond-words, unpicturable in words, so far.

Much of language as articulated consciousness represents and reflects social realities, social and cultural ones: it might be said that language is the common ground, the objective correlative itself, all we have of certain operations of consciousness in a sociocultural sense.

It is perhaps possible to train yourself to work to some extent, large or small, outside your sociocultural background. A kind of evidence for this exists in America where most people who go to college develop a college-trained language that is the language of their greatest seriousness.

An absolutist is not often an adequate theologian or a good rabbi or even a good writer and certainly not a good reviewer. He is rarely an impressive thinker, rarely well-read (in a serious sense), almost never a scientist under the discipline of evidence.

A reviewer, for example, is merely someone chosen by an editor. He is someone who has a career. He should not pretend to be something his style and reasoning do not show him to be, no matter how pleasing to him the falsity of his daydreams are. If he does not respect honesty and honesty of language and if he does not regard language itself as extorting a kind of honesty greater than that asked of him by his sociocultural background—his family, his God, his nation—then he is at best an agent of fear and of the consequent lack of seriousness in regard to language. He can manage, barely, to refer to thought. But he cannot think. . . . He uses a language or irresponsible pseudo-intellectual commentary but he cannot speak. He is perhaps strident but it is a strident silence—that is mostly what his consciousness is.

However, let us say that as an absolutist he believes that any one consciousness matches any other consciousness. That is, he believes all human consciousness, not just his, is primarily irresponsible pseudo-intellectual commentary. He doesn't know why he thinks this: he thinks this is a truism.

And this may be so vital to him that he pleads cruelty in others if they menace this thought.

But the real existence of a real audience, if that audience is untyrannized over, menaces that thought. . . .

That is to say, the existence of propaganda shows the presence of oppressive and abstract generality as a governing principle of personal ego in someone who has a semi-ruling, semi-governing position.

When such absolutism is functioning, then *position* is the only form of relativism recognized by the absolutists in place.

A certain dwelling on position as secular truth—*the* secular truth—marks the absolutist who ought not to be acting as a judge of anything in an actually secular society.

.   .   .

Language throughout the duration of any use of it never ceases to be a form of consciousness. It does not become God or some stream of abstract utility and of absolute unity of meaning and of discourse. It is a real thing throughout the duration of its use.

And it is heard in its arcs of procedure by speaker and listener, which is to say, on either end, by the ears, or physically, or read (and perhaps imaginarily sounded) by a potentially articulate, momentarily passive consciousness.

Not only the ears but consciousness in part forms a device for funneling sounds to consciousness. And the sounds represent meaning, intended or stolen from the jumble.

Again, language represents a public (or communal) aspect of consciousness. And as an expression of community, statistically, language, represents listening more than speaking or writing—this helps create a pressure in the self to write (or speak).

Consciousness grows up, I would think, through listening and through acting—the latter means some form of language (of gesture).

In any case of gesture or of speech or of the use of any of the formal arrangements of consciousness used in listening, language remains an example of individual consciousness throughout the duration of any use of it.

The actual matter involves the relation of hearer and speaker as well as the mechanisms of language and the mechanisms of a cultural engagement given over to the putative use of language.

A solecism represents a misuse of language with the misuse defined by the larger communal aspect, but the misuse is always on the part of a smaller unit, a single person: i.e., a solipsism underlies a solecism.

Absolutists try to change all this—all of it—by making solecisms a breach of universal principle (and not of social principle) and by making solipsism universal and inescapable.

This should be seen as an attempt by absolutists to maintain not merely some authority, but all authority—universal, omnipotent authority—in their own hands, since to admit to social discipline is to bring in other judges; and universal solipsism again obviates any real need for social discipline other than that of collusion and agreement.

Someone who submits to "universal" law, of course, submits to nothing since there is no such thing.

An individual, R, tries to make his experience universal but one must see that he tries to see his experience as such and his language as pure and that both matters are life-and-death to him.

But, surely, he also sees that his language and his experience then devour mine. However, he thinks I deserve to be so devoured.

He devours even my experience and not just the interpretation of it. He is the final writer of the stories and the true arbiter of my existence as a man who is a writer but who is chiefly a character in R's writing.

In that writing, in R's writing, the writer and the protagonist of the stories are absolutely the same person, which, in various ways, may very well often be the case; and R perhaps sees that clearly, much more clearly than I can, or than I do; but the matter cannot be unwound without study.

Let me say here that this procedure of identification ties interpretation to biographical, biological fact as such facts are expressed by the reviewer.

In the topographical argument Freud made at various times (and, therefore, in various ways) about the *I* and the *more-than-I*—the ego and superego are the terms used in Strachey's unwise translation—the *I* and the *more-than-I* might be seen as applying chiefly to that part of consciousness that is worded or that one might say is potentially worded, eloquently or not, but that still is not consciousness as a whole but is on the way to being it.

That is, the translation shrinks and absolutizes the matter.

I am proposing, as a translation then, that in any use or anticipation (on any plane) of the use of language the *I* is constrained by the *other-than-I* or by the *more-than-I* all the time, willy-nilly: and in this regard, absolute power is madness—not imperial madness but like it, an undue amount of power exercised—and is, at the same time, comforting and permissive for the nerves in regard to any performance in public.

The language structures used in listening and those used in what might be called pre-speech seem to be much of what Freud meant by internalized otherness.

Which is to say, conscience. Conscience, which is to say moral choice, is built on structures of listening.

Furthermore, language, conceived as a dialectical object in essence (to speak in old-fashioned terms) and irretrievably relative (to use modern terms), is, either way, the essential building block of what has been called the conscience.

Another way to say this is that the categorical imperative might not apply in cases (the case that Büchner proposes in *Woyzeck*) of people inarticulate or mute; and the application of justice to them becomes an act of often unperformed charity.

By extension, since we are all inarticulate, the application of justice to us (Büchner argues) is forgetful.

Hence the rights of rebellion often ascribed to the *silenced* undermen (and underwomen) and granted by Nietzsche to the articulate *übermenschen*.

Language can be taken to include mathematical, gestural, inflectional (musical), elements when such elements are expressive in a way that clearly includes the possibility of words directly or by implication, or a meaningful admission that words do not apply.

Language includes long- and short-term contextuality and purposes, as well as long- and short-term associations (meanings) in such layerings and changes (in purposes, in meaning, and in intent) as moments pass. So that all psychological and behavioral reality in geographical space within an admittedly temporal reality that is referred to is, truly, an immense human structure and adequate for many purposes.

And, of course, it is inadequate for some.

That is, what is signified (if I might be permitted the use of that term) must be considered as a very real element of language, even in theoretical considerations of language itself.

This brings us again to the reality of the speech occurrence and the actuality (or real-life basis) of what is signified (often taken as biographical or autobiographical elements), sometimes rightly, sometimes wrongly, and the need for one to exercise judgment toward these matters in any piece of writing.

The exercise of judgment is a form of citizenship and no matter how constrained such an exercise is by social forces and psychological limits, one must consider it as having at its center free will, since it does have just that, doesn't it?

Once again, among the elements of language, the moral element of conscience is built in.

Whatever is known as expressive consciencelessness must be understood as a real example of actual negation—negation in actuality. Negation of actuality but relying on actuality; otherwise it becomes (Wittgensteinian) *nonsense*.

What Freud called consciousness—*ego* and *superego* atop the *id*, the idiot-whatever—can be seen to have an analogue in what is called proper language; and unconsciousness can be seen as a most peculiar analogue (but an analogue nevertheless) to what is called improper language—and poetry.

Improper and failed language—language that fails to be poetry in the light of the soul and of at least one listener—might represent to us a failure of the conscience.

Errors of speech represent unconscious language—an id confession—unrestrained private ego lyingly proposed or felt to be communal ego and responsible, but, essentially, out of control, dangerous, and ugly (in Freud's judgment).

One would like to risk a figure of speech. It would seem at some level that consciousness is as susceptible to language as it is to a child of its own.

A child might be called articulated purpose or an articulated explanation of the self. Anyway, language is the sometimes favored child of consciousness.

. . .

Then this: articulated consciousness as the sometimes favored child of consciousness is analagous to the cultural idea of the more seriously articulate male, the male who is favored in so many biblical narratives in the First and Second Testaments.

The failure of one's language is felt in childhood as injustice.

Then someone more articulate may be the one to be courted, at least for a while, but, then, will ultimately be attacked and deposited in a pit, sold into Egypt, and so on.

Like a child, language asserts itself in relation to its parent consciousness within the home of consciousness itself. Language is the child of one's most private consciousness crossbred with a sense of others and of the community and of communal experience—sports, say, or the *yeshiva*.

A wordless part of the mind is not to be described as *hidden*. Much of the Talmud consists of error and of the correction of earlier error, but in a claim made for the Talmud of finality is further error.

Furthermore, the Talmud represents the painful and lengthy superimposition of relativism and rule on the more or less unbridled absolutism of portions of the Holy Text.

Thought that attempts to hold all of reality and all of literature and all of music (in the singular lunacies of ideas) as substantive and as without time (or narrative) but caught and held in a single apothegmatic and complex point taken to be an eternal particle of the *all* is plainly a madness, often fertile, but not lastingly so: rather, it is doomed to defeat because of its banishment of reality.

The final secular importance, after all, is that reality is life and death for all of us.

1990

THE ANIMAL LIFE
OF IDEAS

My mind is entirely time-ridden. If someone were to ask me, *Why do you write the way you do?* I would say something on the order of "What other way is there for me to write at the end of the twentieth century?" Or I can be cryptic and say, "I write the way I do because it is the end of the twentieth century." One has outgrown photographs and media notions of reality—and fear of Picasso's success. One is this way whether one names it or not: one is captivated by movies—the correction of the photograph, of absolutism—and by common speech, as Wittgenstein pointed out: I think it is like this for everyone.

Take one's sense of time. Almost all Western writing of *lasting merit* agrees that bodies are time-ridden. Well, I write in a time-ridden way.

I have extended the notion of time to include everything: ideas, minds, ultimate meanings (if they exist), and further meanings (which certainly do exist). But, of course, this is not a *transcription* of reality or of what the eye sees: it is a change in the *technology*—and spirit—of *representation*.

One's failures are obvious, one's successes are always dubious for a number of years until it is known on rereading that such representation, such perspectives, really do work effectively to convey meaning and pleasure—the Horatian duo sometimes translated as *delight and instruction*—

but one's successes and failures can't be measured by professional mediocrity, unfortunately. . . .

This century's alterations in representation forbid simple portraiture
or simpleminded transcriptions of reality: to deny the revolution is rather
sad. A sense of reality is also a sense of truth, in the Keatsian sense. If what
I do were transcriptions of reality, someone else would have done it—a
number of writers are trying to do it now.

That is because mediocrity has its rules and its realities and cannot
ever match itself to what is required of it: success or largeness of spirit
would automatically make mediocrity unmediocre. So you always have a
body, or corps, or corpus, of the third-rate who are passionately devoted to
what is third-rate.

Among the things I do is form sentences and paragraphs and narratives in such a way, or ways, that it can be seen one is structuring prose
in order to convey meaning—so much meaning per phrase, per sentence,
per page.

I have been asked if I have a name for the way I write. I have none that
I use daily that is not private and silly. Silly? Hyphenated: *It-is-time-to-
write-this-way-now.* . . . That's my private name for how I write.

Am I a realist? Yes. But a realist who considers reality to be psychologically and spiritually—and politically—complex. A realist must be a
relativist—consider painting and music, opera, and so on: epic poetry,
drama, and the novel. Someone who draws from nature as well as from
earlier texts to form a text (if he, or she, works with intelligence) deals
with relativism, deals in comparison.

It shouldn't be necessary to say that relativism is not nihilism.
Nihilism is absolute, is a form of reversed, or dark, absolutism, based on a
negativism of belief that the Final Truth is one of defeat and of meaninglessness. Relativism is far too relative to do that.

Relativism is relative in every fact, which means it often consists of
relative absolutisms—absolutes in relation to each other—as in English
politics or as in a job.

Or as in a narration concerned with degrees of *absolute* honesty—
absolute under certain circumstances, as honest as is humanly possible, or
true cosmologically, apparently, but faced with another cosmological
truth, claiming to be equally final—a war of eschatologies, you might say,
with death camps at stake, or, more modestly, a marriage—or an orgasm.

The Theory of Relativity seems at our current stage of investigations to be truer—more honest?—than the Newtonian pictures of things were, but it does not entirely (or absolutely) dismiss Newtonian physics. The relative truths of Newtonian physics survive. The Newtonian universe, however, is a shameful superstition and still appears often in novels.

Novels are not good fantasy structures. Neither, for that matter, are paintings. One can make rather odd generalizations. Few of the front-rank novelists have been very blond. No critic who does not *write* very well has ever lasted in interest for very long (so far).

With paintings, one responds to color and line, representation or the avoidance of representation, but what one responds to most forcefully, I believe, is the often concealed, sometimes overt, representation of *time.* . . . I refer you, for the moment, only to the idea. And I hurry on to say that relativism is the temporal medium in which life occurs, must occur, has always occurred, and will continue to occur.

This is difficult for some egos to accept since it argues a political organization of God's reality and a sort of implicit competition of forms, methods, and beings, in that everything that is known and felt is known and felt by means of comparison, by intrinsically egocentric measurement that can, of course, be transcended, such transcendence, when demonstrated, being, of course, a demonstration of grace.

But there are other forms of grace, as well.

Language is articulated consciousness. Consciousness and articulation and language are all set in time, and not simultaneously, or in simple relation to one another. If one is considering a text, then one can consider the reader's consciousness and articulation and language and the writer's consciousness and articulation and language; and one can, with greater or lesser discipline, chart some of the patterns of how those things relate and how that leads to a sense of meaning, a sense of truth, a sense of aesthetic excitement or interest or satisfaction.

But so, too, for individual phrases and sentences, for grammar throughout the text, and for observation and plot as they *unfold*—as they move in the streams of time, metrical tempi, tempi of comprehension, and the like.

One does not comprehend in a blow: speech, say, or a text; comprehension, too, occurs over time—as any civilized teacher knows. As any civilized editor or critic knows. One can measure the intellectual rapacity of the third-rate critic by his or her claim of comprehension without crediting time and by the implication that comprehension is final whereas we all know or suspect that it is not, that if we are to write about a poem, we must stop reading it, since, with every reading, our sense of it and of its parts changes.

One might here speak of the *false* use of stillness—as in photographs, where the pattern of reference to reality is formed mechanically. One might argue that a photograph is known fantasy, an overt lie, about physically factual reality, with certain ill-defined elements of truth in it.

Much of what all art does—and most politics—can be called the escape from the photograph (but in opposed directions; art proceeds toward a more complete sense of fact; politics distorts and lies about fact for political reasons).

If we compare two photographs, do we have, almost automatically as it were, the foundation of a story?

Perhaps we have the rudiments of the structures of a number of stories—for instance, if the photographs were taken by the same man, we have the change of circumstances in the man between the moments of taking and developing the two photographs.

This change of circumstances, if used as the basis of a story, must be set in relation to time: all stories use time, they *unfold* in sequences of moments; they, like all acts (and moments) of interpretation, are actually portraits of time.

Relativism then suggests the presence of more truth and more reality than are present in narratives that attempt to be absolutist or that use absolutist devices more often than is advisable in serious work. Few of the major texts are absolutist: I cannot think of any.

But many of them show a longing for absolutism. And they have moments of describing or indicating a possible absolutism that complicates the matter of describing them in these terms—*La divina commedia*, for instance, is absolutely relative in technique, but it is about the great beauty of absolutism and of finality (and it is, perhaps, still the premier self-conscious work about the absolute and human actions.)

. . .

What governs my work is a simple notion, all in all: the primacy of time.

And this echoes a great deal of work, in antiquity and in Western Europe and in this century from just before the beginning of the century until now—Rilke, Musil, Proust, Freud, Nietzsche, Wittgenstein, Bergson, Kafka, Benjamin, to mention just the Jews and Germans.

But in many cases, such work argues for absolutism as superior or as what is longed for, or it argues that the loss of it wrecks this or that, or it argues that the absolute, while it is that which is longed for, is essentially incomprehensible, whereas I do none of those things.

I do not long for it. I do not think it is or ever was the basis of language or the truth of at least secular religion or the basis of mind.

I associate it with dreaming, arrogance, and failure.

It used to be the case with me that I would argue with myself, *Well, fart-brain, it is not likely you are right. . . .* But I tried not to let that feeling control the formation of the texts I was working on.

Nowadays I believe that no absolute ever existed and that the absolutist bits and pieces in good work are remnants of dreams and of dream formulas, formulations, and the like, and interfere with the portrayal of things—acts and plots—and, of course, with the creation of characters.

Time is everything. Is awareness, too.

But then the *dream* intervenes: it is probably the case that such a simple notion, so basic, carries the seeds or perhaps already is a culminating structure of a radical change in sensibility.

So many people in this century have said they were engineering such a change that I am reluctant to say it *might* be the case that now I am attempting to do it or that I am doing something else, which may bring this other revolution about.

One advocates a wakefulness, a curtailment to sleepwalking, at least as an exercise of political and aesthetic will. One hopes for an extension, an increase of wakefulness in relation to dreams and will.

Subjects: gender, childhood, the interpretation of doctrine. Success in the world (worldly success). Love; sex; politics. Political realities. Money. The moments.

Technical considerations: nothing exists abstractly.

.   .   .

A story line: someone who is not often loved chases someone who is
often loved.

Part of the plot must be the pursuer's failure or success in realizing a
useful amount about the reality of his/her pursuit and the reality of the
person loved. . . . His/her failure to have this sense is the story—not some
fantastic difficulty in love itself or in life not permitting anyone to love.

If one cannot see the person loved with any clarity, one cannot hope for
success. . . .

Realism equals love when realism is clarity of observation. Clarity and
charity blur into one another.

Anyone can claim clarity for his work. Minimalism is not clear—it is
sourly cryptic, if you ask me.

Writing cannot create, cannot reproduce, specific realities. If writing
gives you that sense of itself, then it is writing of an excellent order and of
an excellent order of imagination.

The reality set forth in the text must be the product, to a considerable
extent, of imagination. (Theory. Technical fancy. Philosophy of reality. A
technical mastery of impression and of the force of hallucination.)

The positivist world of photographs, of tape recordings, and of video-
taped moments, and the positivist world of Ayer and Waugh, have nothing to do with my writing. The shadow, the light of the longing for
absolutes, for an absolute, for a single correctness. . . . But the workings of
consciousness—I am here, you are there—as a landscape of time and as a
mock spatial landscape: they do not and will not synchronize. . . . And
not all consciousnesses are the same. Two consciousnesses are not much
alike—a child knows this—we all know this.

Language is variable, expandable, contractible—tractable, intractable,
well worth one's attention.

The absolute is not the parent of concision. Time is. Here, one might
mention that the succinct is usually not the best work of a given period,
era, century, or decade.

An absolute can never be true—except perhaps psychologically.

Wittgenstein points out that biologically general statements have the proviso of *so far* (or *so far as we know*), since a single contrary example changes everything in this sort of universal.

The moment of collapse of theological absolutism, by the way, was the beginning of European success in the world.

Absolute political structures lose wars.

And they fail to maintain prosperity. They mostly succeed only in undercutting the functioning of the society they are part of: they precede failure and revolution.

Any notion of relativism and of secular truth must honor the English. *The English Revelation.*

What other legitimator of truth is there except actuality?

The opposite of truth is nothingness.

Literary thought in the West follows the line of political success, unfortunately. (The line of success that I most admire is the line of the anti-Napoleonic: Baudelaire, Flaubert, Stendhal; Tolstoy—some of the time—Proust, Lawrence, et al.)

The influence of Byron on Goethe equals Nietzsche. (Nietzsche's resemblance to Wordsworth should be explored—Nietzsche as the Wordsworth who went mad.)

The centrality of temporal obsession in Kafka explains Kafka—if you want to explain Kafka.

The novel, with its sorts of traffic with time, is replaced by movies and photographs with their sorts of traffic with time.

One might compare James to Hemingway—the notions of impotence and of potency in each.

Subversion in art: a conscious experiment with time.

It is not possible to discuss mediocrity anymore.

Modernism as *Jewish*:

1. The untheocratic nature of the new universalism. A Baconian construct.

2. The journalistic nature of modern consciousness. The redefinition of nations (and social class) as media entities.
3. Modernism's reliance on its sense of observable time. Such his-
   toricity undercuts earlier notions of fate and of social class.

These elements have a noticeable similarity to certain elements in
rabbinic (Diaspora) Judaism.

And may have partly arisen from it through Oliver Cromwell's philo-
Semitism. . . .

Maimonides may be more important in European history than scholars have yet indicated.

Sequential realities, momentums, velocities, histories, outcomes.
Relative voices.

Some people prefer *apocalypse* to the continuance of reality.

Mediocrity and relativism: realistic comparisons do not work in favor
of mediocrity.

Nihilism may be the simplest—and most absolute—absolutism. (It
may be a basic linguistic—and psychological—stance.)

Immediacy, often rightly, places a higher value on journalism than on
art. The word *glamour* is a corruption of the word *grammar*. (Of such
importance it has been for the freedom to rise in social class.) I am
opposed to shrewdness, and to *classroom logic*.

Classroom logic goes like this: Something—a statement—is true
or not true. But in actuality, the statement in question is sometimes
true, sometimes not true. So far as we know, only an absolute statement is
never true.

The technological resources of government, the resources of political
will, mean that the world is endangered nowadays. We do not have
any intellectual or moral choice: we are realists or we are murderers of
the world.

Language exists only in individual purpose.

Mediocrity has a great many levels. It can be vastly able. It can
be outgrown. (Through suffering and love, self-sacrifice, adventure, et
cetera.)

Mediocrity (in a quick definition) is not a friend of life, even of its own
existence.

. . .

It is extremely dangerous to be brief. But I would like to risk saying that T. S. Eliot is Gothic, not *classic*. He is *Christian* and in a far from gentlemanly sense. He is in a state of longing for absolutism.

His work suggests that the attempt to be Christian (rather than any boast of being it) is to be it, in this life, in a passionate sense.

Our language, our schooled and conscious thoughts, are in modes that are out-of-date and that are dangerous to us and to everyone.

Everything moves in time and everything contains time and everything itself is a form of time.

By time, we understand motion, individuation, death and life.

Absolutism? Well, take the idea of nine: for it to exist as a serious idea in someone in actual time—for you at this moment say—it must exclude everything else while you consider it. The idea of nine is only truly the idea of nine when it is *absolutely* nothing else—when it is not the idea of ten or the idea of political democracy. It is an actual question whether you can consider ideas *seriously*, profoundly, with any sort of democracy of relativism at the moment you are considering them.

The hierarchy of attention here is what underlies the hierarchical nature of pure and impure absolutism. The absolutism of *attention* is a mental construct, very like the reality of one's self dreaming, or daydreaming, and never complete; and when seen from a distance (from outside itself) can be seen to be faultily double. Thought, reverie, a brown study, are terms that refer to this.

Also, faith, discipline, having values (of a fixed sort), and so on.

The high repute of absolutism comes from one's sense of the fineness of attention—the order, the orderly effort—to be found in the regard, the contemplation of absolutes, the disciplined effort of dealing with and in them. Faith and conviction are then said to rest on this discipline of attention. An absolute idea is said to be the finest or ultimate training or purpose or reality for attention, for consciousness.

And fantasy, fant'see, fancy, represent thought, privilege, merit, et cetera—as in architecture, masquerade, haute couture. . . .

I say that it is our respect for focused attention, on singleness of focus, as when we ask each other, *Do you love me best?* that causes the trouble.

(In real time, no one, perhaps, loves anyone best all the time.)

But let us be very clear: absolutism is part of us; it underlies the structures of dreams, indeed of sleep itself, and of many kinds of love, and of most kinds of attention. A fine performance, a handsome public square, can elicit a "fascist" sort of attention. . . .

What are we to do?

Now, relativism is very odd. It is, simply put, Keats's formulation about truth being beauty and beauty truth. Wateriness caught in a partly stone representation. Formal considerations of attention and time. *Repentance, paganism, political majesty.*

If you consider the idea of *nine fingers*, it is, relatively speaking, a signal about how split and rapid attention actually is, how riddled with multiplicities, so riddled that it is never without multiplicity even if it can concentrate on an idea of *nine fingers* and on nothing else.

The game or sport of relativistic realism has to do with meaning here, as in life, and not there, as in death, in unalertness, in dreaming, in heaven, in doctrines, or in systems. Only in life.

The presence of reality is the difference. But we know from our own lives that such attention is cheated on, except at the rarest moments, unless extreme pain is involved.

Pain focuses the attention, but it is rarely clear what that focus involves—the reality of power? The reality of death?

The reality of flesh?

Should dialogue be written differently nowadays?

Adam's garden, considered as an image of a text, of a written thought, represents sincerity of belief.

During periods of a rapid expansion of democratic notions, art will tend to be more and more absolutist—more like the essay, less like a multi-voiced drama or many-voiced book.

Solipsistic self-liberation is not possible in real life.

. . .

The texture, or substance, of writing about love as part of a universe of motions among the mind's attempts to rule as in dream, the dream monarchies of love—do you know? And the plight of intelligence then? And of attention? And of judgment? And the body's versions of those things?

These represent the mechanisms of plot of a love story.

Each moment in which one experiences love is enclosed in a history of the actualities of attention and inattention within the frame of (historical) reality as well as within a history of attentive (and inattentive) actions.

Fantasies—and absolutes—specific gestures by people, characters, voices that crush or maim any truthful representation . . .

Generalities cannot love each other. One can say that logic loves geometry, but it is not interesting.

If God is a matter of favorable method—let's leave that thought alone.

If in a novel the chief attachment is between the writer and the reader, can one expect it to be a lasting attachment?

The love story and the narrative of adventure: each should be enclosed in the actual motions of actual people, in a streaky or dappled actuality of lightedness. Some speeds confer invisibility. Some are visible, are in the range of display. They are elements of visible existence. But they are mounted on invisible velocities. In life, feelings are known as motions, but not, however, in bad writing. In life, feelings arise from an abundance of beloved and boring and hateful and beloved, again, motions of events, moods, people, and states of soul. . . .

Thought does not leave time and become timeless. Poetry can be concerned with timelessness but mostly as what is sought for but not gained. The poetic line has a meter in it. And one should be aware that one has learned something since the last reading and is finding something new this time; and one should know one breathes and reads in a slightly new rhythm each time.

One should realize that Plato is, unfortunately, guilty of what Plato condemns.

Any reference to the absence of time is an error and a source of further error. It gives rise to the time-riddled horror of the dismissal of the human. Truth is not leftist or rightist: it is relative and never absolutist. Error here is the source of massacre.

Consider, for a moment, what an attempt to be absolute in real time must involve, the deafness, the death-bringing, the ignoring of real moments, the lust for the simple victory possible in apocalypse-made-real. It is all anger and horror and God-summoning wrongness—of the *actuality* of absolutist notions.

(In painting, the nineteenth century begins its major line of development, we now feel, with portraits of massacre and of death.)

Narrowed attention, concentration at a given moment, in their beauty, have a willful thematic and sensual discipline. Honestly regarded, the question posed in such attention can be seen as: what in this world can a *Pure Idea* be?

I imagine ideas as having visible skins, as existent physically—this is Christian (it is pseudotactful to say *perhaps this is Christian*). The notion of *God-for-a-while* interests me—*God-for-a-while* here, embodied, but I would not *dream* of attempting to define the nature of Christ or of God.

Have you ever imagined print as lips speaking and whispering confidingly to you?

Do ideas replace women—and the reality of men—when they replace the reality of moments with an aeriality of pretension?

Women's eyes: delicacies of evoked knowledge. Experience shows us ideas in real time as the gambler's ground for quick decisions; but what ideas help us to feel, to recognize what goes on in us in relation to women's eyes?

The use of idea to explain a perception will, often, trigger a recognition in a viewer.

This is difficult to explain unless one posits a reality beyond idea.

Then: an idea known in time. One exclaims, *Oh, I get it. I see it!*

The silky feel and thrust of idea, its small haunches, like those of an ermine.

When someone says he, or she, has thought about something, they may mean they thought about it for eighteen minutes.

In the outward play of theater of someone's face there is often the visible attempt at a fixity of mind: a dictatorship of the sensual real.

An escape from the pressure of others choosing or not choosing you becomes you making your choice, as in dreams: you establish, willfully, mentally, the primary building blocks of time and truth in the universe so that you can wake at your will, a massacre of the images, plausible-seeming as real, of your dreaming, obliterating everyone, everything in the dream.

(The problem with style is that one may become trapped in the success of one's manner—if one has success with it.)

What the adults did and said when one was young was beyond one's understanding—this is a pattern of intimidation—and it allows one, later in life, to believe in thoughts that one knows to be inaccurate and inadequate.

The masquerade of art is, despite its specialness, actually a matter of an experiment in useful language—in useful clothes: it would be better if this were less dreamlike for a while.

Art: the romantically mysterious legacy left us by dexterous exhibitionists in the past: only some of it is useful in any given age (or arc of style).

The extension of the will regarded—seen and felt—as success is dreamlike—dreamlike is tiresome as praise, but perhaps one will never tire enough of it.

The Villa Lante at Bagnaia, northwest of Rome: in a wood of casually placed trees of various sizes—with the complexity of their branching—is a square reflecting pool. It is broad rimmed, with tallish obelisks set at the four corners of the broad rim. It is astoundingly geometrical—and among trees on the uneven ground, the sky seen glancingly in the woods is also reflected in the wind-rippled, two-dimensional reality of the surface of the geometrically framed pool, holding the complexity of the twisting branches:

The *truth* is startlingly beautiful here at the pool.

The actual counterpoint of symbolic time and self-willed time (invented by oneself watching) and the actual time (ticking on), once it is noticed, gives the pool, and one's response—one is lost in the woods of response—a true otherness of sensual dimension. It is almost clear that to think and to be moved by thought is to be asleep, awake, in a peculiar way—with various degrees of counterfeiting of this state to make the matter complicated—and that to dream when asleep, or to daydream, or to think a little but sincerely is to be awake asleep. The laws of the universe predicate more change than our formulations allow.

Any illusion of stillness perhaps gives some pleasure—it certainly gives one a sense of one's own will and one's superiority in terms of the ability to destroy the stillness or the stilled thing.

Idea is a discipline of attention. Perhaps no more than that.

Stories are a landscape of talk and involve the animal life of idea: the words, statements, scenes, and alternations and poses in a story are like horses in a herd, which, as they move, outline the drift of the hollows and knolls of a meadow, a pasture, in this case, a landscape of language and of possible meaning.

The thin, vibrant, vivid line of conscious attention—the principles of attention—is a species matter. This is not insulting. A species' truth, the biological singularity of the species, the attributes of a species, should not be considered to be insulting simply because they are not absolute in the universe. Indeed, I would think that as a matter of faith, such singularities would seem holy—like individually talented but sensibly human voices in a choir.

Words. A word has its dream nature, its capacity for motion, a poetry of its command of attention. One has a perhaps insufficiently complete terror of coerced attention. One is essentially opposed to absolutism because absolutism as part of its would-be claim to omniscience develops, always, a science of contempt that does not permit any given word (or other people) to live for very long; or oneself to exist as a student among relative decisions.

Relativism includes absolutes as part of the mechanisms of the disturbances and reactions—and the light of others—and the stages of hallucination or wakefulness. An absolute relativism would be merely yet another form of absolutism. A measure (or symptom) that relativism was operating would be to notice that the doctrine in command allows us all to live.

Mindlessness, like most forms of elegance and all forms of high style, is a form of confession. Mindlessness, elegance, high style, and confession are select forms of relativity—of inconsistent momenta that fools, alone among us, ever present as consistency, as perfection. One must be honest from the ground up, or how can one understand that there are varieties of self-forgiveness, some of which are vile as well as too faulty to be borne? One says *perfectly elegant* and *perfectly witty* since dreamlike ways of indicating contempt are impossible for an absolutist here (although we know that contempt, hatred, and disapproval are never impossible for an absolutist).

It is a source of joy to start to pretend, but when the pretense is carried out in reality it becomes obvious that it is unwise to pretend.

Shrewdness, however, merchandises pretense as a common denominator among consumers, voters, readers, intellects.

I say shrewdness will destroy us all.

Love indicates great faith in a possible meaning to be found among human relations. It is relatively easy to see why love is usually taken to be a justification for life, for what life turns out to be. It might be simpler just to see love as life. Or to say love is life. Deathiness, unlove, are attempts to be abstract while still being present in the flesh. Motion as ambition can be taken to be a love of something. Love, as I said earlier, can be taken to be an ambition as well as ambitious while it exists. Life, too, is an ambition.

(But ambition, separated from motion, love, and life, is death itself: not unattractive, not always to be avoided—but it is real.)

This is enough—too much?—for now.

1992

THE GENTEELY
OBSTINATE SHAWN

It is much too soon to try to write about William Shawn. To attempt respect and a summing up is impossible. His influence was enormous. And it lives on. And rebellion and antagonism and dislike and competition continue. He was a man whose story will be in medias res for another sixty years.

I envied him the admiration I thought surrounded him. I became sensibly aware in time of the controversies and efforts he faced every day and what a high-wire performance his career was.

He rarely showed strain. He showed amusement and polite emotion. He wasn't interested in a full range of emotions. And temperament wasn't a card he played. He was a pacifist and a man of reason.

But he was a very realistic pacifist who felt that the point was that pacifism brought you realer triumphs than those gained by any form of violence, including psychic violence. He was very sure of his causes and very, very sure of his ground. In the suspense of some of his battles, he was willing to risk the ruin of his reputation. His anti-pesticide and anti-nuclear campaigns moved me the most.

He was a pacifist who used charm and factual reliability and humor and cartoons and who, although he wasn't clearly an optimist, wanted and intended to win.

Part of the seductiveness of his *New Yorker* was the absence of violence in it. I mean the absence of violence of spirit in its workmanship—even in accounts of violence.

And part of the seductiveness of the magazine came from a nearly absolute ban on sympathy for or even mention of any white male patriarchy. He himself never played the patriarch; he was only ever an editor figure.

He wasn't interested in white male patriarchs. Such men were rarely if ever profiled, and certainly not in any way that supported such patriarchy. *New Yorker* fiction largely ignored their existence. This early rebelliousness, now a part of the sociological landscape everywhere, helped create the atmosphere of thoughtfulness and gentility that the magazine had, and it was part of the oddity of the magazine that repelled some writers and outside editors. But it aroused sympathy consciously and unconsciously in many others.

Under William Shawn, the magazine was an offshoot of the world of the white patriarchy while being opposed to it and perhaps being a bit patriarchal in its own way. This was part of yet something else, a utopianism that was purely American, that had a sweetness of disposition or of the heart. It was actually a political program, religious in structure, and of no mean dimension, and derived from Tolstoy and Gandhi, but modified by Shawn both in terms of spirit and degree of practicality in the contemporary world.

The almost bloodless revolutions in Eastern Europe were in their way an enormous justification of his theories and strategies and a lifetime of work.

The *New Yorker* covers indicated the scope and the nature of his campaign, his political program, his realistic sweetness. The concern for the reader, the frequency of idyllic pieces or of idyllic descriptions in the fiercer pieces, the quality and content of the ads, the pungency and relevance of the cartoons, the promise of a certain egalitarian superiority if you lived right and were sensitive (this one of Shawn's inventions, a notion of a modest aristocracy without pretensions but not without assertion and duties) carried out this motif page after page.

It was a decent world within the covers of William Shawn's magazine from the late 1950s on, and it was a coherent and doctrinaire magazine of urbane integrity. . . . That last phrase is Robert Gottlieb's.

I'm not the right person to describe William Shawn. I thought he was quietly combative, smilingly obstinate, brave to the point of lunacy, and so proud and fastidious as to seem mad sometimes even to those who doted on him. I never came across anyone with a firmer ego. Or a cleverer person. He was so clever that actually he was impossible to deal with. You mostly gave in to his influence. Or withdrew into antagonism.

He didn't often compromise, and even then he didn't compromise much. Reality being what it is, one has to bend, but I think William Shawn compromised less than most and then almost only on his own terms in the light of reason.

He was more than aware, he was profoundly aware, as only a claustrophobe can be, of the width of reality. He was aware all the time of at least a dozen things while being undistracted. He was profoundly aware of you if he was talking to you, of me when he was talking to me, and of what I'd written in the last five or ten or twenty years. I have a blessed amnesia about what I've written. But he remembered, and he knew what I was working on, and he knew how the world might regard it. He was so intelligent in what he said and in how he phrased it that he was less wrong, day in and day out, and year after year, than anyone I've known so far.

He was aware of the office and of the lives in it. And of the lives of people in the media in New York and elsewhere. And of the lives that made up a large part of my circle. He went out rarely and saw only a few people outside his family and *New Yorker* people, and yet for me to talk to him was to see and be in touch with more of the world than my own personal experience in several years of traveling could match.

His mind dealt in wide scope and in narrow focus. He couldn't help you do work of a sort antipathetic to his taste or abilities. His imprimatur made you famous, up to a point, and not without controversy, but it meant a good deal.

And he shaped the *New Yorker* into an institution that amplified skills. The proofreading, the copyediting, the editing for sense, the sophistication toward diction, the research and checking departments made, so some of us joked, short men tall and Fords into Ferraris.

At one time, by showing your *New Yorker* card or by using the magazine's name and giving the telephone number there of someone who could identify you, you could cash a check in any store in this city. The assumption was that you were honest and solvent or close to it. And everyone knew it.

In relation to news and factual pieces and issues and opinions, Shawn worked in months and years. In the great pesticide war, he calculated that it took approximately ten years to make an unpopular subject generally discussed, which is what it did take.

His discretion and self-control were such that I know of no instance of his slipping into indiscretion. He had a monumental charm that was insolent and unshowy (but so great that it was more insolent than ordinary insolence can ever be; he seemed to be patient with his own deftness like someone walking a very handsome dog, someone modest who was resigned to the dog's splendor). The fame of the magazine issue by issue made him awesome enough, but there was more.

"People judge us by the cartoons," he said. "We work very hard on the cartoons." He was always funny. He was a good psychologist. The things he said privately to a writer were often so personal and so valuable that he insured the privacy of his conversation by the very wit and applicability of what he said. He was patient toward neurosis and ingratitude.

Add that up and then add further the number of personalities he dealt with in the course of a day and then the complex individual quality of his responses to each one, and you can see what led to the aura of implicit and at times quite nerve-shattering and terrifying authority he had.

I have seen people blinded and silent in his presence. It happened to me a couple of times. He was so good at his work and he was so influential in the world that I could respond to him at times only with lousy awe or with cranky or corrupt rebellion or with monstrous but nonsensical ingratitude.

Everyone at the magazine had both a public and a secret attitude toward Shawn. His success was so great that it had a deleterious effect. Other editors were squeezed into untenable positions aesthetically or into corners of supposed preference, of attaching themselves to fiction of suspense, say, or supermacho fiction in order to have a publicly noticeable editorial identity different from his.

I will tell just one anecdote. In the early seventies, William Shawn asked if I would accept him as my direct editor. I couldn't actually function very easily at first in relation to such intelligent attention. Of course, he figured me out very early. I did listen to him. And some of my stories are for me the *Shawn* stories.

We were copyediting a long story in his office and sitting side by side at his desk, and we came to the obligatory four-letter word one was always trying to get into the *New Yorker*. He put down his pencil and turned to me and said, "Harold, you can have this word if you want it. You have certainly earned the right. But I think I ought to warn you in a worldly way that this is a very good story, but it won't matter, since, as you know this will be the first time this word has appeared in the magazine, and this story—which really is a good story, will always be known as the story in which that word first appeared in the magazine and not as the good story it is."

"Please," I said. "Take the word out."

I tried not to be a drag on his energies or to be someone he had to lug around among his other burdens. Of course, I was, anyway. I have not liked or admired any man more or been more tangled up inside over anyone in mingled resistance and affection and admiration. I tried not to be jealous of the two hundred other people on the magazine; as I wrote this, I have tried not to be angry with him for dying. I feel sorrier for the world that he's gone than I do for myself, but I loved him a hell of lot, and I feel really lousy that he's dead.

1993

HOW ABOUT SALINGER AND
NABOKOV FOR STARTERS?

Gore Vidal announced recently in the *New York Times* that we no longer had examples of the category "famous novelist."

Putting aside the mischief and wit, that remark was a way of talking about modern culture. Factually, of course, he's wrong. Tom Wolfe is a famous novelist, and so is Stephen King.

But Mr. Vidal meant something on the order of what Mary McCarthy was referring to on a now half-famous television broadcast with Joseph Brodsky and George Steiner and A. A. Alvarez when she said that in the West the novelist felt that "no one is listening."

She differed from Mr. Steiner, who gently condemned the West and admired, even envied, the situation in the East where Aleksandr Solzhenitsyn or really Mr. Solzhenitsyn's work represented an "alternative state" to that of the Soviets. And a man could be killed for having written a disrespectful poem about the cockroach Stalin. These circumstances represented a truly serious art and how, under some circumstances, the novel was *really* important.

Mr. Brodsky protested that that was an ugly romanticism and, anyway, freedom was worth a novel, or the novel. McCarthy refused to agree that the novel in the West was inferior. McCarthy instead complained of "the noise" in Western culture.

Mr. Vidal's comment is related to that argument. But his comment was without reference to what Mr. Steiner indicated was the finer and deeper writing that he felt arose in oppressive and dangerous conditions or at any rate in the East. A discussion of the relative merits of Vladimir Nabokov and Mr. Solzhenitsyn might have extended the question a bit on the television program, but McCarthy held no brief for Nabokov and, indeed, had attacked *Lolita* savagely. Looking back, it seems now rather astonishing how consistently McCarthy was wrong with no great loss of status, but one does see why "no one [was] listening."

But Mr. Brodsky didn't compare Yeats to Zbigniew Herbert perhaps because Mr. Brodsky prefers Auden to Yeats, or perhaps because comparisons are odious.

Perhaps, too, the issue was what can be written now, what sort of writing, novel or essay or poem, can influence things and gain a hearing at this moment. That is, what is the relative standing of the people on the panel, relative to great fame and the status of greatness?

A state-endangered writer is, willy-nilly, a more romantic object of contemplation and aesthetically a more satisfying one since the problem of aesthetics doesn't quite enter in. But in time the question of aesthetic merit does dominate. Meanwhile, the argument is that political attitude is art, is the new art, a famous life of danger is talent, and so on. This does rather open the door for a great many more high reputations to exist than at present, but those reputations do not last. The welcome relief for busy critics and novelists and people in general of not being bothered by the pressure of having to read actually good books soon collapses, as does that whole literary scene. And writers do have to produce good books or go unattended to.

The phrase *lyric sensationalism* was used by critic Robert Alter as a slam in a piece he did in the *New Republic* not long ago. Apparently he was unaware of what art in the West is. If not unaware, then set on another agenda. I mention it here in order to rip off the phrase in order to say that to be politically important is more worthwhile, the argument runs, for writers and critics—and readers—than to be mired in the problems and awe of creating and reacting to the lyrically sensational and sensationally lyric which make up, in all the arts, painting, drama, music and poetry, and the novel, the high culture of the West.

Critics are often wrong. They are often well beside the point but not always. And when they are wrong, it is not always entirely their fault, although we might as well treat them as culprits since they are culpable in so many ways.

But critics, too, must be educated and policed by controversy and competition, and often that education must come to them through novels. If novels and novelists go astray, then most critics, dear sheep that they are, wander into folly. Gore Vidal is addressing this problem but from another angle, one he knows a very great deal about, being as famous as he is but without being "a famous novelist," merely a famous writer.

But he can see and compare sensibly from his own experience. He knows what he is talking about, up to a point. At that point he is perhaps a bit hasty and, while hardly ill-informed, he is as if ill-informed.

You see, all of us who talk about books have a problem in that we do not have enough terms handy in general use or in specialized use to describe what we are really talking about. We fall back on clichés and clearly mistaken statements that at best are clear only in a codified way.

For instance, we have no good term for a *serious* novelist. I know of no novelist who isn't serious. Such terms as *a real novelist* or *a good novelist* or *an artist* don't signify much. The word *poet* is actually, I think, a term of higher praise than the phrase *a great poet* is. But that is hardly true of the term *novelist*. The murky area in which you try to set up classes or categories of seriousness of attempt on the part of the writer is riddled with snobbery and self-interest. Often in the course of a novel, the nature of the attempt and the degree of seriousness change as the writer's mood and condition do.

And at what point are we talking about technical competence? About moral depth? Or moral elevation? A kind of success in matching meaning to "lyric sensationalism"? Are we talking about our own prejudices mostly, in terms of religion, stolidity of talent, or flightiness of talent, gender? The currently politically correct charge about Western culture reflecting the interests of white males is very largely true, with one exception being the English novel.

But how do you distinguish between writers who are very interesting at moments and who are interesting as lives and careers but who have never written—here is another problem—a book that seems really to matter in its own time or later or both?

In my adult lifetime, in English, I can think of only two writers who wrote in English whose books have achieved that sort of rank so far: J. D. Salinger with *Catcher in the Rye* and Nabokov with *Lolita*, both very odd books—and lyrically sensational.

And of translations, I can think offhand only of *The Leopard*, by Giuseppe di Lampedusa, and Boris Pasternak's *Dr. Zhivago*. But four is quite a lot. And a number of other books are in the running although it doesn't look now as if they will make it. I am not complaining of the number of successes. I am merely pointing out that Mr. Vidal seems to be mistaken.

I will complain of literary discussions that omit these examples of triumph, or to use a more tendentious word, these successes. And point out that *triumphs* and *successes* are poor terms for what we mean here, a *serious* or massive entry into the culture.

Careerism has various forms. Every level of literary ability has its warlike nature so that the most banal mediocrity is as vicious as the great writers are. Each individual, each group, pursues an agenda and struggles to establish the fame and status of its work. Milton's phrase is *fame is the spur*, but you might say that ego is preternaturally human and inescapable in everything.

Despite Mr. Vidal's comment and McCarthy's remarks, fame and close listening and broadscale cultural effectuality still attend successful books. But here the term *successful* really is impossibly inadequate. Take a nonfiction book, one that may not be *immortal* (another inadequate term), Rachel Carson's *Silent Spring*. Its success stretches over a span of thirty years. And *The Leopard* is still not a great best-seller.

The other category of literary attempt is very important and very *successful*, too, but not in the same way. Many famous writers are very good and are technically adroit in reaching an audience but they are usually not good novelists. Their books reverberate for a while, but not greatly. But such *writers* are important as lives, as voices, as careers. Those elements do enter the culture even if the texts don't. Mr. Vidal's argument, I think, is that such figures don't rank as they used to in the world.

Novels are culture whether they are good or bad. The importance of the novel in the nineteenth century was not that it was the dominant popular form. George Eliot's *Middlemarch* sold only sixteen thousand copies. The novel never was dominant in the way that movies and television are said to be today and that sports and politics and business news actually are. The movies and television are forms of popularization. They deal inadequately with subject matter and matters of interest, and they do not create the verbal terms or ideas they present. Nor do they create the initial interest in the subject matter.

The novel in its heyday was the dominant form of argument and may be so still in the long run, but it would seem that in the twentieth century it was displaced by Marxist and Freudian and Fascist and Nazi texts and then by nonfiction and literary texts imitating the "success" of those texts.

The novel is the longest and most coherent form of extended argument that any culture has developed. Its argument is embodied in events and personalities narrated in relation to the passage of time. Novelistic coherence is still, it seems after recent events, the best means, in a good novel, to show real-life logic.

A good novel demonstrates the unnatural power of coherence to prove a point, not by opinion or by rhetoric, but by illustration, by embodiment—to use a Christian term. What is embodied is reason, but reason of a complicatedly self-proving order that contains leaps and jokes and odd perceptions. This quality of reason, of truth, if you will, shows in a good novel from the first page.

The agreed-on good novels are self-provingly radiant even when they are dark in mood.

Textbooks rely on claims of evidence and factuality, and always have a bit of the swindle about them. So-called evidence can never be coherent except for short stretches or in terms of added examples or near-repetition and tautology. This lack of coherence is masked by claims of system. Imitation of that, claims of system, are what led postmodernism astray.

A novel's coherence is thematic and expansive. It spreads out from itself through the intelligence and convincingness of its portrayals of events and its show of meanings to embrace the lives and understanding of a great many divergent individual readers. Readers are always individuals. A good novel cannot have a mass audience no matter how many people read it. A novel is a one-to-one proposition.

This is part of what makes novels difficult to write and talk about. Movies, however, are collective enterprises, and offer handholds everywhere on their surfaces.

To write an honestly coherent novel while not offending reviewers and critics, bottom feeders, macho-ninny ideologues, blind mouths, and the like, is impossible. To offend them is no guarantee of merit, either. But the half-popular serious American novel is only half-serious, or half-baked, and the writer of such books is, of course, despite publicity, in the end, only half-famous.

By definition, though, a half-good book is not bad.

Ludwig Wittgenstein brought philosophy into alignment with novelistic practices. The twentieth century saw the displacement of the novel for a while—and perhaps permanently—as dominant argument. It was replaced by books that propounded systems and were clearly propaganda as well as argument. But the novel may be finding its way back to dominance now.

1992

SOME NOTES ON
CHEKHOV

The idea of there being a category of beings who are contemporary writers implies similarity of date, occasionally simultaneity. It includes a notion of similar effects of history on them, similarities in style up to a point, related approaches to and interests in approximately the same aesthetic and political and ethical or moral and religious issues; and it suggests similar techniques, similar attitudes toward form, more similar than between writers of different eras; and similar suggestions for the amelioration or salvation of life. That is, there is a theory implied of detectable kinship among the members of such a category.

I am not sure this holds for American writing at this time. I mean I think the stories and books produced in this country in the last decade, let's say, indicate a literary universe so fragmented, so individual, that I cannot easily think, offhand, of two writers I would say were really contemporary with each other. Perhaps it's something that shows best after one is dead or when one is very old.

Similarity is a dangerous term anyway, linguistically and logically. Despite Aristotle's dictum that intelligence sees relationships, much of the most powerfully argued, and so far as I know, accepted as such, modern philosophy and mathematics seems to incline to the hypothesis that similarity is merely a predilection of the beholder, that it is a quality that usually is arbitrarily ascribed unless one is careful to state one is dealing with inches and the length of poles for staking tomatoes. After all, similarity implies *some* dissimilarity or there is identity or sameness—which is, I think, impossible, except rhetorically. (Pragmatically what we intend when we say two things are the same is that the differences don't matter for our purposes.)

I exclude poetry: the situation may be different there. And, I might very well be wrong about prose writers—I claim no authority in this field. There may be groups. The zeitgeist may have twinned us all as in a Vonnegut fable. But take this example: Barthelme and Updike both write for the *New Yorker* and do so quite often. Some critics for some time have spoken of a *New Yorker* school of writers; but if they include Updike, they exclude Barthelme as an aberrance; and vice versa; and sometimes they exclude them both and include only writers they dislike. Or like. It hardly matters. I find it difficult to see similarities between Barthelme and Updike or those two and Eudora Welty or those two and me, for that matter. Of the two, Barthelme and Updike still, I might say both write careful but unlike sentences, predominantly Romance-language-oriented in grammatical structure and syntactical effects striven for, rather than the Teutonic; neither is particularly vernacular—both seem to me formalists but not in the same way; Updike uses metaphor frequently, Barthelme hardly at all except to parody it, but sometimes an entire Barthelme story is a metaphor and so on. In short, I do not see that they are alike. I also consider Malamud and Bellow more dissimilar than similar, Sukenick and Coover also, Reynolds Price and Eudora Welty. . . . I think it can be more convincingly argued—this is, of course, an opinion—that in a very clear sense, none of these is quite contemporary with the others: they do not occupy the same world, the same dates: there is a lack of synchronization.

How much I have been influenced in this by reading and probably misunderstanding Wittgenstein, Russell, bits and pieces of the logical positivists, I can't tell. It would seem they exert on the mind a fairly powerful pull to see only individual cases and only difficulty in generalization or in categorization. I am told that mathematicians, because of some recent work, have given up on the old notion of "mathematical proof"—that is, they are reduced to saying, "from certain points of view" and "in special circumstances, we can say that so-and-so is the case." They are refraining from generalization too.

This splintering of authority—authority in the sense of believing there is an authority—that there is a correct language, that there is a truth from which lesser truths are derived—is part of the current age and has also been going on for some time, in other ages. Of the current situation, here is one small illustration—pronunciation. There is no central authority that I can think of, no dominant university, no dominant social class, no royal court; and certainly the movies and television don't convince us—or perhaps they do. As for dictionaries, they are commercial publishing ventures—the extent of one's belief in them is comparatively slight: they initiate, I would say, one's own thoughts on the matter—of pronunciation and of definition: they settle arguments only because it is convenient to have the arguments settled for a moment. Meanwhile, language changes, is changing—and books and stories do not reflect the vernacular very well. For one thing, the vernacular relies heavily on facial expression, human context, and vocal inflection, on a whole series of habits and styles in a given milieu. Take a situation such as an associate professor bucking for promotion and a junior officer in a corporation also bucking for promotion and saying hello in the morning to their immediate superiors: they will speak differently because of the milieu, because of the past histories of the men, the politics as they understand it of their immediate situations; and furthermore, this will vary from college to college, corporation to corporation, and in a college or corporation from individual or set of individuals to individual or other pair of individuals. This kind or degree of variation can sometimes be hinted at in a novel or short story but it depends, if it is to be understood—this reporting or creation of a variation—on the reader knowing about such things too: someone at Cornell knows Cornell and can detect misreporting easily; but is perhaps not so good on variations at Berkeley or Ann Arbor, say. This tends to push American writers toward an American version of Mandarin, often heavily disguised as vernacular—I don't mean Henry James Mandarin but rather the conventions, say, that are common in political speeches, or the conventions associated at the moment with "serious" or less serious writing.

But the conventions of serious writing are not agreed upon—what is serious writing is not agreed upon: murder mysteries, gothics, and science fiction press in upon us, as do Westerns; after all, *The Brothers Karamazov* is a murder mystery, among other things; *Wuthering Heights*, a gothic, and *Huckleberry Finn* a sort of a western.

To list some of the issues of the present age is to give a distorted picture but I don't see what else to do: the conflict between the almost-capitalist nations, or whatever they should be called, and the socialized or communized nations—but there is little unity in either camp; perhaps one can say between the pietists and the utopians. There is a certain anger or rage at history; there are various sorts of moral explosions. Journalism and our own discomfort tell us of the ecological threat, the population bloating, the technological wilderness we are in. There is the moral and political tension between what seems possible and what-is; there is polarization, racial, religious and political—breakdown, experimentation, all sorts of things. It is different nowadays, I would think, to be a man, a woman, a child, an old man, an old woman—if one makes it that far.

Chekhov, a mere seventy years ago, hoped for change but would not have approved of all of the change that has occurred: what would he have thought of modern Sweden, for instance? Or of an American suburb? He might not have been surprised at the Holocaust or the Gulag Archipelago—he was, after all, a major poet in prose about inhumanity, about inhumanity flourishing sometimes after a crime: I refer you to a story called "In the Ravine."

He seems to have found language already in difficulty—I don't mean only when he says directly such things as he does at the end of a story called "Gusev"—"—colors for which it is hard to find a name in human speech"—but in the very structure of his stories and his construction of character, which usually rest on nineteenth-century conventions, often quite melodramatic or trashy ones: I refer you to the plot of "In the Ravine," which contains a child murder; a saintly, simple girl; a police-informer forger who goes to jail; and perhaps eleven other melodramatic plot elements: this seems to indicate a need to stay close to what his audience knew as language-referring-to-something, and then he altered it, often removing romance and applying a truthfulness—even of romance: he does write love stories, he does picture "irresistible" women—a wakefulness: he tries to extend the language out, let's say, from middle-class nineteenth-century conventions toward a truthfulness that, while it does not omit joy or pleasure, does omit optimism. Perhaps one can say he corrects Tolstoy.

I would like to argue—but I am too ill-educated, too ill-informed, and so I must state, must theorize—that he dealt with the situation I attempted clumsily to outline at the beginning of this paper. He saw the fragmentation—both literary and moral: who is of the school of Chekhov? Isaac Babel? Solzhenitsyn? Any American writer you can think of? Apparently he accepted it: I feel a strain of loneliness in the writing or shaping of his stories—it is a feeling. . . . As for character, his notions of character, he often, it seems to me, is physical, clinically physical, in his description, and then he relies on gesture or tone, which he interprets morally as many times as not. But it seems to me he hinted that character was beyond speech or description: in the opening paragraph of a story called "A Dreary Story," someone is describing in the third person the honorable career, the highly successful career of a Russian scholar; it begins, "There is in Russia an emeritus Professor Nikolay Stepanovitch, a chevalier and privy councilor—" It mentions his Russian and foreign decorations, and that for the last twenty-five years there "has not been one single distinguished man of learning in Russia with whom he has not been intimately acquainted." He goes on to list other honors and signs of merit; and then suddenly he skips to the first person and says, "All that and a great deal more that might be said makes up what is called my 'name.' "

"A Dreary Story" is about dying: you might do well to read it and then read "The Death of Ivan Ilyich" in which Tolstoy makes the coming of death a spiritual judgment and the actuality of death a possible moment of illumination (Tolstoy has other death scenes too, the one in *Anna Karenina* of Levin's brother, not to speak of Anna's, which seem to me similarly treated; so too Andrei's near death and then death in *War and Peace*). I don't know what more modern death scene to suggest you read— death scenes are out of style: Willa Cather has *Death Comes for the Archbishop*. People die brutally or briefly in a great many novels: Patrick White's *Eye of the Storm* has a dying in it: Gide's *Symphonie Pastorale*. But what Chekhov does strikes me as the best and most convincing: he pictures a man who cannot any longer love first this, then that, part of his life; bit by bit he ceases to love; he ceases to love not only himself but everyone and everything he has loved best or loved to the slightest degree. In this fashion he prepares for death. The story ends with him apostrophizing in his own mind his ward, a girl he has admired for her courage and charm: he says to her within himself, "Farewell, my treasure!"

It seems to me Chekhov could not have written a novel, considering his linguistic and characterological techniques; his plays seem to me to use short-story techniques.

Now, there are mysteries about the short story. One is that the short narrative existed a long time ago—the short, quasi-historical narrative first, perhaps—and of course myths are narratives. The kind of fictional, "realistic" account we—I—associate with Chekhov does not really appear until the nineteenth century; and when it does, it is the child of the new periodicals and the new audience. That is to say, all the various kinds of revolution—social, religious, philosophical, military, technological—that went into the creation of the nineteenth century and of the middle class as a paramount world force seem to have gone into the creation at last of the short story: its function was to entice readers—it was a variation on the news stories of the newspapers and the articles of magazines; and in my view so it has remained, even the most-experimental short story being, for me anyway, a parody of a scholarly article, or of some written, news-giving, middle-class-invented (so far as I can judge) form.

More than a novel, the short story relies on what the reader knows, on a community of interests and background between reader and writer: the writer doesn't have time to start from the beginning—neither actually does the novel writer but he can come closer.

It is a theory of mine which I cannot go into at any length that the human sense of form—of symmetry and such things—comes from the probability that in earliest infancy and on until language is spoken, the infant may not have the will to abstract patterns from reality: what happens is that he dreams: and in the dreams of infants, actuality is reproduced—with great error, of course, and with emotion often, and this occurs under the command of the barely existent infant ego; this reproduction is in a sense two-dimensional—time is altered, is subject to ego; and space is played with, is subject to the requirements eventually of dream reproduction: I would argue that nearly any dream reproduction would in itself represent an act of learning; and that such learning would be of patterns, structures, ghosts, forms; I believe that the mind is never able subsequently to hold more than a small amount of actuality in itself in wakefulness but pretty much constantly bolsters and fills out with forms, formal representations, prior decisions about, prior notions of the structure of this or that part of what the mind is trying to contemplate or deal with now; and finally, that much of our sense and knowledge of actuality can never get into language because language is a set of forms—it may be derived from infant's dreams as well—and it is hard for us to *hold* a thought we cannot express or that we cannot summarize or hint at as with a caption but made up of words, forms.

The forms in a short story tend to be crowded and brief with, I would say, one dominating or overriding form, so that unlike a novel or poem, or some poems, which I think are impossible to describe, a short story can be described in a way: a bishop is dying; his mother, a peasant, is at his bedside but cannot be brought to recognize in the grown man, ennobled by the church, her son; she sees him as the Bishop and will not address him except as "Sir."

If this is true, it would imply that the short story was constrained to play with forms, with conventions, to be conventional, or perverse toward its own conventionality, or to make perverse use of the conventions it relies on for communication in the first place. I can think of an example but it might not convey much to anyone but me: in a short story in the *New Yorker*, a writer spoke of a man giving "his son a father's glance." Well, that is quite general on the face of it, but it becomes less general if you take into consideration the *New Yorker* at the time that story appeared—it had certain conventions about relationships—and also the work of that writer, other work of his, suggested his attitudes, gave some of the conventions he worked by or with. I cannot imagine "a father's glance" except as an invention of sentimentality: each father would be different, I think.

This leads me to the last few remarks I want to make. "A father's glance" is by modern standards, as I said, a sentimental phrase; and there are not many writers nowadays who risk sentiment or emotion. Think of the limited emotional range in so good a writer as John Barth, or in Pynchon, or in another generation, Mary McCarthy: in forty years of writing, she has produced so few scenes of emotion other than exasperation or of ironic anger that I, who admire her work, can't think of any. So too in William Gass's novel, *Omensetter's Luck*: it has power—truly considerable power—but a very limited range of emotion. This is not true of Joyce's short stories or his *Ulysses* or of Virginia Woolf or even Proust—I say, even Proust, because the structure of that immense book, and its comedy, require a limit set on the number of emotions he can treat—but he often breaks his form. I am not sure, of course, how emotion is generated in fiction—or poetry—but I would advocate its return on the grounds that to claim superiority to it or to assert alienation or to rely merely on indignation is maybe self-righteous.

I don't know. I think it is time for me to be silent.

I want to close with a very short description of another Chekhov story: a man meets a woman at a resort and they fall in love with each other; but then they don't fall out of love as time passes; and they realize they're not going to fall out of love any time soon; Chekhov says, "—it was clear to both of them that they had still a long, long way to go, and that the most complicated and difficult part of it was just beginning."

Now that they know that some meaning and truth exist for them, how do they live? How do they live now that this is true?

1978

GRAMMAR AND
AMERICAN REALITY

Grammar is a term designed to cover the sets of linguistic structures held to be effectual and persuasive for conveying meaning (sense). A purposeful lie may be ironic, which is to say, that the grammar of the overt meaning is meaningless. The linguistic commune is an inordinately complex structure even among native tribes.

Honest instruction in grammar would have to deal with issues such as real and implicit meaning, multiplicities of meaning, and social structures.

No "polite" American English has been agreed upon; and the variants, Texas and Chicago, Colorado and California and Massachusetts, Washington and Boston, have not been canonically established as dialects. We have no real over-tongue, no equivalent to *hochdeutsch* or serious standard-British English or to Tuscan.

Crudity of spirit (in the sense of not anciently derived spirit) and aesthetic hubris (in the same sense) mark any intelligent use of English. English, in any of its forms inside or outside literature, is not a language greatly parallel to Russian or German, to French, Latin, or Italian. We seriously remake literary language writer by writer: Stein, Eliot, Whitman, Dickinson, Salinger, Hemingway, Lincoln, West. We unconsciously admit that a proper use of English is, ipso facto, an eccentric use; and, so, we overpraise proper or seemingly proper writers who write a rather poor but pretentiously schooled English.

Consider this: when the movie *From Here to Eternity* was made, Montgomery Clift, whose diction was Boston and New York of an educated kind, spoke his way; and Burt Lancaster and Sinatra each in his own trained show-business way spoke with a lower-class background audible and visible, a different lower-class background in each case; and then a higher social class, an officer's wife class, was represented by Deborah Kerr using an acted *American* tone with a theatrical British–English base; and that mess, that potpourri, has not dated or aged into absurdity: it is a part of the movie that works still, as does Donna Reed's portrait of a whore as a matter of vocal inflection and facial expressions and of extreme ladylikeness using schoolteachery English.

Similarly, serious people sometimes wonder what Americans think when they contemplate the language of American politics. I say we think in several steps of translation—with suspicion, approval, guesswork, anger, or rage—of the many levels of shrewd secrets involved through which we guess at, untangle, read purpose in the language *relatively*, guess at what might happen—that is how we listen to the words: realistically. We consider this to be part of being grown-up. And we often show off to each other our powers of cynical and deep comprehension of speech and grammar, as in Hemingway, for instance, or Eliot.

Ours are grammars of reality largely untouched by churchliness or historical theory, and we demonstrate an automatic extremity of response: extreme gullibility or extreme cynicism. Our political reality, like our language, is relativist and Nietzschean, willy-nilly, but gawpingly, soppily American as well.

It is possible that Nietzsche was embodying American reality. He was exploring reason and reality and making a hermetic (and hermeneutical) analysis of social, or cultural, reality by considering the American example.

But put that aside. Consider this possibility: that for us, whatever passes for clarity and truth, in our political context, is hardly realistic—real life we treat as obscure—but is, instead, snobbish, ideal, and foreign, of foreign derivation. Also, we do not think of clarity and truth as reflecting *male* interests.

Indeed, *clarity and truth* reflect subversion and specifically feminine or feminist interests—what one might call the *French* influence on American writing. Any American use of English is relativist: this helps establish it as a major linguistic structure, the one that might lead to a world language.

The human use of language is so complex that each use always carries beyond grammar and beyond-the-(old) rules. . . . We make estimates of the future as we carelessly or carefully calibrate our speech in terms of wished-for effects—always fanciful or imaginary in part. . . .

Speech, properly understood, would indicate that we cannot expect the future to be like our pasts or to be like any past except for purposes of comparison (relatively). This beyond-grammar-ness can be called generative since it indicates and does generate new meanings. It is comparative-indicative; it uses one kind of relative structure to indicate comparatively how another, temporal, relative structure functions and can be used or guessed at.

Classroom procedures, judging from our popular arts and from our cultural carryings-on, are out-of-date worldwide. We expect social mobility, social relativism and a kind of absolutist intimidation to exist in most discourse. At times we expect a final, or lasting, factuality, an apocalyptically towering conclusiveness, an answer, a final rightness.

An American might vote with her or his life for economic freedom—the factors that go into a real decision have the nature of a moment in them and the reality of an individual life set among its near recurrences of idea and of situations. One also has to admit that one is inevitably culturally unstable outside the locality of the immediate field of relevance of one's upbringing(s)—the plural being from friends and their families and from college opposed to lower schools and so on. We are too unlettered and too unletteredly giddy for Nietszchean *gaiety*: it is doubtful if we can understand him but, nonetheless, we are Nietszchean. But we have had no dictatorship—yet.

We have had cruelty and cheapness, however.

. . .

Philosophy speaks of people through metonymy glorifyingly, as if *upward*, and not downward as statistics or details. Religion and philosophy and most advertising do not see women and men as swooping toward the grave but as lasting abstractions menaced by the grave—this is perhaps not a wise thing.

Our art, our lives, our thoughts, the adequacy of our awareness, the inadequacy of our kindness: if the woman who cleans your house is ill, you don't, feudally, stay home with her—not without arousing resentment in others. And it is not necessarily nobler to stay with her. The merit of the act throughout its spread of moments depends on feeling and on details of the actuality of feeling. The idioms *track record* and *batting average* refer to character over time.

This is Nietzschean but is not subject to Nietzsche: this is what Nietzsche wrote about. The symptomatic presence of light tends to define the realities of appearance for us. But whole things are difficult, or impossible, to see as wholes. We see parts—facets, angles, parts of planes. And memory and projections fill in the gaps of what we see. Visibility in real life always has a personal heat in it. A heat of experience and the unique way a unique accumulation of experience is used in each of us.

If you see light as color, you can see that what is visible is lit by yellow light or blue light or, here and there, by white light. The detail, the representative bit or aspect, is truer in that it can be seen in a given moment, while the whole thing in the representation of what is known in a given moment is partly unknown.

But this is useless information if it is said to be absolute or absolutely correct: it must be eccentric, admittedly flawed, *humble*. The parts of something that are visible, the symptoms of its presence, can be said to be attributes. Attributes, which include similarities, which, in turn, include *number*, are on both sides of what was in the past sometimes called *essence*, a compressed, small, potent reduction to an elemental intellectual summary, a solidity of nonexistence felt to be existence; always a *reduction* only destructively thought of as the truer whole—the truer whole is the true whole: the universe of an entire soul should not be reduced to verbal formulations of varying merit having to do with inexistent essences.

Because it has contingently identified elements of substantive existence, particle physics asserts that it is better to think of a number of things than of any one thing when you want to think of that one thing. That is, for the semi-primal elements of physical existence, particle physics uses such terms as things-and-events (particles that become energy and then reassemble themselves as particles and that seem to have an identity, to be the same thing whatever state or whatever arc of motion they are in). Paradox; self-contradiction; things unexpectedly, contrarily so; opposites-being-the-same; opposites having an identity-with; symmetries; rhythms; echoes—these are, so far as we know, practical reality. This is what *event* means. The bottommost items of physical reality are not small solidities but are sets-of-changing-circumstances-which-yet-have-an-identity-seemingly.

If we want to be old-fashioned (and absolutist), we carelessly consider things to be the same when they are not the same, and we use force, coercion, death, to enforce the notion. To say the subject is closed is to say that much of our conscious existence is without event.

A person, famous, infamous, anonymous, is knowingly and often self-destructively, in a given moment, an entire life bound up in being one un-ideal example, one with hypocritically *ideal* aspects.

If you accept the notion that the change inherent in an event in a given passage of time is inevitably sufficient to be jolting and perilous to some notion of the reality of purpose and identity, then you accept the idea of a person as a lifelong event.

And then your reading, too, is inevitably subject to being thought of as a continuing event, lifelong, time-ridden—part of the moment's adventure. And you can see where deconstruction is interestingly relativist but, in its attempt to be a universal system, is systematically wrong.

Nietzsche, who is not entirely right, is more right than any American thinker since his time about America.

The minimum for the avoidance of nonsense involves us in relativism. We are lifelong totals expressing ourselves in present-tense behavior. Absolute repetition is impossible: the second time by being the second time has a materially different meaning. Each moment is a stage of our expressing something new in the moment and correcting and emending the past.

If one thinks of this in terms of an old-fashioned metaphor—balls in motion or arrows shot into the air—or in terms of yet freer movement or motions—ideas as silken, small-haunched animals breathing rapidly and scurrying in the grip of the mind—one is at the verge of being a Nietszchean-American.

1991

I THINK OF
WHAT I WRITE

I think of what I write as an amalgam of language and the politics of moral procedure sifted through common life. By common life I mean something along the lines of what in experience might be commonly known by readers: the portrayal of the real, making full acknowledgment of time as reality—rather than literary evasions of the reality of time—so that statements and the evidence for those statements are recognizable in one's own experience; and the relation of writer and reader is changed, making it more nearly equal. The reader in his or her life has more access to the real than the author does, which counters the author's more practiced access to language. This is *Momentism*, an experiment with the sayable in regard to what is overwhelmingly present but has usually been held to be relegated to silence—or to be lied about, i.e., distorted for the sake of personal advantage.

Since the evidence for statements of opinion lies in how what is observed, is observed, a sort of prose is created that is not propaganda. If reality is presented in a way heretofore held to be impossible, then truths of a more complete and interesting order can be dealt in. The literal reality of American lives, including that of the narrator, is proposed; and this is done as an antidote, or counterweight, to the stale misunderstand-

ings of American life when American existence is looked at in stale and
unsuitable frames and is not taken for what it is (or for any one true thing
it is of the many things it is).

So the events pictured are accessible but are not laid out in the techniques or familiar shapes and forms of old or recent literary tradition. The
safe, and largely idle, keys of satire and lament are avoided; and the author
behind the narrator is not assumed to be a scion of language with some
sort of artificial claim to rightness as a matter of course, in the claim of
being a narrator in more or less intellectually stylish English. When that
privilege is laid aside, the obstreperous falsity of false auctorial claims (of
knowledge, of ascription of character, even of sequences) becomes much
harder: one is less likely to be bearing false witness.

The work, the text, then becomes an open subject with some kind of
meaning required as its purpose other than that of claiming the right to
hold the rank of author or knower. The meaning, then, that is offered is
the grounds for licensing the privilege—even for writers who claim to be
nihilistic solipsists or religiously devout or who use any of those dodges
rather than take the responsibility for meaning something—and is necessary morally and aesthetically once silence has been broken by an attempt
at narration.

Politics and psychology depend on the use of language so that
one becomes, if one pursues such a program, a political writer and a psychological theoretician—and every man's enemy.

In the 1950s, I wrote simpler, younger, somewhat lyrical versions
of the above. In the 1960s, I wrote third-person narratives in which the
same questions were addressed but the element of the truth-proposition
was placed in relation to some identifiable and unarguable element of
illusion—moviemaking, drug taking, projections of personal happiness
as daydream (the subject being false and real emotions, felt, or known,
to be such). In the 1970s, the truth element became the active element
of narration—that is, the core of each narrative was scandal, usually
multiple, of tone and of language and of subject and of event and of truthfulness. (These stories were misread as being in opposition to the New
Novel and the postmodernist effort because so much of American postmodernism relished and flaunted untruth as evidence of honesty as such,
whatever the merit of the truth as storytelling or as fantasy or as symbol.)

The purpose of what I do is a more equitable and flexible language and a just world, of course; an increase in the spirit of charity among us; greater happiness for a widening number of people; and an enlargement of one's sense of amusement and interest in life, more of which can be spoken about sensibly, more of which can find its way into language.

1980

BIBLIOGRAPHICAL NOTE

These essays first appeared, some of them in different form, in the following publications:

"Translating Brando": *The New Yorker*, October 24, 1994

"Why Is This Woman Funny?": *Esquire*, June 1972

"The Last Word on Winchell": *The New Yorker*, January 30, 1995

"The Kaelification of Movie Reviewing": *The New York Observer*, October 5, 1992

"Hollywood Close-up": *The New Yorker*, May 3, 1993

"Variations on Sex": *The New Yorker*, May 21, 1994

"Box Populi": *The New Yorker*, October 26, 1992

"A Frightening Chasm between the Rulers": *The New York Observer*, November 2, 1992

"Shy MWM Writer, 61, Seeks Cultural Elite": *The New York Observer*, July 13–20, 1992

"The Weather of the Spirit": "The Talk of the Town," *The New Yorker*, April 6, 1987

"Thanksgiving": "The Talk of the Town," *The New Yorker*, December 14, 1987

"A Good Blizzard": "The Talk of the Town," *The New Yorker*, March 2, 1987

"The Subway at Christmas": "The Talk of the Town," *The New Yorker*, January 5, 1987

"Companions in New York Unlikelihood": "The Talk of the Town," *The New Yorker*, December 29, 1986

"Bad Streets": "The Talk of the Town," *The New Yorker*, February 15, 1993

"The Video Vault": "The Talk of the Town," *The New Yorker*, January 13, 1992

"White Dust and Black Dust": "The Talk of the Town," *The New Yorker*, November 3, 1986

"The Return of the Native": *The New Yorker*, February 15, 1993

"Spring 1989": *Fiction*, Volume 9, Number 3, 1990

"My Time in the Garden": *Mirabella*, May 1995

"Family": *The New Yorker*, November 23, 1987

"Love Speeches": *Ms.*, September 1986

"Sex and Looks": *Allure*, June 1993

"The Second Skin": *The New Yorker*, November 7, 1994

"AIDS and Loss in a City of Ghosts": *The New York Observer*, February 22, 1993

"Jane Austen vs. Henry James": *The Threepenny Review*, Spring 1988

"Reading, the Most Dangerous Game": *The New York Times Book Review*, November 24, 1985

"The One Who Writes": *Anteaus*, June 1994

"The Roar of the Canon": *The New Yorker*, September 13, 1993

"Stanley Elkin, the Story Man": Afterword to *Criers and Kibbitzers, Kibbitzers and Criers*, Thunder's Mouth Press, 1990

"Max Frisch: The Ability to Be Ordinary": *du* magazine, December 1991

"The Rustle of Language: Roland Barthes": *The New York Times Book Review*, April 20, 1986

"The Animal Life of Ideas": *Twenty-First Century*, Winter 1992

"The Genteely Obstinate Shawn": *The New York Observer*, January 4, 1993

"How about Salinger and Nabokov": *The New York Observer*, September 14, 1992

"Some Notes on Chekhov": From *Chekhov and Our Age*, Cornell University Press, 1985

"A Man Enraptured with the Seasons": *The New Yorker*, September 15, 1986